KV-437-582

# Stage 2

# Operational Cost
# Accounting

# Examination Kit

1404/J00

**British Library Cataloguing-in-Publication Data**

A catalogue record for this book is available from the British Library.

Published by AT Foulks Lynch Ltd
Number 4
The Griffin Centre
Staines Road
Feltham
Middlesex
TW14 OHS

ISBN 0 7483 4140 4

© AT Foulks Lynch Ltd, 2000

**Acknowledgements**

We are grateful to the Chartered Institute of Management Accountants, the Association of Chartered Certified Accountants and the Institute of Chartered Accountants in England and Wales for permission to reproduce past examination questions. The answers have been prepared by AT Foulks Lynch Ltd.

All rights reserved. No part of this publication may be reproduced, stored in a retrieval system, or transmitted, in any form or by any means, electronic, mechanical, photocopying, recording or otherwise, without the prior written permission of AT Foulks Lynch Ltd.

# CONTENTS

# PREFACE

This is the 2000 edition of the CIMA Kit for this paper. It is fully up to date for legislation as at 1 December 1999 which is the legislation date for the May and November 2000 exams, the last two exams under the current Syllabus.

The Kit includes questions from all exams up to November 1999. It gives thorough, balanced coverage of the syllabus, as a glance at the contents page will quickly demonstrate, and has been designed to give you practice at all the major topic areas as well as providing an excellent means of revision as the exams approach.

Each kit features:

- the Syllabus

- 80+ questions - you can start practising some now and still leave plenty for final revision

- all current syllabus exam questions including November '99

- answers all provided by AT Foulks Lynch with numerous workings and tutorial notes to show how the answers are constructed and to help with your examination technique.

**Complementary Textbooks, Lynchpins and Audio Tapes**

**Textbooks** - complete coverage of the Syllabus and Syllabus Guidance Notes, with self-test questions at the end of each chapter.

**Lynchpins** - pocket-sized revision aids which can be used throughout your course, contain revision notes of all main syllabus topics, all fully indexed, plus numerous examples and diagrams. They provide invaluable focus and assistance in keeping key topics in the front of your mind.

**Audio Tapes** - our 'Tracks' audio tapes are fully integrated with our other publications, providing a clear explanation of key aspects of the Syllabus, invaluable throughout your studies.

To find out more or place an order, please contact us by:

Phone: 0208 831 9990
Fax:    0208 831 9991
Email: atfl4main@aol.com

Why not visit our website today – www.foulkslynch.com

# FORMAT OF THE EXAMINATION

The examination paper will be divided into three sections.

*Section A* will contain one compulsory question composed of ten multiple-choice sub-questions worth 20 marks.

*Section B* will contain two compulsory questions of 30 and 25 marks.

*Section C* will offer candidates a choice of one question from two, worth 25 marks.

Questions in Section B and Section C may be in either a numerical or essay format or in a combination of these styles.

# THE SYLLABUS

## ABILITIES REQUIRED IN THE EXAMINATION

Each examination paper contains a number of topics.  Each topic has been given a number to indicate the level of ability required of the candidate.

The numbers range from 1 to 4 and represent the following ability levels:

*Appreciation*                                                                                                                          ***Ability level***

To understand a knowledge area at an early stage of learning, or outside the core of management accounting, at a level which enables the accountant to communicate and work with other members of the management team.                                                                                                            1

*Knowledge*

To have detailed knowledge of such matters as laws, standards, facts and techniques so as to advise at a level appropriate to a management accounting specialist.                                                                          2

*Skill*

To apply theoretical knowledge, concepts and techniques to the solution of problems where it is clear what technique has to be used and the information needed is clearly indicated.                                        3

*Application*

To apply knowledge and skills where candidates have to determine from a number of techniques which is the most appropriate and select the information required from a fairly wide range of data, some of which  might not be relevant; to exercise professional judgement and to communicate and work with members of the management team and other recipients of financial reports.                                          4

## EXAMINATION PROCEDURE

The examination will be set in accordance with the provisions of relevant UK legislation passed and case law established up to and including 1 December preceding the examination.  This is especially relevant to the following five papers:

- Business Environment and Information Technology (Stage 1)
- Financial Accounting & Business and Company Law (Stage 2)
- Financial Reporting & Business Taxation (Stage 3)

This means that the Business Taxation paper will be set in accordance with the Finance Act 1998 for the November 1999 examination and with the Finance Act 1999 for the May and November 2000 examinations.

The examination will also be set in accordance with relevant Statements of Standard Accounting Practice and Financial Reporting Standards issued up to and including 1 December preceding the examination.  These are especially relevant to the following papers:

- Financial Accounting
- Financial Reporting

This criterion also applies to material contained in Financial Reporting Exposure Drafts, which are especially relevant to the Financial Reporting paper.

Students are advised to refer to the notice of examinable legislation published regularly in the monthly *CIMA Student.*

Where examinations are not based  on UK legislation and practice, overseas candidates may take appropriate opportunities to cite examples of local practice in their answers.  Such examples should be supported with references which will validate the answers.

A credit accumulation strategy was introduced with effect from the November 1997 examination.  There is now a degree of flexibility to structure your sittings to suit your personal circumstances, and to apply for papers of your choice, subject to the examination timetable.  Students can choose to sit between one and six papers with the timetable ensuring that students apply for the correct Stage and core paper combinations.  The core papers must be taken in strict sequence and are as follows:  CQM, OCA and MAA; FAF, FNA and FRP.  Stage 1 must be completed before Stage 3 is attempted and all three Stages must be completed before attempting Stage 4.

**Stage 2, Paper 6: OPERATIONAL COST ACCOUNTING**

## Syllabus overview

This syllabus covers the underpinning knowledge necessary for a student to apply a range of cost accounting techniques within the context of organisation-wide databases and information systems.

Students should seek the opportunity to learn cost accounting techniques in a computer environment.

## Aims

To test the candidate's ability to:

- apply cost accounting principles and techniques to all kinds of organisations

- analyse and critically evaluate information for cost ascertainment, planning, control and decision making

- interpret cost accounting statements.

## Content

| | *Ability required* |
|---|---|
| **6a    COST ACCOUNTING (study weighting 35%)** | |
| Use of relevant, opportunity and notional costs; classification and coding of costs; cost behaviour | 3 |
| Cost accounting appropriate to service and production-based organisations; specification, design and operation of databases for the collection of and storage of cost accounting data; use of relevant applications software to extract data and prepare management information | 3 |
| Integrated and non-integrated systems, including their reconciliation | 3 |
| Job, batch, contract and service costing, including work in progress | 3 |
| Process costing: the principle of equivalent units; treatment of normal and abnormal losses and gains; joint products and by-products; problems of common costs | 3 |
| **6b    INFORMATION FOR DECISIONS (study weighting 25%)** | |
| Marginal costing compared with absorption costing | 3 |
| The concept of contribution; relevant costs | 3 |
| Product sales pricing and mix | 2 |
| Break-even analysis, break-even and profit/volume graphs | 3 |
| Limiting factors, single scarce resource problems including situations with demand constraints | 2 |
| Decisions about alternatives, such as make or buy | 3 |

| Content | Ability required |
|---|---|

**6c**    **BUDGETS AND BUDGETARY CONTROL**
**(study weighting 20%)**

| | |
|---|---|
| The budget manual; preparation and monitoring procedures; reporting against actual financial data | 3 |
| Flexible budgets | 3 |
| Preparation of functional budgets for operating and non-operating functions; cash budgets; the master budget | 3 |
| Principal budget factors | 3 |

**6d**    **STANDARD COSTING (study weighting 20%)**

| | |
|---|---|
| Types of standard and sources of standard cost information | 3 |
| Evolution of standards: continuous improvement; keeping standards meaningful and relevant | 3 |
| Variance analysis covering material (price/usage), labour (rate/efficiency), variable overhead (expenditure/efficiency), fixed overhead (expenditure/volume) and sales (price/volume) variances | 3 |
| Standard cost book-keeping | 3 |

# THE MEANING OF EXAMINERS' INSTRUCTIONS

The examinations department of the CIMA has asked the Institute's examiners to be precise when drafting questions. In particular, examiners have been asked to use precise instruction words. It will probably help you to know what instruction words may be used, and what they mean. With the Institute's permission, their list of recommended requirement words, and their meaning, is shown below. "The following instruction words are recommended to examiners as being precise and likely to elicit the required response. The definitions given here are deliberately short and to the point rather than lengthy. It is recommended that examiners do not ring the changes between instructions in order to be literary. If the answers to all questions in a particular paper require discussion, it is felt there is nothing against using the word 'discuss' in each requirement."

**Recommended requirement words are:**

| | |
|---|---|
| Advise/recommend | Present information, opinions or recommendations to someone to enable that recipient to take action. |
| Amplify | Expand or enlarge upon the meaning of (a statement or quotation) |
| Analyse | Determine and explain the constituent parts of |
| Appraise/assess/evaluate | Judge the importance or value of |
| Clarify | Explain more clearly the meaning of |
| Comment (critically) | Explain |
| Compare (with) | Explain similarities and differences between |
| Contrast | Place in opposition to bring out difference(s) |
| Criticise | Present the faults in a theory or policy or opinion |
| Demonstrate | Show by reasoning the truth of |
| Describe | Present the details and characteristics of |
| Discuss | Explain the opposing arguments |
| Distinguish | Specify the differences between |
| Explain/interpret | Set out in detail the meaning of |
| Illustrate | Use an example, chart, diagram, graph or figure as appropriate, to explain something |
| Justify | State adequate grounds for |
| List | Itemise |
| Prove | Show by testing the accuracy of |
| Reconcile | Make compatible apparently conflicting statements or theories |
| Relate | Show connections between separate matters |
| State | Express |
| Summarise | State briefly the essential points (dispensing with examples and details) |
| Tabulate | Set out facts or figures in a table. |

**Requirement words which will be avoided**

Examiners have been asked to avoid instructions which are imprecise or which may not specifically elicit an answer. The following words will not be used:

| | |
|---|---|
| Consider | As candidates could do this without writing a word |
| Define | In the sense of stating exactly what a thing is, as CIMA wishes to avoid requiring evidence of rote learning |
| Examine | As this is what the examiner is doing, not the examinee |
| Enumerate | 'List' is preferred |
| Identify | |
| Justify | When the requirement is not 'to state adequate grounds for' but 'to state the advantage of' |
| List | On its own, without an additional requirement such as 'list and explain' |
| Outline | As its meaning is imprecise. The addition of the word 'briefly' to any of the suggested action words is more satisfactory |
| Review | |
| Specify | |
| Trace | |

# ANALYSIS OF PAST PAPERS

| Topics | M95 | N95 | M96 | N96 | M97 | N97 | M98 | N98 | M99 | N99 |
|---|---|---|---|---|---|---|---|---|---|---|
| Cost classification | | | | | ● | | | | | |
| Cost accounting systems and overhead costs | | | | ○ | | | ○ | ● | | ○ |
| Computerised systems | | | | ○ | | | | ○ | ● | |
| Specific order costing | | ○ | ○ | ● | ○ | | ● | | ● | |
| Service costing | | | | | | | | ● | ○ | ● |
| Process costing | ○ | | | | ● | ○ | | | | |
| Marginal v Absorption costing | | | ○ | ○ | | | | | | |
| Contribution and relevant costs | ○ | | ● | ● | | | ● | ○ | ● | |
| Product pricing/mix | | | | | | | ● | | | |
| Breakeven analysis | | | ● | ○ | | | ● | | | ○ |
| Limiting factor decisions | | ○ | | | | ○ | | | ○ | |
| Make v Buy decisions | | ● | | | | | | | ● | |
| Relevant cost decisions | | | | | | ○ | ● | ● | | |
| Budgeting procedures | ○ | | | | | | ● | | | ● |
| Flexible budgeting | | | | ○ | ○ | | | | ○ | |
| Budget preparation | | | ○ | ○ | | ○ | ○ | ○ | | ○ |
| Types of standard cost | | | ● | | | | | | ● | |
| Variance analysis | ○ | ○ | ● | ○ | ○ | ○ | ○ | ○ | ○ | ○ |
| Standard cost book-keeping | | ● | ● | | | | | | | |

*Key*

○      This topic formed the whole or a substantial part of the question.

●      This topic formed a non-substantial part of a question.

# PRACTICE QUESTIONS

## 1    TRUE COSTS

"It is probably impossible to obtain an absolutely accurate true cost of a product or service" said a speaker at a students' society meeting.

**You are required** to comment on the above statement, referring in your answer to

(a)     an explanation of your understanding of the word 'cost' in the above statement;                    **(3 marks)**

(b)     whether or not you are in agreement with the statement, supporting your conclusion with an explanation;                                                                                                              **(3 marks)**

(c)     the purposes for which costs are needed by business.                                                      **(9 marks)**
                                                                                                      **(Total:  15 marks)**
                                                                                                        *(CIMA Nov 92)*

## 2    ECONOMIC ORDER

Most textbooks consider that the optimal re-order quantity for materials occurs when 'the cost of storage is equated with the cost of ordering'.  If one assumes that this statement is acceptable and also, in attempting to construct a simple formula for an optimal re-order quantity, that a number of basic assumptions must be made, then a recognised formula can be produced using the following symbols:

$C_o$   =   cost of placing an order
$C_h$   =   cost of storage per annum, expressed as a percentage of stock value
$D$    =   demand in units for a material, per annum
$Q$    =   re-order quantity, in units
$Q/2$  =   average stock level, in units
$p$    =   price per unit

**You are required**

(a)     to present formulae, using the symbols given above, representing:

(i)     total cost of ordering,
(ii)    total cost of storage,
(iii)   total cost of ordering and storage,
(iv)    optimal re-order quantity;                                                                              **(4 marks)**

(b)     to state the limitations experienced in practice which affect the user of the formula for optimal re-order quantity as expressed in (a) (iv) above;                                                             **(4 marks)**

(c)     to calculate the optimal re-order quantity from the following data:

Cost of storage is 20% per annum of stock value
Cost of placing an order is £30 each
Demand for material is 2,000 units per annum
Price of material is £70 per unit;                                                                              **(3 marks)**

(d)    to explain a system of stock usage which renders economic order quantity re-ordering obsolete.

**(4 marks)**
**(Total: 15 marks)**
*(CIMA Nov 93)*

| 3 | MACHINISTS |
|---|---|

A businessman employs 20 sewing machinists but he is aware that ten are better workers than the others. He is considering a training programme for his ten 'less efficient' machinists to increase their efficiency to be equal to that achieved by his 'better' workers.

Relevant data are:

- All the 20 machinists are paid on a piece work system and are engaged on similar work; £0.22 per garment is paid for each good garment produced.

- To rectify each rejected garment costs £0.40; this work is done by sub-contractors (outworkers at home).

- There is one sewing machine for each machinist.

- The garment machining department operates for 2,000 hours per year.

- Average output per machinist is 12 good garments per hour with 1 reject per worker per hour. However, ten 'less efficient' machinists averaged only 10 good garments per hour with 1.5 rejects per worker per hour while the other ten 'better' machinists averaged 14 good garments per hour with 0.5 rejects per worker per hour.

- Depreciation for each sewing machine is £1,000 per year and the variable cost for power, cleaning and preventive maintenance is £0.50 per hour per machine.

- Fixed production overhead, other than depreciation, is being absorbed at £3 per sewing machine hour.

- Selling price per garment is £1.90.

- Direct material cost per garment is £1.20.

- Training will not reduce productive hours because it will be undertaken outside the normal working week.

- The demand for output is increasing so it can be assumed that what can be made can be sold.

**You are required**

(a)    to prepare a statement of annual comparative costs for the 'better' workers and the 'less efficient' workers, **excluding** direct material costs:    **(7 marks)**

(b)    to state the financial benefit to the business, over a one-year period, if £10,000 is spent on a training course for the 'less efficient' workers, assuming that their efficiency would then match that of the 'better' workers;    **(6 marks)**

(c)     to state **two** non-financial benefits, other than an increase in productivity, which may arise if the training programme is undertaken.                                                                      **(2 marks)**
**(Total:  15 marks)**
*(CIMA Nov 93)*

---

## 4     WAGES CONTROL

(a)     Describe briefly the purpose of the 'wages control account'.                                       **(3 marks)**

(b)     A manufacturing company has approximately 600 weekly paid direct and indirect production workers.  It incurred the following costs and deductions relating to the payroll for the week ended 2 May:

|  | £ | £ |
|---|---|---|
| Gross wages |  | 180,460 |
| Deductions |  |  |
|     Employees' National Insurance | 14,120 |  |
|     Employees' pension fund contributions | 7,200 |  |
|     Income tax (PAYE) | 27,800 |  |
|     Court order retentions | 1,840 |  |
|     Trade union subscriptions | 1,200 |  |
|     Private health care contributions | 6,000 |  |
| Total deductions |  | 58,160 |
| Net wages paid |  | 122,300 |

The employer's National Insurance contribution for the week was £18,770.

From the wages analysis the following information was extracted:

|  | Direct workers £ | Indirect workers £ |
|---|---|---|
| Paid for ordinary time | 77,460 | 38,400 |
| Overtime wages at normal hourly rates | 16,800 | 10,200 |
| Overtime premium (treat as overhead) | 5,600 | 3,400 |
| Shift premiums/allowances | 8,500 | 4,500 |
| Capital work-in-progress expenditure* | - | 2,300* |
| Statutory sick pay | 5,700 | 3,300 |
| Paid for idle time | 4,300 | - |
|  | 118,360 | 62,100 |

*Work done by building maintenance workers concreting floor area for a warehouse extension.

**You are required** to show journal entries to indicate clearly how each item should be posted into the accounts

(i)     from the payroll, and
(ii)    from the wages control account to other accounts, based on the wages analysis.

*Note:* narrations for the journal entries are not required.                                       **(12 marks)**
**(Total:  15 marks)**
*(CIMA May 92)*

# 5    EXPERIMENT

Having attended a CIMA course on activity based costing (ABC) you decide to experiment by applying the principles of ABC to the four products currently made and sold by your company. Details of the four products and relevant information are given below for one period:

| Product | A | B | C | D |
|---|---|---|---|---|
| Output in units | 120 | 100 | 80 | 120 |
| Costs per unit | £ | £ | £ | £ |
| Direct material | 40 | 50 | 30 | 60 |
| Direct labour | 28 | 21 | 14 | 21 |
| Machine hours (per unit) | 4 | 3 | 2 | 3 |

The four products are similar and are usually produced in production runs of 20 units and sold in batches of 10 units.

The production overhead is currently absorbed by using a machine hour rate, and the total of the production overhead for the period has been analysed as follows:

|  | £ |
|---|---|
| Machine department costs (rent, business rates, depreciation and supervision) | 10,430 |
| Set up costs | 5,250 |
| Stores receiving | 3,600 |
| Inspection/quality control | 2,100 |
| Materials handling and dispatch | 4,620 |

You have ascertained that the 'cost drivers' to be used are as listed below for the overhead costs shown:

| Cost | Cost driver |
|---|---|
| Set up costs | Number of production runs |
| Stores receiving | Requisitions raised |
| Inspection/quality control | Number of production runs |
| Materials handling and dispatch | Orders executed |

The number of requisitions raised on the stores was 20 for each product and the number of orders executed was 42, each order being for a batch of 10 of a product.

**You are required**

(a)     to calculate the total costs for each product if all overhead costs are absorbed on a machine hour basis;                                                                                   **(4 marks)**

(b)     to calculate the total costs for each product, using activity based costing;            **(7 marks)**

(c)     to calculate and list the unit product costs from your figures in (a) and (b) above, to show the differences and to comment briefly on any conclusions which may be drawn which could have pricing and profit implications.                                                                 **(4 marks)**

                                                                                                **(Total: 15 marks)**
                                                                                                **(CIMA Nov 91)**

# 6    DISTORTIONS

"It is now fairly widely accepted that conventional cost accounting distorts management's view of business through unrepresentative overhead allocation and inappropriate product costing.

This is because the traditional approach usually absorbs overhead costs across products and orders solely on the basis of the direct labour involved in their manufacture. And as direct labour as a proportion of total manufacturing cost continues to fall, this leads to more and more distortion and misrepresentation of the impact of particular products on total overhead costs."

*(From an article in the Financial Times, 2 March 1990)*

**You are required** to discuss the above and to suggest what approaches are being adopted by management accountants to overcome such criticism. **(15 marks)**

*(CIMA May 92)*

## 7    RH LTD

RH Ltd makes and sells one product, the standard production cost of which is as follows for one unit:

|  |  | £ |
|---|---|---|
| Direct labour | 3 hours at £6 per hour | 18 |
| Direct materials | 4 kilograms at £7 per kg | 28 |
| Production overhead | Variable | 3 |
|  | Fixed | 20 |
| Standard production cost |  | 69 |

Normal output is 16,000 units per annum and this figure is used for the fixed production overhead calculation.

Costs relating to selling, distribution and administration are

| Variable | 20 per cent of sales value |
|---|---|
| Fixed | £180,000 per annum. |

The only variance is a fixed production overhead volume variance. There are no units in finished goods stock at 1 October 19X2. The fixed overhead expenditure is spread evenly throughout the year. The selling price per unit is £140.

For the two six-monthly periods detailed below, the number of units to be produced and sold are budgeted as:

|  | *Six months ending 31 March 19X3* | *Six months ending 30 September 19X3* |
|---|---|---|
| Production | 8,500 | 7,000 |
| Sales | 7,000 | 8,000 |

**You are required**

(a)    to prepare statements for management showing sales, costs and profits for **each** of the six-monthly periods, using

    (i)    marginal costing, **(6 marks)**
    (ii)    absorption costing; **(9 marks)**

(b)    to prepare an explanatory statement reconciling for **each** six-monthly period the profit using marginal costing with the profit using absorption costing; **(4 marks)**

(c)    to state and explain **three** business situations where the use of marginal costing may be beneficial to management in making a decision. **(6 marks)**

**(Total: 25 marks)**
*(CIMA Nov 92)*

## 8    SERVICE DEPARTMENT COSTS

"Attributing direct costs and absorbing overhead costs to the product/service through an activity-based costing approach will result in a better understanding of the true cost of the final output."

*[Source: A CIMA publication on costing in a service environment]*

**You are required** to explain and comment on the above statement.                **(15 marks)**

*(CIMA Nov 94)*

## 9    DC LTD

DC Ltd is an engineering company which uses job costing to attribute costs to individual products and services provided to its customers.  It has commenced the preparation of its fixed production overhead cost budget for 1999 and has identified the following costs:

|             | £'000 |
|-------------|------:|
| Machining   |   600 |
| Assembly    |   250 |
| Finishing   |   150 |
| Stores      |   100 |
| Maintenance |    80 |
|             | 1,180 |

The stores and maintenance departments are production service departments.  An analysis of the services they provide indicates that their costs should be apportioned accordingly:

|             | *Machining* | *Assembly* | *Finishing* | *Stores* | *Maintenance* |
|-------------|-------------|------------|-------------|----------|---------------|
| Stores      | 40%         | 30%        | 20%         | -        | 10%           |
| Maintenance | 55%         | 20%        | 20%         | 5%       | -             |

The number of machine and labour hours budgeted for 1999 is:

|              | *Machining* | *Assembly* | *Finishing* |
|--------------|-------------|------------|-------------|
| Machine hours | 50,000      | 4,000      | 5,000       |
| Labour hours  | 10,000      | 30,000     | 20,000      |

**Requirements:**

(a)    Calculate appropriate overhead absorption rates for each production department for 1999.

**(9 marks)**

(b)    Prepare a quotation for job number XX34, which is to be commenced early in 1999, assuming that it has:

|                  |         |        |
|------------------|---------|--------|
| Direct materials | costing | £2,400 |
| Direct labour    | costing | £1,500 |

and requires:

|                      | *Machine hours* | *Labour hours* |
|----------------------|-----------------|----------------|
| Machining department | 45              | 10             |
| Assembly department  | 5               | 15             |
| Finishing department | 4               | 12             |

and that profit is 20% of selling price.                **(5 marks)**

(c)     Assume that in 1999 the actual fixed overhead cost of the assembly department totals £300,000, and that the actual machine hours were 4,200 and actual labour hours were 30,700.

Prepare the fixed production overhead control account for the assembly department, showing clearly the causes of any over/under absorption.                                      **(5 marks)**

(d)     Explain how activity based costing would be used in organisations like DC Ltd.     **(6 marks)**

**(Total: 25 marks)**

*(CIMA May 98)*

## 10     DIRECT SERVICES ORGANISATION

The Direct Services Organisation (DSO) of a large local authority has been trading commercially for several years. Through the competitive tendering system now employed, it is seeking to obtain larger building contracts than have previously been undertaken. The Director of the DSO is concerned about the amount of profit that can be included in each year on uncompleted contracts.

He has asked you, as the management accountant to the DSO, to prepare a report for him stating what factors need to be taken into consideration when determining the amount of profit which should be included at the end of a financial year on uncompleted contracts (the figure which could legitimately be included in the ordinary surplus).

In addition, he specifically asks what profit could be reported at the end of the second year in relation to a three-year contract of which two years have elapsed and fifty per cent of the estimated profit is expected to be earned in the final year of the contract.

For purposes of illustration, to make your explanation clear, use the undermentioned figures.

|                                                                       | £ million |
|-----------------------------------------------------------------------|-----------|
| Estimated three-year contract price                                   | 10.0      |
| Estimated three-year contract total costs                             | 7.0       |
| Estimated contract costs at end of second year                        | 6.0       |
| Estimated value of completed work on the contract at the end of the second year | 7.5 |

**You are required** to prepare the report requested by the Director of the Direct Services Organisation of the local authority.                                      **(20 marks)**

*(CIMA May 93)*

## 11     FAST REPAIRS

The Strategic Planning Department of your company has suggested that a separate division be created in order to enter the market providing a fast repair service for cars.

Enquiries made suggest that one typical fast repair service centre* would have sales and costs as follows, for one year:

|                                          | £       | £       |
|------------------------------------------|---------|---------|
| Sales                                    |         | 540,000 |
| Components and consumable stores         | 301,600 |         |
| Wages and salaries                       | 78,160  |         |
| Bonuses (profit sharing scheme)          | 30,400  |         |
| Pension scheme costs                     | 5,600   |         |
| Staff health scheme                      | 2,840   |         |
| National Insurance contributions         | 7,000   |         |

| A | Rent | 14,000 |
| B | Rates on business premises | 8,000 |
| C | Power, heating and lighting | 6,000 |
| D | Advertising | 10,000 |
| E | Telephones and stationery | 1,600 |
| F | Customer 'creature comforts' (waiting room with coffee and magazines) | 2,000 |

Depreciation on plant and equipment - 10% straight-line
method with nil residual value                            13,280
Charges from Head Office for
    Financing costs                                          4,000
    Administration and share of divisional office expenses    10,000

Total cost                                                              494,480

Net profit before tax                                                    45,520

*Note:* VAT is excluded from the above figures.

*It is envisaged that such a centre would provide for replacement tyres, batteries, exhausts, clutches, brake pads, sparking plugs, filters and oil changes. Mechanics of semi-skilled grades would be employed.

The following data are based on information published by a public company with a nationwide chain of centres which specialises in supplying replacement tyres and exhaust systems.
The figures relate to the supply and fitting of four tyres and an exhaust system for a small family car:

|  | £ | % | £ | % |
|---|---|---|---|---|
| Sales (excluding VAT) |  |  | 154.60 | 100.00 |
| Stocks: spent on buying replacement stocks from suppliers | 77.48 | 50.12 |  |  |
| Staff: wages, pensions, staff health scheme and employer's National Insurance contributions | 30.96 | 20.03 |  |  |
| Operating costs: the costs of running the business - rent, rates, heating, lighting, stationery, advertising and the like | 27.38 | 17.71 |  |  |
| Depreciation | 3.33 | 2.15 |  |  |
| Interest paid on money borrowed | 1.33 | 0.86 |  |  |
| Taxes - paid to the Government | 3.04 | 1.97 |  |  |
| Dividends | 3.80 | 2.46 |  |  |
| Retained profits | 7.28 | 4.70 |  |  |

**You are required**

(a)    to compare the cost structure of one typical fast repair service centre with the information given by the public company specialising in tyre and exhaust replacements. Comment on significant differences and state possible reasons for these differences;                                **(12 marks)**

to indicate which **two** of the six costs listed above (A-F) for the typical fast service repair centre ᵘld be classified as discretionary fixed costs;                                                                 **(3 marks)**

ᵔ costs you have identified as your answer to (b) above could be avoided and if so, to ᵗkely effect on profitability;                                                                                          **(3 marks)**

.ting method(s) or costing technique(s) you would recommend be used by the fast centre

(i)      initially, bearing in mind this is the start of a new operation, and

(ii)     after 12 months' experience of operating.         **(7 marks)**

                                                  **(Total: 25 marks)**

                                                    *(CIMA Nov 90)*

## 12    JOBBING COMPANY

You have just taken up the position as the first full-time accountant for a jobbing engineering company. Previously the accounting work had been undertaken by the company's auditors who had produced the following summarised profit and loss statement for the financial year which ended on 31 March of this year.

|  | £ | £ | £ |
|---|---|---|---|
| Sales |  |  | 2,400,000 |
| Direct material |  | 1,000,000 |  |
| Direct labour: |  |  |  |
| Grinding department | 200,000 |  |  |
| Finishing department | 260,000 | 460,000 |  |
| Production overhead: |  |  |  |
| Grinding | 175,000 |  |  |
| Finishing | 208,000 | 383,000 |  |
| Administration costs |  | 118,500 |  |
| Selling costs |  | 192,000 | 2,153,500 |
| Net profit |  |  | 246,500 |

The sales manager is currently negotiating a price for an enquiry for a job which has been allocated number 878 and he has been given the following information by his staff:

| | |
|---|---|
| Preferred price to obtain a return of $16\frac{2}{3}$% on selling price | £22,656 |
| Lowest acceptable price | £18,880 |

These prices have been based on the following estimated costs for proposed Job 878:

|  | £ | £ |
|---|---|---|
| Direct material |  | 9,000 |
| Direct labour: |  |  |
| Grinding department 400 hours @ £5 | 2,000 |  |
| Finishing department 300 hours @ £6 | 1,800 | 3,800 |
|  |  | 12,800 |
| Add: 47.5% to cover all other costs |  | 6,080 |
| Total cost |  | 18,880 |

The sales manager seeks your advice about the validity of the method he is using to quote for Job 878.

The company is currently busy with a fairly full order book but the Confederation of British Industry has forecast that a recession is imminent for the engineering industry.

**You are required**, as the accountant:

(a)      to criticise the method adopted for estimating the costs which are used as the basis for quoting prices for jobs;                                        **(8 marks)**

(b)     to suggest a better method of estimating job costs and to calculate a revised job cost and price, based on the information available, to give to the sales manager;                                              **(8 marks)**

(c)     to suggest how you would propose to improve the accounting information to assist with controlling costs and providing information for pricing purposes.                                              **(9 marks)**

**(Total:  25 marks)**

*(CIMA Nov 91)*

---

# 13     A PRIVATE HOSPITAL

A private hospital has three main revenue earning departments - maternity, surgical and orthopaedic.  These departments are supported by many other departments, some of which also earn revenue  by charging for services undertaken for external customers.

The radiology department is one of these departments - in addition to undertaking x-ray work for the above three hospital departments, it charges for external work involved in carrying out x-rays on patients who have been referred to it by doctors in general practice.  After this work has been done, patients may continue their treatment within the hospital.

**You are required**, as a cost adviser, to prepare a *report*, addressed to the hospital administrator (bearing in mind the *principles* associated with cost control and responsibility accounting), setting out the information which ought to be provided within the hospital for:

(a)     operational control; and

(b)     making proper charges for services.                                              **(20 marks)**

*(CIMA Nov 94)*

---

# 14     SMALL BUSINESS

Knowing that you are studying for the CIMA qualification, a friend who manages a small business has sought your advice about how to produce quotations in response to the enquiries which her business receives.  Her business is sheet metal fabrication - supplying ducting for dust extraction and air-conditioning installations.  She believes that she has lost orders recently through the use of a job cost estimating system which was introduced, on the advice of her auditors, seven years ago.  You are invited to review this system. Upon investigation, you find that a plant-wide percentage of 125% is added to prime costs in order to arrive at a selling price.   The percentage added is intended to cover all overheads for the three production departments (departments P, Q and R), all the selling, distribution and administration costs, and the profit.

You also discover that the selling, distribution and administration costs equate to roughly 20% of total production costs and that to achieve the desired return on capital employed, a margin of 20% of sales value is necessary.

You recommend an analysis of overhead cost items be undertaken with the objective of determining a direct labour hour rate of overhead absorption for each of the three departments the work passes through. (You think about activity-based costing but feel this would be too sophisticated and difficult to introduce at the present time.)

There are 50 direct workers in the business plus five indirect production people.

From the books, records and some measuring, you ascertain the following information which will enable you to compile an overhead analysis spreadsheet, and to determine overhead absorption rates per direct labour hour for department overhead purposes:

| Cost/expense | Annual amount £ | Basis for apportionment where allocation not given |
|---|---|---|
| Repairs and maintenance | 62,000 | Technical assessment: P £42,000, Q £10,000, R £10,000 |
| Depreciation | 40,000 | Cost of plant and equipment |
| Consumable supplies | 9,000 | Direct labour hours |
| Wage-related costs | 87,000 | 12.5% of direct wages costs |
| Indirect labour | 90,000 | Direct labour hours |
| Canteen/rest/smoke room | 30,000 | Number of direct workers |
| Business rates and insurance | 26,000 | Floor area |

**Other estimates/information**

| | Dept P | Dept Q | Dept R |
|---|---|---|---|
| Estimated direct labour hours | 50,000 | 30,000 | 20,000 |
| Direct wages costs | £386,000 | £210,000 | £100,000 |
| Number of direct workers | 25 | 15 | 10 |
| Floor area in square metres | 5,000 | 4,000 | 1,000 |
| Plant and equipment, at cost | £170,000 | £140,000 | £90,000 |

**You are required** to:

(a)    calculate the overhead absorption rates for each department, based on direct labour hours;

**(9 marks)**

(b)    prepare a sample quotation for Job 976, utilising information given in the question, your answer to (a) above, and the following additional information:

Estimated direct material cost        £800
Estimated direct labour hours:        30 in Department P
                                      10 in Department Q
                                      5 in Department R                        **(3 marks)**

(c)    calculate what would have been quoted for Job 976 under the 'auditor's system' and to comment on whether your friend's suspicions about lost business could be correct.        **(3 marks)**

**(Total: 15 marks)**

*(CIMA Nov 94)*

---

## 15      MR G & MRS H

Mr G and Mrs H have recently formed a consultancy business, and have sought your advice concerning costs and fees. Mr G and Mrs H each wishes to receive a salary of £20,000 in the first year of trading. They have purchased two cars at a cost of £13,000 each and expect to use them for three years. At the end of this time each of the cars has an expected resale value of £4,000. Straight-line depreciation is to be applied.

Mr G and Mrs H each expect to work for 8 hours per day, 5 days per week for 45 weeks per year. They refer to this as available time. 25% of the available time is expected to be used dealing with administrative matters related to their own business, and in the first year it is expected that there will be idle time which will average 22.5% of the available time. The remainder of the available time is expected to be chargeable to clients.

Mr G and Mrs H agreed that their fee structure should comprise:

an hourly rate for productive client work;
an hourly rate for travelling to/from clients; and
a rate per mile travelled to/from clients.

They expect that the travelling time will equal 25% of their chargeable time, and will amount to a total of 18,000 miles. They have agreed that this time should be charged at one-third of their normal hourly rate.

Apart from the costs referred to above, Mr G and Mrs H have estimated their other costs for the first twelve months as follows:

|  | £ |
|---|---|
| Electricity | 1,200 |
| Fuel for vehicles | 1,800 |
| Insurance - professional liability and office | 600 |
| Insurance - vehicles | 800 |
| Mobile telephones | 1,200 |
| Office rent and rates | 8,400 |
| Office telephone/facsimile | 1,800 |
| Postage and stationery | 500 |
| Secretarial costs | 8,400 |
| Servicing and repairs of vehicles | 1,200 |
| Vehicle road tax | 280 |

**You are required** to

(a)     in order that the consultancy business breaks even after paying the required salaries, classify the costs between professional services and vehicle costs, and then, using the above costs and data, calculate the following:

an hourly rate for productive client work,
an hourly rate for travelling to/from clients, and
a rate per mile travelled to/from clients.                          **(15 marks)**

(b)     explain how Mr G and Mrs H may monitor their income and costs during the year to see if they are achieving their objectives.                          **(5 marks)**

(c)     explain the method of cost accounting which should be used by Mr G and Mrs H in order to ensure that each of their clients is charged correctly for the services provided.          **(5 marks)**
                                                                 **(Total:  25 marks)**
                                                                 *(CIMA Nov 95)*

## 16     HR CONSTRUCTION PLC

HR Construction plc makes up its accounts to 31 March each year. The following details have been extracted in relation to two of its contracts:

|  | Contract A | Contract B |
|---|---|---|
| Commencement date | 1 April 1994 | 1 December 1994 |
| Target completion date | 31 May 1995 | 30 June 1995 |
| Retention % | 4 | 3 |
|  | £'000 | £'000 |
| Contract price | 2,000 | 550 |
| Materials sent to site | 700 | 150 |
| Materials returned to stores | 80 | 30 |
| Plant sent to site | 1,000 | 150 |
| Materials transferred | (40) | 40 |
| Materials on site 31 March 1995 | 75 | 15 |
| Plant hire charges | 200 | 30 |

| Labour cost incurred | 300 | 270 |
| Central overhead cost | 75 | 18 |
| Direct expenses incurred | 25 | 4 |
| Value certified | 1,500 | 500 |
| Cost of work not certified | 160 | 20 |
| Cash received from client | 1,440 | 460 |
| Estimated cost of completion | 135 | 110 |

Depreciation is charged on plant using the straight-line method at the rate of 12% per annum.

**Requirements:**

(a) Prepare contract accounts, in columnar format, for EACH of the contracts A and B, showing clearly the amounts to be transferred to profit and loss in respect of each contract. **(20 marks)**

(b) Show balance sheet extracts in respect of EACH contract for fixed assets, debtors and work-in-progress. **(4 marks)**

(c) Distinguish between job, batch and contract costing.

Explain clearly the reasons why these methods are different. **(6 marks)**
**(Total: 30 marks)**
*(CIMA May 96)*

## 17    ST HOTEL

You have recently been appointed as management accountant of the ST hotel, an establishment having capacity for 100 guests. The hotel is open for business for 40 weeks per annum (7 days per week), and is well-known for its restaurant service and friendly lounge bar.

Charges for accommodation are £30 per person per night. The hotel occupancy percentage is budgeted at 70%.

In the restaurant, the average expenditure on meals is £15 per person (excluding drinks) and the target gross profit is 60% of sales. Any drinks ordered with restaurant meals are supplied from the bar which is accounted for separately. The budgeted number of restaurant meals to be sold in the year to 31 December 1997 is 12,000.

The bar sells light meals and snacks which are supplied from the kitchen, in addition to selling drinks via the restaurant and to its own customers. The expected gross profit on bar sales (food and drinks) is 45% of sales value.

The hotel functions are Accommodation, Restaurant, Bar, Kitchen services, Maintenance services, and General administration. Costs are collected and where possible allocated to the different functions of the hotel. However, it is not possible to allocate all of the costs, so some have to be apportioned between the various functional areas of the hotel which benefit from them.

The following costs have been predicted for the year ending 31 December 1997:

| | £ | £ |
|---|---|---|
| Wages and salaries | | |
| Restaurant | 12,000 | |
| Bar | 9,000 | |
| Kitchen | 20,000 | |
| Maintenance | 18,000 | |
| General administration | 12,000 | |
| | | 71,000 |

Food purchases
   Kitchen                                     96,000
Drinks purchases
   Bar                                          50,000
Rates                                      20,250
Electricity                                  8,000
Telephone                             5,000
Insurance                              4,600
Depreciation                         8,000
Laundry                               4,500
Maintenance materials             3,000
Miscellaneous                       3,000

The following bases of cost apportionment are to be used:

Rates - floor area occupied:

| | |
|---|---|
| Accommodation | 600 square metres |
| Restaurant | 30 square metres |
| Bar | 15 square metres |
| Kitchen | 20 square metres |
| Administration | 10 square metres |

Electricity is to be shared on a percentage basis:

| | |
|---|---|
| Accommodation | 25% |
| Restaurant | 5% |
| Bar | 4% |
| Kitchen | 50% |
| Administration | 16% |

Telephone cost is to be shared on a percentage basis:

| | |
|---|---|
| Kitchen | 20% |
| Administration | 80% |

Insurance and depreciation:

| | |
|---|---|
| Accommodation | 30% |
| Restaurant | 15% |
| Bar | 10% |
| Kitchen | 40% |
| Administration | 5% |

Laundry:

| | |
|---|---|
| Accommodation | 90% |
| Restaurant | 10% |

Miscellaneous costs are to be treated as an administration item.

The costs of the service departments are to be apportioned as follows:

| | |
|---|---|
| Kitchen | 75% to the Restaurant and 25% to the Bar. |
| Maintenance | 50% to Accommodation; 20% to Kitchen; 10% each to Restaurant, Bar and Administration. |
| Administration | 70% to Accommodation; 20% to Restaurant and 10% to Maintenance. |

**Requirements:**

(a)    Prepare a departmental profit and loss account, showing clearly, in columns, the budgeted profit from each of Accommodation, Restaurant and Bar.

(Note: You may use the full width of your answer book to lay out this answer.)    **(15 marks)**

(b)    Calculate

   (i)     the cost per guest-night,
   (ii)    the overhead cost per meal served in the Restaurant, and
   (iii)   the overhead cost as a percentage of the sales value for the Bar.    **(6 marks)**

(c)    Explain how the hotel management may make use of the departmental profit and loss account, AND of your calculations in (b) above.    **(4 marks)**

**(Total:  25 marks)**

*(CIMA Nov 96)*

---

## 18    PZ PLC

(a)    PZ plc undertakes work to repair, maintain and construct roads. When a customer requests the company to do work, PZ plc supplies a fixed price to the customer, and allocates a works order number to the customer's request. This works order number is used as a reference number on material requisitions and timesheets to enable the costs of doing the work to be collected.

PZ plc's financial year ends on 30 April. At the end of April 1997, the data shown against four of PZ plc's works orders were:

| Works order number | 488 | 517 | 518 | 519 |
|---|---|---|---|---|
| Date started | 1/3/96 | 1/2/97 | 14/3/97 | 18/3/97 |
| Estimated completion date | 31/5/97 | 30/7/97 | 31/5/97 | 15/5/97 |
| | £'000 | £'000 | £'000 | £'000 |
| Direct labour costs | 105 | 10 | 5 | 2 |
| Direct materials costs | 86 | 7 | 4 | 2 |
| Selling price | 450 | 135 | 18 | 9 |
| Estimated direct costs to complete orders: | | | | |
|   Direct labour | 40 | 60 | 2 | 2 |
|   Direct materials | 10 | 15 | 1 | 1 |
| Independent valuation of work done up to 30 April 1997 | 350 | 30 | 15 | 5 |

Overhead costs are allocated to works orders at the rate of 40% of direct labour costs.

It is company policy not to recognise profit on long-term contracts until they are at least 50% complete.

**Requirements:**

(i)    State, with reasons, whether the above works orders should be accounted for using contract costing or job costing.

**(4 marks)**

(ii)    Based on your classification at (i) above, prepare a statement showing CLEARLY the profit to be recognised and balance sheet work-in-progress valuation of EACH of the above works orders in respect of the financial year ended 30 April 1997.

**(10 marks)**

(iii)    Comment critically on the policy of attributing overhead costs to works orders on the basis of direct labour cost.

**(6 marks)**

(b)    Explain the main features of process costing. Describe what determines the choice between using process costing or specific order costing in a manufacturing organisation.

**(10 marks)**
**(Total:  30 marks)**
*(CIMA May 97)*

## 19    ABC CONSULTING LTD

ABC Consulting Ltd employs four full-time consultants, together with two support staff, and provides a business consultancy service to engineering companies.

Each consultant earns a salary, which, together with related employment costs, is expected to total £63,000 in 1999.  Each consultant is expected to work for 35 hours per week, 45 weeks per year.

ABC Consulting Ltd's work is project-based and costs are collected against projects (WIP) on the following bases:

| | |
|---|---|
| Consulting time | £45 per consulting hour |
| Administration overhead | £15 per consulting hour |
| Travel costs – motor | £0.40 per mile |
| Rechargeable project expenses | At cost |

Clients are charged according to the following fee scale:

| | |
|---|---|
| Consulting time | £80.00 per consulting hour |
| Travel costs – motor | £0.50 per mile |
| Rechargeable project expenses | At cost |

The following balances have been extracted from the accounting records of ABC Consulting Ltd at 31 March 1999.

| | DR £ | CR £ |
|---|---|---|
| Uncompleted projects (work-in-progress) | 16,425 | |
| Debtors' control | 15,800 | |
| Creditors' control | | 1,400 |

The following data relates to April 1999:

(1)    Costs incurred:

| | |
|---|---|
| Consultants' salaries and related costs | £22,200 |
| Travel costs – motor | £2,100 |
| Rechargeable project expenses | £1,350 |
| Administration overhead | £6,900 |

(2)     Details extracted from project records:

| | |
|---|---|
| Consultancy hours | 485 |
| Chargeable mileage | 4,477 miles |

(3)     Invoices were issued to clients based on:

| | |
|---|---|
| Consultancy hours | 575 |
| Chargeable mileage | 5,888 miles |
| Rechargeable project expenses | £939 |

(4)     Receipts from clients totalled £14,120.

(5)     Payments made to creditors:

| | |
|---|---|
| Consultants' salaries and related costs | £22,200 |
| Travel costs – motor | £1,800 |
| Rechargeable project expenses | £1,450 |
| Administration overhead | £7,420 |

Ignore VAT

**Requirements:**

(a)     Write up the transactions for April 1999 using the following ledger accounts:

- Uncompleted projects (work-in-progress)
- Debtors' control
- Creditors' control
- Travel costs – motor control
- Consultants' salary cost control
- Administration overhead control
- Fees invoiced (sales)
- project costs invoiced (cost of sales)          **(17 marks)**

(b)     Prepare a profit/loss statement for April 1999.          **(5 marks)**

(c)     Explain, using examples, the different types of specific order costing methods used by organisations. Your explanation should make reference to the characteristics of each method, and why it may be appropriate.          **(8 marks)**

                                                         **(Total: 30 marks)**

                                                         *(CIMA May 99)*

---

## 20    SEQUENTIAL PROCESSES

Product P63 is made by three sequential processes, I, II and III. In process III a by-product arises and after further processing in process BP, at a cost of £2 per unit, by-product BP9 is produced.

Selling and distribution expenses of £1 per unit are incurred in marketing BP9 at a selling price of £9 per unit.

| | Process I | Process II | Process III |
|---|---|---|---|
| Standards provide for | | | |
|     Normal loss in process, of input, of | 10% | 5% | 10% |
|     Loss in process, having a scrap value, | | | |
|        per unit of | £1 | £3 | £5 |

For the month of April 19X8 the following data are given:

|  | Process I | Process II | Process III | Process BP |
|---|---|---|---|---|
| Output, in units | 8,800 | 8,400 | 7,000 of P63 | 420 of BP9 |

|  | £ | £ | £ | Total £ |
|---|---|---|---|---|
| Costs |  |  |  |  |
| Direct materials introduced (10,000 units) | 20,000 |  |  | 20,000 |
| Direct materials added | 6,000 | 12,640 | 23,200 | 41,840 |
| Direct wages | 5,000 | 6,000 | 10,000 | 21,000 |
| Direct expenses | 4,000 | 6,200 | 4,080 | 14,280 |

Budgeted production overhead for the month was £84,000.

Absorption is based on a percentage of direct wages.

There were no stocks at the beginning or end of the month.

**You are required**, using the information given, to prepare accounts for

(a)    each of processes I, II and III;

(b)    process BP;

(c)    (i)    abnormal losses;
        (ii)   abnormal gains;

        showing the balances to be transferred to the profit and loss statement.          **(25 marks)**

## 21    QR LTD

QR Ltd operates a chemical process which produces four different products Q, R, S and T from the input of one raw material plus water. Budget information for the forthcoming financial year is as follows:

|  | £'000 |
|---|---|
| Raw materials cost | 268 |
| Initial processing cost | 464 |

| Product | Output in litres | Sales £'000 | Additional processing cost £'000 |
|---|---|---|---|
| Q | 400,000 | 768 | 160 |
| R | 90,000 | 232 | 128 |
| S | 5,000 | 32 | - |
| T | 9,000 | 240 | 8 |

The company policy is to apportion the costs prior to the split-off point on a method based on net sales value.

Currently, the intention is to sell product S without further processing but to process the other three products after the split-off point. However, it has been proposed that an alternative strategy would be to sell all four products at the split-off point without further processing. If this were done the selling price obtainable would be as follows:

|   | Per litre £ |
|---|---|
| Q | 1.28 |
| R | 1.60 |
| S | 6.40 |
| T | 20.00 |

**You are required**

(a)    to prepare a budgeted profit statement showing the profit or loss for each product, and in total, if the current intention is proceeded with;                                    **(10 marks)**

(b)    to show the profit or loss by product, and in total, if the alternative strategy were to be adopted;                                    **(6 marks)**

(c)    to recommend what should be done and why, assuming that there is no more profitable alternative use for the plant.                                    **(4 marks)**

**(Total: 20 marks)**

*(CIMA May 90)*

## 22    BK CHEMICALS

BK Chemicals produces three joint products in one common process but each product is capable of being further processed separately after the split-off point. The estimated data given below relate to June:

|  | Product B | Product K | Product C |
|---|---|---|---|
| Selling price at split-off point (per litre) | £6 | £8 | £9 |
| Selling price after further processing (per litre) | £10 | £20 | £30 |
| Post-separation point costs | £20,000 | £10,000 | £22,500 |
| Output in litres | 3,500 | 2,500 | 2,000 |

Pre-separation point joint costs are estimated to be £40,000 and it is current practice to apportion these to the three products according to litres produced.

(a)    **You are required**

(i)    to prepare a statement of estimated profit or loss for each product and in total for June if all three products are processed further, and

(ii)    to advise how profits could be maximised if one or more products are sold at the split-off point. Your advice should be supported by a profit statement.                                    **(11 marks)**

(b)    It has been suggested that responsibility accounting would be more relevant in BK Chemicals with the process incurring the common cost being treated as a profit centre.

**You are required**

(i)    to explain briefly how this could best be achieved,
(ii)    to state the resulting profit to be shown for the common process, and
(iii)    to state **two** advantages of this approach.                                    **(5 marks)**

(c)    Discuss the problems associated with joint cost apportionment in relation to

   (i)    planning,
   (ii)   control, and
   (iii)  decision making.

                                                                    **(9 marks)**
                                                              **(Total:  25 marks)**
                                                                  *(CIMA May 92)*

## 23    CHEMICAL COMPOUND

A chemical compound is made by raw material being processed through two processes.  The output of Process A is passed to Process B where further material is added to the mix.  The details of the process costs for the financial period number 10 were as shown below:

**Process A**
   Direct material           2,000 kilograms at £5 per kg
   Direct labour             £7,200
   Process plant time        140 hours at £60 per hour
**Process B**
   Direct material           1,400 kilograms at £12 per kg
   Direct labour             £4,200
   Process plant time        80 hours at £72.50 per hour

The departmental overhead for Period 10 was £6,840 and is absorbed into the costs of each process on direct labour cost.

|                        | *Process A*      | *Process B*     |
|------------------------|------------------|-----------------|
| Expected output was    | 80% of input     | 90% of input    |
| Actual output was      | 1,400 kgs        | 2,620 kgs       |

Assume no finished stock at the beginning of the period and no work-in-progress at either the beginning or the end of the period.

Normal loss is contaminated material which is sold as scrap for £0.50 per kg from Process A and £1.825 per kg from Process B, for both of which immediate payment is received.

**You are required** to prepare the accounts for Period 10, for

(i)     Process A,
(ii)    Process B,
(iii)   Normal loss/gain,
(iv)    Abnormal loss/gain,
(v)     Finished goods,
(vi)    Profit and loss (extract).

                                                                    **(15 marks)**
                                                                  *(CIMA Nov 92)*

## 24    PRODUCT COSTS

(a)    'Whilst the ascertainment of product costs could be said to be one of the objectives of cost accounting, where joint products are produced and joint costs incurred the total cost computed for the product may depend upon the method selected for the apportionment of joint costs, thus making it difficult for management to make decisions about the future of products.'

   **You are required** to discuss the above statement and to state **two** different methods of apportioning joint costs to joint products.                                        **(8 marks)**

(b)    A company using process costing manufactures a single product which passes through two processes, the output of process 1 becoming the input to process 2.  Normal losses and abnormal losses are defective units having a scrap value and cash is received at the end of the period for all such units.

The following information relates to the four-week period of accounting period number 7.

Raw material issued to process 1 was 3,000 units at a cost of £5 per unit.

There was no opening or closing work-in-progress but opening and closing stocks of finished goods were £20,000 and £23,000 respectively.

|  | *Process 1* | *Process 2* |
|---|---|---|
| Normal loss as a percentage of input | 10% | 5% |
| Output in units | 2,800 | 2,600 |
| Scrap value per unit | £2 | £5 |
| Additional components | £1,000 | £780 |
| Direct wages incurred | £4,000 | £6,000 |
| Direct expenses incurred | £10,000 | £14,000 |
| Production overhead as a percentage of direct wages | 75% | 125% |

**You are required** to present the accounts for

Process 1
Process 2
Finished goods
Normal loss
Abnormal loss
Abnormal gain
Profit and loss (so far as it relates to any of the accounts listed above).          **(17 marks)**
**(Total:  25 marks)**
*(CIMA Nov 89)*

## 25    PQR LTD

PQR Ltd produces two joint products - P and Q - together with a by-product R, from a single main process (process 1).  Product P is sold at the point of separation for £5 per kg whereas product Q is sold for £7 per kg after further processing into product Q2.  By-product R is sold without further processing for £1.75 per kg.

Process 1 is closely monitored by a team of chemists who planned the output per 1,000 kg of input materials to be as follows:

| Product P | 500 kg |
|---|---|
| Product Q | 350 kg |
| Product R | 100 kg |
| Toxic waste | 50 kg |

The toxic waste is disposed of at a cost of £1.50 per kg, and arises at the end of processing.

Process 2, which is used for further processing of product Q into product Q2, has the following cost structure:

| Fixed costs | £6,000 per week |
|---|---|
| Variable costs | £1.50 per kg processed |

The following actual data relate to the first week of accounting period 10:

*Process 1*

| | |
|---|---:|
| Opening work in process | Nil |
| Materials input  10,000 kg costing | £15,000 |
| Direct labour | £10,000 |
| Variable overhead | £4,000 |
| Fixed overhead | £6,000 |

*Outputs:*

| | |
|---|---:|
| Product P | 4,800 kg |
| Product Q | 3,600 kg |
| Product R | 1,000 kg |
| Toxic waste | 600 kg |
| Closing work in process | Nil |

*Process 2*

| | |
|---|---:|
| Opening work in process | Nil |
| Input of product Q | 3,600 kg |
| Output of product Q2 | 3,300 kg |
| Closing work in process | 300 kg, 50% converted |

Conversion costs were incurred in accordance with the planned cost structure.

**You are required to**

(a)    prepare the main process account for the first week of period 10 using the final sales value method to attribute pre-separation costs to joint products.                                  **(12 marks)**

(b)    prepare the toxic waste account and process 2 account for the first week of period 10.      **(9 marks)**

(c)    comment on the method used by PQR Ltd to attribute pre-separation costs to its joint products.
                                                                                      **(4 marks)**

(d)    advise the management of PQR Ltd whether or not, on purely financial grounds, it should continue to process product Q into product Q2

    (i)    if product Q could be sold at the point of separation for £4.30 per kg and

    (ii)    if 60% of the weekly fixed costs of process 2 were avoided by not processing product Q further.                                                                         **(5 marks)**
                                                                          **(Total:  30 marks)**
                                                                          *(CIMA May 95)*

## 26   ABC LTD

ABC Ltd operates an integrated accounting system.  It is a chemical processing company, which converts three raw materials - W, X and Y - into a final product Z which is used as a fertiliser in the farming industry.

On 30 September 1993 an extract of the trial balance taken from its ledgers was as follows:

|  | £ | £ |
|---|---|---|
| Raw material control account | 15,400 |  |
| Work-in-progress control account | 21,520 |  |
| Production overhead control account |  | 2,360 |
| Abnormal loss account | 1,685 |  |
| Abnormal gain account |  | 930 |
| Finished goods control account | 27,130 |  |

The following notes are also relevant:

(1)    ABC Ltd prepares its financial accounts to 31 October each year.

(2)    The raw material control account balance comprises:

| Direct materials | | £ |
|---|---|---|
| Material X | 4,200 kg @ £2 per kg | 8,400 |
| Material Y | 1,050 kg @ £4 per kg | 4,200 |
| Indirect materials | | 2,800 |
| | | 15,400 |

(3)    The work-in-progress control account balance comprises:

| Process 2 | 8,400 kg | Process 1 | 8,720 |
|---|---|---|---|
| | | Materials | 2,000 |
| | | Labour | 3,600 |
| | | Overhead | 7,200 |
| | | | 21,520 |

During October 1993, the following transactions occurred:

(a)    Indirect materials purchased on credit amounted to £1,300.

(b)    Indirect materials purchased on credit as follows:

| Material W | 10,500 kg costing | £4,960 |
|---|---|---|
| Material X | 10,000 kg costing | £21,000 |
| Material Y | 5,000 kg costing | £19,000 |

(c)    Direct wages were incurred as follows:

| Process 1 | £17,160 |
|---|---|
| Process 2 | £8,600 |

(d)    Indirect wages were incurred amounting to £2,980.

(e)    Production overhead costs incurred (excluding materials and labour costs) amounted to £31,765.

(f)    Indirect materials consumed in the month amounted to £1,450.

(g)    Direct materials were issued to production as follows:

| Process 1 | 10,500 kg of W costing | £4,960 |
|---|---|---|
| | 7,200 kg of X costing | £14,700 |

Process 2                 4,050 kg of Y costing        £15,600

There was no opening or closing stock of material W.

(h)      The cost of finished goods sold during the month amounted to £125,740.

The completed output from the two process for October 1993 amounted to

Process 1                 13,100 kg
Process 2                 20,545 kg

Closing work-in-progress, which is 100% complete as to materials but only 50% completed as to conversion cost, amounted to

Process 1                 2,000 kg
Process 2                 1,500 kg

Normal losses, caused by evaporation and occurring at the end of processing, are expected in each of the processes as follows:

Process 1                            15% of throughput
Process 2                            10% of throughput

*Note:* Throughput equals opening work-in-progress plus materials introduced less closing work-in-progress.

Production overhead is absorbed using the following absorption rates:

Process 1                            150% of direct labour cost
Process 2                            200% of direct labour cost

**You are required** to

(a)      Prepare the accounts for EACH of the TWO processes for the month of October 1993.     **(16 marks)**

(b)      Prepare the SIX ledger accounts for which opening balances have been given, commencing with those balances, entering the transactions for the month of October 1993 and making entries in those accounts for 31 October 1993 as appropriate.                                              **(9 marks)**

(c)      State the differences between using an integrated accounting system compared to an interlocking system, and explain the advantages and disadvantages caused by those differences.     **(5 marks)**

**(Total:  30 marks)**
*(Specimen paper)*

## 27    PAINT MANUFACTURER

XYZ plc, a paint manufacturer, operates a process costing system.  The following details relate to process 2 for the month of October 1997:

Opening work-in-progress          5,000 litres fully complete as to transfers from process 1 and 40% complete as to labour and overhead, valued at £60,000.

Transfer from process 1          65,000 litres valued at cost of £578,500
Direct labour                    £101,400
Variable overhead                £80,000
Fixed overhead                   £40,000

Normal loss                      5% of volume transferred from process 1, scrap value £2.00 per litre.

| | |
|---|---|
| Actual output | 30,000 litres of Paint X (a joint product) |
| | 25,000 litres of Paint Y (a joint product) |
| | 7,000 litres of by-product Z |
| | |
| Closing work-in-progress | 6,000 litres fully complete as to transfers from process 1 and 60% complete as to labour and overhead. |

The final selling prices of products X, Y and Z are:

| | |
|---|---|
| Paint X | £15.00 per litre |
| Paint Y | £18.00 per litre |
| Product Z | £4.00 per litre |

There are no further processing costs associated with either Paint X or the by-product, but Paint Y requires further processing at a cost of £1.50 per litre.

All three products incur packaging costs of £0.50 per litre before they can be sold.

**Requirements:**

(a) Prepare the process 2 account for the month of October 1997, apportioning the common costs between the joint products, based upon their values at the point of separation. **(20 marks)**

(b) Prepare the abnormal loss / gain account showing clearly the amount to be transferred to profit and loss account. **(4 marks)**

(c) Describe one other method of apportioning the common costs between the joint products, AND explain why it is necessary to make such apportionments, and their usefulness when measuring product profitability. **(6 marks)**

**(Total: 30 marks)**

*(CIMA Nov 97)*

---

## 28    ABC PLC

---

ABC plc operates an integrated cost accounting system and has a financial year which ends on 30 September. It operates in a processing industry in which a single product is produced by passing inputs through two sequential processes. A normal loss of 10% of input is expected in each process.

The following account balances have been extracted from its ledger at 31 August 1998:

| | Debit £ | Credit £ |
|---|---|---|
| Process 1 (Materials £4,400; Conversion costs £3,744) | 8,144 | |
| Process 2 (Process 1 £4,431; Conversion costs £5,250) | 9,681 | |
| Abnormal loss | 1,400 | |
| Abnormal gain | | 300 |
| Overhead control account | | 250 |
| Sales | | 585,000 |
| Cost of sales | 442,500 | |
| Finished goods stock | 65,000 | |

ABC plc uses the weighted average method of accounting work in process.

During September 1998 the following transactions occurred:

| Process 1 | materials input | 4,000 kg costing | £22,000 £5. 5/kg each. |
|---|---|---|---|
| | labour cost | | £12,000 |
| | transfer to process 2 | 2,400 kg | |
| Process 2 | transfer from process 1 | 2,400 kg | |
| | labour cost | | £15,000 |
| | transfer to finished goods | 2,500 kg | |

| | |
|---|---|
| Overhead costs incurred amounted to | £54,000 |
| Sales to customers were | £52,000 |

Overhead costs are absorbed into process costs on the basis of 150% of labour cost.

The losses which arise in process 1 have no scrap value: those arising in process 2 can be sold for £2 per kg.

Details of opening and closing work in process for the month of September 1998 are as follows:

| | Opening | Closing |
|---|---|---|
| Process 1 | 3,000 kg | 3,400 kg |
| Process 2 | 2,250 kg | 2,600 kg |

In both processes closing work in process is fully complete as to material cost and 40% complete as to conversion cost.

Stocks of finished goods at 30 September 1998 were valued at cost of £60,000.

**Requirements:**

(a)     Prepare the ledger accounts for September 1998 and the annual profit and loss account of ABC plc. (Commence with the balance given above, balance off and transfer any balances as appropriate.)

                                                                     **(25 marks)**

(b)     Prepare a transaction record layout which would be suitable for ABC plc if it were to use a computerised database system to record its accounting transactions.

         Your answer should indicate the fields to be used, their length, and the type of data which they would contain (ie, alphabetic, numeric, or alpha-numeric).        **(5 marks)**

                                                            **(Total: 30 marks)**

                                                             **(CIMA Nov 98)**

## 29    XY LTD

*opening Bal = zero.*

XY Ltd commenced trading on 1 February with fully paid issued share capital of £500,000, Fixed Assets of £275,000 and Cash at Bank of £225,000. By the end of April, the following transactions had taken place:

(1)     Purchases on credit from suppliers amounted to £572,500 of which £525,000 was raw materials and £47,500 was for items classified as production overhead.

(2)     Wages incurred for all staff were £675,000, represented by cash paid £500,000 and wage deductions of £175,000 in respect of income tax etc.

(3)     Payments were made by cheque for the following overhead costs:

| | £ |
|---|---|
| Production | 20,000 |
| Selling | 40,000 |
| Administration | 25,000 |

(4) Issues of raw materials were £180,000 to Department A, £192,500 to Department B and £65,000 for production overhead items.

(5) Wages incurred were analysed to functions as follows:

|  | £ |
|---|---|
| Work-in-progress – Department A | 300,000 |
| Work-in-progress – Department B | 260,000 |
| Production overhead | 42,500 |
| Selling overhead | 47,500 |
| Administration overhead | 25,000 |
|  | 675,000 |

(6) Production overhead absorbed in the period by Department A was £110,000 and by Department B £120,000.

(7) The production facilities, when not in use, were patrolled by guards from a security firm and £26,000 was owing for this service. £39,000 was also owed to a firm of management consultants which advises on production procedures; invoices for these two services are to be entered into the accounts.            indirect cost of production

(8) The cost of finished goods completed was

|  | Department A £ | Department B £ |
|---|---|---|
| Direct labour | 290,000 | 255,000 |
| Direct materials | 175,000 | 185,000 |
| Production overhead | 105,000 | 115,000 |
|  | 570,000 | 555,000 |

(9) Sales on credit were £870,000 and the cost of those sales were £700,000.
(10) Depreciation of productive plant and equipment was £15,000.
(11) Cash received from debtors totalled £520,000.
(12) Payments to creditors were £150,000.

**You are required**

(a) to open the ledger accounts at the commencement of the trading period;
(b) using integrated accounting, to record the transactions for the three months ended 30 April;
(c) to prepare, in vertical format, for presentation to management,

 (i) a profit statement for the period;
 (ii) the balance sheet at 30 April. **(20 marks)**
*(CIMA May 91)*

## 30   VARIOUS POINTS

(a) One of the weaknesses, it is often argued, of operating an integrated accounting system is that 'notional costs' cannot be entered into the accounting records.

**You are required** to discuss the above statement, to explain the meaning of notional costs and to illustrate with two examples why their inclusion in cost accounts may be desirable. **(7 marks)**

(b)    Knowing that you are studying for the CIMA examinations, a friend seeks your advice on the following problem. He owns and manages a small unincorporated business and is concerned at the high level of charges made by his bank for the business account even though it is seldom overdrawn. Querying the charge with his Bank Manager, he was told that the charge was based on the costs of handling his business account. Your friend does not see how the bank can possibly arrive at a cost of handling his business account.

**You are required** to explain to your friend the problems faced by the bank at arriving at a cost, as suggested by the Bank Manager, including any limitations attaching to such a cost.    **(9 marks)**

(c)    The reduced price of personal computers has undoubtedly led to a growth in their use for cost and management accounting purposes.

**You are required** to list and explain very briefly four benefits which have followed from this increased use of personal computers.    **(4 marks)**
**(Total: 20 marks)**
*(CIMA May 92)*

## 31    NB LTD

NB Ltd operates an integrated accounting system. At the beginning of October, the following balances appeared in the trial balance:

|  | £'000 | £'000 | £'000 |
|---|---|---|---|
| Freehold buildings | | 800 | |
| Plant and equipment, at cost | | 480 | |
| Provision for depreciation on plant and equipment | | | 100 |
| Stocks: | | | |
| Raw materials | | 400 | |
| Work in Process 1: | | | |
| direct materials | 71 | | |
| direct wages | 50 | | |
| production overhead | 125 | 246 | |
| Work in Process 2: | | | |
| direct materials | 127 | | |
| direct wages | 70 | | |
| production overhead | 105 | 302 | |
| Finished goods | | 60 | |
| Debtors | | 1,120 | |
| Capital | | | 2,200 |
| Profit retained | | | 220 |
| Creditors | | | 300 |
| Bank | | | 464 |
| Sales | | | 1,200 |
| Cost of sales | | 888 | |
| Abnormal loss | | 9 | |
| Production overhead under/over absorbed | | | 21 |
| Administration overhead | | 120 | |
| Selling and distribution overhead | | 80 | |
| | | 4,505 | 4,505 |

The transactions during the month of October were:

|  | £'000 |
|---|---|
| Raw materials purchased on credit | 210 |
| Raw materials returned to suppliers | 10 |
| Raw materials issued to: |  |
| Process 1 | 136 |
| Process 2 | 44 |
| Direct wages incurred: |  |
| Process 1 | 84 |
| Process 2 | 130 |
| Direct wages paid | 200 |
| Production salaries paid | 170 |
| Production expenses paid | 250 |
| Received from debtors | 1,140 |
| Paid to creditors | 330 |
| Administration overhead paid | 108 |
| Selling and distribution overhead paid | 84 |
| Sales, on credit | 1,100 |
| Cost of goods sold | 844 |

|  | Direct materials £'000 | Direct wages £'000 |
|---|---|---|
| Abnormal loss in: |  |  |
| Process 1 | 6 | 4 |
| Process 2 | 18 | 6 |
| Transfer from Process 1 to Process 2 | 154 | 94 |
| Transfer from Process 2 to finished goods | 558 | 140 |

Plant and equipment is depreciated at the rate of 20% per annum, using the straight-line basis. Production overhead is absorbed on the basis of direct wages cost.

**You are required**

(a) to ascertain and state the production overhead absorption rates used for Process 1 and for Process 2;

**(2 marks)**

(b) to write up the ledger accounts; **(25 marks)**

(c) to explain the nature of abnormal losses and **two** possible reasons for their occurrence. **(3 marks)**

**(Total: 30 marks)**

*(CIMA Nov 93)*

## 32 RETAIL DEPARTMENT STORE

The directors of a family-owned retail department store were shocked to receive the following profit statement for the year ended 31 January 19X0:

|  | £'000 | £'000 | £'000 |
|---|---|---|---|
| Sales |  | 5,000 |  |
| Less: Cost of sales |  | 3,398 |  |
|  |  |  | 1,602 |
| Wages – Departments | 357 |  |  |
| Office | 70 |  |  |
| Restaurant | 26 |  |  |
|  |  | 453 |  |
| Delivery costs |  | 200 |  |
| Departmental expenses |  | 116 |  |
| Salaries – Directors and management |  | 100 |  |

| | |
|---|---:|
| Directors' fees | 20 |
| Sales promotion and advertising | 120 |
| Store capacity costs ie, rent, rates and energy | 488 |
| Interest on bank overdraft | 20 |
| Discounts allowed | 25 |
| Bad debts | 15 |
| Miscellaneous expenses | 75 |
| | —— |
| | 1,632 |

Net loss  (30)

Management accounting has not been employed but the following breakdown has been extracted from the financial records:

| | Ladies' wear £'000 | Men's wear £'000 | General £'000 | Toys £'000 | Restaurant £'000 |
|---|---|---|---|---|---|
| Sales | 800 | 400 | 2,200 | 1,400 | 200 |
| Purchases | 506 | 220 | 1,290 | 1,276 | 167 |
| Opening stock | 90 | 70 | 200 | 100 | 5 |
| Closing stock | 100 | 50 | 170 | 200 | 6 |
| Wages | 96 | 47 | 155 | 59 | 26 |
| Departmental expenses | 38 | 13 | 35 | 20 | 10 |
| Sales promotion and advertising | 10 | 5 | 30 | 75 | - |
| Floor space occupied | 20% | 15% | 20% | 35% | 10% |

(Departments: Ladies' wear, Men's wear, General, Toys. Restaurant.)

The directors are considering two separate proposals which are independent of each other:

(1)    Closing the Toys Department
(2)    Reducing selling prices on Ladies' Wear and Men's Wear by 5% in the hope of boosting sales.

**You are required**

(a)    to present the information for the year to 31 January 19X0 in a more meaningful way to aid decision making.  Include any statistics or indicators of performance which you consider to be useful;**(12 marks)**

(b)    to show and explain the change in profit for a full year if the Toys Department were closed and if all other costs remain the same;                                                                                       **(4 marks)**

(c)    to show for the Ladies' Wear and Men's Wear Departments, if selling prices are reduced by 5% and unit costs remain the same,

   (i)    the increase in sales value (to the nearest thousand pounds) that would be required for a full year to maintain the gross profits, in £s, earned by each of these Departments; and

   (ii)   the increase in (i) above expressed as a percentage of the sales for each Department to 31 January 19X0;                                                                                       **(8 marks)**

(d)    to state your views on both the proposals being considered by the directors and recommend any alternative action you think appropriate.                                                                        **(6 marks)**
                                                                                       **(Total:  30 marks)**
                                                                                       *(CIMA May 90)*

## 33    GLASS BOTTLES

A manufacturer of glass bottles has been affected by competition from plastic bottles and is currently operating at between 65 and 70 per cent of maximum capacity.

The company at present reports profits on an absorption costing basis but with the high fixed costs associated with the glass container industry and a substantial difference between sales volumes and production in some months, the accountant has been criticised for reporting widely different profits from month to month. To counteract this criticism, he is proposing in future to report profits based on marginal costing and in his proposal to management lists the following reasons for wishing to change:

(1)     Marginal costing provides for the complete segregation of fixed costs, thus facilitating closer control of production costs.

(2)     It eliminates the distortion of interim profit statements which occur when there are seasonal fluctuations in sales volume although production is at a fairly constant level.

(3)     It results in cost information which is more helpful in determining the sales policy necessary to maximise profits.

From the accounting records the following figures were extracted: standard cost per gross (A gross is 144 bottles and is the cost unit used within the business.):

|  | £ |
|---|---|
| Direct materials | 8.00 |
| Direct labour | 7.20 |
| Variable production overhead | 3.36 |
| Total variable production cost | 18.56 |
| Fixed production overhead | 7.52* |
| Total production standard cost | 26.08 |

*The fixed production overhead rate was based on the following computations:

Total annual fixed production overhead was budgeted at £7,584,000 or £632,000 per month.

Production volume was set at 1,008,000 gross bottles or 70 per cent of maximum capacity.

There is a slight difference in budgeted fixed production overhead at different levels of operating:

| Activity level Per cent of maximum capacity | Amount per month |
|---|---|
|  | £'000 |
| 50 - 75 | 632 |
| 76 - 90 | 648 |
| 91 - 100 | 656 |

You may assume that actual fixed production overhead incurred was as budgeted.

Additional information:

|  | September | October |
|---|---|---|
| Gross sold | 87,000 | 101,000 |
| Gross produced | 115,000 | 78,000 |
| Sales price, per gross | £32 | £32 |
| Fixed selling costs | £120,000 | £120,000 |
| Fixed administrative costs | £80,000 | £80,000 |

There were no finished goods in stock at 1 September.

**You are required**

(a)    to prepare monthly profit statements for September and October using

    (i)    absorption costing; and
    (ii)    marginal costing;    **(16 marks)**

(b)    to comment briefly on the accountant's three reasons which he listed to support his proposal.

**(9 marks)**
**(Total:  25 marks)**
*(CIMA Nov 90)*

## 34   THREE PRODUCTS

Three products - X, Y and Z - are made and sold by a company; information is given below:

|  | *Product X* £ | *Product Y* £ | *Product Z* £ |
|---|---|---|---|
| Standard costs |  |  |  |
|   Direct materials | 50 | 120 | 90 |
|   Variable overhead | 12 | 7 | 16 |

| *Direct labour:* | *Rate per hour* £ | *Hours* | *Hours* | *Hours* |
|---|---|---|---|---|
| Department A | 5 | 14 | 8 | 15 |
| Department B | 6 | 4 | 3 | 5 |
| Department C | 4 | 8 | 4 | 15 |

Total fixed overhead for the year was budgeted at £300,000.

The budget for the current financial year, which was prepared for a recessionary period, was based on the following sales:

| *Product* | *Sales in units* | *Selling price per unit* £ |
|---|---|---|
| X | 7,500 | 210 |
| Y | 6,000 | 220 |
| Z | 6,000 | 300 |

However, the market for each of the products has improved and the Sales Director believes that without a change in selling prices, the number of units sold could be increased for each product by the following percentages:

| *Product* | *Increase* |
|---|---|
| X | 20% |
| Y | 25% |
| Z | 33⅓% |

When the Sales Director's views were presented to a management meeting, the Production Director declared that although it might be possible to sell more units of product, output could not be expanded because he was unable to recruit more staff for Department B, there being a severe shortage of the skills needed by this department.

**You are required**

(a)    to show in the form of a statement for management, the unit costs of each of the three products and the total *profit* expected for the current year based on the original sales figures;    **(4 marks)**

(b)      to state the profit if the most profitable mixture of the products was made and sold, utilising the higher sales figures and the limitation on Department B;                                           **(6 marks)**

(c)      to identify and to comment on *three* possible problems which may arise if the mixture in (b) above were to be produced;                                                                                  **(6 marks)**

**(Total: 16 marks)**
*(CIMA Nov 91)*
*(amended)*

---

## 35      CD LTD

The opportunities afforded by the European Union have created a pleasant problem for CD Ltd, which is considering concentrating its production on one of two products - 'Robroy' or 'Trigger' - both of which are currently made and sold.  With the expansion in sales possible, either product can be sold in quantities which exceed the capacity of the present production facilities.  Therefore, the use of sub-contractors is being considered.

Sub-contractor Jason can produce up to a maximum of 10,000 units of Robroy **or** 8,000 units of Trigger in a year **for the type of work done by Department 1**.  Jason's prices would be £110 for Robroy and £170 for Trigger, both prices being inclusive of the raw materials.

Sub-contractor Nadira can produce up to a maximum of 6,400 units of Robroy **or** 4,000 units of Trigger in a year **for the type of work done by Department 2**.  Nadira's prices would be £120 for Robroy and £154 for Trigger, both prices being inclusive of the raw materials.

A market research study has shown that for more than 22,000 units of Robroy to be sold in a year, the price of the total quantity sold would need to be reduced to £270 each.  If more than 18,000 units of Trigger are to be sold in a year, the price of the total quantity sold would need to be reduced to £390 each.

CD Ltd has stated that its standard selling prices and standard prime costs for each product for the forthcoming year are:

|  | *Robroy* | | *Trigger* | |
| --- | --- | --- | --- | --- |
|  | *Hours* | *£* | *Hours* | *£* |
| Selling prices |  | 300 |  | 430 |
| Costs - Department 1: |  |  |  |  |
| Direct materials |  | 45 |  | 75 |
| Direct wages | 5 | 40 | 7.5 | 60 |
| Costs - Department 2: |  |  |  |  |
| Direct materials |  | 15 |  | 20 |
| Direct wages | 7.5 | 75 | 10 | 100 |

Production overheads are to be absorbed on a direct labour hour basis and the budgeted overheads for the forthcoming year are:

|  | *Department 1* | *Department 2* |
| --- | --- | --- |
| Fixed | £400,000 | £800,000 |
| Variable - per direct labour hour | £2.00 | £2.40 |
| Budgeted maximum labour hours available | 100,000 | 160,000 |

**You are required**

(a)      to state, with supporting calculations and estimated PROFIT figures, whether CD Ltd should concentrate its resources on Robroy **or** Trigger if:

(i)  it does not use sub-contractors; **(9 marks)**

(ii) it does use sub-contractors and restricts its sales to **either** 22,000 units of Robroy **or** 18,000 units of Trigger; **(9 marks)**

(b)  to describe briefly **one** possible problem arising for **each** of the following situations:

(i)  if your conclusion in (a) (i) above is followed;
(ii) if your conclusion in (a) (ii) above is followed; **(2 marks)**

(c)  to comment briefly on the usefulness of marginal costing for decision-making. **(5 marks)**
**(Total: 25 marks)**
*(CIMA May 94)*

## 36  PQ LTD

(a)  PQ Ltd makes and sells a single product, X, and has budgeted the following figures for a one-year period:

Sales, in units                                                   160,000

|  | £ | £ |
|---|---|---|
| Sales |  | 6,400,000 |
| Production costs |  |  |
| Variable | 2,560,000 |  |
| Fixed | 800,000 |  |
| Selling, distribution and administration costs |  |  |
| Variable | 1,280,000 |  |
| Fixed | 1,200,000 |  |
| Total costs |  | 5,840,000 |
| Net profit |  | 560,000 |

Fixed costs are assumed to be incurred evenly throughout the year.

At the beginning of the year, there were no stocks of finished goods. In the first quarter of the year, 55,000 units were produced and 40,000 units were sold.

**You are required** to prepare profit statements for the first quarter, using:

(i)  marginal costing; and
(ii) absorption costing. **(6 marks)**

(b)  There is a difference in the profit reported when marginal costing is used compared with when absorption costing is used.

**You are required** to discuss the above statement and to indicate how *each* of the following conditions would affect the net profit reported:

(i)   when sales and production are in balance at standard (or expected) volume;
(ii)  when sales exceed production;
(iii) when production exceeds sales.

Use the figures from your answer to (a) above to support your discussion; you should also refer to SSAP 9. **(9 marks)**

(c)    WF Ltd makes and sells a range of plastic garden furniture. These items are sold in sets of one table with four chairs for £80 per set.

The variable costs per set are £20 for manufacturing and £10 for variable selling, distribution and administration.

Direct labour is treated as a fixed cost and the total fixed costs of manufacturing, including depreciation of the plastic-moulding machinery, are £800,000 per annum. Budgeted profit for the forthcoming year is £400,000.

Increased competition has resulted in the management of WF Ltd engaging market research consultants. The consultants have recommended three possible strategies, as follows:

|  | Reduce selling price per set by % | Expected increase in sales (sets) % |
|---|---|---|
| Strategy 1 | 5 | 10 |
| Strategy 2 | 7.5 | 20 |
| Strategy 3 | 10 | 25 |

**You are required** to assess the effect on profits of *each* of the three strategies, and to recommend which strategy, if any, ought to be adopted.  **(10 marks)**
**(Total: 25 marks)**
*(CIMA Nov 94)*

## 37    AZ TRANSPORT GROUP PLC

AZ Transport Group plc comprises three divisions — AZ Buses; AZ Taxis; and Maintenance.

AZ Buses operates a fleet of eight vehicles on four different routes in Ceetown. Each vehicle has a capacity of 30 passengers. There are two vehicles assigned to each route, and each vehicle completes five return journeys per day, for six days each week, for 52 weeks per year.

AZ Buses is considering its plans for the year ending 31 December 1999. Data in respect of each route is as follows:

|  | Route W | Route X | Route Y | Route Z |
|---|---|---|---|---|
| Return travel distance (km) | 42 | 36 | 44 | 38 |
| Average number of passengers: |  |  |  |  |
| Adults | 15 | 10 | 25 | 20 |
| Children | 10 | 8 | 5 | 10 |
| Return journey fares: |  |  |  |  |
| Adults | £3.00 | £6.00 | £4.50 | £2.20 |
| Children | £1.50 | £3.00 | £2.25 | £1.10 |

The following cost estimates have been made:

| | |
|---|---|
| Fuel and repairs per kilometre | £0.1875 |
| Drivers' wages per vehicle per work-day | £120 |
| Vehicle fixed cost per annum | £2,000 |
| General fixed cost per annum | £300,000 |

**Requirements**

(a)     Prepare a statement showing the planned contribution of each route and the total contribution and profit of the AZ Buses division for the year ending 31 December 1999.          **(6 marks)**

(b)     (i)     Calculate the effect on the contribution of route W of increasing the adult fare to £3.75 per return journey if this reduces the number of adult passengers using this route by 20%, and assuming that the ratio of adult to child passengers remains the same.  (Assume no change in the child fare.)

        (ii)    Recommend whether or not AZ Buses should amend the adult fare on route W.

                                                                                **(4 marks)**

(c)     The Maintenance division comprises two fitters who are each paid an annual salary of £15,808, and a transport supervisor who is paid an annual salary of £24,000.

        The work of the Maintenance division is to repair and service the buses of the AZ Buses division and the taxis of the AZ Taxis division.  In total there are eight buses and six taxis which need to be maintained.  Each vehicle requires routine servicing on a regular basis on completion of 4,000 kilometres: every two months each vehicle is fully tested for safety.  The Maintenance division is also responsible for carrying out any breakdown work, though the amount of regular servicing is only 10% of the Maintenance division's work.

        The annual distance travelled by the taxi fleet is 128,000 kilometres.

        The projected material costs associated with each service and safety check are £100 and £75- - respectively, and the directors of AZ Transport Group plc are concerned over the efficiency and cost of its own Maintenance division.  The company invited its local garage to tender for the maintenance contract for its fleet and the quotation received was for £90,000 per annum Including parts and labour.

        If the maintenance contract is awarded to the local garage then the Maintenance division will be closed down, and the two fitters made redundant with a redundancy payment being made of 6 months' salary to each fitter.  The transport supervisor will be retained at the same salary and will be redeployed elsewhere in the Group instead of recruiting a new employee at an annual salary cost of £20,000.

**Requirements:**

(i)     Calculate the cost of the existing maintenance function.                     **(6 marks)**

(ii)    Advise the directors of AZ Transport Group plc whether to award the maintenance contract to the local garage on financial grounds.                                        **(4 marks)**

(iii)   State clearly the other factors which need to be considered before making such a decision, commenting on any other solutions which you consider may be appropriate.          **(5 marks)**

                                                                        **(Total:  25 marks)**
                                                                        *(CIMA Nov 98)*

## 38     JK LTD

JK Ltd has prepared a budget for the next 12 months when it intends to make and sell four products, details of which are shown below:

| Product | Sales in units (thousands) | Selling price per unit £ | Variable cost per unit £ |
|---------|----------------------------|--------------------------|--------------------------|
| J | 10 | 20 | 14.00 |
| K | 10 | 40 | 8.00 |
| L | 50 | 4 | 4.20 |
| M | 20 | 10 | 7.00 |

Budgeted fixed costs are £240,000 per annum and total assets employed are £570,000.

**You are required**

(a)     to calculate the total contribution earned by each product and their combined total contributions;

**(2 marks)**

(b)     to plot the data of your answer to (a) above in the form of a contribution to sales graph (sometimes referred to as a profit-volume graph) on the graph paper provided;                    **(6 marks)**

(c)     to explain your graph to management, to comment on the results shown and to state the break-even point;                                                                                             **(4 marks)**

(d)     to describe briefly three ways in which the overall contribution to sales ratio could be improved.

**(3 marks)**
**(Total:  15 marks)**
*(CIMA May 91)*

## 39     PE LTD

PE Ltd produces and sells two products, P and E.  Budgets prepared for the next six months give the following information:

|  | Product P per unit £ | Product E per unit £ |
|--|----------------------|----------------------|
| Selling price | 10.00 | 12.00 |
| Variable costs: production and selling | 5.00 | 10.00 |

Common fixed costs: production and selling - for six months £561,600.

(a)     **You are required**, in respect of the forthcoming six months,

(i)     to state what the break-even point in £s will be and the number of each product this figure represents if the two products are sold in the ratio 4P to 3E;                    **(3 marks)**

(ii)     to state the break-even point in £s and the number of products this figure represents if the sales mix changes to 4P to 4E (ignore fractions of products);                    **(3 marks)**

(iii)     to advise the sales manager which product mix should be better, that in (a)(i) above or that in (a)(ii) above, and why;                                                                     **(2 marks)**

(iv)     to advise the sales manager which of the two products should be concentrated on and the reason(s) for your recommendation - assume that whatever can be made can be sold, that both products go through a machining process and that there are only 32,000 machine hours available, with product P requiring 0.40 hours per unit and product E requiring 0.10 hours per unit.                                                                                             **(2 marks)**

(b)   **You are required** to compare and contrast the usefulness of a conventional break-even chart with a contribution break-even chart. Your explanation should include illustrative diagrams drawn within your answer book and not on graph paper.

**(5 marks)**
**(Total:  15 marks)**
*(CIMA May 92)*

## 40   PREMIER HOTEL

(a)   **You are required**, using the accountants' conventional breakeven chart as a 'model', to explain how and why a breakeven chart drawn by an economist would differ. Illustrative diagrams should be adjacent to your answer and NOT on separate graph paper. **(10 marks)**

(b)   PM Ltd owns the Premier Hotel which is on a busy main road near an international airport. The hotel has 40 rooms which are let at a rental of £35 per day.

Variable costs are £6 per room occupied per day.

Fixed costs **per month** are:

|  | £ |
|---|---|
| Depreciation | 9,000 |
| Insurance | 5,500 |
| Maintenance | 4,800 |
| Services | 2,700 |
| Management | 3,000 |

Business is not as good in the period October to March as it is in the period April to September. The figures below relate to the two six-monthly periods for 19X3/X4.

|  | *April to September* *(183 days)* £ | *October to March* *(182 days)* £ |
|---|---|---|
| Potential room lettings | 256,200 | 254,800 |
| Budgeted room lettings | 218,400 | 165,200 |

**You are required**

(i)     to calculate the budgeted room occupancy ratio to the nearest percentage figure for **each** six-month period; **(2 marks)**

(ii)    to prepare a statement showing budgeted profit or loss for each of the two six-monthly periods. **(5 marks)**

(iii)   to state the number of room days per month which must be let on average each month to break even; **(2 marks)**

(iv)   to state with reason(s) whether or not you believe the hotel should be closed during January and February because in these two particularly poor trading months the fixed costs are not covered by the receipts from letting the rooms; **(3 marks)**

(v)    to state briefly how you would investigate the costs for insurance and maintenance; the Manager of the hotel believes these two costs are too high and should be capable of being reduced. **(3 marks)**
**(Total:  25 marks)**
*(CIMA May 93)*

# 41    BUDGET PROFIT STATEMENT

A summary of a manufacturing company's budgeted profit statement for its next financial year, when it expects to be operating at seventy five per cent of capacity, is given below:

|  | £ | £ |
|---|---|---|
| Sales: | | |
| 9,000 units at £32 | | 288,000 |
| Less: | | |
| Direct materials | 54,000 | |
| Direct wages | 72,000 | |
| Production overhead: | | |
| Fixed | 42,000 | |
| Variable | 18,000 | |
| | | 186,000 |
| Gross profit | | 102,000 |
| Less: | | |
| Administration, selling and distribution costs: | | |
| Fixed | 36,000 | |
| Varying with sales volume | 27,000 | |
| | | 63,000 |
| Net profit | | 39,000 |

(a)    **You are required**

(i)    to calculate the breakeven point in units and in value;          **(4 marks)**

(ii)    to draw a contribution volume (profit volume) graph on graph paper;          **(4 marks)**

(iii)    to ascertain from your graph answer to (ii) above, what profit could be expected if the company operated at full capacity.          **(2 marks)**

(b)    It has been estimated that:

(i)    if the selling price per unit were reduced to £28, the increased demand would utilise 90% of the company's capacity without any additional advertising expenditure; and

(ii)    to attract sufficient demand to utilise full capacity would require a 15% reduction in the current selling price and a £5,000 special advertising campaign.

**You are required** to present a statement showing the effect of the two alternatives compared with the original budget and to advise management which of the three possible plans ought to be adopted ie, the original budget plan or (i) above or (ii) above.          **(8 marks)**

(c)    An independent market research study shows that by spending £15,000 on a special advertising campaign, the company could operate at full capacity and maintain the selling price at £32 per unit.

**You are required** to:

(i)    advise management whether this proposal should be adopted; and
(ii)    state any reservations you might have.          **(7 marks)**
          **(Total:  25 marks)**
          *(CIMA Nov 88)*

## 42    BUDGETED PROFIT STATEMENT

The following budgeted profit statement has been prepared using absorption costing principles:

|  | *January to June 1997* | | *July to December 1997* | |
|---|---|---|---|---|
|  | £'000 | £'000 | £'000 | £'000 |
| Sales |  | 540 |  | 360 |
| Opening stock | 100 |  | 160 |  |
| Production costs |  |  |  |  |
| Direct materials | 108 |  | 36 |  |
| Direct labour | 162 |  | 54 |  |
| Overhead | 90 |  | 30 |  |
|  | 460 |  | 280 |  |
| Closing stock | 160 |  | 80 |  |
|  |  | 300 |  | 200 |
| GROSS PROFIT |  | 240 |  | 160 |
| Production overhead |  |  |  |  |
| (Over)/Under absorption | (12) |  | 12 |  |
| Selling costs | 50 |  | 50 |  |
| Distribution costs | 45 |  | 40 |  |
| Administration costs | 80 |  | 80 |  |
|  |  | 163 |  | 182 |
| NET PROFIT/(LOSS) |  | 77 |  | (22) |
| Sales units |  | 15,000 |  | 10,000 |
| Production units |  | 18,000 |  | 6,000 |

The members of the management team are concerned by the significant change in profitability between the two six-month periods. As management accountant, you have analysed the data upon which the above budget statement has been produced, with the following results:

1.    The production overhead cost comprises both a fixed and a variable element, the latter appears to be dependent on the number of units produced. The fixed element of the cost is expected to be incurred at a constant rate throughout the year.

2.    The selling costs are fixed.

3.    The distribution cost comprises both fixed and variable elements, the latter appears to be dependent on the number of units sold. The fixed element of the cost is expected to be incurred at a constant rate throughout the year.

4.    The administration costs are fixed.

**Requirements:**

(a)    Present the above budgeted profit statement in marginal costing format.                    **(10 marks)**

(b)    Reconcile EACH of the six-monthly profit/loss values reported respectively under marginal and absorption costing.                    **(4 marks)**

(c)      Reconcile the six-monthly profit for January to June 1997 from the absorption costing statement with the six-monthly loss for July to December 1997 from the absorption costing statement.

**(4 marks)**

(d)      Calculate the annual number of units required to break even.                    **(3 marks)**

(e)      Explain briefly the advantages of using marginal costing as the basis of providing managers with information for decision making.                                          **(4 marks)**

**(Total:  25 marks)**

*(CIMA May 96)*

## 43    Z PLC

Z plc operates a single retail outlet selling direct to the public. Profit statements for August and September 1996 are as follows:

|                              | *August* £ | *September* £ |
|------------------------------|-----------|---------------|
| Sales                        | 80,000    | 90,000        |
| Cost of sales                | 50,000    | 55,000        |
| Gross profit                 | 30,000    | 35,000        |
| Less:                        |           |               |
| Selling and distribution     | 8,000     | 9,000         |
| Administration               | 15,000    | 15,000        |
| Net profit                   | 7,000     | 11,000        |

**Requirements:**

(a)      Use the high and low points technique to identify the behaviour of

(i)      cost of sales,
(ii)     selling and distribution costs, and
(iii)    administration costs.

**(4 marks)**

(b)      Using the graph paper provided, draw a contribution breakeven chart and identify the monthly breakeven sales value, and area of contribution.

**(10 marks)**

(c)      Assuming a margin of safety equal to 30% of the breakeven value, calculate Z plc's annual profit.

**(2 marks)**

(d)      Z plc is now considering opening another retail outlet selling the same products. Z plc plans to use the same profit margins in both outlets and has estimated that the specific fixed costs of the second outlet will be £100,000 per annum.

Z plc also expects that 10% of its annual sales from its existing outlet would transfer to this second outlet if it were to be opened.

**Requirement:**

Calculate the annual value of sales required from the new outlet in order to achieve the same annual profit as previously obtained from the single outlet.

**(5 marks)**

(e)     Briefly describe the cost accounting requirements of organisations of this type.

**(4 marks)**
**(Total: 25 marks)**
**(CIMA Nov 96)**

## 44   EXE PLC

Exe plc makes and sells four products. The profit and loss statement for April 1998 is as follows:

| Product | W £ | X £ | Y £ | Z £ | Total £ |
|---|---|---|---|---|---|
| Sales | 30,000 | 20,000 | 35,000 | 15,000 | 100,000 |
| Cost of sales | 16,000 | 8,000 | 22,000 | 10,000 | 56,000 |
| Gross profit | 14,000 | 12,000 | 13,000 | 5,000 | 44,000 |
| Overhead cost: | | | | | |
| Selling | 8,000 | 7,000 | 8,500 | 6,500 | 30,000 |
| Admin | 2,000 | 2,000 | 2,000 | 2,000 | 8,000 |
| Net profit | 4,000 | 3,000 | 2,500 | (3,500) | 6,000 |

The management team is concerned about the results, particularly those of product Z, and it has been suggested that Exe plc would be better off if it ceased production of product Z. The production manager has said that if product Z were discontinued the resources which would become available could be used to increase production of product Y by 40%.

You have analysed the cost structures of each of the products and discovered the following:

Cost of sales

| | W £ | X £ | Y £ | Z £ | Total £ |
|---|---|---|---|---|---|
| Variable costs | 4,800 | 1,600 | 13,200 | 5,000 | 24,600 |
| Fixed costs | 11,200 | 6,400 | 8,800 | 5,000 | 31,400 |
| | 16,000 | 8,000 | 22,000 | 10,000 | 56,000 |

The total fixed costs figure includes £20,000 which is not specific to any one product, and which has been apportioned to each product on the basis of sales values. If the quantity of any product increases by more than 25%, then the specific production fixed costs of the product will increase by 30%.

The selling overhead comprises a fixed cost of £5,000 per product plus a variable cost which varies in proportion to sales value. The fixed cost is not specific to any product but the sales director believes that it should be shared equally by the four products.

The administration cost is a central overhead cost; it is not affected by the products made.

**Requirements:**

(a)     Prepare a statement which shows clearly the results of continuing to produce products W, X, Y and Z at the same volumes as were achieved in April 1998. Present your statement in a format suitable for management decision-making.                                              **(6 marks)**

(b)     (i)     Prepare a statement showing clearly the results if product Z is discontinued, and the number of units of Y is increased in accordance with the production manager's statement.

Assume that no change in selling price per unit is necessary to sell the additional units.

**(4 marks)**

(ii)     Reconcile the profit calculated in (a) and (b) (i) above; advise the management team as to whether product Z should be discontinued.     **(2 marks)**

(c)     Explain briefly any non-financial factors which should be considered before discontinuing a product.     **(3 marks)**

(d)     Prepare a contribution breakeven chart for product Y only, showing clearly the sales value at which the product recovers fully its specific fixed costs, but provides a nil contribution towards non-specific overhead costs:

(i)     if Exe plc continues to produce product Z;

(ii)     if Exe plc discontinues product Z and increases production of product Y in accordance with the production director's statement.

From the chart, determine the effect on the breakeven point and margin of safety which occur because of the change in the use of resources. State these values clearly in sales values of product Y.     **(10 marks)**

**(Total: 25 marks)**

*(CIMA May 98)*

---

## 45    X LTD

(a)     Costs may be classified as fixed or variable. This classification method is useful for decision making because variable costs are relevant costs whereas fixed costs are irrelevant.

**You are required** to discuss this statement.     **(5 marks)**

(b)     (i)     X Ltd manufactures four liquids - A, B, C and D. The selling price and unit cost details for these products are as follows:

| | A | B | C | D |
| --- | --- | --- | --- | --- |
| | *£/litre* | *£/litre* | *£/litre* | *£/litre* |
| Selling price | 100 | 110 | 120 | 120 |
| Direct materials | 24 | 30 | 16 | 21 |
| Direct labour(£6/hour) | 18 | 15 | 24 | 27 |
| Direct expenses | - | - | 3 | - |
| Variable overhead | 12 | 10 | 16 | 18 |
| Fixed overhead *(note 1)* | 24 | 20 | 32 | 36 |
| Profit | 22 | 35 | 29 | 18 |

*Note 1:*

Fixed overhead is absorbed on the basis of labour hours, based on a budget of 1,600 hours per quarter.

During the next three months the number of direct labour hours is expected to be limited to 1,345. The same labour is used for all products.

The marketing director has identified the maximum demand for each of the four products during the next three months as follows:

| A | 200 litres |
|---|---|
| B | 150 litres |
| C | 100 litres |
| D | 120 litres |

These maximum demand levels include the effects of a contract already made between X Ltd and one of its customers, Y Ltd, to supply 20 litres of each of A, B, C and D during the next three months.

**You are required** to determine the number of litres of products A, B, C and D to be produced/sold in the next three months in order to maximise profits, and calculate the profit that this would yield.

Assume that no stock is held at the beginning of the three months which may be used to satisfy demand in the period.                                        **(15 marks)**

(ii)     After completing the production plan in (i) above, you receive two memos.

The first is from the research director

'New environmental controls on pollution must be introduced with effect from the start of next month to reduce pollution from the manufacture of product D. These will incur fixed costs of £6,000 per annum.'

The second memo is from the sales director:

'An overseas supplier has developed a capacity to manufacture products C and D on a sub-contract basis, and has quoted the following prices to X Ltd:

| C | £105/litre |
|---|---|
| D | £100/litre' |

**You are required** to use the information from *both* of these memos and state and quantify the effect (if any) on X Ltd's plans.                                 **(10 marks)**
                                                                       **(Total:  30 marks)**
                                                                       *(CIMA Nov 95)*

## 46     BVX LTD

BVX Limited manufactures three garden furniture products - chairs, benches and tables. The budgeted unit cost and resource requirements of each of these items is detailed below:

|  | Chair £ | Bench £ | Table £ |
|---|---|---|---|
| Timber cost | 5.00 | 15.00 | 10.00 |
| Direct labour cost | 4.00 | 10.00 | 8.00 |
| Variable overhead cost | 3.00 | 7.50 | 6.00 |
| Fixed overhead cost | 4.50 | 11.25 | 9.00 |
|  | 16.50 | 43.75 | 33.00 |
| Budgeted volumes per annum | 4,000 | 2,000 | 1,500 |

- These volumes are believed to equal the market demand for these products.
- The fixed overhead costs are attributed to the three products on the basis of direct labour hours.
- The labour rate is £4.00 per hour.
- The cost of the timber is £2.00 per square metre.

The products are made from a specialist timber. A memo from the purchasing manager advises you that because of a problem with the supplier, it is to be assumed that this specialist timber is limited in supply to 20,000 square metres per annum.

The sales director has already accepted an order for 500 chairs, 100 benches and 150 tables which if not supplied would incur a financial penalty of £2,000. These quantities are included in the market demand estimates above.

The selling prices of the three products are:

|        |        |
|--------|--------|
| Chair  | £20.00 |
| Bench  | £50.00 |
| Table  | £40.00 |

**Requirements:**

(a)     Determine the optimum production plan AND state the net profit that this should yield per annum.

**(10 marks)**

(b)     Calculate AND explain the maximum prices which should be paid per square metre in order to obtain extra supplies of the timber.

**(5 marks)**

(c)     The management team has accused the accountant of using too much jargon.

**Requirement:**

Prepare a statement which explains the following terms in a way that a multi-disciplinary team of managers would understand. The accountant will use this statement as a briefing paper at the next management meeting. The terms to be explained are

- variable costs;
- relevant costs;
- avoidable costs;
- incremental costs;
- opportunity costs.

**(10 marks)**
**(Total: 25 marks)**
*(CIMA May 97)*

---

## 47     PRINCIPAL BUDGET FACTORS

You are the assistant management account of ZED plc. Preliminary discussions concerning the company budgets for the year ended 30 June 1999 have already taken place, and the sales and production directors have produced the following forecasts:

Sales Director:

'I forecast that the total sales for the year will be 24,000 units of product A if we continue to sell them at £10.00 per unit for the first six months of the year and increase the price to £11.00 per unit thereafter. I estimate the quarterly sales to be:

|                     |             |
|---------------------|-------------|
| July - September    | 7,200 units |
| October - December  | 3,000 units |
| January - March     | 4,800 units |
| April - June        | 9,000 units |

This represents a 20% increase over our present quarterly sales targets, and I expect that within each quarter the monthly demand will be equal. We can also sell up to 2,000 units of product B per month at a selling price of £8.00 per unit. This is a less profitable product, so we should concentrate on product A.'

Production Director:

'Our maximum capacity is at present limited by the available machine hours. Each unit of product A requires 2 machine hours, and on this basis we can usually produce 2,000 units per month. However, because of employee holidays in August, the number of machine operators is reduced, and in that month we can produce only 1,000 units. We have placed an order for new semi-automatic machines which are being installed in August 1998. These should be capable of producing a further 2,000 units per month starting on 1 September 1998.

Product B requires 4 machine hours per unit. The quantity that we can produce is limited because of the demands on the available machine time by making product A.'

You have predicted the costs per unit of the two products for the 1999 budget year as follows:

|                   | A £/unit | B £/unit |
|-------------------|----------|----------|
| Direct materials  | 1.50     | 1.60     |
| Direct labour     | 2.50     | 3.00     |
| Variable overhead | 1.50     | 3.00     |
|                   | 5.50     | 7.60     |

**Requirements:**

(a)  Use the above information to calculate the extent of the limiting factor during the budget period.
                                                                                     **(5 marks)**

(b)  Prepare monthly sales and production budgets, expressed in units, for the period JULY TO DECEMBER 1998, based upon the limiting factor you determined in (a) above. Assume that stocks of products A and B cannot be held, and that ZED plc wishes to concentrate on production of product A.                                                                    **(8 marks)**

(c)  Prepare monthly sales and production budgets, expressed in units, for the period JULY TO DECEMBER 1998, based upon the limiting factor you determined in (a) above. Assume that stocks of products A and B can now be held, and assume that ZED plc decided to sell equal quantities of product A and product B each month.                                                      **(10 marks)**

(d)  Determine the effect on profits of the change in sales mix proposed in part (c) above.    **(2 marks)**
                                                                            **(Total: 25 marks)**
                                                                               *(CIMA Nov 97)*

## 48    PDR PLC

PDR plc manufactures four products using the same machinery. The following details relate to its products:

|                   | Product A £ per unit | Product B £ per unit | Product C £ per unit | Product D £ per unit |
|-------------------|----------|----------|----------|----------|
| Selling price     | 28       | 30       | 45       | 42       |
| Direct material   | 5        | 6        | 8        | 6        |
| Direct labour     | 4        | 4        | 8        | 8        |
| Variable overhead | 3        | 3        | 6        | 6        |
| Fixed overhead *  | 8        | 8        | 16       | 16       |

| | | | | |
|---|---|---|---|---|
| Profit | 8 | 9 | 7 | 6 |
| Labour hours | 1 | 1 | 2 | 2 |
| Machine hours | 4 | 3 | 4 | 5 |
| | *Units* | *Units* | *Units* | *Units* |
| Maximum demand per week | 200 | 180 | 250 | 100 |

\* Absorbed based on budgeted labour hours of 1,000 per week.

There is a maximum of 2,000 machine hours available per week.

**Requirement:**

(a)   Determine the production plan which will maximise the weekly profit of PDR plc and prepare a profit statement showing the profit your plan will yield.   **(10 marks)**

(b)   The marketing director of PDR plc is concerned at the company's inability to meet the quantity demanded by its customers.

Two *alternative* strategies are being considered to overcome this:

(i)   to increase the number of hours worked using the existing machinery by working overtime. Such overtime would be paid at a premium of 50% above normal labour rates, and variable overhead costs would be expected to increase in proportion to labour costs.

(ii)   to buy product B from an overseas supplier at a cost of £19 per unit including carriage. This would need to be re-packaged at a cost of £1 per unit before it could be sold.

**Requirement:**

Evaluate EACH of the two alternative strategies and, as management accountant, prepare a report to the marketing director, stating your reasons (quantitative and qualitative) as to which, if either, should be adopted.   **(15 marks)**
**(Total: 25 marks)**
*(CIMA May 99)*

## 49   CHOICE OF CONTRACTS

A company in the civil engineering industry with headquarters located 22 miles from London undertakes contracts anywhere in the United Kingdom.

The company has had its tender for a job in north-east England accepted at £288,000 and work is due to begin in March 19X3. However, the company has also been asked to undertake a contract on the south coast of England. The price offered for this contract is £352,000. Both of the contracts cannot be taken simultaneously because of constraints on staff site management personnel and on plant available. An escape clause enables the company to withdraw from the contract in the north-east, provided notice is given before the end of November and an agreed penalty of £28,000 is paid.

The following estimates have been submitted by the company's quantity surveyor:

**Cost estimates**

| | North-east £ | South coast £ |
|---|---|---|
| Materials: | | |
| In stock at original cost, Material X | 21,600 | |
| In stock at original cost, Material Y | | 24,800 |

| | | |
|---|---:|---:|
| Firm orders placed at original cost, Material X | 30,400 | |
| Not yet ordered - current cost, Material X | 60,000 | |
| Not yet ordered - current cost, Material Z | | 71,200 |
| Labour - hired locally | 86,000 | 110,000 |
| Site management | 34,000 | 34,000 |
| Staff accommodation and travel for site management | 6,800 | 5,600 |
| Plant on site - depreciation | 9,600 | 12,800 |
| Interest on capital, 8% | 5,120 | 6,400 |
| Total local contract costs | 253,520 | 264,800 |
| Headquarters costs allocated at rate of 5% on total contract costs | 12,676 | 13,240 |
| | 266,196 | 278,040 |
| Contract price | 288,000 | 352,000 |
| Estimated profit | 21,804 | 73,960 |

**Notes:**

(1)    X, Y and Z are three building materials. Material X is not in common use and would not realise much money if re-sold; however, it could be used on other contracts but only as a substitute for another material currently quoted at 10% less than the original cost of X. The price of Y, a material in common use, has doubled since it was purchased; its net realisable value if re-sold would be its new price less 15% to cover disposal costs. Alternatively it could be kept for use on other contracts in the following financial year.

(2)    With the construction industry not yet recovered from the recent recession, the company is confident that manual labour, both skilled and unskilled, could be hired locally on a sub-contracting basis to meet the needs of each of the contracts.

(3)    The plant which would be needed for the south coast contract has been owned for some years and £12,800 is the year's depreciation on a straight-line basis. If the north-east contract is undertaken, less plant will be required but the surplus plant will be hired out for the period of the contract at a rental of £6,000.

(4)    It is the company's policy to charge all contracts with notional interest at 8% on estimated working capital involved in contracts. Progress payments would be receivable from the contractee.

(5)    Salaries and general costs of operating the small headquarters amount to about £108,000 each year. There are usually ten contracts being supervised at the same time.

(6)    Each of the two contracts is expected to last from March 19X3 to February 19X4 which, coincidentally, is the company's financial year.

(7)    Site management is treated as a fixed cost.

**You are required,** as the management accountant to the company,

(a)    to present comparative statements to show the net benefit to the company of undertaking the more advantageous of the two contracts;    **(12 marks)**

(b)    to explain the reasoning behind the inclusion in (or omission from) your comparative financial statements, of each item given in the cost estimates and the notes relating thereto.    **(13 marks)**
    **(Total: 25 marks)**
    *(CIMA Nov 92)*

## 50    JASON

(a)    Distinguish between 'opportunity cost' and 'out of pocket cost' giving a numerical example of each using your own figures to support your answer.                                        **(6 marks)**

(b)    Jason travels to work by train to his 5-day week job. Instead of buying daily tickets he finds it cheaper to buy a quarterly season ticket which costs £188 for 13 weeks.

Debbie, an acquaintance, who also makes the same journey, suggests that they both travel in Jason's car and offers to give him £120 each quarter towards his car expenses. Except for weekend travelling and using it for local college attendance near his home on three evenings each week to study for his CIMA Stage 2, the car remains in Jason's garage.

Jason estimates that using his car for work would involve him, each quarter, in the following expenses:

| | |
|---|---|
| Depreciation (proportion of annual figure) | £200 |
| Petrol and oil | £128 |
| Tyres and miscellaneous | £52 |

**You are required** to state whether Jason should accept Debbie's offer and to draft a statement to show clearly the monetary effect of your conclusion.                                        **(5 marks)**

(c)    A company with a financial year 1 September to 31 August prepared a sales budget which resulted in the following cost structure:

| | *% of sales* |
|---|---|
| Direct materials | 32 |
| Direct wages | 18 |
| Production overhead: | |
|   Variable | 6 |
|   Fixed | 24 |
| Administrative and selling costs: | |
|   Variable | 3 |
|   Fixed | 7 |
| Profit | 10 |

After ten weeks, however, it became obvious that the sales budget was too optimistic and it has now been estimated that, because of a reduction in sales volume, for the full year sales will total £2,560,000 which is only 80% of the previously budgeted figure.

**You are required** to present a statement for management showing the amended sales and cost structure in £s and percentages, in a marginal costing format.                                        **(4 marks)**
                                        **(Total: 15 marks)**
                                        *(CIMA Nov 91)*

## 51    PUBLISHING COMPANY

You are the management accountant of a publishing and printing company which has been asked to quote for the production of a programme for the local village fair. The work would be carried out in addition to the normal work of the company. Because of existing commitments, some weekend working would be required to complete the printing of the programme. A trainee accountant has produced the following cost estimate based upon the resources required as specified by the production manager:

|  |  |  | £ |
|---|---|---|---|
| Direct materials | - paper (book value) |  | 5,000 |
|  | - inks (purchase price) |  | 2,400 |
| Direct labour | - skilled | 250 hours @ £4.00 | 1,000 |
|  | - unskilled | 100 hours @ £3.50 | 350 |
| Variable overhead |  | 350 hours @ £4.00 | 1,400 |
| Printing press depreciation |  | 200 hours @ £2.50 | 500 |
| Fixed production costs |  | 350 hours @ £6.00 | 2,100 |
| Estimating department costs |  |  | 400 |
|  |  |  | 13,150 |

You are aware that considerable publicity could be obtained for the company if you are able to win this order and the price quoted must be very competitive.

The following notes are relevant to the cost estimate above:

(1)    The paper to be used is currently in stock at a value of £5,000. It is of an unusual colour which has not been used for some time. The replacement price of the paper is £8,000, whilst the scrap value of that in stock is £2,500. The production manager does not foresee any alternative use for the paper if it is not used for the village fair programmes.

(2)    The inks required are not held in stock. They would have to be purchased in bulk at a cost of £3,000. 80% of the ink purchased would be used in printing the programmes. No other use is foreseen for the remainder.

(3)    Skilled direct labour is in short supply, and to accommodate the printing of the programmes, 50% of the time required would be worked at weekends for which a premium of 25% above the normal hourly rate is paid. The normal hourly rate is £4.00 per hour.

(4)    Unskilled labour is presently under-utilised, and at present 200 hours per week are recorded as idle time. If the printing work is carried out at a weekend, 25 unskilled hours would have to occur at this time, but the employees concerned would be given two hours time off (for which they would be paid) in lieu of each hour worked.

(5)    Variable overhead represents the cost of operating the printing press and binding machines.

(6)    When not being used by the company, the printing press is hired to outside companies for £6.00 per hour. This earns a contribution of £3.00 per hour. There is unlimited demand for this facility.

(7)    Fixed production costs are those incurred by and absorbed into production, using an hourly rate based on budgeted activity.

(8)    The cost of the estimating department represents time spent in discussions with the village fair committee concerning the printing of its programme.

**You are required** to

(a)    prepare a revised cost estimate using the opportunity cost approach, showing clearly the minimum price that the company should accept for the order. Give reasons for each resource valuation in your cost estimate.    **(16 marks)**

(b)    explain why contribution theory is used as a basis for providing information relevant to decision making.    **(4 marks)**

(c)    explain the relevance of opportunity costs in decision making.    **(5 marks)**
**(Total: 25 marks)**
*(CIMA May 95)*

| 52 | EXE PLC |
|----|---------|

You have received a request from EXE plc to provide a quotation for the manufacture of a specialised piece of equipment. This would be a one-off order, in excess of normal budgeted production. The following cost estimate has already been prepared:

|  |  | Note | £ |
|---|---|---|---|
| Direct materials: | | | |
| Steel | 10m$^2$ @ £5.00 per m$^2$ | (1) | 50 |
| Brass fittings | | (2) | 20 |
| Direct labour: | | | |
| Skilled | 25 hours @ £8.00 per hour | (3) | 200 |
| Semi-skilled | 10 hours @ £5.00 per hour | (4) | 50 |
| Overhead | 35 hours @ £10.00 per hour | (5) | 350 |
| Estimating time | | (6) | 100 |
| | | | 770 |
| Administration overhead @ 20% of production cost | | (7) | 154 |
| | | | 924 |
| Profit @ 25% of total cost | | (8) | 231 |
| Selling price | | | 1,155 |

*Notes:*

(1)     The steel is regularly used, and has a current stock value of £5.00 per square metre. There are currently 100m$^2$ in stock. The steel is readily available at a price of £5.50 per square metre.

(2)     The brass fittings would have to be bought specifically for this job: a supplier has quoted the price of £20 for the fittings required.

(3)     The skilled labour is currently employed by your company and paid at a rate of £8.00 per hour. If this job were undertaken it would be necessary either to work 25 hours overtime which would be paid at time plus one half OR reduce production of another product which earns a contribution of £13.00 per hour.

(4)     The semi-skilled labour currently has sufficient paid idle time to be able to complete this work.

(5)     The overhead absorption rate includes power costs which are directly related to machine usage. If this job were undertaken, it is estimated that the machine time required would be ten hours. The machines incur power costs of £0.75 per hour. There are no other overhead costs which can be specifically identified with this job.

(6)     The cost of the estimating time is that attributed to the four hours taken by the engineers to analyse the drawings and determine the cost estimate given above.

(7)     It is company policy to add 20% on to the production cost as an allowance against administration costs associated with the jobs accepted.

(8)     This is the standard profit added by your company as part of its pricing policy.

**Requirements:**

(a)    Prepare, on a relevant cost basis, the lowest cost estimate that could be used as the basis for a quotation.

Explain briefly your reasons for using EACH of the values in your estimate.        **(12 marks)**

(b)    There may be a possibility of repeat orders from EXE plc which would occupy part of normal production capacity.

What factors need to be considered before quoting for this order?        **(7 marks)**

(c)    When an organisation identifies that it has a single production resource which is in short supply, but is used by more than one product, the optimum production plan is determined by ranking the products according to their contribution per unit of the scarce resource.

Using a numerical example of your own, reconcile this approach with the opportunity cost approach used in **(a)** above.        **(6 marks)**
**(Total: 25 marks)**
*(CIMA Nov 97)*

## 53    CASH BUDGET

The following figures have been extracted from a manufacturing company's budget schedules:

|  | Sales including VAT £'000 | Wages and salaries £'000 | Purchases of materials £'000 | Production overhead £'000 | Selling and administration overhead £'000 |
|---|---|---|---|---|---|
| 19X2 Oct | 1,200 | 55 | 210 | 560 | 125 |
| Nov | 1,100 | 50 | 280 | 500 | 125 |
| Dec | 1,000 | 65 | 240 | 640 | 125 |
| 19X3 Jan | 1,400 | 60 | 210 | 560 | 125 |
| Feb | 1,200 | 60 | 240 | 500 | 130 |
| Mar | 1,100 | 60 | 230 | 560 | 130 |

Other relevant information:

(1)    All sales are on credit terms of net settlement within 30 days of the date of the sale.

However,
    only 60% of indebtedness is paid by the end of the calendar month in which the sale is made;
    another 30% is paid in the following calendar month;
    5% in the second calendar month after the invoice date;
    and 5% become bad debts.

(2)    Assume all months are of equal number of 30 days for the allocation of the receipts from debtors.

(3)    Wages and salaries are paid within the month they are incurred.

(4)    Creditors for materials are paid within the month following the purchase.

(5)    Of the production overhead, 35% of the figure represents variable expenses which are paid in the month after they were incurred.  £164,000 per month is depreciation and is included in the 65%

which represents fixed costs. The payment of fixed costs is made in the month in which the cost is incurred.

(6)     Selling and administration overhead which is payable is paid in the month it is incurred. £15,000 each month is depreciation.

(7)     Corporation tax of £750,000 is payable in January.

(8)     A dividend is payable in March: £500,000 net. (Ignore advance corporation tax.)

(9)     Value added tax (VAT), payable monthly one month later than the sales are made, is to be calculated as follows:

> Output Tax
>
> $\frac{7}{47}$ ths of the sales including VAT figure
> less     Input Tax of  £136,000 for January
>                         £125,000 for February and
>                         £121,000 for March.

(10)    Capital expenditure commitments are due for payment:

> £1,000,000 in January and £700,000 in March.

Both are payments for machinery to be imported from Japan and thus no VAT is involved.

(11)    Assume that overdraft facilities, if required, are available.

(12)    The cash at bank balance at 31 December is expected to be £1,450,000.

**You are required**

(a)     to prepare, in columnar form, cash budgets for **each** of the months of January, February and March (working to nearest £'000);                                                                **(15 marks)**

(b)     to recommend action which could be suggested to management to effect

    (i)      a permanent improvement in cash flow, and

    (ii)     a temporary solution to minimise any overdraft requirements revealed by your answer to (a) above.                                                                                       **(5 marks)**
                                                                                      **(Total:  20 marks)**
                                                                                      *(CIMA Nov 92)*

 ## 54    D LTD

D Ltd is preparing its annual budgets for the year to 31 December 1994. It manufactures and sells one product, which has a selling price of £150. The marketing director believes that the price can be increased to £160 with effect from 1 July 1994 and that at this price the sales volume for each quarter of 1994 will be as follows:

|                | Sales volume |
|----------------|--------------|
| Quarter 1      | 40,000       |
| Quarter 2      | 50,000       |
| Quarter 3      | 30,000       |
| Quarter 4      | 45,000       |

Sales for each quarter of 1995 are expected to be 40,000 units.

Each unit of the finished product which is manufactured requires four units of component R and three units of component T, together with a body shell S. These items are purchased from an outside supplier. Currently prices are:

| | |
|---|---|
| Component R | £8.00 each |
| Component T | £5.00 each |
| Shell S | £30.00 each |

The components are expected to increase in price by 10% with effect from 1 April 1994; no change is expected in the price of the shell.

Assembly of the shell and components into the finished product requires 6 labour hours: labour is currently paid £5.00 per hour. A 4% increase in wage costs is anticipated to take effect from 1 October 1994.

Variable overhead costs are expected to be £10 per unit for the whole of 1994; fixed production overhead costs are expected to be £240,000 for the year, and are absorbed on a per unit basis.

Stocks on 31 December 1993 are expected to be as follows:

| | |
|---|---|
| Finished units | 9,000 units |
| Component R | 3,000 units |
| Component T | 5,500 units |
| Shell S | 500 units |

Closing stocks at the end of each quarter are to be as follows:

| | |
|---|---|
| Finished units | 10% of next quarter's sales |
| Component R | 20% of next quarter's production requirements |
| Component T | 15% of next quarter's production requirements |
| Shell S | 10% of next quarter's production requirements |

**You are required** to

(a)    Prepare the following budgets of D Ltd for the year ending 31 December 1994, showing values for each quarter and the year in total:

    (i)      sales budget (in £s and units)
    (ii)     production budget (in units)
    (iii)    material usage budget (in units)
    (iv)    production cost budget (in £s).

                                                                                    **(15 marks)**

(b)    Sales are often considered to be the principal budget factor of an organisation.

**You are required** to

Explain the meaning of the "principal budget factor" and, assuming that it is sales, explain how sales may be forecast making appropriate reference to the use of statistical techniques and the use of microcomputers.

                                                                                    **(10 marks)**
                                                                                    **(Total: 25 marks)**
                                                                                    *(Specimen paper)*

## 55    SUPERMARKET

A supermarket which sells numerous food and grocery items has eight check-out points. There is also a separate wines and spirits section which operates as 'a shop within a shop' and has its own check-out point. Each check-out has electronic point-of-sale terminals.

The manager is not satisfied that she is being given all the information that she ought to receive in order to manage and control the supermarket efficiently. She seeks your advice.

**You are required**, as the management accountant, to write a report which contains lists of the information you think should be provided for her on

(a)    a daily basis,
(b)    a weekly basis,
(c)    a monthly basis.

You may assume that computer facilities are available to assist with the provision of the information.

**(15 marks)**
*(CIMA Nov 93)*

## 55    TJ LTD

TJ Ltd is in an industry sector which is recovering from the recent recession. The directors of the company hope next year to be operating at 85% of capacity, although currently the company is operating at only 65% of capacity. 65% of capacity represents output of 10,000 units of the single product which is produced and sold. One hundred direct workers are employed on production for 200,000 hours in the current year.

The flexed budgets for the current year are:

| *Capacity level* | 55% | 65% | 75% |
|---|---|---|---|
| | £ | £ | £ |
| Direct materials | 846,200 | 1,000,000 | 1,153,800 |
| Direct wages | 1,480,850 | 1,750,000 | 2,019,150 |
| Production overhead | 596,170 | 650,000 | 703,830 |
| Selling and distribution overhead | 192,310 | 200,000 | 207,690 |
| Administration overhead | 120,000 | 120,000 | 120,000 |
| Total costs | 3,235,530 | 3,720,000 | 4,204,470 |

Profit in any year is budgeted to be $16^{2/3}\%$ of sales.

The following percentage increases in costs are expected for next year:

| | *Increase* % |
|---|---|
| Direct materials | 6 |
| Direct wages | 3 |
| Variable production overhead | 7 |
| Variable selling and distribution overhead | 7 |
| Fixed production overhead | 10 |
| Fixed selling and distribution overhead | 7.5 |
| Administration overhead | 10 |

**You are required** to:

(a)    prepare for next year a flexible budget statement on the assumption that the company operates at 85% of capacity; your statement should show both contribution and profit;    **(14 marks)**

(b)    discuss briefly *three* problems which may arise from the change in capacity level;    **(6 marks)**

(c)    state who is likely to serve on a budget committee operated by TJ Ltd and explain the purpose of such a committee.    **(5 marks)**

**(Total: 25 marks)**
*(CIMA Nov 94)*

## 57 XYZ LTD

XYZ Ltd has the following forecast sales at list price for the nine months to 29 February 19X6:

| | | | | | |
|---|---|---|---|---|---|
| June | £40,000 | September | £48,000 | December | £44,000 |
| July | £44,000 | October | £40,000 | January | £42,000 |
| August | £50,000 | November | £45,000 | February | £50,000 |

60% of the company's sales are on credit, payable in the month after sale. Cash sales attract a 5% discount off list price.

Purchases amount to 40% of selling price, and these are paid for two months after delivery.

Stock is maintained at a level equal to 50% of the following month's sales except that in November stock is to be increased by £2,000 (at cost prices) to ensure that XYZ Ltd has a safety stock during the period when its major supplier shuts down. This safety stock will be released in March.

Wages comprise a fixed sum of £2,000 per month plus a variable element equal to 10% of sales; these are payable in the month they are incurred.

Fixed costs amount to £7,500 per month, payable one month in arrears, of which £1,500 is depreciation.

XYZ Ltd has capital expenditure/receipts scheduled as follows:

| Acquisitions: | £ |
|---|---|
| September | 15,000 |
| November | 10,000 |
| February | 4,000 |
| Disposal: | |
| October | 8,000 |

Corporation tax, payable in November, amounts to £44,000.

The bank balance on 1 September 19X5 is expected to be £5,000.

**You are required** to

(a)  prepare a cashflow forecast for XYZ Ltd for EACH of the six months from September 19X5 to February 19X6, using a row and column format. **(10 marks)**

(b)  explain clearly, using your answer to (a) above, how a spreadsheet may be used to assist in the preparation of cash forecasts. **(10 marks)**

(c)  explain how a cash forecast is an example of both feedforward and feedback control mechanisms. **(5 marks)**

**(Total: 25 marks)**
*(CIMA May 95)*

## 58    BUDGETED SALES VALUES

The following budgeted sales values have been extracted from the budget of AZ Ltd for the year ending 31 December 1997:

|          | £       |
|----------|---------|
| April    | 400,000 |
| May      | 450,000 |
| June     | 520,000 |
| July     | 420,000 |
| August   | 480,000 |

The contribution/sales ratio is 40%. Fixed costs are budgeted to be £1,200,000 for the year arising at a constant rate per month and including depreciation of £300,000 per annum.

40% of each month's sales are produced in the month prior to sale, and 60% are produced in the month of sale. 50% of the direct materials required for production are purchased in the month prior to their being used in production.

30% of the variable costs are labour costs, which are paid in the month they are incurred.

60% of the variable costs are direct material costs. Suppliers of direct materials are paid in the month after purchase.

The remaining variable costs are variable overhead costs. 40% of the variable overhead costs are paid in the month they are incurred, the balance being paid in the month after they are incurred.

Fixed costs are paid in the month they are incurred.

Capital expenditure expected in June is £190,000.

Sales receipts for the three months of May, June and July are budgeted as follows:

|       | £       |
|-------|---------|
| May   | 401,700 |
| June  | 450,280 |
| July  | 425,880 |

The bank balance on 1 May 1997 is expected to be £40,000.

**Requirement:**

Prepare a cash budget for AZ Ltd.

Your budget should be in columnar format showing separately the receipts, payments and balances for EACH of the months of May, June and July 1997.                                    **(25 marks)**

*(CIMA May 96)*

## 59    FLEXIBLE

(a)    Explain briefly the differences between fixed and flexible budgets.                **(5 marks)**

(b)    Prepare a report, addressed to the Board of Directors, clearly explaining the advantages/ disadvantages of using fixed/flexible budgets as part of a budgetary control system.    **(10 marks)**

(c)    Spreadsheets are often used by accountants to assist in the preparation of budgets.

Describe how a spreadsheet may be used to prepare a sales budget AND explain the advantages of using spreadsheets to assist in this task.

(Your answer should refer to input, use of formulae, and output reports.)       **(10 marks)**

**(Total: 25 marks)**

*(CIMA Nov 96)*

## 60    Q PLC

The following budgeted profit and loss account has been prepared for Q plc for the four months January to April 1999:

|  | January £'000 | February £'000 | March £'000 | April £'000 |
|---|---|---|---|---|
| Sales | 60 | 50 | 70 | 60 |
| Production cost | 50 | 55 | 32.5 | 50 |
| Stock adjustment | (5) | (17.5) | 20 | (5) |
| Cost of sales | 45 | 37.5 | 52.5 | 45 |
| Gross profit | 15 | 12.5 | 17.5 | 15 |
| Admin/selling overhead | 8 | 7.5 | 8.5 | 8 |
| Net profit before interest | 7 | 5 | 9 | 7 |

The working papers provide the following additional information:

(i)    40% of the production cost relates to direct materials. Materials are bought in the month prior to the month in which they are used, and 50% of them are paid for in the month of purchase. The remainder are paid for one month later.

(ii)    30% of the production cost relates to direct labour which is paid for when it is used.

(iii)    The remainder of the production cost is production overhead. £5,000 per month is a fixed cost which includes £3,000 depreciation. Fixed production overhead costs are paid monthly in arrears. The variable production overhead is paid 40% in the month of usage and the balance one month later.

(iv)    The administration and selling costs are paid quarterly in advance on 1 January, 1 April, 1 July and 1 October. The amount payable is £15,000 per quarter.

(v)    Creditors on 1 January 1999 are expected to be:

        Direct materials        £10,000
        Production overheads    £11,000

(vi)    The amounts expected to be received from customers during January to March are:

                    £         Debtor

        January        69,600
        February      56,944
        March         56,470

(vii)    The company intends to purchase capital equipment costing £30,000 in February which will be payable in March.

(viii)    The bank balance on 1 January 1999 is expected to be £5,000 overdrawn. The bank balance on 1 December 1998 is expected to be £5,000 (positive).

(ix)   Interest is payable/receivable on average monthly bank balances $\left(\frac{\text{opening}+\text{closing}}{2}\right)$ at the following rates:

| | | |
|---|---|---|
| Positive balances | interest receivable | 1% per month |
| Overdrawn balances | interest payable | 2% per month |

Interest is payable/receivable in the following month.

**Requirements:**

(a)   Prepare a cash budget for each of the months January to March 1999 for Q plc, showing clearly the bank balance at the beginning and end of each month.     **(17 marks)**

(b)   Explain how cash budgets are used in both feed-forward and feedback control mechanisms. Use your answer to (a) above to assist in your explanation.     **(8 marks)**

**(Total: 25 marks)**

*(CIMA May 98)*

## 61    X PLC

X plc manufactures Product X using three different raw materials. The product details are as follows:

| | | |
|---|---|---|
| Selling price per unit | £250 | |
| Material A | 3 kgs | material price £3.50 per kg |
| Material B | 2 kgs | material price £5.00 per kg |
| Material C | 4 kgs | material price £4.50 per kg |
| Direct labour | 8 hours | labour rate £8.00 per hour |

The company is considering its budgets for next year and has made the following estimates of sales demand for Product X for July to October 1999:

| July | August | September | October |
|---|---|---|---|
| 400 units | 300 units | 600 units | 450 units |

It is company policy to hold stocks of finished goods at the end of each month equal to 50% of the following month's sales demand, and it is expected that the stock at the start of the budget period will meet this policy.

At the end of the production process the products are tested: it is usual for 10% of those tested to be faulty. It is not possible to rectify these faulty units.

Raw material stocks are expected to be as follows on 1 July 1999:

| | |
|---|---|
| Material A | 1,000 kgs |
| Material B | 400 kgs |
| Material C | 600 kgs |

Stocks are to be increased by 20% in July 1999, and then remain at their new level for the foreseeable future.

Labour is paid on an hourly rate based on attendance. In addition to the unit direct labour hours shown above, 20% of *attendance time* is spent on tasks which support production activity.

**Requirements:**

(a)   Prepare the following budgets for the quarter from July 1999 to September 1999 inclusive:

    (i)    sales budget in quantity and value;

    (ii)    production budget in units;

(iii)    raw material usage budget in kgs;
(iv)    raw material purchases budget in kgs and value;
(v)     labour requirements budget in hours and value.                          **(16 marks)**

(b)    Explain the term *"principal budget factor"* and why its identification is an important part of the budget preparation process.                          **(3 marks)**

(c)    Explain clearly, using data from part (a) above, how you would construct a spreadsheet to produce the labour requirements budget for August 1999. Include a specimen cell layout diagram containing formulae which would illustrate the basis for the spreadsheet.                          **(6 marks)**
                          **(Total: 25 marks)**
                          *(CIMA Nov 98)*

## 62     MAZ HOTEL

(a)    'Spreadsheets are suited to the development of planning tools, such as budgets and standard costs, but databases are appropriate for recording actual data and converting it into useful information'.

**Requirements:**

Compare and contrast spreadsheets and databases, using examples to illustrate how each might be used.                          **(10 marks)**

(b)    The following cost per unit data has been extracted from the weekly flexible budgets of the MAZ hotel:

| Number of guests | 100 | 150 | 200 |
|---|---|---|---|
| Cost per guest | £ | £ | £ |
| Food costs | 20.00 | 20.00 | 20.00 |
| Heating, lighting, power | 6.50 | 6.00 | 5.75 |
| Cleaning | 11.00 | 10.67 | 10.50 |
| Administration | 30.00 | 20.00 | 15.00 |

During week 38 there were 120 guests at the MAZ hotel and the costs incurred were as follows:

|  | £ |
|---|---|
| Food costs | 2,490 |
| Heating, lighting, power | 710 |
| Cleaning | 1,440 |
| Administration | 2,850 |

**Requirement:**

Prepare a budgetary control statement for the MAZ hotel for week 38.                          **(15 marks)**
                          **(Total: 25 marks)**
                          *(CIMA May 99)*

## 63     BUDGETS AND STANDARDS

'Budgets and standards are similar but they are not the same.'

**You are required** to explain and expand on the above statement, mentioning differences and similarities.
                          **(15 marks)**
                          *(CIMA May 93)*

---

## 64    RS LTD

RS Ltd makes and sells a single product, J, with the following standard specification for materials:

|  | Quantity kg | Price per kg £ |
|---|---|---|
| Direct material R | 10 | 30 |
| Direct material S | 6 | 45 |

It takes 30 direct labour hours to produce one unit of J with a standard direct labour cost of £5.50 per hour.

The annual sales/production budget is 1,200 units evenly spread throughout the year.

The budgeted production overhead, all fixed, is £252,000 and expenditure is expected to occur evenly over the year, which the company divides into 12 calendar months. Absorption is based on units produced.

For the month of October the following actual information is provided. The budgeted sales quantity for the month was sold at the standard selling price.

|  | £ | £ |
|---|---|---|
| Sales |  | 120,000 |
| Cost of sales |  |  |
| Direct materials used | 58,136 |  |
| Direct wages | 17,325 |  |
| Fixed production overhead | 22,000 |  |
|  |  | 97,461 |
| **Gross profit** |  | 22,539 |
| Administration costs | 6,000 |  |
| Selling and distribution costs | 11,000 |  |
|  |  | 17,000 |
| **Net profit** |  | £5,539 |

Costs of opening stocks, for each material, were at the same price per kilogram as the purchases made during the month but there had been changes in the materials stock levels, viz:

|  | 1 October kg | 30 October kg |
|---|---|---|
| Material R | 300 | 375 |
| Material S | 460 | 225 |

Material R purchases were 1,100 kg for £35,000.

Material S purchases were 345 kg for £15,180.

The number of direct labour hours worked was 3,300 and the total wages incurred £17,325.

Work-in-progress stocks and finished goods stocks may be assumed to be the same at the beginning and end of October.

**You are required**

(a)     to present a standard product cost for one unit of product J showing the standard selling price and standard gross profit per unit;                                                     **(3 marks)**

(b)     to calculate appropriate variances for the materials, labour and fixed production overhead, noting that it is company policy to calculate material price variances *at time of issue to production*;

**(11 marks)**

(c)     to present a statement for management reconciling the budgeted gross profit with the actual gross profit;                                                                                        **(5 marks)**

(d)     to suggest a possible cause for each of the labour variances you show under (b) above, stating whether you believe each variance was controllable or uncontrollable and, if controllable, the job title of the responsible official.  Please state the name and amount of each variance about which you write and explain the variance, quantifying it, where possible, in non-financial terms which might be better understood by line management.                                                    **(6 marks)**

**(Total:  25 marks)**

*(CIMA Nov 91)*

## 65     USES AND LIMITATIONS

(a)     Discuss the uses and limitations of standard costs, ignoring inflation.                      **(8 marks)**

(b)     "A high rate of inflation tends to make standard costing a waste of time" said the production manager to her managing director.

**You are required**, as the assistant accountant, to draft a brief memorandum to the production manager in reply to her statement.

*Notes:*

(1)     Do not repeat any part of your answer to (a) above.

(2)     Do not refer to planning and operational variances because such variances are outside the syllabus.                                                                                        **(5 marks)**

(c)     The following information relates to the standard cost and selling price of product Y.

|  |  | *£ per unit (kg)* |
|---|---|---|
| Direct materials | 1 kilogram | 8.00 |
| Direct labour | 2 hours at £6 per hour | 12.00 |
| Variable overhead | 2 hours at £1.20 per hour | 2.40 |
| Fixed overhead |  | 4.00 |
| Production royalty, per kilogram |  | 0.80 |
|  |  | 27.20 |
| Selling and distribution costs at £2 per kg |  | 2.00 |
|  |  | 29.20 |
| Total cost |  | 29.20 |
| Sales margin |  | 5.80 |
| Standard selling price |  | 35.00 |

Variable overhead is deemed to vary with hours worked.

The budget for Period 9, on which the fixed overhead rate per kilogram was based, was 10,000 kilograms. Sales budget was 7,000 kg. After the standard had been set, the royalty was increased to £1 per kilogram.

Actual sales, production and costs for Period 9 were as follows:

| | |
|---|---|
| Sales | 7,000 kilograms at £37 per kg |
| Production | 8,000 kilograms |
| Costs | |
| Direct materials, purchased and used | 8,300 kilograms at £7.90 per kg |
| Direct wages incurred | 17,000 hours at a cost of £107,100 |
| Variable overhead | £18,800 |
| Fixed overhead | £39,000 |
| Royalties | £8,000 |
| Selling and distribution costs | £12,000 |

Assume opening finished goods stock to be nil and the closing stock for *both* the statements required for (i) and (ii) below is to be valued at standard cost.

**You are required** to present in **columnar format**, using two facing pages in the answer book,

(i)      actual revenues and costs;

(ii)     standard revenues and costs;

(iii)    variances analysed into price and usage/efficiency.            **(12 marks)**

                                                         **(Total: 25 marks)**

                                                         *(CIMA May 91)*

---

## 66     JB PLC

(a)     JB plc operates a standard marginal cost accounting system. Information relating to product J, which is made in one of the company's departments, is given below.

**Product J**       **Standard marginal product cost**

| | | *Unit* |
|---|---|---|
| | | *£* |
| Direct material | 6 kilograms at £4 per kg | 24 |
| Direct labour | 1 hour at £7 per hour | 7 |
| Variable production overhead* | | 3 |
| | | — |
| Total variable production cost | | 34 |
| | | — |

*Variable production overhead varies with units produced.

Budgeted fixed production overhead, per month: £100,000.

Budgeted production for product J: 20,000 units per month.

Actual production and costs for *month 6* were as follows:

| | | |
|---|---|---|
| Units of J produced | | 18,500 |
| | | £ |
| Direct materials purchased and used | 113,500 kgs | 442,650 |
| Direct labour | 17,800 hours | 129,940 |
| Variable production overhead incurred | | 58,800 |
| Fixed production overhead incurred | | 104,000 |
| | | ——— |
| | | 735,390 |
| | | ——— |

**You are required**

(i)    to prepare a columnar statement showing, by element of cost, the

      (I)    original budget
      (II)   flexed budget
      (III)  actual costs
      (IV)   total variances;                                          **(9 marks)**

(ii)   to sub-divide the variances for direct material and direct labour shown in your answer to **(a)(i)(IV)** above to be more informative for managerial purposes.          **(4 marks)**

(b)    Explain the meaning and use of a 'rolling forecast'.                  **(2 marks)**
                                                                **(Total:  15 marks)**
                                                                *(CIMA May 93)*

---

## 67    SK LTD

---

SK Ltd makes and sells a single product 'Jay' for which the standard cost is as follows:

|  |  | £ per unit |
|---|---|---|
| Direct materials | 4 kilograms @ £12 per kg | 48 |
| Direct labour | 5 hours @ £7 per hour | 35 |
| Variable production overhead | 5 hours @ £2 per hour | 10 |
| Fixed production overhead | 5 hours @ £10 per hour | 50 |
|  |  | 143 |

The variable production overhead is deemed to vary with the hours worked.

Overhead is absorbed into production on the basis of standard hours of production and the normal volume of production for the period just ended was 20,000 units (100,000 standard hours of production).

For the period under consideration, the actual results were:

| Production of 'Jay' | 18,000 units |
|---|---|
|  | £ |
| Direct material used - 76,000 kgs at a cost of | 836,000 |
| Direct labour cost incurred - for 84,000 hours worked | 604,800 |
| Variable production overhead incurred | 172,000 |
| Fixed production overhead incurred | 1,030,000 |

**You are required** to:

(a)    calculate and show, by element of cost, the standard cost for the output for the period;          **(2 marks)**

(b)    calculate and list the relevant variances in a way which reconciles the standard cost with the actual cost;

      *Note:* fixed production overhead sub-variances of capacity and volume efficiency (productivity) are *not* required.          **(9 marks)**

(c)    comment briefly on the usefulness to management of statements such as that given in your answer to (b) above.          **(4 marks)**
                                                                **(Total:  15 marks)**
                                                                 *(CIMA Nov 94)*

## 68    DL HOSPITAL TRUST

You have been appointed as the management accountant of the DL Hospital Trust, a newly-formed organisation with specific responsibility for providing hospital services to its local community. The hospital trust is divided into a number of specialist units: one of these, unit H, specialises in the provision of a particular surgical operation.

Although the trust does not have profit maximisation as its objective, it is concerned to control its costs and to provide a value-for-money service. To achieve this, it engages teams of specialist staff on a sub-contract basis and pays them an hourly rate based upon the direct hours attributable to the surgical operation being carried out.

Surgical team fees (ie labour costs) are collected and attributed to each surgical operation, whereas overhead costs are collected and attributed to surgical operations using absorption rates. These absorption rates are based on the surgical team fees. For the year ended 31 December 1993, these rates were:

|  |  |
|---|---|
| Variable overhead | 62.5% of surgical team fees; and |
| Fixed overhead | 87.5% of surgical team fees. |

Each surgical operation is expected to take ten hours to complete, and the total fees of the team for each operation are expected to be £2,000.

The budget for the year ended 31 December 1993 indicated that a total of 20 such surgical operations were expected to be performed each month, and that the overhead costs were expected to accrue evenly throughout the year.

During November 1993 there were 22 operations of this type completed. These took a total of 235 hours and the total surgical team fees amounted to £44,400.

Overhead costs incurred in unit H in November 1993 amounted to:

|  |  |
|---|---|
| Variable overhead | £28,650 |
| Fixed overhead | £36,950. |

**You are required** to

(a)    Prepare a statement which reconciles the original budget cost and the actual cost for this type of operation within unit H for the month of November 1993, showing the analysis of variances in as much detail as possible from the information given.    **(15 marks)**

(b)    Distinguish between the use of budgetary control and standard costing as a means of cost control in service-based organisations.

Explain clearly the arguments in favour of using BOTH of these methods simultaneously. **(5 marks)**

(c)    The DL Hospital Trust has been preparing its budgets for 1994, and the finance director has questioned the appropriateness of using surgical team fees as the basis of attributing overhead costs to operations.

**You are required** to

Write a brief report to her explaining the arguments for and against the use of this method.

**(5 marks)**
**(Total: 25 marks)**
*(Specimen paper)*

## 69    ABC LTD

The following profit reconciliation statement has been prepared by the management accountant of ABC Ltd for March 19X5:

|  |  | £ |  |
|---|---|---|---|
| Budgeted profit |  | 30,000 |  |
| Sales volume profit variance |  | 5,250 | A |
| Selling price variance |  | 6,375 | F |
|  |  | 31,125 |  |

| Cost variances: | | A £ | F £ |
|---|---|---|---|
| Material: | price | 1,985 | |
| | usage | | 400 |
| Labour: | rate | | 9,800 |
| | efficiency | 4,000 | |
| Variable overhead: | expenditure | | 1,000 |
| | efficiency | 1,500 | |
| Fixed overhead: | expenditure | | 500 |
| | volume | 24,500 | |
| | | 31,985 | 11,700 |

|  |  |
|---|---|
| | 20,285  A |
| Actual profit | 10,840 |

The standard cost card for the company's only product is as follows:

|  |  | £ |
|---|---|---|
| Materials | 5 litres @ £0.20 | 1.00 |
| Labour | 4 hours @ £4.00 | 16.00 |
| Variable overhead | 4 hours @ £1.50 | 6.00 |
| Fixed overhead | 4 hours @ £3.50 | 14.00 |
|  |  | 37.00 |
| Standard profit |  | 3.00 |
| Standard selling price |  | 40.00 |

The following information is also available:

(1)    There was no change in the level of finished goods stock during the month.
(2)    Budgeted production and sales volumes for March 19X5 were equal.
(3)    Stocks of materials, which are valued at standard price, decreased by 800 litres during the month.
(4)    The actual labour rate was £0.28 lower than the standard hourly rate.

**You are required** to

(a)    calculate the following:

|  |  |  |
|---|---|---|
| (i) | the actual production/sales volume, | **(4 marks)** |
| (ii) | the actual number of hours worked, | **(4 marks)** |
| (iii) | the actual quantity of materials purchased, | **(4 marks)** |
| (iv) | the actual variable overhead cost incurred, | **(2 marks)** |
| (v) | the actual fixed overhead cost incurred. | **(2 marks)** |

(b)     ABC Ltd uses a standard costing system whereas other organisations use a system of budgetary control.

          **You are required** to explain the reasons why a system of budgetary control is often preferred to the use of standard costing in non-manufacturing environments.     **(9 marks)**

                                                                     **(Total: 25 marks)**

                                                                     *(CIMA May 95)*

---

## 70    TUR PLC

---

TUR plc uses an integrated standard costing system, with stocks being valued at standard cost. The standard cost card of one of its products, K, is shown below. This product is the only one of TUR plc's products which uses raw material F.

**Standard cost card of product K**
**Year ended 31 October 19X5**

|  |  |  | £ |
|---|---|---|---|
| Raw material F | 5 kilos | @ £3.50 per kilo | 17.50 |
| Direct labour | 4 hours | @ £4.50 per hour | 18.00 |
| Overhead: |  |  |  |
|   Variable | 4 hours | @ £1.50 per hour | 6.00 |
|   Fixed | 4 hours | @ £2.50 per hour | 10.00 |
|  |  |  | 51.50 |

TUR plc prepares its annual accounts to 31 October each year. The trial balance at 30 September 19X5 shows that the stock of raw material F at that date was valued at £8,750.

Raw material F is added to the process continuously at a constant flow rate until the final product K is complete. Any price variances which arise are calculated and recorded in the material stock account at the time of purchase.

Company policy is to enter actual labour and overhead costs into the work-in-progress account, from which appropriate variances are extracted at the month end.

The budgeted production of product K during October 19X5 was 1,000 units. There was no opening or closing work-in-progress, and 965 units were transferred into finished goods stocks during October 19X5.

The following transactions occurred during October 19X5:

| | |
|---|---|
| Purchased raw material F on credit | 4,800 kilos costing £18,240 |
| Issued raw material F to production | 4,840 kilos |
| Direct wages | 4,000 hours @ £4.60 |
| Variable overhead incurred | £5,950 |
| Fixed overhead incurred | £9,900 |

**You are required** to

(a)     Calculate the following variances for the month of October 19X5:

          (i)     Material price variance - raw material F
          (ii)    Material usage variance - raw material F
          (iii)   Direct labour rate variance
          (iv)   Direct labour efficiency variance
          (v)    Variable overhead expenditure variance

| | | |
|---|---|---|
| (vi) | Variable overhead efficiency variance | |
| (vii) | Fixed overhead expenditure variance | |
| (viii) | Fixed overhead volume variance. | **(17 marks)** |

(b)    Prepare the ledger accounts for

      (i)      stock of raw material F

      (ii)     work-in-progress - product K.

**(8 marks)**
**(Total: 25 marks)**
*(CIMA Nov 95)*

---

## 71    Q PLC

Q plc uses a standard absorption costing system which it developed five years ago. Three years ago, the specification of Q plc's material requirements changed and its standard costs were revised. Apart from this, the only change made to Q plc's material standards is to update its standard prices each year when preparing its annual budgets. Q plc calculates its material price variances at the time of purchase.

One of Q plc's products - product 2258 - uses material R. It is the only product made by Q plc which uses this material. According to the standard cost card, 5.00 kgs of material R are required per unit of product 2258, and the standard price of material R during the year ending 30 June 1996 is £3.00 per kg.

During April 1996, seven hundred units of product 2258 were manufactured. There was no opening stock of material R on 1 April 1996. During April 1996, 4,000 kgs of material R were purchased at a cost of £12,800. At the end of the month, on 30 April 1996, there were 320 kgs of material R in stock.

**Requirements:**

(a)    Calculate the material price and usage variances for April 1996 using the standard cost data shown on the standard cost card.                                                                                     **(4 marks)**

(b)    Prepare journal entries to record the transactions in material R during April 1996, using your answer to part (a) above.                                                                                                         **(4 marks)**

(c)    Explain the advantages and disadvantages of calculating the material price variance at the time of purchase.                                                                                                                                  **(6 marks)**

(d)    The standard shown on the standard cost card assumes 0% material wastage, though 5% wastage is considered normal.

      Recalculate the material usage variance using a more appropriate standard, AND explain why this is more useful to management than the usage variance calculated in your answer to (a) above.

**(5 marks)**

(e)    Explain the difference between

      (i)      attainable standards; and

      (ii)     ideal standards.

      Use the information in the question to assist in your explanation.                                **(6 marks)**
**(Total: 25 marks)**
*(CIMA May 96)*

## 72   SALES/OVERHEAD VARIANCES

You have been provided with the following data for S plc for September 1996:

| Accounting method | Absorption | Marginal |
|---|---|---|
| VARIANCES | £ | £ |
| Selling price | 1,900 (A) | 1,900 (A) |
| Sales volume | 4,500 (A) | 7,500 (A) |
| Fixed overhead expenditure | 2,500 (F) | 2,500 (F) |
| Fixed overhead volume | 1,800 (A) | not applicable |

During September 1996 production and sales volumes were as follows:

| | Sales | Production |
|---|---|---|
| Budget | 10,000 | 10,000 |
| Actual | 9,500 | 9,700 |

**Requirements:**

(a) Calculate

    (i) the standard contribution per unit,
    (ii) the standard profit per unit,
    (iii) the actual fixed overhead cost total.

**(9 marks)**

(b) Using the information presented above, explain why different variances are calculated depending upon the choice of marginal or absorption costing.

**(8 marks)**

(c) Explain the meaning of the fixed overhead volume variance and its usefulness to management.

**(5 marks)**

(d) Fixed overhead absorption rates are often calculated using a single measure of activity. It is suggested that fixed overhead costs should be attributed to cost units using multiple measures of activity (Activity Based Costing).

Explain 'Activity Based Costing' and how it may provide useful information to managers.

(Your answer should refer to both the setting of cost driver rates and subsequent overhead cost control.)

**(8 marks)**
**(Total: 30 marks)**
*(CIMA Nov 96)*

## 73   PDC LTD

(a) The following report has been prepared, relating to one product for March 1997. This has been sent to the appropriate product manager as part of PDC Limited's monitoring procedures.

### Monthly variance report - March 1997

| | Actual | Budget | Variance | % |
|---|---|---|---|---|
| Production volume (units) | 9,905 | 10,000 | 95 A | 0.95 A |
| Sales volume (units) | 9,500 | 10,000 | 500 A | 5.00 A |

| | | | | |
|---|---|---|---|---|
| Sales revenue (£) | 27,700 | 30,000 | 2,300 A | 7.67 A |
| Direct material (kgs) | 9,800 | 10,000 | 200 F | 2.00 F |
| Direct material (£) | 9,600 | 10,000 | 400 F | 4.00 F |
| Direct labour (hours) | 2,500 | 2,400 | 100 A | 4.17 A |
| Direct labour (£) | 8,500 | 8,400 | 100 A | 1.19 A |
| Contribution (£) | 9,600 | 11,600 | 2,000 A | 17.24 A |

The product manager has complained that the report ignores the principle of flexible budgeting and is unfair.

**Requirement:**

Prepare a report addressed to the management team which comments critically on the monthly variance report.

Include as an appendix to your report the layout of a revised monthly variance report which will be more useful to the product manager.

Include row and column headings, but do NOT calculate the contents of the report.

**(15 marks)**

(b)     Explain the differences between budgetary control and standard costing / variance analysis. In what circumstances would an organisation find it beneficial to operate both of these cost control systems?

**(5 marks)**

(c)     Explain briefly how a database may be used to collect the information required to prepare a report such as that illustrated in part (a) above.

**(5 marks)**
**(Total: 25 marks)**
**(CIMA May 97)**

# 74    SEW

The following profit reconciliation statement summarises the performance of one of SEW's products for March 1997.

|  | £ |
|---|---|
| Budgeted profit | 4,250 |
| Sales volume variance | 850 A |
| Standard profit on actual sales | 3,400 |
| Selling price variance | 4,000 A |
|  | (600) |

| Cost variances: | Adverse £ | Favourable £ |
|---|---|---|
| Direct material price |  | 1,000 |
| Direct material usage | 150 |  |
| Direct labour rate | 200 |  |
| Direct labour efficiency | 150 |  |
| Variable overhead expenditure | 600 |  |
| Variable overhead efficiency | 75 |  |

| | | | |
|---|---|---|---|
| Fixed overhead expenditure | | 2,500 | |
| Fixed overhead volume | | 150 | |
| | 1,175 | 3,650 | 2,475 F |

Actual profit          1,875

The budget for the same period contained the following data:

| | | |
|---|---|---|
| Sales volume | | 1,500 units |
| Sales revenue | £20,000 | |
| Production volume | | 1,500 units |
| Direct materials purchased | | 750 kgs |
| Direct materials used | | 750 kgs |
| Direct material cost | £4,500 | |
| Direct labour hours | | 1,125 |
| Direct labour cost | £4,500 | |
| Variable overhead cost | £2,250 | |
| Fixed overhead cost | £4,500 | |

Additional information:

- stocks of raw materials and finished goods are valued at standard cost;
- during the month the actual number of units produced was 1,550;
- the actual sales revenue was £12,000; and
- the direct materials purchased were 1,000 kgs.

**Requirements:**

(a) Calculate

     (i)      the actual sales volume;
     (ii)     the actual quantity of materials used;
     (iii)    the actual direct material cost;
     (iv)    the actual direct labour hours;
     (v)     the actual direct labour cost;
     (vi)    the actual variable overhead cost;
     (vii)   the actual fixed overhead cost.

**(19 marks)**

(b) Explain the possible causes of the direct materials usage variance, direct labour rate variance, and sales volume variance.

**(6 marks)**
**(Total: 25 marks)**
*(CIMA May 97)*

## 75   OVERHEAD VARIANCES

The following details have been extracted from the standard cost card for product X:

| | £/*unit* |
|---|---|
| Variable overhead | |
| 4 machine hours @ £8.00/hour | 32.00 |
| 2 labour hours @ £4.00/hour | 8.00 |
| Fixed overhead | 20.00 |

During October 1997, 5,450 units of the product were made compared to a budgeted production target of 5,500 units. The actual overhead costs incurred were:

| | |
|---|---|
| Machine-related variable overhead | £176,000 |
| Labour-related variable overhead | £42,000 |
| Fixed overhead | £109,000 |

The actual number of machine hours was 22,000 and the actual number of labour hours was 10,800.

**Requirements:**

(a)      Calculate the overhead cost variances in as much detail as possible from the data provided.

**(12 marks)**

(b)      Explain the meaning of, and give possible causes for, the variable overhead variances which you have calculated.
**(8 marks)**

(c)      Explain the benefits of using multiple activity bases for variable overhead absorption.      **(5 marks)**

**(Total: 25 marks)**
*(CIMA Nov 97)*

---

## 76      T PLC

You are the management accountant of T plc. The following computer printout shows details relating to April 1998:

| | | | *Actual* | *Budget* |
|---|---|---|---|---|
| Sales volume | | | 4,900 units | 5,000 units |
| Selling price per unit | | | £11.00 | £10.00 |
| Production volume | | | 5,400 units | 5,000 units |
| | | | | |
| Direct materials | - | kgs | 10,600 | 10,000 |
| | | price per kg | £0.60 | £0.50 |
| | | | | |
| Direct labour | - | hours per unit | 0.55 | 0.50 |
| | | rate per hour | £3.80 | £4.00 |
| | | | | |
| Fixed overhead: | | | | |
| Production | | | £10,300 | £10,000 |
| Administration | | | £3,100 | £3,000 |

T plc uses a standard absorption costing system.
There was no opening or closing work-in-progress.

**Requirements:**

(a)      Prepare a statement which reconciles the budgeted profit with the actual profit for April 1998, showing individual variances in as much detail as the above data permit.      **(20 marks)**

(b)      Explain briefly the possible causes of

      (i)      the material usage variance;
      (ii)     the labour rate variance; and
      (iii)    the sales volume profit variance.

**(6 marks)**

(c)    Explain the meaning and relevance of inter-dependence of variances when reporting to managers.

**(4 marks)**
**(Total:  30 marks)**
*(CIMA May 98)*

---

## 77    RESTAURANT

A local restaurant has been examining the profitability of its set menu.  At the beginning of the year the selling price was based on the following predicted costs:

|  |  | £ |
|---|---|---|
| *Starter* | *Soup of the day* | |
| | 100 grams of mushrooms @ £3.00 per kg | 0.30 |
| | Cream and other ingredients | 0.20 |
| *Main course* | *Roast beef* | |
| | Beef 0.10 kgs @ £15.00 per kg | 1.50 |
| | Potatoes 0.2 kgs @ £0.25 per kg | 0.05 |
| | Vegetables 0.3 kgs @ £0.90 per kg | 0.27 |
| | Other ingredients and accompaniments | 0.23 |
| *Dessert* | *Fresh tropical fruit salad* | |
| | Fresh fruit 0.15 kgs @ £3.00 per kg | 0.45 |

The selling price was set at £7.50, which produced an overall gross profit of 60%.

During October 1998 the number of set menus sold was 860 instead of the 750 budgeted: this increase was achieved by reducing the selling price to £7.00.  During the same period an analysis of the direct costs incurred showed:

|  | £ |
|---|---|
| 90 kgs of mushrooms | 300 |
| Cream and other ingredients | 160 |
| 70 kgs of beef | 1,148 |
| 180 kgs of potatoes | 40 |
| 270 kgs of vegetables | 250 |
| Other ingredients and accompaniments | 200 |
| 140 kgs of fresh fruit | 450 |

There was no stock of ingredients at the beginning or end of the month.

**Requirements:**

(a)    Calculate the budgeted profit for the month of October 1998.                                **(2 marks)**

(b)    Calculate the actual profit for the month of October 1998.                                      **(3 marks)**

(c)    Prepare a statement which reconciles your answers to (a) and (b) above, showing the variances in as much detail as possible.                                                                                       **(14 marks)**

(d)    Prepare a report, addressed to the restaurant manager, which identifies the two most significant variances, and comments on their possible causes.                                             **(6 marks)**
**(Total:  25 marks)**
*(CIMA Nov 98)*

---

## 78    RBF TRANSPORT LTD

RBF Transport Ltd, a haulage contractor, operates a standard costing system and has prepared the following report for April 1999:

**Operating statement**

|  |  |  | £ | £ | £ |
|---|---|---|---|---|---|
| BUDGETED PROFIT | | | | | 8,000 |
| Sales volume profit variance | | | | | 880 (A) |
| | | | | | 7,120 |
| Selling price variance | | | | | 3,560 (F) |
| | | | | | 10,680 |
| COST VARIANCES | | | *A* | *F* | |
| Direct labour | - | rate | | 1,086 | |
| | - | efficiency | 240 | | |
| Fuel | - | price | 420 | | |
| | - | usage | 1,280 | | |
| Variable overhead | - | expenditure | | 280 | |
| | - | efficiency | 180 | | |
| Fixed overhead | - | expenditure | | 400 | |
| | - | volume | 1,760 | | |
| | | | 3,880 | 1,766 | 2,114 (A) |
| ACTUAL PROFIT | | | | | 8,566 |

The company uses delivery miles as its cost unit, and the following details have been taken from the budget working papers for April 1999:

|  |  |  |
|---|---|---|
| (1) | Expected activity | 200,000 delivery miles |
| (2) | Charge to customers | £0.30 per delivery mile |
| (3) | Expected variable cost per delivery mile: | |
| | Direct labour (0.02 hours) | £0.08 |
| | Fuel (0.1 litres) | £0.04 |
| | Variable overhead (0.02 hours) | £0.06 |

The following additional information has been determined from the actual accounting records for April 1999.

- Fixed overhead cost        £15,600
- Fuel price                 £0.42 per litre
- Direct labour hours        3,620

**Requirements:**

(a)   Calculate for April 1999:

   (i)     the actual number of delivery miles;
   (ii)    the actual direct labour rate per hour;
   (iii)   the actual number of litres of fuel consumed;
   (iv)    the actual variable overhead expenditure.                        **(16 marks)**

(b)   Prepare a report, addressed to the transport operations manager, explaining the different types of standard which may be set, and the importance of keeping standards meaningful and relevant.

**(9 marks)**
**(Total: 25 marks)**
*(CIMA May 99)*

## 79   MULTIPLE CHOICE QUESTIONS

1    A company's existing production plan is as follows

|  |  | A | B |
|---|---|---|---|
| Units |  | 1,000 | 750 |
|  |  | £ | £ |
| Unit selling price |  | 13.00 | 21.00 |
| Unit variable costs |  |  |  |
| Direct material |  | 1.00 | 1.00 |
| Direct labour at £2 per hour |  | 5.00 | 12.00 |
| Overhead |  | 0.50 | 1.20 |
|  |  | £6.50 | £14.20 |

This represents the maximum demand for each product. The company is limited to 7,000 labour hours availability. A contract to produce 200 units of product C is under review. These are required by a customer who will provide his own materials. Net proceeds from the contract after deducting labour and overhead costs amount to £3,000 and will utilise 1,500 labour hours.

Assuming that the company wishes to maximise profit, which is the optimum production plan?

|  | A | B | C |
|---|---|---|---|
| **A** | 400 | 750 | 200 |
| **B** | 1,000 | 750 | 0 |
| **C** | 1,000 | 500 | 200 |
| **D** | 0 | 750 | 200 |

2    Carrell Ltd produces two types of jacket, Blouson and Bomber, in its factory which is divided into two departments, cutting and stitching. The firm wishes to calculate a fixed overhead cost per unit figure from the following budgeted data

|  | Cutting dept | Stitching dept |
|---|---|---|
| Direct and allocated fixed overheads | £120,000 | £72,000 |
| Labour hours per unit |  |  |
| Blouson | 0.05 hours | 0.20 hours |
| Bomber | 0.10 hours | 0.25 hours |
| Budgeted production |  |  |
| Blouson | 6,000 units | 6,000 units |
| Bomber | 6,000 units | 6,000 units |

If fixed overheads are absorbed by reference to labour hours, the fixed overhead cost of a bomber would be

**A**   £5.33        **B**   £6.67        **C**   £12.00        **D**   £20.00

3    The following data relate to Rose's major production process

|                                               | Units  |
|-----------------------------------------------|--------|
| Opening work in progress (40% complete)       | 1,500  |
| Goods completed in the period                 | 18,000 |
| Closing work in progress (80% complete)       | 3,000  |

How many equivalent units were produced during the period?

A    21,300        B    20,400        C    19,800        D    16,200

---

4    Carter Ltd assembles personal computers.  During July 1,900 computers were completed of which 100 were 30% complete at the start of the month.  At the end of the month there were 200 units which were 40% finished.  Costs for July were

|                              | £          |
|------------------------------|------------|
| Costs brought forward        | 38,600     |
| Costs incurred this period   | 1,930,500  |
| Total costs                  | £1,969,100 |

If the factory chooses the FIFO method of spreading costs, what is the cost per unit for production completed in July?

A    £1,010        B    £995        C    £990        D    £975

---

5    The following data for last week relate to a production process

|                                                          | Units  |
|----------------------------------------------------------|--------|
| Opening work in process (each 60% complete), cost £12,000 | 2,000  |
| Entered process                                          | 9,500  |
| Satisfactorily completed                                 | 8,500  |
| Closing work in process (each 50% complete)              | 3,000  |

The manufacturing costs of the process last week were £100,000.

What is the cost of the closing work in process using the FIFO method of valuation (to the nearest £100)?

A    £17,000        B    £16,800        C    £16,300        D    £14,600

---

6    A cleaning fluid is produced by a series of processes.  The following information relates to the final process

|                                   | Litres |
|-----------------------------------|--------|
| Opening work in progress          | 2,000  |
| Closing work in progress          | 1,500  |
| Input                             | 42,300 |
| Transfer to finished goods stock  | 40,100 |
| Normal loss                       | 400    |

The abnormal loss is

| | |
|---|---|
| A | 800 litres |
| B | 1,300 litres |
| C | 1,800 litres |
| D | 2,300 litres |

---

7    Two types of plastic piping are produced in a joint production process. UB-1 may be sold immediately after split off. UB-2 requires further processing before it is ready for sale. There is no opening stock. The following production data are available

| | |
|---|---|
| Total joint cost | £80,000 |
| Additional cost of processing UB-2 | £38,400 |

| | Sales quantity (metres) | Sales price (per metre) | Closing stock (metres) |
|---|---|---|---|
| UB-1 | 200,000 | £0.30 | 8,000 |
| UB-2 | 180,000 | £0.40 | 12,000 |

What is the cost of closing stock using the final sales revenue method of joint cost allocation (to the nearest £100)?

A    £4,000      B    £6,400      C    £6,500      D    £7,200

---

8    A factory manufactures model cars. During October work commenced on 110,000 new cars. This was in addition to 20,000 which were 50% complete at the start of the month. At the end of October there were 40,000 cars which were 50% complete.

Costs for October were

| | £ |
|---|---|
| Brought forward | 11,000 |
| Incurred this period | 121,000 |
| | £132,000 |

If this factory chooses the weighted average method of spreading costs, what is the cost per car for October production?

A    £1.10      B    £1.20      C    £1.21      D    £1.32

---

9    The standard cost of the only type of quartz watch made in the Wells factory of a jewellery firm based on an expected monthly level of production and sales of 1,000 is as follows

| | £ |
|---|---|
| Variable production costs | 5.60 |
| Fixed production costs | 5.80 |
| Variable selling costs | 3.40 |
| Fixed selling costs | 4.60 |
| Profit | 5.50 |
| Selling price | £24.90 |

The break-even point (in units) is

**A**      365            **B**      513            **C**      654            **D**      920

---

10      Hibernian Liquids makes a product Q which sells for £20 a litre and as a by-product of the process, R, which can be sold for £0.50 per litre. In the first period joint costs of production were £300,000 and 10,000 litres of Q and 3,000 litres of R were produced. 8,000 litres of Q and all the 3,000 litres of R were sold.

If by-product income realised is treated as a reduction in the costs of the main product, the value of stocks at the end of the period, to the nearest £10, was

**A**      £58,960        **B**      £59,260        **C**      £59,700        **D**      £60,000

---

11      A company produces Inverness in a continuous process. At the beginning of November work in progress of 400 litres was 30% complete as regards labour and overheads. At the end of the month, work in progress was 200 litres and was 60% complete. During the month 2,000 litres were introduced to the process.

If the labour and overheads in November cost £3,300, the cost per equivalent unit in the month was

**A**      £1.42          **B**      £1.50          **C**      £1.62          **D**      £1.65

---

12      A company makes three products as follows

|                              | *Kilts* | *Skirts* | *Dresses* |
|                              | £       | £        | £         |
|------------------------------|---------|----------|-----------|
| Material @ £5/square metre   | 5       | 2.50     | 10        |
| Labour @ £2/hour             | 6       | 2.00     | 2         |
| Fixed costs absorbed         | 6       | 2.00     | 2         |
| Profit                       | 6       | 3.50     | 5         |
| Selling price                | £23     | £10.00   | £19       |

Maximum demand is 1,000 for each product, but supplies of material are limited to 4,000 square metres while the labour force will only work 1,000 hours.

To maximise its profits the company should produce

**A**      1,000 kilts    **B**      1,000 skirts    **C**      1,000 dresses    **D**      333 kilts

---

13      Raith sells three products, X, Y and Z

|   | *Selling price* | *Maximum demand* | *Variable cost of production* |
|---|-----------------|------------------|-------------------------------|
| X | £10             | 30,000           | £8                            |
| Y | £15             | 10,000           | £10                           |
| Z | £5              | 20,000           | £4                            |

Fixed costs are £26,000

If Raith always sells its products in the same proportions as the maximum demand for each, the amount made and sold of X when the company breaks even is

**A**     6,000          **B**     6,545          **C**     12,000          **D**     13,000

---

14     Vare Ltd produces various inks at its Normanton factory. Production details for Process 1 are as follows

| | | |
|---|---|---|
| Opening work in progress, 1 April | 400 units | 60% complete |
| Closing work in progress, 30 April | 600 units | 20% complete |
| Units started | 1,000 | |
| Units finished | 800 | |

The degree of completion quoted relates to labour and overhead costs. Three-quarters of the materials are added at the start of the process and the remaining quarter added when the process is 50% complete.

The equivalent units of production for materials in the period are

**A**     1,250          **B**     1,000          **C**     850          **D**     680

---

15     The following data are available for Scott's production in September

Budget
| | |
|---|---|
| Selling price per unit | £120 |
| Variable cost per unit | £80 |
| | |
| Production and sales | 18,000 units |

Actual for April
| | |
|---|---|
| Sales | 21,000 units |
| Sales price variance | £50,000 F |
| Fixed costs | £580,000 |
| Fixed costs expenditure variance | £20,000 F |
| Variable cost per unit | £60 |

What was the budgeted profit for September?

**A**     £120,000     **B**     £140,000     **C**     £160,000     **D**     £190,000

---

16     An error was made in a firm's computation of the percentage of completion of closing work in progress. The error resulted in assigning a lower percentage of completion than actually was the case.

What was the effect of this error upon the cost per equivalent unit and the cost of goods completed for the period?

| | *Cost per equivalent unit* | *Cost of goods completed* |
|---|---|---|
| **A** | understated | understated |
| **B** | understated | overstated |
| **C** | overstated | understated |
| **D** | overstated | overstated |

17    Trim Ltd's materials price variance for the month of January was £1,000 F and the usage variance was £200 F. The standard material usage per unit is 3 kg, and the standard material price is £2 per kg. 500 units were produced in the period. Opening stocks of raw materials were 100 kg and closing stocks 300 kg.

Material purchases in the period were

| A | 1,200 kg | B | 1,400 kg | C | 1,600 kg | D | 1,800 kg |

18    MacFarlane is preparing a cash budget for July. His credit sales are

|  |  | £ |
|---|---|---|
| April | (actual) | 80,000 |
| May | (actual) | 60,000 |
| June | (actual) | 40,000 |
| July | (estimated) | 50,000 |

His recent debt collection experience has been as follows

| Current month's sales | 20% |
|---|---|
| Prior month's sale | 60% |
| Sales two months prior | 10% |
| Cash discounts taken | 5% |
| Bad debts | 5% |

How much may MacFarlane expect to collect from debtors during July?

| A | £48,000 | B | £42,000 | C | £40,000 | D | £36,000 |

19    Quintin is preparing a cash budget for July. His credit sales are

|  |  | £ |
|---|---|---|
| April | (actual) | 40,000 |
| May | (actual) | 30,000 |
| June | (actual) | 20,000 |
| July | (estimated) | 25,000 |

His recent debt collection experience has been as follows

| Current month's sales | 20% |
|---|---|
| Prior month's sale | 65% |
| Sales two months prior | 10% |
| Cash discounts taken | 2.5% |
| Bad debts | 2.5% |

How much may Quintin expect to collect from debtors during July?

| A | £19,000 | B | £20,000 | C | £21,000 | D | £24,000 |

20  A company manufactures special electrical equipment. The company employs a standard costing system with separate standards established for each product.

A special transformer is manufactured in the transformer department. Production volume is measured by direct labour hours in this department, and a flexible budget system is used to plan and control departmental overheads.

Standard costs for the special transformer are determined annually. The standard cost of a transformer is shown below

| Direct materials | | | £ |
|---|---|---|---|
| Iron | 5 sheets | @ £2 | 10 |
| Copper | 3 spools | @ £3 | 9 |
| Direct labour | 4 hours | @ £7 | 28 |
| Variable overhead | 4 hours | @ £3 | 12 |
| Fixed overhead | 4 hours | @ £2 | 8 |
| | | | — |
| Total | | | £67 |
| | | | — |

Overhead rates were based upon normal and expected monthly capacity, both of which were 4,000 direct labour hours. Practical capacity for this department is 5,000 direct labour hours per month. The variable overhead costs are expected to vary with the number of direct labour hours actually used.

During the month 800 transformers were produced.

The following costs were incurred in the month

Direct materials

| Type | Quantity purchased | Used |
|---|---|---|
| Iron | 5,000 sheets @ £2.00 per sheet | 3,900 sheets |
| Copper | 2,200 spools @ £3.10 per spool | 2,600 spools |

Direct labour

2,000 hours @ £7.00
1,400 hours @ £7.20

Overheads

| Variable overheads | £10,000 |
|---|---|
| Fixed overheads | £8,800 |

(a)  The total material usage variance is

A   £200 A   **B**   £400 A   **C**   £600 A   **D**   £800 A

(b)  The labour rate variance is

A   £280 A   **B**   £340 A   **C**   £1,680 A   **D**   £2,440 A

(c)  The variable overhead rate variance is

A   £200 F   **B**   £400 A   **C**   £600 A   **D**   £1,600 A

(d)    The expenditure variance for fixed overhead is

**A**    £2,400 A    **B**    Nil    **C**    £800 A    **D**    £1,000 F

(e)    The fixed overhead volume variance is

**A**    £400 A    **B**    £2,200 A    **C**    £2,400 A    **D**    £1,600 A

---

21    A firm is trying to find a relationship between its sales volume in a quarter and its telephone expense in that quarter.

If a sales volume of 2m units corresponds to a telephone expense of £5,000 and sales volume of 4m corresponds to a telephone expense of £6,000, then if the sales volume is 5m, the telephone expense is likely to be

**A**    £2,500    **B**    £6,500    **C**    £7,000    **D**    £7,500

---

22    If both the selling price per unit and variable cost per unit of a company rise by 10%, the break-even point will

**A**    remain constant
**B**    increase
**C**    fall
**D**    be impossible to determine

---

23    Tindall Ltd sells a single product for £40 per unit. Fixed costs are £48,000 and variable costs 80% of revenue. If fixed costs increase by £8,000 the break-even number of units will increase by

**A**    10,000 units    **B**    5,000 units    **C**    1,000 units    **D**    200 units

---

24    The following information relates to job PG 200 which is being carried out by Duke Ltd to meet a customer's order

|                                          | Dept A              | Dept B       |
| ---------------------------------------- | ------------------- | ------------ |
| Direct materials consumed                | £20,000             | £16,000      |
| Direct labour hours                      | 4,000 hours         | 5,000 hours  |
| Direct labour rate per hour              | £6                  | £4           |
| Production overhead per direct labour hour | £5                | £5           |
| Administration and other overhead        | 20% of full production cost | |
| Profit mark-up                           | 20% of sales price  |              |

What is the selling price to the customer for job PG 200?

**A**    £150,000    **B**    £156,250    **C**    £180,000    **D**    £187,500

25      Which one of the following statements is *incorrect*?

    A       Job costs are collected separately, whereas process costs are averages

    B       In job costing the progress of a job can be ascertained from the materials requisition notes and job tickets or time sheet

    C       In process costing information is needed about work passing through a process and work remaining in each process

    D       In process costing, but not job costing, the cost of normal loss will be incorporated into normal product costs

---

26      The following statements relate to the effects or advantages of using a pre-determined overhead absorption rate, rather than calculating overhead costs on the basis of actual costs and actual activity levels.

    (a)      SSAP 9 requires the absorption of production overhead to be based on normal levels of activity rather than actual levels of activity.

    (b)      Using a pre-determined absorption rate avoids fluctuations in unit costs caused by abnormally high or low overhead expenditure or activity levels.

    (c)      The net profit each year, allowing for the under- or over-absorbed overhead adjustment to profit, will be the same with pre-determined overhead rates as with actual rates.

    (d)      Using a pre-determined absorption rate offers the administrative convenience of being able to record full production costs sooner.

All of these statements are correct *except*

    A       Statement (a)
    B       Statement (b)
    C       Statement (c)
    D       Statement (d)

---

27      A company manufactures and sells a single product. The following data have been extracted from this year's budget

| | |
|---|---|
| Sales and production | 1,000 units |
| Variable cost per unit | £60 |
| Fixed cost per unit | £25 |
| Contribution margin ratio | 52% |

The selling price per unit for the next year is budgeted to increase by 8% whereas both the variable cost per unit and the total fixed costs are expected to increase by only 5%.

The objective for next year is that the total budgeted profit should remain the same as that budgeted for this year.

Calculate the minimum number of whole units which should be produced and sold next year in order to achieve the objective

    A       650        B       883        C       903        D       921

---

28     What is cost apportionment?

    **A**     The charging of discrete identifiable items of cost to cost centres or cost units

    **B**     The collection of costs attributable to cost centres and cost units using the costing methods, principles and techniques prescribed for a particular business entity

    **C**     The process of establishing the costs of cost centres or cost units

    **D**     The division of costs amongst two or more cost centres in proportion to the estimated benefit received, using a proxy eg, square feet.

---

29     Grumpy & Dopey Ltd estimated that during the year 75,000 machine hours would be used and it has been using an overhead absorption rate of £6.40 per machine hour in its machining department. During the year the overhead expenditure amounted to £472,560 and 72,600 machine hours were used.

    Which one of the following statements is correct?

    **A**     Overhead was under-absorbed by £7,440
    **B**     Overhead was under-absorbed by £7,920
    **C**     Overhead was over-absorbed by £7,440
    **D**     Overhead was over-absorbed by £7,920

---

30     The overhead expenses of Larchwood Fences plc, a large public company, are coded using a 7-digit coding system, as follows

| *Location* | *Code no* | *Type of expense* | *Code no* | *Function* | *Code no* |
|---|---|---|---|---|---|
| London | 30 | Rent | 123 | Buying | 10 |
| Birmingham | 31 | Machinery depreciation | 214 | Production | 12 |
| Cardiff | 32 | Factory depreciation | 450 | Marketing | 15 |
| Glasgow | 37 | Travel | 521 | Finance | 17 |
| Manchester | 38 | Entertainment | 632 | | |
| Bristol | 39 | Subsistence | 920 | | |

The coding for entertaining expenses of the production manager from the Glasgow office is 3712632.

    (a)     The coding for the depreciation cost of the factory in Birmingham is

    **A**     3110214     **B**     3112214     **C**     3110450     **D**     3112450

    (b)     The coding for hotel expenses incurred by the accountant of the Cardiff office on a recent visit to head office in London is

    **A**     3217632     **B**     3210632     **C**     3217920     **D**     3210920

---

31     Cost centres are

    **A**     units of product or service for which costs are ascertained

    **B**     amounts of expenditure attributable to various activities

    **C**     functions or locations for which costs are ascertained and related to cost units

    **D**     a section of an organisation for which budgets are prepared and control exercised

32  What is the name given to a system of stocktaking, whereby a stock count is made each day of a number of items in store, and the count is checked against stock records, so that every item in store is checked at least once a year?

     A      continuous stocktaking
     B      perpetual inventory
     C      ABC inventory analysis
     D      annual stock accounting

33  Gross wages incurred in Department 1 in June were £135,000. The wages analysis shows the following summary breakdown of the gross pay

| | Paid to direct labour £ | Paid to indirect labour £ |
|---|---|---|
| Ordinary time | 62,965 | 29,750 |
| Overtime | | |
|   Basic pay | 13,600 | 8,750 |
|   Premium | 3,400 | 2,190 |
| Shift allowance | 6,750 | 3,495 |
| Sick pay | 3,450 | 650 |
| | £90,165 | £44,835 |

What is the direct wages cost for Department 1 in June?

   A    £62,965      B    £76,565      C    £86,715      D    £90,165

34  In a period of continual price inflation for materials purchases

     A      the LIFO method will produce lower profits than the FIFO method, and lower closing stock values

     B      the LIFO method will produce lower profits than the FIFO method, and higher closing stock values

     C      the FIFO method will produce lower profits than the LIFO method, and lower closing stock values

     D      the FIFO method will produce lower profits than the LIFO method, and higher closing stock values

35  A company makes regular purchases of a particular material. The price of this material has been increasing steadily during the last period, and this trend is likely to continue into the foreseeable future.

Which of the following methods will produce the lowest closing stock valuation?

     A      first in, first out
     B      last in, first out
     C      next in, first out
     D      average price

36    Capri Ltd purchases and re-sells a single item of product. Opening stock on 1 March was 200 units, valued at £1.80 each. Further receipts and sales during the month were as follows

|            |          | Units | £ per unit |
|------------|----------|-------|------------|
| 8 March    | Receipts | 300   | 2.10       |
| 14 March   | Receipts | 250   | ?          |
| 25 March   | Sales    | 625   | 4.00       |

The company uses the FIFO method of stock valuation. Gross trading profit for March was £1,250.

What was the cost per unit of the 500 units received on 14 March?

A    £1.94        B    £2.00        C    £2.04        D    £2.08

---

37    Receipts and issues of part number JS100 for the month of April are as follows

|          | Receipts units | Total value £ | Issues units |
|----------|----------------|---------------|--------------|
| 3 April  | 2,000          | 12,000        |              |
| 7 April  | 3,000          | 19,800        |              |
| 11 April | 2,000          | 16,000        |              |
| 16 April |                |               | 4,000        |
| 24 April | 3,000          | 21,000        |              |
| 30 April |                |               | 5,000        |

Opening stocks of part number JS100 were 1,000 units, valued at £5,600

(a)    Using a FIFO method of stock valuation, the cost of the issued parts in the month was

A    £60,400        B    £60,800        C    £61,800        D    £62,200

(b)    Using a LIFO method of stock valuation, the cost of the issued parts in the month was

A    £61,800        B    £62,200        C    £62,800        D    £66,200

---

38    The 'high-low' method of cost estimation can be used to

A        calculate the budget cost for the actual activity
B        calculate the highest and lowest costs in the budget period
C        measure the actual cost for the budget activity
D        predict the range of costs expected in the budget period

---

39    For operational purposes, for a company operating a fleet of delivery vehicles, which of the following would be most useful?

A        Cost per mile run
B        Cost per driver hour
C        Cost per tonne mile
D        Cost per kilogram carried

40    When comparing the performance of two factories, one of which is owned and the other rented, the inclusion of rent as an expense in the profit statement of the factory owned is known as the inclusion of

     **A**     a relevant cost.
     **B**     a normal cost.
     **C**     a notional cost.
     **D**     a controllable cost.
     **E**     an indirect cost.

---

41    Q Ltd has in stock 10,000 kg of V, a raw material which it bought for £5/kg five years ago. This was bought for a product line which was discontinued four years ago. At present, V has no use in its existing state but could be sold as scrap for £1.50 per kg. One of the company's current products (QX) requires 2 kg of a raw material which is available for £4.50 per kg. V can be modified at a cost of £1 per kg so that it may be used as a substitute for this material. However, after modification, 3 kg of V is required for every unit of QX to be produced.

Q Ltd has now received an invitation to tender for a product which could use V in its present state.

The relevant cost per kg of V to be included in the cost estimate for the tender is

     **A**    £1.00     **B**    £1.50     **C**    £2.00     **D**    £4.50     **E**    £5.00

*(Specimen paper)*

---

42    F Ltd has the following budget and actual data:

| | |
|---|---:|
| Budget fixed overhead cost | £100,000 |
| Budget production (units) | 20,000 |
| Actual fixed overhead cost | £110,000 |
| Actual production (units) | 19,500 |

The fixed overhead volume variance

     **A**     is £500 adverse.
     **B**     is £2,500 adverse.
     **C**     is £10,000 adverse.
     **D**     is £17,500 adverse.
     **E**     cannot be calculated from the data given.

*(Specimen paper)*

---

43    J Ltd operates a standard cost accounting system. The following information has been extracted from its standard cost card and budgets:

| | |
|---|---:|
| Budgeted sales volume | 5,000 units |
| Budgeted selling price | £10.00 per unit |
| Standard variable cost | £5.60 per unit |
| Standard total cost | £7.50 per unit |

If it used a standard marginal cost accounting system and its actual sales were 4,500 units at a selling price of £12.00, its sales volume variance would be

     **A**     £1,250 adverse.
     **B**     £2,200 adverse.
     **C**     £2,250 adverse.
     **D**     £3,200 adverse.
     **E**     £5,000 adverse.

*(Specimen paper)*

44    When comparing the profits reported using marginal costing with those reported using absorption costing in a period when closing stock was 1,400 units, opening stock was 2,000 units, and the actual production was 11,200 units at a total cost of £4.50 per unit compared to a target cost of £5.00 per unit, which of the following statements is correct?

A       Absorption costing reports profits £2,700 higher.
B       Absorption costing reports profits £2,700 lower.
C       Absorption costing reports profits £3,000 higher.
D       Absorption costing reports profits £3,000 lower.
E       There is insufficient data to calculate the difference between the reported profits.

*(Specimen paper)*

---

45    A Ltd has fixed costs of £60,000 per annum. It manufactures a single product which it sells for £20 per unit. Its contribution to sales ratio is 40%.

A Ltd's breakeven point in units is

A    1,200    B    1,800    C    3,000    D    5,000    E    7,500

*(Specimen paper)*

---

46    A company operates a process which produces three joint products - K, P and Z. The costs of operating this process during September 1993 amounted to £117,000. During the month the output of the three products was

| | |
|---|---|
| K | 2,000 litres |
| P | 4,500 litres |
| Z | 3,250 litres |

P is further processed at a cost of £9.00 per litre. The actual loss of the second process was 10% of the input which was normal. Products K and Z are sold without further processing.

The final selling prices of each of the products are

| | |
|---|---|
| K | £20.00 per litre |
| P | £25.00 per litre |
| Z | £18.00 per litre |

Joint costs are attributed to products on the basis of output volume.

The profit attributed to product P was

A    £6,750    B    £12,150    C    £13,500    D    £16,200    E    £18,000

*(Specimen paper)*

---

47    A construction company has the following data concerning one of its contracts:

| | |
|---|---|
| Contract price | £2,000,000 |
| Value certified | £1,300,000 |
| Cash received | £1,200,000 |
| Costs incurred | £1,050,000 |
| Cost of work certified | £1,000,000 |

The profit (to the nearest £1,000) to be attributed to the contract is

A    £250,000   B    £277,000   C    £300,000   D    £950,000   E    £1,000,000

*(Specimen paper)*

48    When a standard cost bookkeeping system is used and the actual price paid for raw materials exceeds the standard price, the double entry to record this is

     **A**      debit raw material control account, credit raw material price variance account.
     **B**      debit work-in-progress control account, credit raw material price variance account.
     **C**      debit creditor for raw materials, credit raw material price variance account.
     **D**      debit raw material price variance account, credit raw material control account.
     **E**      debit raw material price variance account, credit work-in-progress control account.

*(Specimen paper)*

---

49    State which of the following are characteristics of job costing:

     (i)       homogenous products,
     (ii)      customer-driven production,
     (iii)     complete production possible within a single accounting period.

     **A**      (i) only
     **B**      (i) and (ii) only
     **C**      (ii) and (iii) only
     **D**      (i) and (iii) only
     **E**      All of them                                 *(CIMA May 95)*

---

50    H Ltd manufactures and sells two products - J and K. Annual sales are expected to be in the ratio of J:1 K:3. Total annual sales are planned to be £420,000. Product J has a contribution to sales ratio of 40% whereas that of product K is 50%. Annual fixed costs are estimated to be £120,000.

The budgeted breakeven sales value (to the nearest £1,000)

     **A**      is £196,000
     **B**      is £200,000
     **C**      is £253,000
     **D**      is £255,000
     **E**      cannot be determined from the above data           *(CIMA May 95)*

---

51    Z Ltd manufactures three products, the selling price and cost details of which are given below:

| | Product X | Product Y | Product Z |
|---|---|---|---|
| | £ | £ | £ |
| Selling price per unit | 75 | 95 | 95 |
| Costs per unit: | | | |
|    Direct materials (£5/kg) | 10 | 5 | 15 |
|    Direct labour (£4/hour) | 16 | 24 | 20 |
|    Variable overhead | 8 | 12 | 10 |
|    Fixed overhead | 24 | 36 | 30 |

In a period when direct materials are restricted in supply, the most and the least profitable uses of direct materials are

| | Most profitable | Least profitable |
|---|---|---|
| **A** | X | Z |
| **B** | Y | Z |
| **C** | X | Y |
| **D** | Z | Y |
| **E** | Y | X |

*(CIMA May 95)*

52     State which of the following are characteristics of contract costing:

     (i)      homogeneous products,
     (ii)     customer-driven production,
     (iii)    short timescale from commencement to completion of the cost unit.

     A     None of them
     B     (i) and (ii) only
     C     (ii) and (iii) only
     D     (i) and (iii) only
     E     (ii) only                                   *(CIMA May 95)*

---

53     T plc uses a standard costing system, with its material stock account being maintained at standard costs. The following details have been extracted from the standard cost card in respect of direct materials:

     8 kg @ £0.80/kg = £6.40 per unit

     Budgeted production in April 19X5 was 850 units.

     The following details relate to actual materials purchased and issued to production during April 19X5 when actual production was 870 units:

| | |
|---|---|
| Materials purchased | 8,200 kg costing £6,888 |
| Materials issued to production | 7,150 kg |

     Which of the following correctly states the material price and usage variances to be reported?

     A     £286 (A)     £152 (A)
     B     £286 (A)     £280 (A)
     C     £286 (A)     £294 (A)
     D     £328 (A)     £152 (A)
     E     £328 (A)     £280 (A)                   *(CIMA May 95)*

---

54     The following details have been extracted from the debtor collection records of C Ltd:

| | |
|---|---|
| Invoices paid in the month after sale | 60% |
| Invoices paid in the second month after sale | 25% |
| Invoices paid in the third month after sale | 12% |
| Bad debts | 3% |

     Invoices are issued on the last day of each month.

     Customers paying in the month after sale are entitled to deduct a 2% settlement discount.

     Credit sales values for June to September 19X5 are budgeted as follows:

| June | July | August | September |
|---|---|---|---|
| £35,000 | £40,000 | £60,000 | £45,000 |

     The amount budgeted to be received from credit sales in September 19X5 is

     A  £47,280    B  £47,680    C  £48,850    D  £49,480    E  £50,200    *(CIMA May 95)*

55      State which of the following are characteristics of service costing:

        (i)     high levels of indirect costs as a proportion of total cost.
        (ii)    use of composite cost units.
        (iii)   use of equivalent units.

        A       (i) only
        B       (i) and (ii) only
        C       (ii) only
        D       (ii) and (iii) only
        E       All of them ·                                      *(CIMA May 95)*

56      The following extract is taken from the production cost budget of S Ltd:

        | Production (units) | 2,000 | 3,000 |
        |---|---|---|
        | Production cost (£) | 11,100 | 12,900 |

        The budget cost allowance for an activity level of 4,000 units is

        A       £7,200
        B       £14,700
        C       £17,200
        D       £22,200
        E       none of these values                               *(CIMA May 95)*

57      Z Ltd manufactures a single product, the budgeted selling price and variable cost details of which are as follows:

        |  | £ |
        |---|---|
        | Selling price | 15.00 |
        | Variable costs per unit: | |
        |   Direct materials | 3.50 |
        |   Direct labour | 4.00 |
        |   Variable overhead | 2.00 |

        Budgeted fixed overhead costs are £60,000 per annum charged at a constant rate each month. Budgeted production is 30,000 units per annum.

        In a month when actual production was 2,400 units and exceeded sales by 180 units, the profit reported under absorption costing was

        A   £6,660    B   £7,570    C   £7,770    D   £8,200    E   £8,400    *(CIMA May 95)*

58      PQ Ltd operates a standard costing system for its only product. The standard cost card is as follows:

        | Direct materials | (4 kg @ £2/kg) | £8.00 |
        |---|---|---|
        | Direct labour | (4 hours @ £4/hour) | £16.00 |
        | Variable overhead | (4 hours @ £3/hour) | £12.00 |
        | Fixed overhead | (4 hours @ £5/hour) | £20.00 |

        Fixed overheads are absorbed on the basis of labour hours. Fixed overhead costs are budgeted at £120,000 per annum arising at a constant rate during the year.

Activity in period 3 of 19X5 is budgeted to be 10% of total activity for the year. Actual production during period 3 was 500 units, with actual fixed overhead costs incurred being £9,800 and actual hours worked being 1,970.

The fixed overhead expenditure variance for period 3 of 19X5 was

A £2,200 (F)  B £200 (F)   C £50 (F)    D £200 (A)   E £2,200 (A)   *(CIMA May 95)*

---

59    In a non-integrated accounting system, the balance shown on the cost ledger control account at the beginning of a financial year is

A    equal to the value of accumulated reserves shown in the financial accounts.

B    equal to the value of stocks and work-in-progress shown in the financial accounts.

C    equal to the value of stocks and work-in-progress shown in the cost accounts.

D    equal but opposite to the value of the stocks and work-in-progress shown in the financial accounts.

E    equal but opposite to the value of the stocks and work-in-progress shown in the cost accounts.                                                   *(CIMA Nov 95)*

---

60    XYZ plc manufactures its product through a series of processes. The FIFO method of valuing opening work in process is used, and the following details relate to September 19X5.

Opening work in process was 600 units, each 80% processed as to materials and 60% processed as to conversion costs.

Normal loss was 500 units, fully completed.

Finished output was 14,500 units; there were no abnormal losses or gains.

Closing work in process was 800 units, each 70% processed as to materials and 40% processed as to conversion costs.

When calculating the costs per equivalent unit, the number of equivalent units to be used are:

|   | Materials | Conversion |
|---|---|---|
| A | 14,580 | 14,460 |
| B | 14,940 | 14,580 |
| C | 15,180 | 15,060 |
| D | 15,540 | 15,180 |
| E | 16,040 | 15,680 |

*(CIMA Nov 95)*

---

61    In process costing, where losses have a positive scrap value, when an abnormal gain arises the abnormal gain account is

A    debited with the normal production cost of the abnormal gain units.

B    debited with the normal production cost of the abnormal gain units and credited with the scrap value of the abnormal gain units.

C    credited with the normal production cost of the abnormal gain units and debited with the scrap value of the abnormal gain units.

D    debited with the normal production cost of the abnormal gain units and credited with the scrap value of the abnormal gain units.

E    credited with the normal production cost of the abnormal gain units.    *(CIMA Nov 95)*

62      When deciding, purely on financial grounds, whether or not to process a joint product, the information required is

   (i)      the value of the common process costs;
   (ii)     the method of apportioning the common costs between the joint products;
   (iii)    the sales value of the joint product at the separation point;
   (iv)     the final sales value of the joint product;
   (v)      the further processing cost of the joint product.

Which of the above statements are correct?

   A      (i), (ii) and (iii) only.
   B      (iii), (iv) and (v) only.
   C      (iv) and (v) only.
   D      (i), (ii), (iv) and (v) only.
   E      All of them.                                                    *(CIMA Nov 95)*

---

63      A Ltd makes a single product which it sells for £10 per unit. Fixed costs are £48,000 per month and the product has a contribution to sales ratio of 40%.

In a period when actual sales were £140,000, A Ltd's margin of safety, in units, was

   A 2,000.        B 6,000.        C 8,000.        D 12,000.        E 14,000.        *(CIMA Nov 95)*

---

64      The following data have been extracted from the budget working papers of BL Ltd:

| Production volume | 1,000 | 2,000 |
|---|---|---|
|  | £/unit | £/unit |
| Direct materials | 4.00 | 4.00 |
| Direct labour | 3.50 | 3.50 |
| Production overhead - department 1 | 6.00 | 4.20 |
| Production overhead - department 2 | 4.00 | 2.00 |

The total fixed cost and variable cost per unit are

|  | Total fixed cost | Variable cost per unit |
|---|---|---|
|  | £ | £ |
| A | 3,600 | 7.50 |
| B | 3,600 | 9.90 |
| C | 4,000 | 11.70 |
| D | 7,600 | 7.50 |
| E | 7,600 | 9.90 |

*(CIMA Nov 95)*

---

65      The following details relate to component 1256:

| | |
|---|---|
| Maximum usage per day | 10 units |
| Minimum usage per day | 4 units |
| Maximum lead time | 5 days |
| Minimum lead time | 3 days |
| Ordering cost | £50 per order |
| Stock holding cost | £2 per item per year |
| Annual demand | 1,750 units |

The budget for December 19X5 is currently being revised to take account of these details. The stock is budgeted to be 170 units on 1 December, and the production manager has requested that the stock be at maximum on 31 December 19X5.

Assuming that the usage of this component is expected to be 140 units during December, the number of units to be purchased during December is closest to

A 296 units    B 304 units.    C 334 units.    D 350 units.    E 474 units.    *(CIMA Nov 95)*

---

66    Z plc uses a standard costing system and has the following labour cost standard in relation to one of its products:

   4 hours skilled labour @ £6.00 per hour          £24.00

During October 19X5, 3,350 of these products were made which was 150 units less than budgeted. The labour cost incurred was £79,893 and the number of direct labour hours worked was 13,450.

The direct labour variances for the month were

|   | Rate | Efficiency |
|---|---|---|
| A | £804 (F) | £300 (A) |
| B | £804 (F) | £300 (F) |
| C | £807 (F) | £297 (A) |
| D | £807 (F) | £300 (A) |
| E | £840 (F) | £3,300 (F) |

*(CIMA Nov 95)*

---

67    J Ltd uses a standard costing system and has the following data relating to one of its products:

|   | £ | £ |
|---|---|---|
| Selling price | | 9.00 |
| Variable costs | 4.00 | |
| Fixed costs | 3.00 | |
| | | 7.00 |
| Profit per unit | | 2.00 |

Its budgeted sales for October 19X5 were 800 units, but the actual sales were 850 units. The revenue earned from these sales was £7,480.

If a profit reconciliation statement were to be drawn up using marginal costing principles, the sales variances would be

|   | Price | Volume |
|---|---|---|
| A | £160 (A) | £100 (F) |
| B | £160 (A) | £250 (F) |
| C | £170 (A) | £240 (F) |
| D | £170 (A) | £100 (F) |
| E | £170 (A) | £250 (F) |

*(CIMA Nov 95)*

68    Q Ltd uses an integrated standard costing system. In October, when 2,400 units of the finished product were made, the actual material cost details were:

Material purchased                     5,000 units @ £4.50 each
Material used                             4,850 units

The standard cost details are that 2 units of the material should be used for each unit of the completed product, and the standard price of each material unit is £4.70.

The entries made in the variance accounts would be:

|   | Material price variance a/c | Material usage variance a/c |
|---|---|---|
| A | Debit   £970 | Debit £225 |
| B | Debit £1,000 | Debit £225 |
| C | Credit   £970 | Debit £235 |
| D | Credit £1,000 | Debit £235 |
| E | Credit £1,000 | Debit £900 |

                                                                       *(CIMA Nov 95)*

69    C Ltd uses a standard costing system. The standard cost card for one of its products shows that the product should use 4 kgs of material B per finished unit and that the standard price per kg is £4.50. C Ltd values its stock of materials at standard prices.

During April 1996, when the budgeted production level was 1,000 units, 1,040 units were made. The actual material quantity of material B used was 4,100 kgs and material B stocks were reduced by 300 kgs. The cost of the material B which was purchased was £14,400.

The material price and usage variances for April 1996 were

|   | Price £ | Usage £ |
|---|---|---|
| A | 2,700 F | 450 A |
| B | 2,700 F | 270 F |
| C | 4,050 F | 270 F |
| D | 2,700 F | 1,620 F |
| E | 4,050 F | 1,620 F |

                                                                       *(CIMA May 96)*

70    The following details relate to three products made by F Ltd:

|   | H £ | J £ | K £ |
|---|---|---|---|
| Selling price per unit | 60 | 85 | 88 |
| | | | |
| Direct materials per unit | 15 | 20 | 30 |
| Direct labour per unit | 10 | 15 | 10 |
| Variable overhead per unit | 5 | 8 | 10 |
| Fixed overhead per unit | 10 | 16 | 20 |
| | 40 | 59 | 70 |
| Profit per unit | 20 | 26 | 18 |

All three products use the same direct labour and direct materials, but in different quantities.

In a period when the labour used on these products is in short supply, the most and least profitable use of the labour is

|   | *Most profitable* | *Least profitable* |
|---|---|---|
| **A** | K | H |
| **B** | K | J |
| **C** | H | J |
| **D** | J | K |
| **E** | H | K |

*(CIMA May 96)*

---

71    When comparing the profits reported under marginal and absorption costing during a period when the level of stocks increased,

**A**    absorption costing profits will be higher and closing stock valuations lower than those under marginal costing

**B**    absorption costing profits will be higher and closing stock valuations higher than those under marginal costing

**C**    marginal costing profits will be higher and closing stock valuations lower than those under absorption costing

**D**    marginal costing profits will be lower and closing stock valuations higher than those under absorption costing

**E**    there is no difference in the profit reported or the valuation of closing stock between the two systems

*(CIMA May 96)*

---

72    A single product company has a contribution to sales ratio of 40%. Fixed costs amount to £90,000 per annum.

The number of units required to break even is

**A**    3,000
**B**    4,500
**C**    150,000
**D**    225,000
**E**    impossible to calculate without further information

*(CIMA May 96)*

---

73    In order to utilise some spare capacity, Z Ltd is preparing a quotation for a special order which requires 1,000 kgs of material R.

Z Ltd has 600 kgs of material R in stock (original cost £5.00 per kg). Material R is used in the company's main product Q. Each unit of Q uses 3 kgs of material R and, based on an input value of £5.00 per kg of R, each unit of Q yields a contribution of £9.00.

The resale value of material R is £4.00 per kg. The present replacement price of material R is £6.00 per kg. Material R is readily available in the market.

The relevant cost of the 1,000 kgs of material R to be included in the quotation is

|   |        |
|---|--------|
| A | £4,000 |
| B | £5,000 |
| C | £5,400 |
| D | £6,000 |
| E | £8,000 |

*(CIMA May 96)*

74      In process costing, the value attributed to any abnormal gain units is

A       debited to the process account and credited to the abnormal gain account
B       debited to the abnormal gain account and credited to the normal loss account
C       debited to the normal loss account and credited to the abnormal gain account
D       debited to the abnormal gain account and credited to the process account
E       debited to the scrap sales account and credited to the abnormal gain account

*(CIMA May 96)*

75      S Ltd has extracted the following details from the standard cost card of one of its products:

Direct labour                              4.5 hours @ £6.40 per hour

During March 1996, S Ltd produced 2,300 units of the product and incurred direct wages costs of £64,150. The actual hours worked were 11,700.

The direct labour rate and efficiency variances were

|   | *Rate* <br> £ | *Efficiency* <br> £ |
|---|-----------|------------|
| A | 2,090 F   | 7,402 A    |
| B | 2,090 F   | 8,640 A    |
| C | 10,730 F  | 7,402 A    |
| D | 10,730 F  | 8,640 A    |
| E | 10,730 F  | 10,350 A   |

*(CIMA May 96)*

76      The following details relate to product T, which has a selling price of £44.00:

|                          | *£/unit* |
|--------------------------|---------|
| Direct materials         | 15.00   |
| Direct labour (3 hours)  | 12.00   |
| Variable overhead        | 6.00    |
| Fixed overhead           | 4.00    |
|                          | 37.00   |

During April 1996, the actual production of T was 800 units, which was 100 units fewer than budgeted. The budget shows an annual production target of 10,800, with fixed costs accruing at a constant rate throughout the year. Actual overhead expenditure totalled £8,500 for April 1996.

The overhead variances for April 1996 were

|   | Expenditure<br>£ | Volume<br>£ |
|---|---|---|
| A | 367 A | 1,000 A |
| B | 500 A | 400 A |
| C | 100 A | 1,000 A |
| D | 367 A | 400 A |
| E | 100 A | 400 A |

*(CIMA May 96)*

77   The following data have been taken from the books of CB plc, which uses a non-integrated accounting system:

|   | Financial accounts<br>£ | Cost accounts<br>£ |
|---|---|---|
| Opening stock of materials | 5,000 | 6,400 |
| Closing stock of materials | 4,000 | 5,200 |
| Opening stock of finished goods | 9,800 | 9,600 |
| Closing stock of finished goods | 7,900 | 7,600 |

The effect of these stock valuation differences on the profit reported by the financial and cost accounting ledgers is

A    the financial accounting profit is £300 greater than the cost accounting profit
B    the financial accounting profit is £2,100 greater than the cost accounting profit
C    the cost accounting profit is £300 greater than the financial accounting profit
D    the cost accounting profit is £900 greater than the financial accounting profit
E    the cost accounting profit is £2,100 greater than the financial accounting profit

*(CIMA May 96)*

78   The following details relate to the main process of X Ltd, a chemical manufacturer:

| Opening work-in-progress | 2,000 litres, fully complete as to materials and 40% complete as to conversion |
|---|---|
| Material input | 24,000 litres |
| Normal loss is 10% of input. | |
| Output to process 2 | 19,500 litres |
| Closing work-in-progress | 3,000 litres, fully complete as to materials and 45% complete as to conversion |

The numbers of equivalent units to be included in X Ltd's calculation of the cost per equivalent unit, using a *weighted average basis* of valuation, are

|   | Materials | Conversion |
|---|---|---|
| A | 21,400 | 19,750 |
| B | 21,400 | 20,850 |
| C | 22,500 | 21,950 |
| D | 22,500 | 20,850 |
| E | 23,600 | 21,950 |

*(CIMA May 96)*

79     In process costing, if an abnormal loss arises, the process account is generally

     A      debited with the scrap value of the abnormal loss units
     B      debited with the full production cost of the abnormal loss units
     C      credited with the scrap value of the abnormal loss units
     D      credited with the full production cost of the abnormal loss units
     E      credited with the full production cost less the scrap value of the abnormal loss units

*(CIMA Nov 96)*

80     E plc operates a marginal costing system. For the forthcoming year, variable costs are budgeted to be 60% of sales value and fixed costs are budgeted to be 10% of sales value.

     If E plc increases its selling prices by 10%, but if fixed costs, variable costs per unit and sales volume remain unchanged, the effect on E plc's contribution would be

     A      a decrease of 2%
     B      an increase of 5%
     C      an increase of 10%
     D      an increase of 25%
     E      an increase of $66\frac{2}{3}$%

*(CIMA Nov 96)*

81     A flexible budget is

     A      a budget of variable production costs only
     B      a budget which is updated with actual costs and revenues as they occur during the budget period
     C      a budget which shows the costs and revenues at different levels of activity
     D      a budget which is prepared using a computer spreadsheet model
     E      a budget which is prepared for a period of six months and reviewed monthly. Following such review a further one month's budget is prepared

*(CIMA Nov 96)*

82     D plc operates a standard absorption costing system. Its standard fixed overhead absorption rate, based on a monthly budget of 2,400 standard hours, is £5.00 per standard hour.

     During October 1996 the actual fixed overhead cost incurred was £13,100 when the standard hours produced were 2,350.

     The variance entries in D plc's ledgers are:

A     

| *Account name* | *Dr*<br>£ | *Cr*<br>£ |
|---|---|---|
| Fixed overhead expenditure variance | 1,100 | |
| Fixed overhead volume variance | 250 | |
| Work-in-progress | | 1,350 |

B     

| *Account name* | *Dr*<br>£ | *Cr*<br>£ |
|---|---|---|
| Work-in-progress | | 850 |
| Fixed overhead expenditure variance | 1,100 | |
| Fixed overhead volume variance | | 250 |

| **C** | Account name | Dr £ | Cr £ |
|---|---|---|---|
| | Fixed overhead expenditure variance | 1,350 | |
| | Fixed overhead volume variance | 250 | |
| | Fixed overhead control | | 1,600 |

| **D** | Account name | Dr £ | Cr £ |
|---|---|---|---|
| | Fixed overhead expenditure variance | 1,350 | |
| | Fixed overhead volume variance | | 250 |
| | Fixed overhead control | | 1,100 |

| **E** | Account name | Dr £ | Cr £ |
|---|---|---|---|
| | Fixed overhead expenditure variance | 1,100 | |
| | Fixed overhead volume variance | 250 | |
| | Fixed overhead control | | 1,350 |

*(CIMA Nov 96)*

---

83    Direct costs are

**A**    costs which can be identified with a cost centre but not identified to a single cost unit
**B**    costs which can be identified with a single cost unit
**C**    costs incurred as a direct result of a particular decision
**D**    costs incurred which can be attributed to a particular accounting period
**E**    none of the above

*(CIMA Nov 96)*

---

84    The following details relate to products made by K Ltd:

| | L £ | M £ | N £ |
|---|---|---|---|
| Selling price per unit | 60 | 85 | 88 |
| | | | |
| Direct materials per unit | 15 | 20 | 30 |
| Direct labour per unit | 10 | 15 | 10 |
| Variable overhead per unit | 5 | 8 | 10 |
| Fixed overhead per unit | 10 | 16 | 20 |
| | 40 | 59 | 70 |
| Profit per unit | 20 | 26 | 18 |

All three products use the same direct labour and direct materials, but in different quantities.

In a period when the material used on these products is in short supply, the most and least profitable use of the material is

| | *Most profitable* | *Least profitable* |
|---|---|---|
| **A** | N | L |
| **B** | N | M |
| **C** | L | M |
| **D** | M | L |
| **E** | M | N |

*(CIMA May 96)*

---

85      A master budget comprises

      **A**      the budgeted profit and loss account
      **B**      the budgeted cashflow, budgeted profit and loss account and budgeted balance sheet
      **C**      the budgeted cashflow
      **D**      the capital expenditure budget
      **E**      the entire set of budgets prepared

*(CIMA Nov 96)*

---

86      The following details relate to the main process of W Limited, a chemical manufacturer:

| | |
|---|---|
| Opening work-in-progress | 2,000 litres, fully complete as to materials and 40% complete as to conversion |
| Material input | 24,000 litres |
| Normal loss is 10% of input | |
| Output to process 2 | 19,500 litres |
| Closing work-in-progress | 3,000 litres, fully complete as to materials and 45% complete as to conversion |

The number of equivalent units to be included in W Limited's calculation of the cost per equivalent unit using a **FIFO basis** of valuation are:

| | *Materials* | *Conversion* |
|---|---|---|
| **A** | 19,400 | 18,950 |
| **B** | 20,500 | 20,050 |
| **C** | 21,600 | 21,150 |
| **D** | 23,600 | 20,750 |
| **E** | 23,600 | 21,950 |

*(CIMA Nov 96)*

---

87      Q plc makes two products - Quone and Qutwo - from the same raw material. The selling price and cost details of these products are as shown below:

| | *Quone* £ | *Qutwo* £ |
|---|---|---|
| Selling price | 20.00 | 18.00 |
| Direct material (£2.00/kg) | 6.00 | 5.00 |
| Direct labour | 4.00 | 3.00 |
| Variable overhead | 2.00 | 1.50 |
| | 12.00 | 9.50 |
| Contribution per unit | 8.00 | 8.50 |

The maximum demand for these products is:

      Quone             500 units per week
      Qutwo             unlimited number of units per week

If materials were limited to 2,000 kgs per week, the shadow price of these materials would be

A    £ nil
B    £2.00 per kg
C    £2.66 per kg
D    £3.40 per kg
E    none of these

*(CIMA Nov 96)*

88    P Limited is considering whether to continue making a component or buy it from an outside supplier. It uses 12,000 of the components each year.

The internal manufacturing cost comprises:

|  | £/unit |
|---|---|
| Direct materials | 3.00 |
| Direct labour | 4.00 |
| Variable overhead | 1.00 |
| Specific fixed cost | 2.50 |
| Other fixed costs | 2.00 |
|  | 12.50 |

If the direct labour were not used to manufacture the component, it would be used to increase the production of another item for which there is unlimited demand. This other item has a contribution of £10.00 per unit but requires £8.00 of labour per unit.

The maximum price per component at which buying is preferable to internal manufacture is

A    £8.00
B    £10.50
C    £12.50
D    £13.00
E    £15.50

*(CIMA Nov 96)*

89    When preparing a production budget, the quantity to be produced equals

A    sales quantity + opening stock + closing stock
B    sales quantity - opening stock + closing stock
C    sales quantity - opening stock - closing stock
D    sales quantity + opening stock - closing stock
E    sale quantity

*(CIMA May 97)*

90    A standard marginal costing system

(i)     calculates fixed overhead variances using the budgeted absorption rate per unit.
(ii)    records adverse variances as debt entries in variance accounts within the ledger.
(iii)   values finished goods stock at the standard variable cost of production.

Which of the above statements is/are correct?

| A | (i) and (iii) only. |
|---|---|
| B | (ii) only. |
| C | (ii), and (iii) only. |
| D | (i) and (ii) only. |
| E | All of them. |

*(CIMA May 97)*

---

91　PT plc uses a standard marginal costing system. In April 1997 its sales variances were:

| Selling price | £1,000 adverse |
|---|---|
| Sales volume | £1,200 favourable |

The entries to be made in PT plc's ledgers are:

|  |  | Debit £ | Credit £ |
|---|---|---|---|
| A | Selling price variance | 1,000 | |
|  | Sales volume variance | | 1,200 |
|  | Profit and loss | 200 | |
| B | Sales volume variance | 1,200 | |
|  | Selling price variance | | 1,000 |
|  | Profit and loss | | 200 |
| C | Selling price variance | 1,000 | |
|  | Sales volume variance | | 1,200 |
|  | Sales | 200 | |
| D | Sales volume variance | 1,200 | |
|  | Selling price variance | | 1,000 |
|  | Sales | | 200 |
| E | None of the above. | | |

*(CIMA May 97)*

---

92　QR Limited uses a standard absorption costing system. The following details have been extracted from its budget for April 1997:

| Fixed production overhead cost | £48,000 |
|---|---|
| Production (units) | 4,800 |

In April 1997 the fixed production overhead cost was under-absorbed by £8,000 and the fixed production overhead expenditure variance was £2,000 adverse.

The actual number of units produced was

| A | 3,800 |
|---|---|
| B | 4,000 |
| C | 4,200 |
| D | 5,400 |
| E | 5,800 |

*(CIMA May 97)*

---

93　Your company regularly uses material X and currently has in stock 500 kgs for which it paid £1,500 two weeks ago. If this were to be sold as raw material, it could be sold today for £2.00 per kg. You are aware that the material can be bought on the open market for £3.25 per kg, but it must be purchased in quantities of 1,000 kgs.

You have been asked to determine the relevant cost of 600 kgs of material X to be used in a job for a customer. The relevant cost of the 600 kgs is

| | |
|---|---|
| A | £1,200 |
| B | £1,325 |
| C | £1,825 |
| D | £1,950 |
| E | £3,250 |

*(CIMA May 97)*

94   KL Processing Limited has identified that an abnormal gain of 160 litres occurred in its refining process last week. Normal losses are expected and have a scrap value of £2.00 per litre. all losses are 100% complete as to material cost and 75% complete as to conversion costs.

The company uses the weighted average method of valuation and last week's output was valued using the following costs per equivalent unit:

| | |
|---|---|
| Materials | £9.40 |
| Conversion costs | £11.20 |

The effect on the profit and loss account of last week's abnormal gain is

| | | |
|---|---|---|
| A | Debit | £2,528 |
| B | Debit | £2,828 |
| C | Credit | £2,528 |
| D | Credit | £2,848 |
| E | Credit | £3,168 |

*(CIMA May 97)*

95   The following details relate to product R:

| Level of activity (units) | 1,000 | 2,000 |
|---|---|---|
| | £/unit | £/unit |
| Direct materials | 4.00 | 4.00 |
| Direct labour | 3.00 | 3.00 |
| Production overhead | 3.50 | 2.50 |
| Selling overhead | 1.00 | 0.50 |
| | 11.50 | 10.00 |

The total fixed cost and variable cost per unit are:

| | Total fixed cost £ | Variable cost per unit £ |
|---|---|---|
| A | 2,000 | 1.50 |
| B | 2,000 | 7.00 |
| C | 2,000 | 8.50 |
| D | 3,000 | 7.00 |
| E | 3,000 | 8.50 |

*(CIMA May 97)*

96    Z plc currently sells products Aye, Bee and Cee in equal quantities and at the same selling price per unit. The contribution to sales ratio for product Aye is 40%; for product Bee it is 50% and the total is 48%. If fixed costs are unaffected by mix and are currently 20% of sales, the effect of changing the product mix to

Aye  40%        Bee  25%        Cee  35%

is that the total contribution/total sales ratio changes to

A       27.4%
B       45.3%
C       47.4%
D       48.4%
E       68.4%

*(CIMA May 97)*

97    A fixed budget is

A       a budget for a single level of activity
B       used when the mix of products is fixed in advance of the budget period
C       a budget which ignores inflation
D       used only for fixed costs
E       an overhead cost budget

*(CIMA May 97)*

98    BDL plc is currently preparing its cash budget for the year to 31 March 1998. An extract from its sales budget for the same year shows the following sales values:

|            | £      |
|------------|--------|
| March      | 60,000 |
| April      | 70,000 |
| May        | 55,000 |
| June       | 65,000 |

40% of its sales are expected to be for cash. Of its credit sales, 70% are expected to pay in the month after sale and take a 2% discount; 27% are expected to pay in the second month after the sale, and the remaining 3% are expected to be bad debts.

The value of sales receipts to be shown in the cash budget for May 1997 is

A       £38,532
B       £39,120
C       £60,532
D       £64,220
E       £65,200

*(CIMA May 97)*

99    A direct cost is a cost which

A       is incurred as a direct consequence of a decision
B       can be economically identified with the item being costed
C       cannot be economically identified with the item being costed
D       is immediately controllable
E       is the responsibility of the Board of Directors

*(CIMA Nov 97)*

100   S plc has the following fixed overhead cost data for October 1997:

| | |
|---|---|
| Budgeted cost | £100,000 |
| Actual cost | £101,400 |
| Budget output | 10,000 standard hours |
| Actual output | 9,000 standard hours |
| Actual efficiency | 96% |

The values of over-absorption/under-absorption caused by volume and expenditure effects are:

| | Volume | Expenditure |
|---|---|---|
| A | £7,650 under | £1,400 under |
| B | £7,650 under | £7,650 under |
| C | £10,000 under | £1,400 under |
| D | £10,000 under | £7,650 under |
| E | £10,000 under | £11,400 under |

*(CIMA Nov 97)*

---

The following data are to be used for questions 101 and 102

M plc makes two products - M1 and M2 - budgeted details of which are as follows:

| | M1 £ | M2 £ |
|---|---|---|
| Selling price | 10.00 | 8.00 |
| Costs per unit: | | |
| Direct materials | 2.50 | 3.00 |
| Direct labour | 1.50 | 1.00 |
| Variable overhead | 0.60 | 0.40 |
| Fixed overhead | 1.20 | 1.00 |
| Profit per unit | 4.20 | 2.60 |

Budgeted production and sales for the year ended 31 December 1998 are:

Product M1   10,000 units
Product M2   12,500 units

The fixed overhead shown above comprises both general and specific fixed overhead costs. The general fixed overhead cost has been attributed to units of M1 and M2 on the basis of direct labour cost.

The specific fixed cost totals £2,500 per annum and relates to product M2 only.

101   Both products are available from an external supplier. If M plc could purchase only one of them, the maximum price which should be paid per unit of M1 or M2 instead of internal manufacture would be

|   | M1 | M2 |
|---|---|---|
|   | £ | £ |
| A | 4.60 | 4.40 |
| B | 4.60 | 4.60 |
| C | 5.80 | 4.40 |
| D | 5.80 | 4.60 |
| E | 5.80 | 5.60 |

*(CIMA Nov 97)*

102    If only product M1 were to be made, the number of units to be sold to achieve a profit of £50,000 per annum (to the nearest unit) would be

A    4,074
B    4,537
C    13,333
D    13,796
E    none of the above

*(CIMA Nov 97)*

103    A company s considering accepting a one-year contract which will require four skilled employees. The four skilled employees could be recruited on a one-year contract at a cost of £40,000 per employee. The employees would be supervised by an existing manager who earns £60,000 per annum. It is expected that supervision of the contract would take 10% of the manager's time.

Instead of recruiting new employees, the company could retrain some existing employees who currently earn £30,000 per year. The training would cost £15,000 in total. If these employees were used they would need to be replaced at a total cost of £100,000.

The relevant labour cost of the contract is

A    £100,000
B    £115,000
C    £135,000
D    £141,000
E    £166,000

*(CIMA Nov 97)*

104    In decision making, costs which need to be considered are said to be RELEVANT COSTS.

Which of the following are characteristics associated with relevant costs?

     (i)      future costs
     (ii)      unavoidable costs
     (iii)      common costs
     (iv)      differential costs

A    (ii) and (iii) only
B    (i) and (ii) only
C    (ii), (iii) and (iv) only
D    (i) and (iv) only
E    (i), (ii), (iii) and (iv)

*(CIMA Nov 97)*

105    The following information relates to R plc for October 1997:

Bought 7,800 kg of material R at a total cost of £16,380.
Stocks of material R increased by 440 kg.
Stocks of material R are valued using standard purchase price.
Material price variance was £1,170 Adverse.

The standard price per kg for material R is:

|   | Price £/kg |
|---|---|
| A | 1.95 |
| B | 2.10 |
| C | 2.23 |
| D | 2.25 |
| E | 2.38 |

*(CIMA Nov 97)*

---

106    P Ltd has the following data relating to its budgeted sales for October 1997:

| | |
|---|---|
| Budgeted sales | £100,000 |
| Budgeted selling price per unit | £8.00 |
| Budgeted contribution per unit | £4.00 |
| Budgeted profit per unit | £2.50 |

During October 1997, actual sales were 11,000 units for a sales revenue of £99,000.

P Ltd uses an absorption costing system.

The sales variances reported for October 1997 were:

|   | Price £ | Volume £ |
|---|---|---|
| A | 11,000 F | 3,750 A |
| B | 11,000 F | 6,000 A |
| C | 11,000 A | 6,000 A |
| D | 12,500 F | 12,000 A |
| E | 12,500 A | 12,000 A |

*(CIMA Nov 97)*

---

107    Z plc manufactures three products which have the following selling prices and costs per unit:

|   | Z1 £ | Z2 £ | Z3 £ |
|---|---|---|---|
| Selling price | 15.00 | 18.00 | 17.00 |
| Costs per unit: | | | |
| Direct materials | 4.00 | 5.00 | 10.00 |
| Direct labour | 2.00 | 4.00 | 1.80 |
| Overhead: | | | |
| Variable | 1.00 | 2.00 | 0.90 |
| Fixed | 4.50 | 3.00 | 1.35 |
| | 11.50 | 14.00 | 14.05 |
| Profit per unit | 3.50 | 4.00 | 2.95 |

All three products use the same type of labour.

In a period in which labour is in short supply, the rank order of production is:

|   | Z1 | Z2 | Z3 |
|---|------|--------|--------|
| **A** | First | Second | Third |
| **B** | Third | Second | First |
| **C** | Second | First | Third |
| **D** | First | Third | Second |
| **E** | Second | Third | First |

*(CIMA Nov 97)*

108    The following details have been extracted from a standard cost card of X plc:

PRODUCT X
Direct labour: 4 hours @ £5.40 per hour

During October 1997, the budgeted production was 5,000 units of product X and the actual production was 4,650 units of product X. Actual hours worked were 19,100 and the actual direct labour cost amounted to £98,350.

The labour variances reported were:

|   | Rate £ | Efficiency £ |
|---|------|--------|
| **A** | 9,650 F | 4,860 F |
| **B** | 9,650 F | 2,700 A |
| **C** | 4,790 F | 2,575 A |
| **D** | 4,790 F | 4,860 F |
| **E** | 4,790 F | 2,700 A |

*(CIMA Nov 97)*

109    Which of the following graphs depicts the cost per unit of a fixed cost, such as depreciation?

(i) 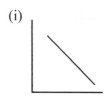  (ii) 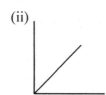  (iii)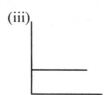

(iv) 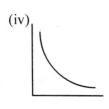  (v)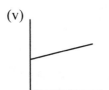

| **A** | (i) |
|---|---|
| **B** | (ii) |
| **C** | (iii) |
| **D** | (iv) |
| **E** | (v) |

*(CIMA May 98)*

110    In process costing, a joint product is

 A    a product which is later divided into many parts

 B    a product which is produced simultaneously with other products but which is of lesser value than at least one of the other products

 C    a product which is produced simultaneously with other products and is of similar value to at least one of the other products

 D    a product which is produced simultaneously with other products but which is of a greater value than any of the other products

 E    a product produced jointly with another organisation

*(CIMA May 98)*

111    Which of the following characteristics are associated with the use of contract costing?

 (i)    A range of items is produced and made available for sale: the customer chooses which item he/she requires

 (ii)    The work is undertaken at the customer's request

 (iii)    Work usually takes a long time to complete, often spanning the contractor's financial year end

 A    (i) and (iii) only
 B    (ii) and (iii) only
 C    (iii) only
 D    (i) only
 E    (ii) only

*(CIMA May 98)*

112    Exe Ltd makes a single product whose total cost per unit is budgeted to be £45. This includes fixed cost of £8 per unit based on a volume of 10,000 units per period. In a period, sales volume was 9,000 units, and production volume was 11,500 units. The actual profit for the same period, calculated using absorption costing, was £42,000.

If the profit statement were prepared using marginal costing, the profit for the period

 A    would be £10,000
 B    would be £22,000
 C    would be £50,000
 D    would be £62,000
 E    cannot be calculated without more information

*(CIMA May 98)*

113    Z Ltd uses a standard absorption costing system. The following details are taken from its budget for March 1998:

|                              |         |
|------------------------------|---------|
| Fixed production overhead cost | £72,000 |
| Production (units)            | 7,200   |

The accounts for March 1998 show that the fixed production overhead cost was over-absorbed by £12,000, and the fixed production overhead expenditure variance was £3,000 adverse.

The actual number of units produced was

A    5,700
B    6,300
C    8,100
D    8,400
E    8,700

*(CIMA May 98)*

---

114    The following details relate to product X in two accounting periods:

| Number of units | 500 | 800 |
|---|---|---|
| | £/unit | £/unit |
| Direct materials | 2.00 | 2.00 |
| Direct labour | 1.50 | 1.50 |
| Production overhead | 2.50 | 1.75 |
| Other overhead | 1.00 | 0.625 |
| | 7.00 | 5.875 |

The fixed cost per period and variable cost per unit are:

| | Period fixed cost | Variable cost/unit |
|---|---|---|
| | £ | £ |
| A | 1,000 | 1.125 |
| B | 1,000 | 3.50 |
| C | 1,500 | 3.50 |
| D | 1,000 | 4.00 |
| E | 1,500 | 4.00 |

*(CIMA May 98)*

---

115    Direct costs are

A    costs which can be identified with a cost centre but not identified to a single cost unit
B    costs which can be economically identified with a single cost unit
C    costs which can be identified with a single cost unit, but it is not economic to do so
D    costs incurred as a direct result of a particular decision
E    costs incurred which can be attributed to a particular accounting period

*(CIMA May 98)*

---

116    In process costing, when a by-product is produced, the usual entries are

A    debit the process account with the resale value of the by-product and credit the profit and loss account

B    debit the process account with the resale value of the by-product and credit the sundry income account

C    credit the process account with the resale value of the by-product and debit the by-product account

D    credit the process account with the resale value of the by-product and debit the profit and loss account

E    none of the above

*(CIMA May 98)*

## THE FOLLOWING DATA RELATE TO QUESTIONS 117 AND 118

KL Processing operates the FIFO method of accounting for opening work in process in its mixing process. The following data relate to April 1998:

| | | | |
|---|---|---|---|
| Opening work in process | 1,000 | litres valued at | £1,500 |
| Input | 30,000 | litres costing | £15,000 |
| Conversion costs | | | £10,000 |
| Output | 24,000 | litres | |
| Closing work in process | 3,500 | litres | |

Losses in process are expected to be 10% of period input. They are complete as to input material costs but are discovered after 60% conversion. Losses have a scrap value of £0.20 per litre.

Opening work in process was 100% complete as to input materials, and 70% complete as to conversion. Closing work in process is complete as to input materials and 80% complete as to conversion.

117 The number of material-equivalent units was

A    26,300 litres
B    26,600 litres
C    27,000 litres
D    28,000 litres
E    29,000 litres

*(CIMA May 98)*

118 The number of conversion-equivalent units was

A    26,400 litres
B    26,600 litres
C    26,800 litres
D    27,000 litres
E    27,400 litres

*(CIMA May 98)*

119 State which of the following are characteristics of contract costing:

(i)     identical products
(ii)    customer-driven production
(iii)   short timescale from commencement to completion of the cost unit.

A    None of them
B    (i) and (ii) only
C    (ii) and (iii) only
D    (i) and (iii) only
E    (ii) only

*(CIMA Nov 98)*

120     The following details have been extracted from the debtor collection records of D Limited:

| | |
|---|---|
| Invoices paid in the month after sale | 70% |
| Invoices paid in the second month after sale | 20% |
| Invoices paid in the third month after sale | 8% |
| Bad debts | 2% |

Invoices are issued on the last day of each month.

Customers paying in the month after sale are entitled to deduct a 3% settlement discount.

Credit sales values for June to September 1999 are budged as follows:

| June | July | August | September |
|---|---|---|---|
| £52,500 | £60,000 | £90,000 | £67,500 |

The amount budged to be received in September 1999 from credit sales is

| | |
|---|---|
| A | £74,610 |
| B | £75,960 |
| C | £77,310 |
| D | £77,850 |
| E | £79,200 |

*(CIMA Nov 98)*

---

121     The following extract is taken from the production cost budget of W Limited:

| | | |
|---|---|---|
| Production units | 2,000 | 3,000 |
| Production cost | £17,760 | £20,640 |

The budget cost allowance for an activity level of 4,000 units is

| | |
|---|---|
| A | £11,520 |
| B | £23,520 |
| C | £27,520 |
| D | £35,520 |
| E | none of these values |

*(CIMA Nov 98)*

---

122     K Limited manufactures three products, the selling price and cost per unit details of which are given below:

| | Product L £ | Product M £ | Product N £ |
|---|---|---|---|
| Selling price | 97.50 | 123.50 | 123.50 |
| Direct materials | 13.00 | 6.50 | 19.50 |
| Direct labour | 20.80 | 31.20 | 26.00 |
| Variable overhead | 10.40 | 15.60 | 13.00 |
| Fixed overhead | 31.20 | 46.80 | 39.00 |

In a period when direct materials are restricted in supply, the most and least profitable uses of direct materials are:

|   | *Most profitable* | *Least profitable* |
|---|---|---|
| **A** | L | N |
| **B** | M | N |
| **C** | L | M |
| **D** | N | M |
| **E** | M | L |

*(CIMA Nov 98)*

---

123  Z plc makes a single product which it sells for £16 per unit. Fixed costs are £76,800 per month and the product has a contribution to sales ratio of 40%.
In a period when actual sales were £224,000, Z plc's margin of safety, in units, was

| **A** | 2,000 |
|---|---|
| **B** | 6,000 |
| **C** | 8,000 |
| **D** | 12,000 |
| **E** | 14,000 |

*(CIMA Nov 98)*

---

124  When deciding, purely on financial grounds, whether or not to process further a joint product, the information required is:

(i)    the value of the common process costs.
(ii)   the method of apportioning the common costs between the joint products.
(iii)  the sales value of the joint product at the separation point.
(iv)   the final sales value of the joint product.
(v)    the further processing cost of the joint product.

Which of the above statements are correct?

| **A** | (i), (ii) and (iii) only. |
|---|---|
| **B** | (iii), (iv) and (v) only. |
| **C** | (iv) and (v) only. |
| **D** | (i), (ii), (iv) and (v) only. |
| **E** | All of them. |

*(CIMA Nov 98)*

---

*The following data relate to sub-questions 125 and 126 below*

---

H Limited operates a standard costing system for its only product. The standard cost card includes:

| Fixed overhead: | 4 hours @ £10 per hour | £40.00 |
|---|---|---|

Fixed overheads are absorbed on the basis of labour hours. Fixed overhead costs are budgeted at £240,000 per annum and are expected to be incurred in equal amounts in each of the twelve accounting periods during the year.

Production is budgeted to be at an equal number of units in each accounting period.

Actual production during period 6 was 450 units, with actual fixed overhead costs incurred being £19,600 and actual hours worked being 1,970.

125    The fixed overhead expenditure variance for period 6 was

    **A**    £4,400    (F)
    **B**    £400    (F)
    **C**    £100    (F)
    **D**    £400    (A)
    **E**    £4,400    (A)

*(CIMA Nov 98)*

126    The fixed overhead volume variance for period 6 was

    **A**    £300    (A)
    **B**    £1,200    (A)
    **C**    £1,700    (A)
    **D**    £2,000    (A)
    **E**    £300    (F)

*(CIMA Nov 98)*

---

*The following data relate to sub-questions 127 and 128 below*

---

R plc uses a standard costing system. The budget for one of its products for September 1998 includes direct labour cost (based on 4 hours per unit) of £117,600. During September 1998 3,350 units were made which was 150 units less than budgeted. The direct labour cost incurred was £111,850 and the number of direct labour hours worked was 13,450.

127    The direct labour rate variance for the month was

    **A**    £5,750    (F)
    **B**    £1,130    (F)
    **C**    £710    (F)
    **D**    £1,130    (A)
    **E**    £5,750    (A)

*(CIMA Nov 98)*

128    The direct labour efficiency variance for the month was

    **A**    £420.00    (A)
    **B**    £415.80    (A)
    **C**    £420.00    (F)
    **D**    £415.80    (F)
    **E**    £4,620.00  (F)

*(CIMA Nov 98)*

129    Direct costs are

    **A**    costs which can neither be identified with a cost centre nor identified with a single cost unit.
    **B**    costs which can be identified with a single cost unit.
    **C**    costs incurred as a direct result of a particular design
    **D**    costs incurred which can be attributed to a particular accounting period.
    **E**    none of the above.

*(CIMA May 99)*

130     A flexible budget is

    **A**      a budget comprising variable production costs only.

    **B**      a budget which is updated with actual costs and revenues as they occur during the budget period.

    **C**      a budget which shows the costs and revenues at different levels of activity.

    **D**      a budget which is prepared using a computer spreadsheet model.

    **E**      a budget which is prepared for a period of six months and reviewed monthly. Following such review a further one month's budget is prepared.

*(CIMA May 99)*

131     A master budget comprises

    **A**      the budgeted profit and loss account.

    **B**      the budgeted cash flow, budgeted profit and loss account and budgeted balance sheet.

    **C**      the budgeted cash flow.

    **D**      the capital expenditure budget.

    **E**      the entire set of budgets prepared.

*(CIMA May 99)*

132     Z Limited manufactures and sells two products – X and Y. Annual sales values are expected to be in the ratio of 2X : 6Y. Total annual sales are planned to be £210,000. Product X has a contribution to sales ratio of 40% whereas that of product Y is 50%. Annual fixed costs are estimated to be £60,000.

The budgeted break-even sales value

    **A**      is £94,500.

    **B**      is £99,750.

    **C**      is £126,316.

    **D**      is £128,571.

    **E**      cannot be determined from the above data.

*(CIMA May 99)*

133     R. Limited manufactures three products, the selling price and cost details of which are given below:

|  | Product P £ | Product Q £ | Product R £ |
|---|---|---|---|
| Selling price per unit | 150 | 190 | 190 |
| Costs per unit: |  |  |  |
| Direct materials (£5/kg) | 20 | 10 | 30 |
| Direct labour (£4/hour) | 32 | 48 | 40 |
| Variable overhead | 16 | 24 | 20 |
| Fixed overhead | 48 | 72 | 60 |

In a period when direct materials are restricted in supply, the most and least profitable uses of direct materials are:

|  | *Most profitable* | *Least profitable* |
|---|---|---|
| **A** | P | R |
| **B** | Q | R |
| **C** | P | Q |
| **D** | R | Q |
| **E** | Q | P |

*(CIMA May 99)*

134    T plc uses a standard costing system, with its material stock account being maintained at standard cost. The following details have been extracted from the standard cost card in respect of direct materials:

> 8 kg @ £0.80/kg = £6.40 per unit
> Budgeted production in April 1999 was 850 units.

The following details relate to actual materials purchased and issued to production during April 1999 when actual production was 870 units:

> Materials purchased           8,200 kg costing £6,888
> Materials issued to production    7,150 kg

Which of the following correctly states the material price and usage variance to be reported?

| | Price | Usage |
|---|---|---|
| A | £286 (A) | £152 (A) |
| B | £286 (A) | £280 (A) |
| C | £286 (A) | £294 (A) |
| D | £328 (A) | £152 (A) |
| E | £328 (A) | £280 (A) |

*(CIMA May 99)*

---

135    XYZ plc manufactures its product through a series of processes. The FIFO method of valuing opening work in process is used and the following details relate to April 1999.

> Opening work in process was 300 units, each unit being 80% processed as to materials and 60% processed as to conversion costs.
>
> Normal loss was 250 units, fully completed.
>
> Finished output was 7,250 units; there were no abnormal losses or gains.
>
> Closing work in process was 400 units, each unit being 70% processed as to materials and 40% processed as to conversion costs.

When calculating the costs per equivalent unit, the number of equivalent units to be used is:

| | Materials | Conversion |
|---|---|---|
| A | 7,290 | 7,230 |
| B | 7,470 | 7,290 |
| C | 7,590 | 7,530 |
| D | 7,770 | 7,590 |
| E | 8,020 | 7,480 |

*(CIMA May 99)*

---

136    The following extract is taken from the production cost budget for S Limited:

| | | |
|---|---|---|
| Production (units) | 4,000 | 6,000 |
| Production cost (£) | 11,100 | 12,900 |

The budget cost allowance for an activity level of 8,000 units is

A     £7,200
B     £14,700
C     £17,200
D     £22,200
E     none of these values.

*(CIMA May 99)*

---

137    Z Limited manufactures a single product, the budgeted selling price and variable cost details of which are as follows:

|                              | £      |
|------------------------------|--------|
| Selling price                | 15.00  |
| Variable costs per unit:     |        |
| Direct materials             | 4.00   |
| Direct labour                | 3.50   |
| Variable overhead            | 2.00   |

Budgeted fixed overhead costs are £60,000 per annum incurred evenly throughout the year.

Budgeted production is 30,000 units per annum.

In a month when actual production was 2,400 units and exceeded sales by 180 units, the profit reported under absorption costing was

A     £6,660     B     £7,570     C     £7,770     D     £8,200     E     £8,400

*(CIMA May 99)*

---

138    Q Limited uses an integrated costing system, with the material stock account being maintained at standard cost. In October, when 2,400 units of the finished product were made, the actual material cost details were:

| Material purchased | 5,000 units @ £4.50 each |
|--------------------|--------------------------|
| Material used      | 4,850 units              |

The standard cost details are that 2 units of the material should be used for each unit of the completed product, and the standard price of each material unit is £4.70.

The entries made in the variance accounts would be:

|   | *Material price* |        | *Material usage* |      |
|---|------------------|--------|------------------|------|
| A | Debit            | £970   | Debit            | £225 |
| B | Debit            | £1,000 | Debit            | £225 |
| C | Credit           | £970   | Debit            | £235 |
| D | Credit           | £1,000 | Debit            | £235 |
| E | Credit           | £1,000 | Debit            | £900 |

*(CIMA May 99)*

# ANSWERS TO PRACTICE QUESTIONS

| 1 | TRUE COSTS |
|---|---|

## Answer plan

(a)   2 definitions, probably noun

(b)   Disagree, overheads, ABC, small vs large business

(c)   Planning
Control purposes vs budget, previous results
Cost comparisons vs external suppliers, alternative methods
Decision making
Different types of cost
Financial reporting - balance sheet/P&L

(a)   The CIMA definition of cost as a noun is "the amount of expenditure (actual or notional) incurred on, or attributable to, a specified thing or activity".

The definition of cost as a verb is "to ascertain the cost of a specified thing or activity".

In the statement, the speaker appears to be using the term as a noun.

(b)   The speaker is correct as far as most companies are concerned, but for very simple situations such as one-person businesses with little or no fixed overhead it may be possible to obtain an absolutely accurate cost.

If a business has fixed overheads, there is a choice of possible accounting methods, absorption costing or marginal costing. The simpler method is marginal costing which avoids the arbitrariness of apportioning and absorbing overheads, but can it really be said to give the true cost of a product or service when it doesn't include all the costs incurred in providing the product or service? If absorption costing is used, the fixed overheads are charged to products by means of subjective apportionment bases and absorption rates. Can this method be said to give a true cost when it charges items such as rent to products when there is no direct relationship between rent and the amount of output?

Activity based costing might be regarded as giving truer costs than under absorption costing as more flexibility is possible in the choice of cost driver rates, and the overheads are charged to specific activities rather than apportioned to departments.

(c)   Whilst there are a variety of different types of cost to choose from and the obtaining of cost information may be said to be subjective, the provision of cost information is vital for a business in many areas.

(1)   Planning

If a company wishes to plan for the future, it will need to know the cost of its products/services in order to know what resources it will need.

(2)   Control

The actual costs of a product/service can be compared with the expected costs and corrective action taken if necessary. The actual costs can also be compared with the costs incurred in previous periods or in different sections of the business.

(3)   Performance evaluation

The cost of providing a product/service internally can be compared with the cost to the company if an external supplier provided the service, eg, should the company have its own information technology section or should it use an external computer bureau?

The company may also compare the cost of providing a product/service in one way with the estimated cost if an alternative method was used.

(4)     Decision making

Product cost information will be necessary for both long term and short term decisions. Different types of cost information will be needed for different decisions and indeed for all the different purposes listed here in part (c).

(5)     Financial reporting

Product cost information will be needed for financial reporting purposes for both the balance sheet and the P&L account, eg, stocks should be valued at the lower of cost and net realisable value.

---

# 2    ECONOMIC ORDER

(a)     (i)     Total cost of ordering $= \dfrac{D}{Q} \times Co$

(*Tutorial note:* $\dfrac{D}{Q}$ is the number of orders per annum.)

(ii)     Total cost of storage $= \dfrac{Q}{2} \times p \times Ch$

(iii)     Total cost of ordering and storage $= \dfrac{D}{Q} \times Co + \dfrac{Q}{2} \times p \times Ch$

(iv)     Optimal re-order quantity $= \sqrt{\dfrac{2 \times Co \times D}{p \times Ch}}$

(*Tutorial note:* The above formula is the formula for the EOQ and can be found in the mathematical tables given in the exam. The formula given, however, includes the term Ch which represents the holding cost (Storage cost here) of one unit for 1 year (or some other period of time). Here the holding cost/unit is represented as p × Ch.

Thus the formula given in the tables is:

$Q = \sqrt{\dfrac{2CoD}{Ch}}$ and we have $Q = \sqrt{\dfrac{2CoD}{p \times Ch}}$

Alternatively for the mathematically adept, the formula in part (iii) could be rearranged and solved using differential calculus to find the optimal order level.)

(b)     The EOQ model makes a number of assumptions which in practice may not hold true:

1     There may not be a constant holding cost per unit.

2     The EOQ model assumes a zero lead time or a known and certain lead time. This assumption may not apply in real life.

3     The total cost per order may be difficult to calculate as there are many different components.

4     Annual demand may be difficult to predict.

5       The total holding cost per unit may be difficult to calculate. It has many different components. The opportunity cost of holding stock may be particularly hard to calculate.

6       The EOQ formula does not consider stockouts.

(c)     Optimal re-order quantity  $= \sqrt{\dfrac{2 \times Co \times D}{p \times Ch}}$  (from part (a))

$$= \sqrt{\dfrac{2 \times 30 \times 2,000}{70 \times 20\%}}$$

$= 93$ units.

(d)     A Just In Time (JIT) system ignores the economic order quantity. It turns conventional stock-holding theory on its head.

A traditional system works on the principle that holding stock is a virtue and that holding a certain amount of stock is necessary in order to cope with operating problems, such as poor quality output or input materials, machine breakdowns, absenteeism or lateness.

A Just In Time system regards the holding of stock as a waste and aims to receive material just before it is needed, thus eliminating the need for stock. The operation of a JIT system will need close cooperation between the company and the supplier and will mean the delivery of small orders, perhaps several times daily. The JIT philosophy is much wider than just the materials purchasing aspect dealt with here.

# 3    MACHINISTS

(a)     **Statement of annual costs**

|  | Better workers | Less efficient workers |
|---|---|---|
| Good output (units) (W1) | 280,000 | 200,000 |
|  | £ | £ |
| Labour (W2) | 61,600 | 44,000 |
| Rectification costs (W3) | 4,000 | 12,000 |
| Variable overheads (W4) | 10,000 | 10,000 |
| Variable production overhead | 75,600 | 66,000 |

*(Tutorial note:* The question does not make it clear whether an absorption costing or marginal costing format is desired. Presumably, a format including fixed overheads would be equally correct.)

(b)

|  | Better workers £ | Less efficient workers £ |
|---|---|---|
| Sales (W5) | 551,000 | 437,000 |
| Direct materials (W6) | (348,000) | (276,000) |
| Variable production overhead | (75,600) | (66,000) |
| Contribution | 127,400 | 95,000 |

The better workers provide £32,400 more contribution. Training the less efficient workers for a cost of £10,000 would thus increase the overall profit of the company by £22,400.

(c)    1      Better training might lead to a greater feeling of self-worth among the workers and thus better morale with perhaps less absenteeism.

        2      Better training might lead to better machine operating practices and less accidents with less maintenance being necessary.

WORKINGS

(1)    **Output**

| Better workers | 2,000 hrs × 14 units/hr × 10 workers = 280,000 units |
|---|---|
| Less efficient workers | 2,000 hrs × 10 units/hr × 10 workers = 200,000 units |

(2)    **Labour cost**

| Better workers | 280,000 units × £0.22/unit = £61,600 |
|---|---|
| Less efficient workers | 200,000 units × £0.22/unit = £44,000 |

(3)    **Rectification costs**

| Better workers | 2,000 hrs × 0.5 units/hr × 10 workers × £0.40/unit = £4,000 |
|---|---|
| Less efficient workers | 2,000 hrs × 1.5 units/hr × 10 workers × £0.40/unit = £12,000 |

(4)    **Variable overheads**

2,000 hours × 10 workers × £0.50/hr = £10,000

(5)    (**Tutorial note:** Sales include both good units and rectified units.)

**Total no of units**

| Better workers | (14 units/hr × 2,000 hrs + 0.5 units/hr × 2,000 hrs) × 10 workers = 290,000 units |
|---|---|
| Less efficient workers | (10 units/hr × 2,000 hrs + 1.5 units/hr × 2,000 hrs) × 10 workers = 230,000 units. |

**Sales**

| Better workers | 290,000 units × £1.90 per unit = £551,000 |
|---|---|
| Less efficient workers | 230,000 units × £1.90 per unit = £437,000 |

(6)    **Direct material**

| Better workers | 290,000 units (W5) × £1.20/unit = £348,000 |
|---|---|
| Less efficient workers | 230,000 units (W5) × £1.20/unit = £276,000 |

# 4   WAGES CONTROL

(a)   A wages control account is used to summarise the wages and related employment costs incurred by an organisation and then to transfer these costs to work in progress or overhead accounts as appropriate.

(b)   (i)

|  |  | DR £ | CR £ |
|---|---|---:|---:|
| Wages control (180,460 + 18,770) | | 199,230 | |
| PAYE/NI creditor (14,120 + 27,800 + 18,770) | | | 60,690 |
| Pension fund | | | 7,200 |
| Court | | | 1,840 |
| Trade union creditor | | | 1,200 |
| Private health creditor | | | 6,000 |
| Bank | | | 122,300 |
| | | 199,230 | 199,230 |

(ii)

|  |  | DR £ | CR £ |
|---|---|---:|---:|
| Work in progress (77,460 + 16,800) | | 94,260 | |
| Capital expenditure | | 2,300 | |
| Statutory sick pay debtor (5,700 + 3,300) | | 9,000 | |
| Production overhead (5,600 + 8,500 + 4,300 + 38,400 + 10,200 + 3,400 + 4,500) | | 74,900 | |
| Wages control | | | 180,460 |
| | | 180,460 | 180,460 |

# 5   EXPERIMENT

(a)   Machine hour absorption rate

$$= \frac{£10,430 + £5,250 + £3,600 + £2,100 + £4,620}{(120 \times 4) + (100 \times 3) + (80 \times 2) + (120 \times 3)}$$

$$= \frac{£26,000}{1,300} \qquad = £20/\text{machine hour.}$$

The total costs for each product are thus:

|  | A £ | B £ | C £ | D £ |
|---|---:|---:|---:|---:|
| Direct materials | 40 | 50 | 30 | 60 |
| Direct labour | 28 | 21 | 14 | 21 |
| Production overhead | 80 | 60 | 40 | 60 |
| Per unit | £148 | £131 | £84 | £141 |
| Total (W4) | £17,760 | £13,100 | £6,720 | £16,920 |

(b)   **Cost driver rates**

| Machine dept costs (m/c hour basis) | = | £10,430/1,300 | | = | £8.023/hr |
|---|---|---|---|---|---|
| Set up costs | = | £5,250/21 | (W1) | = | £250/run |
| Stores receiving | = | £3,600/80 | (W2) | = | £45/requisition |

| | | | | | |
|---|---|---|---|---|---|
| Inspection/quality control | = | £2,100/21 | (W1) | = | £100/run |
| Material handling despatch | = | £4,620/42 | | = | £110/order |

| *Total costs* | A | B | C | D |
|---|---|---|---|---|
| | £ | £ | £ | £ |
| Direct materials | 4,800 | 5,000 | 2,400 | 7,200 |
| Direct labour | 3,360 | 2,100 | 1,120 | 2,520 |
| Machine dep costs | 3,851 | 2,407 | 1,284 | 2,888 |
| Set up costs | 1,500 | 1,250 | 1,000 | 1,500 |
| Stores receiving | 900 | 900 | 900 | 900 |
| Inspection/quality control | 600 | 500 | 400 | 600 |
| Materials handling despatch | 1,320 | 1,100 | 880 | 1,320 |
| | £16,331 | £13,257 | £7,984 | £16,928 |

(c)     **Per unit costs**

| *Product* | A | B | C | D |
|---|---|---|---|---|
| | £ | £ | £ | £ |
| Traditional machine hour method | 148.00 | 131.00 | 84.00 | 141.00 |
| ABC method (W3) | 136.09 | 132.57 | 99.80 | 141.07 |
| Difference | 11.91 | (1.57) | (15.80) | (0.07) |

The most significant differences concern products A and C. The ABC approach, in theory, attributes the cost of resources to each product which uses those resources on a more appropriate basis than the traditional method. The implication is that product A is more profitable than the traditional approach implies whereas C is less profitable. Alternatively the price of C should be increased whereas that of A could be reduced.

WORKINGS

(W1)   (120 + 100 + 80 + 120)/20 = 21
(W2)   4 × 20 = 80
(W3)   Cost/quantity of each product.
(W4)   Unit cost × quantity of each product.

## 6     DISTORTIONS

### Answer plan

Definition of overhead absorption; choice of activity measurement base; use of alternative basis; use of multiple bases; activity based costing.

Overhead absorption is the technique of attributing departmental overhead costs to a cost unit.

Traditionally the basis of overhead absorption was the number of labour hours expected within the budget period and this was then used to calculate an absorption rate per labour hour. This was then used to attribute costs to the cost unit on the basis of the number of labour hours used to produce the cost unit.

Alternative bases of apportionment exist such as the number of machine hours or a percentage of particular elements of prime cost incurred in respect of the cost unit. If the method of manufacture is machine intensive for example, it is more realistic to absorb the overhead cost on the basis of the number of machine hours instead of the number of labour hours.

A further development is to divide the overhead cost into those costs which are labour related and those which are machine hour related and apply a separate absorption rate to each part of the overhead cost. This use of multiple rates is similar to the principles of activity based costing.

Activity based costing is based on the principle that activities cause costs and therefore the use of activities should be the basis of attributing costs to cost units. Costs are identified with particular activities and the performance of those activities is linked with products. The activity is known as the cost driver and the costs associated with that activity are then attributed to cost units using a cost driver rate. This then more accurately reflects the usage of the activity by the product.

---

# 7    RH LTD

(a)    (i)    **Marginal costing statement**

|  | Six months ending 31 March 19X3 | | Six months ending 30 September 19X3 | |
|---|---|---|---|---|
|  | £'000 | £'000 | £'000 | £'000 |
| Sales |  | 980 |  | 1,120 |
| Variable cost of sales |  |  |  |  |
|    opening stock | - |  | 73.5 |  |
|    production cost |  |  |  |  |
|      8,500 units @ £49 | 416.5 |  |  |  |
|      7,000 units @ £49 |  |  | 343 |  |
|   | 416.5 |  | 416.5 |  |
|    less closing stock |  |  |  |  |
|      1,500 units @ £49 | 73.5 |  |  |  |
|      500 units @ £49 |  |  | 24.5 |  |
|   |  | 343 |  | 392 |
|   |  | 637 |  | 728 |
| Variable selling costs |  | 196 |  | 224 |
| Contribution |  | 441 |  | 504 |
| Fixed costs |  |  |  |  |
|    production (W1) | 160 |  | 160 |  |
|    selling, etc | 90 |  | 90 |  |
|   |  | 250 |  | 250 |
| Profit |  | 191 |  | 254 |

(ii)    **Absorption costing statement**

|  | Six months ending 31 March 19X3 | | Six months ending 30 September 19X3 | |
|---|---|---|---|---|
|  | £'000 | £'000 | £'000 | £'000 |
| Sales |  | 980 |  | 1,120 |
| Cost of sales |  |  |  |  |
| opening stock | - |  | 103.5 |  |
| production cost |  |  |  |  |
| 8,500 units @ £69 | 586.5 |  |  |  |
| 7,000 units @ £69 |  |  | 483 |  |
|  | 586.5 |  | 586.5 |  |
| less closing stock |  |  |  |  |
| 1,500 units @ £69 | 103.5 |  |  |  |
| 500 units @ £69 |  |  | 34.5 |  |
|  |  | 483 |  | 552 |
|  |  | 497 |  | 568 |
| (under)/over absorption (W2) |  | 10 |  | (20) |
| Gross profit |  | 507 |  | 548 |
| Selling, etc costs |  |  |  |  |
| variable | 196 |  | 224 |  |
| fixed | 90 |  | 90 |  |
|  |  | 286 |  | 314 |
| Profit |  | 221 |  | 234 |

WORKINGS

(W1)    Fixed production overhead is £20 per unit and the normal level of activity is 16,000 units per annum. The budgeted overhead per annum is therefore $16,000 \times 20 = £320,000$. The budgeted overhead per six-month period is therefore £160,000. The question states that there are no variances apart from a volume variance, therefore, actual overheads are as expected in the budget.

(W2)    Under/over absorption is the difference between overheads incurred and overheads absorbed

**1st 6 months**

|  | £'000 |
|---|---|
| Overhead incurred (W1) | 160 |
| Overhead absorbed |  |
| 8,500 units × £20/unit | 170 |
| Over absorption | 10 |

**2nd 6 months**

|  | £'000 |
|---|---|
| Overhead incurred (W1) | 160 |
| Overhead absorbed |  |
| 7,000 units × £20/unit | 140 |
| Under absorption | 20 |

(b)    The difference in profit = fixed production OAR × change in stock

|  | 1st 6 mths £'000 | 2nd 6 mths £'000 |
|---|---|---|
| Marginal costing profit | 191 | 254 |
| Stock difference | | |
| Increase 1,500 units × £20/unit | 30 | |
| Decrease 1,000 units × £20/unit | | (20) |
| Absorption costing profit | 221 | 234 |

(c)    Marginal costing is useful in the following business situations:

(1)    Shutdown decisions. Using absorption costing it may appear that a product is unprofitable and should be discontinued. The product will have been charged with a share of fixed costs, however, which will usually remain at the same level, regardless of whether the product is continued or not. In the short term at least the focus should be on contribution and if the product has a positive contribution it should be continued.

(2)    Limiting factor decisions. When there is a scarce resource, production should be organised so that those products which give the highest contribution per unit of scarce resource are given the highest priority. Fixed costs can and should be ignored as they will be the same irrespective of which products are made.

(3)    Make or buy decisions. When a company has the choice of making or buying a component/product it should choose the cheaper option. The focus should be on variable costs alone as again the fixed costs will not change whichever option is chosen.

# 8    SERVICE DEPARTMENT COSTS

In order to explain and comment on the statement it is necessary to consider the purposes of cost accounting and the methods used.

The statement refers to "the true cost of the final output". This is considered to be the cost of the resources used to produce the output. The purpose of this information is so that decisions can be made and product profitability measured.

Cost accounting systems identify those costs which can be attributed to the cost unit (direct costs) and separate them from those which cannot be attributed (indirect or overhead costs). It is the treatment of these overhead costs which differs.

A marginal costing system treats such costs as period costs, making no attempt to attribute them to cost units. In the short-run these marginal costs are the costs of the extra units, and these may be used for short-run pricing decisions and when considering output levels.

An absorption costing system attributes overhead costs to cost units using either:

(a)    a measure of output; or
(b)    a measure of input needed to create the output (eg, direct labour hours).

It should be noted that the choice of absorption base is arbitrary but assumes that the cost is related in some way to output. It should also be noted that a single measure is used for a wide variety of costs.

Activity based costing is a form of absorption method in that it attributes indirect costs to cost units. However, this is not done using output measures.

In activity based costing, it is recognised that it is activities which cause costs, not the number of units of output. For example, costs will be incurred in setting up a machine, but these costs are the same whether the machine is then used to produce one unit or a thousand units. Activity based costing therefore identifies the activities which cause costs to be incurred and collects these costs in cost pools. Each cost pool is then attributed to cost units on the basis of its corresponding activity and the extent to which the performance of those activities relate to output. Activity-based costing can therefore be described as absorption costing using multiple absorption rates.

In view of the above, it is considered that activity based costing reflects the resources used in the production of the unit and that its use will therefore provide 'a truer' cost. However, it is an absorption based system and in short-run decisions it may not distinguish between fixed and variable costs. In the long run, however, it may provide a more accurate method of valuing the resources used than single absorption rates.

## 9     DC LTD

(a)     (**Note**: Before calculating the absorption rates the costs of the service dept. must be apportioned to the production departments. This may be done by continuous apportionment **or** by using simultaneous equations. Both alternative solution methods are shown below).

### - Continuous apportionment method

|  | Machining £'000 | Assembly £'000 | Finishing £'000 | Stores £'000 | Maintenance £'000 |
|---|---|---|---|---|---|
| Costs | 600 | 250 | 150 | 100 | 80 |
| Apportion stores | 40 | 30 | 20 | (100) | 10 |
|  | 640 | 280 | 170 | NIL | 90 |
| Apportion maintenance | 49.5 | 18 | 18 | 4.5 | (90) |
|  | 689.5 | 298 | 188 | 4.5 | NIL |
| Apportion stores | 1.8 | 1.35 | 0.9 | (4.5) | 0.45 |
|  | 691.3 | 299.35 | 188.9 | NIL | 0.45 |
| Apportion maintenance | .25 | .10 | .10 | NIL | (0.45) |
|  | 691.55 | 299.45 | 189.0 | NIL | NIL |

### - Simultaneous equations method

$S = £100,000 + 0.05\,M$
$M = £80,000 + 0.10\,S$

$S = £100,000 + 0.05\,(£80,000 + 0.10\,S)$
$\quad = £100,000 + £4,000 + 0.005\,S$

$0.995\,S = £104,000$

$\quad\quad S = £104,523$

By Substitution:

$M = £80,000 + 0.10\,S$
$\quad = £80,000 + 0.10\,(£104,523)$
$\quad = £80,000 + £10,452$
$\quad = £90,452$

| | Machining | Assembly | Finishing | Stores | Maintenance |
|---|---|---|---|---|---|
| | £ | £ | £ | £ | £ |
| Costs | 600,000 | 250,000 | 150,000 | 100,000 | 80,000 |
| Apportion stores | 41,809 | 31,357 | 20,905 | (104,523) | 10,452 |
| Apportion maint. | 49,749 | 18,090 | 18,090 | 4,523 | (90,452) |
| | 691,558 | 299,447 | 188,995 | NIL | NIL |

(**Note**: The differences in the costs of each production department vary slightly due to roundings, both answers are acceptable.)

Appropriate absorption rates are determined by whether the department is labour intensive or machine intensive. This is identified by comparing the relative quantities of machine and labour hours for the year.

Thus the machining department is machine intensive and the other departments are labour intensive. Appropriate absorption rates are:-

Machining: £691,558 / 50,000 = £13.83 per machine hour

Assembly: £299,447 / 30,000 = £9.98 per labour hour

Finishing: £188,995 / 20,000 = £9.45 per labour hour

(b)

| | £ |
|---|---|
| Direct materials | 2,400 |
| Direct labour | 1,500 |
| Production overhead:- | |
| Machining 45 hours × £13.83 | 622 |
| Assembly 15 hours × £9.98 | 150 |
| Finishing 12 hours × £9.45 | 113 |
| Total cost | 4,785 |
| Profit (4,785 × $\frac{20}{80}$) | 1,196 |
| Selling price | 5,981 |

(c)

| | £ |
|---|---|
| Expected cost (per answer (a)) | 299,447 |
| Actual cost | 300,000 |
| Expenditure difference | 553 |

Amount absorbed:

| | £ |
|---|---|
| Expected hours | 30,000 |
| Actual hours | 30,700 |
| Extra hours | 700 hours |
| 700 hours × £9.98* | £6,987 |

Amount absorbed:

30,700 hours × £9.98*                                    306,435

*(**Note**: this uses £9.9816 as the absorption rate to reduce rounding errors)

**Control Account**

|  | £ |  | £ |
|---|---|---|---|
| Costs incurred | 300,000 | Work-In-Progress | 306,435 |
| Volume | 6,987 | Expenditure | 553 |
|  | 306,987 |  | 306,988 |

(difference due to rounding)

(d)    Activity Based Costing is a method of attributing overhead costs to cost units which recognises that costs are caused by activities such as ordering materials, setting up machines.

Each of these activities are identified and costs are budgeted for each activity. For each activity a link is established between the activity and the units of product / service to be provided. This provides the means of connecting the activity costs (known as cost pools) to the output by using cost driver rates. These cost driver rates are similar to traditional absorption rates to the extent that they are based on estimated activity costs and estimates of the number of times the activity is to be performed.

Actual costs are also collected by activity, and actual numbers of activity performance is recorded. These are compared with their respective estimates to identify the reasons why the cost attributed to unit using the cost driver rate differs from the cost incurred for each activity.

For organisations like DC Limited, where there are a large number of different cost units for a number of different customers, activity based costing should attribute overhead costs to individual cost units more fairly than traditional absorption methods because it considers in more detail the activities which are used in respect of each cost unit and attributes the costs of those activities to the item.

# 10    DIRECT SERVICES ORGANISATION

## *Answer plan*

Report; SSAP 9; prudence; true and fair view; three situations.

### REPORT

**To:**        Director

**From:**      Management Accountant

**Date:**      XX-X-19XX

**Subject:**   Profit reporting on long term contracts

In general, profits may not be recognised on ordinary products until the sale is realised ie, the product is finished and sold. This is in accordance with normal financial accounting practice. This prudent approach would have been followed for the DSO's previous smaller contracts.

Long-term contracts span at least two accounting periods and represent a large part of the company's business. If profit is not recognised until the contract is finished, then profits will be high for the years when contracts finish and will be low in the years when no contracts finish. This would not give a true and fair view of the company's performance in the separate years.

SSAP 9 states that "where a business carries out long-term contracts and it is considered that their outcome can be assessed with reasonable certainty before their conclusion, the attributable profit should be calculated on a prudent basis and included in the accounts for the period under review.  The profit taken up needs to reflect the proportion of the work carried out at the accounting date and to take into account any known inequalities of profitability in the various stages of a contract.  The procedure to recognise profit is to include an appropriate proportion of total contract value as turnover in the profit and loss account as the contract activity progresses.  The costs incurred in reaching that stage of completion are matched with this turnover, resulting in the reporting of results that can be attributed to the proportion of work completed.

Where the outcome of long-term contracts cannot be assessed with reasonable certainty before the conclusion of the contract, no profit should be reflected in the profit and loss account in respect of those contracts although, in such circumstances, if no loss is expected it may be appropriate to show as turnover a proportion of the total contract value using a zero estimate of profit.

If it is expected that there will be a loss on a contract as a whole, all of the loss should be recognised as soon as it is foreseen (in accordance with the prudence concept)."

*(Tutorial note:*  Students are most definitely not expected to be able to regurgitate the above lengthy quote from SSAP 9.  As long as the same principles are stated, the exact wording is not important.*)*

Putting the above arguments into simpler terms - SSAP 9 states that profits should be recognised on uncompleted contracts provided that the contract is expected to be profitable and that the outcome is reasonably certain.  Contracts will tend to fall into one of three situations:

1          Contract is profit-making but the outcome is not reasonably certain.

           No profit may be recognised.

2          Contract is profit-making and the end is reasonably certain.

           Profit should be recognised based on the anticipated profit of the contract when finished and the degree of completion so far.  Degree of completion may be judged for instance on:

           (i)        cost of work done;
           (ii)       value of work certified;
           (iii)      any other appropriate basis.

           For the specific example given, anticipated profit is £3 million (contract price £10 million, total cost £7 million), the degrees of completion are six sevenths complete for option (i) (cost so far divided by total cost), 75% complete for option (ii) (value to date divided by total value), and 50% complete according to the particular method used here to judge degree of completion.  The third option seems to be the appropriate one here and reported profit is equal to:

           £3,000,000 × 50% = £1,500,000

3          Contract is loss making.

           Entire anticipated loss should be recognised immediately.

A traditional method of profit reporting not acceptable for financial accounting purposes but which may be used for internal profit reporting is to use the following formula:

$$\text{Reported profit} = \text{Notional profit} \times \frac{2}{3} \times \frac{\text{Cash received}}{\text{Value of work certified}}$$

Notional profit is the profit if the contract could be stopped and sold now.  It is equal to the value of work done - cost of work done.  The $\frac{2}{3}$ is for prudence.

$$\text{The final fraction} = \frac{\text{Cash received}}{\text{Value of work certified}}$$ is for more prudence and is equal to 100% less retention fee percentage.

There is no mention of a retention fee here.

In the specific example:

Notional profit  =  £7,500,000 – £6,000,000 = £1,500,000

Reported profit  =  £1,500,000 × ⅔ × 100% (no retention fee)

            =  £1,000,000

## 11  FAST REPAIRS

(a)

|  | Fast service % | PLC % |
|---|---|---|
| Sale price | 100.00 | 100.00 |
| Materials | 55.85 | 50.12 |
| Staff costs | 22.97 | 20.03 |
| Operating costs | 7.70 | 17.71 |
| Interest and depreciation | 3.20 | 3.01 |
| Head office administration charges | 1.85 | - |
| Pre-tax profit | 8.43 | 9.13 |

The percentages for the fast service are obtained by totalling the relevant groups of costs and expressing each of them as a percentage of the sales value.

The PLC appears to enjoy more favourable material costs that the fast repair service outlet. Since the PLC is a nationwide organisation it is likely to be able to negotiate better prices due to the volume of its purchases nationwide.

The difference in staff costs may be due to a lack of specialisation in the fast repair outlets which increases job times and thereby increases labour costs per job.

The operating costs of the PLC are significantly higher than those of the fast repair service, this could be due to the policies of the PLC with regard to discretionary costs such as advertising, research and training and the location of the PLC's outlets some of which may be in high cost areas.

(b)  Advertising;  Customer creature comforts.

(c)  These costs could be avoided, but to do so may be short-sighted. The reduction in costs would not affect current sales and therefore the profit of the current period would increase, however, future sales may be lost by the discontinuance of advertising and if the customer facilities do not meet a certain minimum acceptable standard certain customers may not return with future work.

(d)  (i)  Initially a form of job costing system is needed to identify the costs of performing each of the repair services which they provide. This should include details of the materials to be used and the amount and type of labour used.

    (ii)  After 12 months a more sophisticated system can be introduced whereby estimated costs are calculated prior to the commencement of each job and actual results are compared with those estimates. If there are jobs which are being performed regularly, the estimates may take the form of a standard cost and may be used for pricing.

## 12  JOBBING COMPANY

(*Tutorial note:* this question involves identifying what is wrong with the method used for calculating the cost of jobs. The main things to note are that

(1)  a single 'blanket' recovery rate (47.5%) is used for all overheads;
(2)  the fact the company uses total cost as the lowest acceptable selling price; and
(3)  a recession is imminent making (2) a dangerous approach to use.)

(a)     **Criticism of method for estimating costs**

The essential feature of job costing is that all jobs are potentially different. The cost is therefore likely to differ. The method used for charging costs to jobs should aim at reflecting the incidence of the costs ie the costs caused by the job. In this case all overheads are charged to products on the basis of a single blanket recovery rate of 47.5% of direct materials, direct labour and department costs. It is extremely unlikely that such a direct method will provide an accurate basis for charging overheads eg, if higher priced higher quality material is used the amount of variable overhead may be less if, for example, less labour time is needed to work on the better quality material. The above absorption rate would result in a higher overhead charge.

Similarly it may be that direct labour rates vary in which case higher wage rates would **not** necessarily result in higher overheads being incurred whereas with this method more overhead is charged to the job.

Another weakness of the existing system is that no attempt is made to split cost between fixed and variable. With the imminent recession it will be extremely important for managers to know the variable cost of jobs so that, with increased competition, it is possible to quote lower prices which will still generate contribution. If the existing total cost plus pricing system is continued the company is likely to start losing jobs to competitors.

As shown for job no. 878 the current system is to use total cost ie, fixed cost and variable costs, as the lowest acceptable price. This is misleading since the lowest price should be as mentioned above the variable cost. This is because a price above variable cost will generate contribution which will increase profit/reduce losses. In a time of recession the firm may be forced to accept very low prices in order to win orders from customers.

A further criticism is the method for calculating the mark up of 47.5%. This is based on the actual costs for the year just ended.

$$\left( \text{ie } \frac{383,000 + 118,500 + 192,000}{1,000,000 + 460,000} \times 100 = 47.5\% \right)$$

There are several factors which will result in costs being different in the current period from the previous period:

(i)     The level of activity may be lower – this will cause average fixed overheads to increase as a proportion of direct costs.

(ii)     Inefficiency may have arisen in the previous year which is not expected to recur.

(iii)     Inflation would cause the level of costs to alter.

(iv)     Changes in production method may have occurred.

(b)     In this circumstance it would be more accurate to calculate separate production overhead recovery rates for each of the production departments ideally based on budgeted figures. Direct labour hours or machine hours would be suitable bases for recovery but the information given means direct labour hours must be used below:

| Based on last year's actual figures | *Grinding* | *Finishing* |
|---|---|---|
| *Direct labour hours* | $\dfrac{200,000}{5} = 40,000$ | $\dfrac{260,000}{6} = 43,333$ |
| *Overhead recovery rates* | | |
| $= \dfrac{\text{Overhead}}{\text{Direct labour cost}} \times 100$ | $\dfrac{175,000}{40,000}$ | $\dfrac{208,000}{43,333}$ |
| | $= £4.375 \text{ per hour}$ | $= £4.80 \text{ per hour}$ |

Administration and selling costs, as a percentage of production costs

$$\frac{118,500 + 192,000}{1,000,000 + 460,000 + 383,000} \times 100$$

$$= 16.85\%$$

$$\text{Mark up} = \frac{\text{net profit}}{\text{sales}} \times 100 \qquad = \frac{246{,}500}{2{,}400{,}000} \times 100$$

$$= 10.27\%$$

Revised estimate for job 878

|  | £ | £ |
|---|---|---|
| Direct material |  | 9,000 |
| Direct labour |  | 3,800 |
| Production overhead: |  |  |
| Grinding:      $400 \times 4.375 =$ | 1,750 |  |
| Finishing:     $300 \times 4.80 =$ | 1,440 | 3,190 |
|  |  | 15,990 |
| Admin. and selling costs |  |  |
| $16.85\% \times 15{,}990 =$ |  | 2,694 |
| Revised total cost |  | 18,684 |
| Mark up $10.27\% \times 18{,}684 =$ |  | 1,919 |
| Revised selling price |  | 20,603 |

or if based on 'preferred return'

| Cost | $83\frac{1}{3}$ |
|---|---|
| Mark up | $16\frac{2}{3}$ |
| Selling price | 100 |

$$\text{Selling price} = 18{,}684 \times \frac{100}{83\frac{1}{3}} = \pounds 22{,}421$$

(c)    The following changes should be made to improve the accounting information:

(i)    Preparation of budgets. This would include calculation of predetermined overhead recovery rates and a separation of fixed and variable costs. The latter will be needed to identify the minimum acceptable selling price for each job. This will enable adoption of a more flexible attitude to pricing (ie, not just use a margin of $16\frac{2}{3}\%$) which will be particularly important in the recession when prices may need to be determined by demand.

(ii)    When actual costs are available for each job these should be compared with budget to identify variances. These variances may indicate that current activities must be amended or that it is necessary to vary future estimates.

(iii)    It could be beneficial to obtain information about competitors eg costs, profits, quality of product and selling prices charged.

(iv)    It may be possible to establish more accurate job costs by using activity based costing.

## 13   A PRIVATE HOSPITAL

**To:**      Hospital administrator (Rep AM2)

**From:**    Cost adviser

**Date:**    23 November 19X4

**Subject:** Operational control and charging for services within the hospital

The costing system used within the hospital can have a significant effect on the control of costs and the pricing of internal hospital services.

(a)   **Operational control**

Control is achieved by the comparison of actual performance with a pre-set target. This target is often in the form of a standard or budget. The target should include both financial and non-financial items and to be of significant use should emphasise controllable items.

In order to facilitate the target setting and control process, the hospital should be divided into areas of responsibility, known as responsibility centres. Each of these would be headed by a manager who takes responsibility for that area's performance.

For managers to accept their responsibilities they must be involved in the target setting process. In this way they will feel some personal responsibility for its achievement.

The hospital is likely to provide a wide variety of surgical operations and services, and as a consequence it may be difficult to set realistic targets. This must be considered when making comparisons of actual performance. Managers will also be required to make judgements between financial and non-financial factors due to the nature of the organisation.

(b)   **Charging for services**

Charging for internal services implies that different departments are to be regarded as profit centres or investment centres.

A profit centre approach charges the manager with the responsibility for achieving a target level of profit.

An investment centre develops the profit centre approach by charging the manager with a responsibility for achieving a target level of profit relative to the level of investment in the department. This is often measured using return on capital employed or residual income.

The pricing of services will affect the profitability of the department and therefore, especially in the area of quoted work, an accurate cost recording system will be required.

Regard must also be had to the behaviour of the costs so that spare capacity may be utilised by marginal cost pricing. Care is required however to ensure that such price setting does not become long-term. This cost behaviour analysis can be used in order to identify breakeven points and activity levels for particular profits.

This shows the importance of the cost accounting system to the hospital. However it should always be remembered that the system will cause costs to be incurred. The benefits from the system should always exceed its costs.

## 14 SMALL BUSINESS

(a) Firstly costs must be attributed to departments, then the overhead absorption rates can be calculated.

**Overhead analysis sheet**

| | | Departments | | | |
|---|---|---|---|---|---|
| *Cost* | *Basis* | *P* £ | *Q* £ | *R* £ | *Total* £ |
| Repairs and maintenance | Technical estimate | 42,000 | 10,000 | 10,000 | 62,000 |
| Depreciation | Cost of plant/equipment | 17,000 | 14,000 | 9,000 | 40,000 |
| Consumable supplies | Direct labour hours | 4,500 | 2,700 | 1,800 | 9,000 |
| Wage related costs | 12.5% of direct wages | 48,250 | 26,250 | 12,500 | 87,000 |
| Indirect labour | Direct labour hours | 45,000 | 27,000 | 18,000 | 90,000 |
| Canteen/rest/smoke room | Number of direct workers | 15,000 | 9,000 | 6,000 | 30,000 |
| Business rates and insurance | Floor area | 13,000 | 10,400 | 2,600 | 26,000 |
| | | 184,750 | 99,350 | 59,900 | 344,000 |

The overhead absorption rates per direct labour hour are:

Department P $\quad \dfrac{£184,750}{50,000} \quad = \quad £3.70$

Department Q $\quad \dfrac{£99,350}{30,000} \quad = \quad £3.31$

Department R $\quad \dfrac{£59,900}{20,000} \quad = \quad £3.00$

(b)

| | | | £ | £ |
|---|---|---|---|---|
| Direct materials | | | | 800.00 |
| Direct wages | | | | |
| Dept P | $30 \times \dfrac{£386,000}{50,000} =$ | | 231.60 | |
| Dept Q | $10 \times \dfrac{£210,000}{30,000} =$ | | 70.00 | |
| Dept R | $5 \times \dfrac{£100,000}{20,000} =$ | | 25.00 | |
| | | | | 326.60 |
| Overhead | | | | |
| Dept P | $30 \times £3.70$ | | 111.00 | |
| Dept Q | $10 \times £3.31$ | | 33.10 | |
| Dept R | $5 \times £3.00$ | | 15.00 | |
| | | | | 159.10 |
| Production cost | | | | 1,285.70 |
| Selling/distribution/administration | | | | 257.14 |
| | | | | 1,542.84 |

To achieve a profit margin of 20% the selling price is:

Total cost × 100/80 = £1,542.84 × 100/80 = £1,928.55

(c)      Using the auditor's system:

|  | £ |
|---|---|
| Direct material cost | 800.00 |
| Direct labour cost | 326.60 |
| Prime cost | 1,126.60 |
| Overhead/profit (125%) | 1,408.25 |
| Selling price | 2,534.85 |

It can be seen that for this particular quotation the auditor's system results in a much higher selling price which may be unacceptable to the market.

If this job is typical of the resource mix required by many jobs, then the price *may* lead to lost sales.

## 15     MR G & MRS H

(a)

|  | Professional services £ | Vehicles £ |
|---|---|---|
| Salaries | 40,000 | |
| Car depreciation | | 6,000 $\left[\dfrac{(13,000-4,000)\times 2}{3 \text{ years}}\right]$ |
| Electricity | 1,200 | |
| Fuel | | 1,800 |
| Insurance | 600 | 800 |
| Telephone   -   mobile | 1,200 | |
| -   office | 1,800 | |
| Rent | 8,400 | |
| Postage and stationery | 500 | |
| Secretarial | 8,000 | |
| Vehicle servicing | | 1,200 |
| Road tax | | 280 |
| | 62,100 | 10,080 |
| Hours available (2 × 8 × 5 × 45) | | 3,600 |
| Administration (25%) | | (900) |
| Idle time (22.5%) | | (810) |
| Chargeable time | | 1,890 |
| Travel time (25% of 1,890) | | 472.5 hours |
| Active time (75% of 1,890) | | 1,417.5 hours |
| Effective chargeable hours (472.5 × ⅓) + 1,417.5 | | 1,575 hours |
| Rates per hour | | |
| Productive £62,100/1,575 | | £39.43 per hour |
| Travel £39.43/3 | | £13.14 per hour |

The vehicle rate per mile is £10,080/18,000 = £0.56 per mile.

(b)     The cost estimates which have already been prepared should be analysed by accounting period, and these used as a basis of comparison with actual results.

Actual costs should be analysed in accord with the expenditure headings and comparison should be made with the target each month. Any differences will need to be investigated to identify the cause.

Mr G and Mrs H should also record their number of hours, and analyse them between administration, idle time, chargeable productive time, and chargeable travel time. The number of miles should also be recorded and these compared with the target set. This will allow Mr G and Mrs H to control their revenue.

(c)     The business is providing a service which is specific to the needs of individual clients, a job costing system is therefore appropriate. ·

Each client should have their own record sheet on which is entered details of time spent, miles travelled and any specific costs.

This will ensure that each client is charged for services received and where fees have been agreed in advance, the profitability of the work can be measured.

## 16    HR CONSTRUCTION PLC

(a)

### Contract accounts

|  | A £'000 | B £'000 |  | A £'000 | B £'000 |
|---|---|---|---|---|---|
| Material sent to site | 700 | 150 | Material returned to stores | 80 | 30 |
| Plant sent to site | 1,000 | 150 | Materials transferred | 40 |  |
| Materials transferred |  | 40 | Materials on site c/d | 75 | 15 |
| Plant hire charges | 200 | 30 | Plant on site c/d (W1) | 880 | 144 |
| Labour cost incurred | 300 | 270 | Cost of work |  |  |
| Central overhead cost | 75 | 18 | Not certified c/d | 160 | 20 |
| Direct expenses incurred | 25 | 4 | Certified c/d (balance) | 1,065 | 453 |
|  | 2,300 | 662 |  | 2,300 | 662 |

### Profit calculation

|  | A £'000 | £'000 | B £'000 | £'000 |
|---|---|---|---|---|
| Contract price |  | 2,000 |  | 550 |
| Costs incurred | 1,225 |  | 473 |  |
| Estimated completion costs | 135 |  | 110 |  |
|  |  | 1,360 |  | 583 |
| Estimated contract profit/(loss) |  | 640 |  | (33) |
| Loss recognised in full |  |  |  | 33 |

### Profit earned to date

$$\frac{\text{Value certified}}{\text{Contract price}} \times £640 = \frac{1,500}{2,000} \times £640 = \textbf{480}$$

*Note:* using $\dfrac{\text{Value certified}}{\text{Contract price}}$ is more prudent than the alternative $\dfrac{\text{Costs incurred}}{\text{Total estimated costs}}$

(b)

|  | | A | | | B | |
|---|---|---|---|---|---|---|
|  | £'000 | £'000 | | £'000 | £'000 |
| Fixed assets | | | | | |
| Plant on site | | 880 | | | 144 |
| | | | | | |
| Debtors | | | | | |
| Value certified | 1,500 | | | 500 | |
| Cash received | 1,440 | | | 460 | |
| | | 60 | | | 40 |

Long-term contract balances:

|  | A | | B | |
|---|---|---|---|---|
|  | £'000 | £'000 | £'000 | £'000 |
| Value certified | 1,500 | | 500 | |
| (Profit)/Loss | (480) | | 33 | |
| Cost of sales | 1,020 | | 533 | |
| Cost incurred | 1,225 | | 473 | |
| | | 205 | | (60) |

(c)     Job, batch and contract costing are all costing methods which are used when goods/services are supplied which meet the specific requirements of the customer. They are therefore all forms of specific order costing.

Job costing is used when the cost unit is a single item. The time taken from commencement to completion of the work is short, the organisation completing a large number of such works throughout its financial year. Consequently the number and value of work in progress at the end of the financial year is small relative to the number started.

Batch costing is similar to job costing in all respects *except* that the customer is supplied with a number of identical items (instead of a single item). It is not cost efficient to treat each item in the batch as a single cost unit and thereby attempt to determine each item's individual cost. Instead the batch is regarded as the cost unit, costs are attributed to the batch, and if required, the cost of an individual item is calculated by a simple average (batch cost/number of items in the batch).

Contract costing is used where the time between commencement and completion of the work is long and may span two or more financial years. In such cases each individual contract is usually of significant value, and in order to fairly report the results of the organisation it is necessary to recognise the profit/loss of the contract before it is fully completed. It is this which distinguishes contract costing from job and batch costing.

**WORKING**

Depreciation is 12% per annum:

A: £1m × 12% = £120,000, so c/f value = £880,000.
B: £150,000 × 12% × $4/12$ = £6,000, so c/f value = £144,000.

## 17    ST HOTEL

(a)

| | Accommodation | Restaurant | Bar | Kitchen | Maintenance | General administration |
|---|---|---|---|---|---|---|
| | £ | £ | £ | £ | £ | £ |
| **Allocated costs** | | | | | | |
| Wages and salaries | | 12,000 | 9,000 | 20,000 | 18,000 | 12,000 |
| Food | | | | 96,000 | | |
| Drinks | | | 50,000 | | | |
| Maintenance materials | | | | | 3,000 | |
| Miscellaneous | | | | | | 3,000 |
| **Apportioned costs** | | | | | | |
| Rates (W1) | 18,000 | 900 | 450 | 600 | | 300 |
| Electricity (W2) | 2,000 | 400 | 320 | 4,000 | | 1,280 |
| Telephone (W2) | | | | 1,000 | | 4,000 |
| Insurance (W2) | 1,380 | 690 | 460 | 1,840 | | 230 |
| Depreciation (W2) | 2,400 | 1,200 | 800 | 3,200 | | 400 |
| Laundry (W2) | 4,050 | 450 | | | | |
| **Total costs** | 27,830 | 15,640 | 61,030 | 126,640 | 21,000 | 21,210 |
| **Service depts:** | | | | | | |
| Gen admin (W3) | 14,847 | 4,242 | | | 2,121 | (21,210) |
| Maintenance (W4) | 11,561 | 2,312 | 2,312 | 4,624 | (23,121) | 2,312 |
| Gen admin (W3) | 1,618 | 463 | | | 231 | (2,312) |
| Maintenance (W4) | 116 | 23 | 23 | 46 | (231) | 23 |
| Gen admin (W3) | 18 | 5 | | | | (23) |
| Kitchen (W5) | | 98,482 | 32,828 | (131,310) | | |
| **Total costs** | 55,990 | 121,167 | 96,193 | Nil | Nil | Nil |
| **Sales (W6)** | 588,000 | 180,000 | 134,545 | | | |
| **Profit** | 532,010 | 58,833 | 38,352 | | | |

*(Tutorial note:* the above solution uses the continuous apportionment method to attribute the service department costs to the profit centres; an alternative solution is to use simultaneous equations:

| | Accommodation | Restaurant | Bar | Kitchen | Maintenance | General administration |
|---|---|---|---|---|---|---|
| Total costs (from above) | 27,830 | 15,640 | 61,030 | 126,640 | 21,000 | 21,210 |
| **Service depts:** | | | | | | |
| Gen admin (W7) | 16,481 | 4,709 | | | 2,355 | (23,545) |
| Maintenance (W8) | 11,679 | 2,335 | 2,335 | 4,671 | (23,355) | 2,335 |
| Kitchen (W5) | | 98,483 | 32,828 | (131,311) | | |
| **Total costs** | 55,990 | 121,167 | 96,193 | Nil | Nil | Nil |

)

## WORKINGS

(W1)    The rates cost to be apportioned to each department is given by:

$$\frac{\text{Total rates cost}}{\text{Total floor area}} = \frac{£20,250}{675m^2} = £30/m^2$$

The area occupied by each department is then multiplied by $£30/m^2$.

(W2)    These costs are apportioned using the percentages given. The cost attributed to each department is the relevant percentage multiplied by the total cost.

(W3)   General administration costs are apportioned using the percentages given. This must be repeated until the cost is fully attributed to the profit centres.

(W4)   Maintenance costs are apportioned using the percentages given. This must be repeated until the cost is fully attributed to the profit centres.

(W5)   Kitchen costs are apportioned using the percentages given. This service department is apportioned last because none of its costs are attributed to other service departments.

(W6)   Sales:
Accommodation:
100 guest capacity × 70% occupancy × 40 weeks × 7 nights × £30/night = £588,000

Restaurant: 12,000 meals × £15 = £180,000

Bar:
Food and drinks cost
= (£96,000 × 25%) + £50,000
= £74,000

Gross profit is 45% of sales value, therefore cost = 55% of sales value

$$\text{Sales} = \frac{£74,000}{55\%} = £134,545$$

(W7)   Admin          =   £21,210 + 10% Maintenance
Maintenance    =   £21,000 + 10% Admin

So Admin       =   £21,210 + 10% (£21,000 + 10% Admin)
               =   £21,210 + £2,100 + 1% Admin

99% Admin  =   £23,310
Admin      =   £23,545

This value of £23,545 is then apportioned using the percentages given (subject to roundings)

(W8)   By substitution:

Maintenance    =   £21,000 + 10% Admin
               =   £21,000 + 10% of £23,545
               =   £21,000 + £2,355
               =   £23,355

This value is then apportioned using the percentages given (subject to roundings).

(b)   (i)   Cost per guest night   =   $\dfrac{\text{Total accommodation cost}}{\text{Number of guest nights}}$

=   $\dfrac{£55,990}{100 \times 70\% \times 40 \times 7}$

=   £2.86

(ii)   Restaurant overhead cost  =   Total cost – Food cost
=   £121,167 – (75% × £96,000)
=   £121,167 – £72,000
=   £49,167

Number of meals   =   12,000

Overhead cost per meal    =    $\dfrac{£49,167}{12,000} = £4.10$

(iii)    Bar overhead cost    =    Total cost − Drink cost − Food cost

   =    £96,193 − £50,000 − (25% × £96,000)

   =    £96,193 − £50,000 − £24,000

   =    £22,193

Bar sales    =    £134,545

Overhead cost %    =    $\dfrac{£22,193}{£134,545} = 16.5\%$

(c)    The profit statement shows the budgeted costs, revenues and profit to be earned during the year ended 31 December 1997. This provides management with guidelines as to the prices to be charged to customers and guests and identifies those areas of the hotel which are more profitable than others.

As a budget it provides the basis against which actual costs and revenues may be compared, thus enabling management to use budgetary control as part of their management of the hotel.

## 18    PZ PLC

(a)    (i)    All four works orders straddle PZ plc's financial year end of 30 April, but this does not automatically mean that they are all to be treated as long-term contracts.

A long-term contract is work of a substantial value for a relatively long period of time, thus works order number 488 being of significant value and of over twelve months duration should be treated as a long term contract.

Works order number 517 is also of significant value even though it is only of six months duration. On the basis of its value it should be treated as a long-term contract.

Works orders numbered 518 and 519 are of only 6 - 7 weeks duration, and are of much lesser value. These should both be treated as jobs in job costing.

(ii)

| Works order | 488 | 517 | 518 | 519 |
|---|---|---|---|---|
|  | £'000 | £'000 | £'000 | £'000 |
| Costs incurred: |  |  |  |  |
| Direct costs | 191 | 17 | 9 | 4 |
| Indirect costs (40% of direct labour) | 42 | 4 | 2 | 0.8 |
|  | 233 | 21 | 11 | 4.8 |
| Completion costs: |  |  |  |  |
| Direct costs | 50 | 75 | n/a | n/a |
| Indirect costs (40% of direct labour) | 16 | 24 | n/a | n/a |
| Total estimated costs | 299 | 120 | n/a | n/a |
| Contract price | 450 | 135 |  |  |
| Estimated profit | 151 | 15 |  |  |
| Profit earned to date (W1) | 117 | n/a | n/a | n/a |
| Turnover | 350 |  |  |  |
| Profit to date | 117 |  |  |  |
| Cost of sales | 233 | n/a | n/a | n/a |

| | | | | |
|---|---|---|---|---|
| Cost incurred | 233 | 21 | 11 | 4.8 |
| Cost of sales | (233) | - | - | - |
| Work in progress | Nil | 21 | 11 | 4.8 |

(iii)     The attribution of overhead costs to works orders on the basis of direct labour cost is an application of absorption costing. The use of direct labour cost is one alternative method of measuring activity.

However, there are a number of matters which should be considered. The use of labour cost instead of labour hours implies that the amount of overhead cost incurred is determined by the labour cost. Whilst this may be true of certain overhead costs it is more common for such overhead costs to be incurred in relation to time and in such circumstances a rate per labour hour may be more appropriate. Furthermore the use of a single basis of absorption takes a simplistic view of reality. Although a single absorption basis is easy to operate from an accounting sense its use assumes that there is only one cause of overhead costs.

In reality there are often many causes of overhead cots, and to this extent a system of Activity Based Costing (ABC) attempts to recognise these causes and the costs they incur by using many cost driver rates to attribute overhead costs to cost units.

Finally, it is surprising that PZ plc seems to be attributing all of its overhead costs to works orders on the arbitrary basis of absorption rates. One of the features of contracting work is that expenses can often be specifically identified with a particular contract. If PZ plc sought to do this it would cause their costing of individual works orders to be more accurate.

(b)     Process costing is a system of cost accounting used when a continuous operation of a series of processes produce a homogenous product.

It is usual for the output of a process to be the input to a subsequent process until the finished product is derived and put into stock from which it is sold to the customer.

Typically the method of manufacture involves the mixing of raw materials and this often gives rise to a chemical reaction such that the output from a process is less than the combined weight or volume of its inputs. Since this is a usual effect of the manufacturing process and is therefore expected it is referred to as a normal loss. No value is attributed to normal losses unless they have a scrap value when this is used.

At the end of each accounting period the output is measured and the extent of the actual loss is determined. In order to measure the total volume of output any partially completed items are converted into an equivalent number of completed items by assessing their degree of completion.

If the actual loss is more than expected the excess is referred to as an abnormal loss; if the actual loss is less than expected the shortfall is referred to as an abnormal gain. Abnormal losses and gains are valued at the same rate per unit as good output. and the total value identified for management control purposes in the periodic profit and loss statement.

The choice between process costing and specific order costing lies chiefly in the nature of the item being manufactured and its method of manufacture. Specific order costing is designed for use when the item being made is specific to the needs of the customer.

In contrast process costing is used for continuous production systems where the items produced are not customer specific. They form a limited range of products made by the organisation and sold, from stock, to many customers. It is not economic to measure the costs of each individual unit produced, instead an average cost per unit is determined based on the periodic cost and output levels achieved.

**WORKINGS**

W1

W.O 488        Degree of completion is measured by:

$$\frac{\text{Value certified}}{\text{Contract price}} = \frac{350}{450}$$

This proportion is used to determine the profit earned to date:

$$\frac{350}{450} \times £151{,}000 = £117{,}000 \text{ (rounded)}$$

W.O 517    The work is less than 50% complete, so company policy is not to recognise any profit this year.

## 19    ABC CONSULTING LTD

(a)

### Uncompleted projects

| | £ | | £ |
|---|---|---|---|
| Balance b/f | 16,425 | Project costs invoiced: | |
| Creditors control | 1,350 | Consultancy hours | 25,875 |
| Motoring costs | 1,791 | Mileage | 2,355 |
| Consultancy hours | 21,825 | Disbursements | 939 |
| Administration | 7,275 | Administration | 8,625 |

### Debtors' control

| | £ | | £ |
|---|---|---|---|
| Balance b/f | 15,800 | Bank | 14,120 |
| Fees invoiced | 49,883 | | |

### Creditors' control

| | £ | | £ |
|---|---|---|---|
| Bank | 32,870 | Balance b/f | 1,400 |
| | | Consultants salary | 22,200 |
| | | Travel costs – motor | 2,100 |
| | | Project WIP | 1,350 |
| | | Administration overhead | 6,900 |

### Travel Costs – Motor control

| | £ | | £ |
|---|---|---|---|
| Creditors control | 2,100 | WIP – mileage | 1,791 |

### Consultants salary cost control

| | £ | | £ |
|---|---|---|---|
| Creditors control | 22,200 | WIP – Consultancy hours | 21,825 |

### Administration overhead control

| | £ | | £ |
|---|---|---|---|
| Creditors control | 6,900 | Uncompleted projects | 7,275 |

### Fees invoiced

| | £ | | £ |
|---|---|---|---|
| | | Debtors control | 49,883 |

### Project costs invoiced

| | £ | | £ |
|---|---|---|---|
| Uncompleted projects | 37,794 | | |

(b)

**Profit/loss statement**
**April 1999**

|  | £ | £ |
|---|---|---|
| Fees invoiced |  | 49,883 |
| Project cost of sales |  | (37,794) |
|  |  | 12,089 |
| Costs under/(over) recovered: |  |  |
| Travel | 309 |  |
| Salary | 375 |  |
| Administration | (375) |  |
|  |  | (309) |
| Profit |  | 11,780 |

(c)     There are three main forms of specific order costing. Each of them may be used on a marginal costing basis though absorption costing is more commonly applied so that any work in progress is valued in accordance with SSAP 9 for financial reporting.

The three methods are:

Job costing;
Batch costing; and
Contract costing

Job costing is used where each item is unique, like the projects undertaken by ABC Consulting Ltd. Each job is of a relatively short duration and the number of uncompleted jobs is small compared to the total number of jobs undertaken.

Batch costing is used where a number of identical items are made. Motor manufacturers use batch costing. Costs are collected for a batch and an average cost per unit calculated.

Contract costing is similar to job costing except that a contract is must larger than a job and takes much longer to complete. Often contracts span more than one financial period. When this occurs profit must be measured on uncompleted contracts in order to present a true and fair view of the state of the business.

# 20    SEQUENTIAL PROCESSES

(a)

**Process I**

|  | Units | £ |  | Units | £ |
|---|---|---|---|---|---|
| Direct materials | 10,000 | 20,000 | Normal loss (W2) | 1,000 | 1,000 |
| Direct materials |  | 6,000 | Output (W4) | 8,800 | 52,800 |
| Direct wages |  | 5,000 | Abnormal loss (W3) | 200 | 1,200 |
| Direct expenses |  | 4,000 |  |  |  |
| Production ohd (W1) |  | 20,000 |  |  |  |
|  | 10,000 | 55,000 |  | 10,000 | 55,000 |

### Process II

| | Units | £ | | Units | £ |
|---|---|---|---|---|---|
| Process 1 | 8,800 | 52,800 | Normal loss (W5) | 440 | 1,320 |
| Direct materials | | 12,640 | Output (W7) | 8,400 | 100,800 |
| Direct wages | | 6,000 | | | |
| Direct expenses | | 6,200 | | | |
| Production ohd (W1) | | 24,000 | | | |
| Abnormal gain (W6) | 40 | 480 | | | |
| | 8,840 | 102,120 | | 8,840 | 102,120 |

### Process III

| | Units | £ | | Units | £ |
|---|---|---|---|---|---|
| Process II | 8,400 | 100,800 | Normal loss (W8) | 840 | 4,200 |
| Direct materials | | 23,200 | Output (W10) | 7,000 | 168,000 |
| Direct wages | | 10,000 | By product (W11) | 420 | 2,520 |
| Direct expenses | | 4,080 | Abnormal loss (W9) | 140 | 3,360 |
| Production ohd (W1) | | 40,000 | | | |
| | 8,400 | 178,080 | | 8,400 | 178,080 |

WORKINGS

(W1)   The overhead absorption rate as a percentage of direct wages is given by:

$$\frac{\text{Budgeted production overhead}}{\text{Direct wages}} \times 100 = \frac{£84,000}{£21,000} \times 100$$

= 400%

Thus the amount of production overhead absorbed into each of processes I-III is:

| Process I | £5,000 × 400% | = £20,000 |
|---|---|---|
| Process II | £6,000 × 400% | = £24,000 |
| Process III | £10,000 × 400% | = £40,000 |

(W2)   The normal loss in process I is 10% of the input quantity:

Input quantity = 10,000 units, therefore the normal loss is 10,000 × 10% = 1,000 units. Each of these units has a scrap value of £1 so the value of the normal loss to be credited to process I is £1,000.

(W3)   The quantity of the abnormal loss is found by balancing the units column in the process account. The abnormal loss is the balancing figure.

It is valued at the same rate per unit as good output. In this question there is no work in progress so the cost per unit can be found by using the short cut method:

$$\frac{\text{(Process I costs incurred - Scrap value of the normal loss)}}{\text{Expected output of process I}}$$

The expected output is equal to the input quantity less the allowance for normal loss, thus in process I it is:

10,000 units – 1,000 units of normal loss = 9,000 units.

The sum of the costs incurred = £55,000, and we have seen above that the scrap value of the normal loss is £1,000 (W2).

Thus the cost per unit to be used to value the abnormal loss and good units is:

$$\frac{£55,000 - £1,000}{9,000} = £6 \text{ per unit.}$$

The value of the abnormal loss is thus:

$$200 \text{ units} \times £6 = £1,200.$$

(W4)  The value of the output which is transferred to process II is:

$$8,800 \text{ units} \times £6 = £52,800.$$

(W5)  The normal loss in process II is 5% of the input quantity:

Input quantity = 8,800 units, therefore the normal loss is 8,800 × 5% = 440 units. Each of these units has a scrap value of £3 so the value of the normal loss to be credited to process II is £1,320.

(W6)  The quantity of the abnormal gain is found by balancing the units column in the process account. The abnormal gain is the balancing figure.

It is valued at the same rate per unit as good output. In this question there is no work in progress so the cost per unit can be found by using the short cut method:

$$\frac{(\text{Process II costs incurred - Scrap value of the normal loss})}{\text{Expected output of process II}}$$

The expected output is equal to the input quantity less the allowance for normal loss, thus in process II it is:

$$8,800 \text{ units} - 440 \text{ units of normal loss} = 8,360 \text{ units.}$$

The sum of the costs incurred = £101,640, and we have seen above that the scrap value of the normal loss is £1,320 (W5).

Thus the cost per unit to be used to value the abnormal loss and good units is:

$$\frac{£101,640 - £1,320}{8,360} = £12 \text{ per unit.}$$

The value of the abnormal gain is thus:

$$40 \text{ units} \times £12 = £480$$

(W7)  The value of the output which is transferred to process II is:

$$8,400 \text{ units} \times £12 = £100,800$$

(W8)  The normal loss in process III is 10% of the input quantity:

Input quantity = 8,400 units, therefore the normal loss is 8,400 × 10% = 840 units. Each of these units has a scrap value of £5 so the value of the normal loss to be credited to process III is £4,200.

(W9)  The quantity of the abnormal gain is found by balancing the units column in the process account. The abnormal gain is the balancing figure.

It is valued at the same rate per unit as good output. In this question there is no work in progress so the cost per unit can be found by using the short cut method, but because there is a by-product in this process the formula used above must be modified to:

$$\frac{\text{Process III costs incurred - Scrap value of normal loss - value of by-product}}{\text{Expected output of process III}}$$

The expected output is equal to the input quantity less the allowance for normal loss and the amount of the by-product, thus in process III it is:

8,400 units – 840 units of normal loss – 420 units of the by-product = 7,140 units.

The sum of the costs incurred = £178,080, and we have seen above that the scrap value of the normal loss is £4,200 (W8).

The value of the by-product is shown in (W11) (below) to be £2,520.

Thus the cost per unit to be used to value the abnormal loss and good units is:

$$\frac{£178,080 - £4,200 - £2,520}{7,140} = £24 \text{ per unit.}$$

The value of the abnormal loss is thus:

140 units × £24 = £3,360.

(W10)   The value of the output which is transferred to finished goods is:

7,000 units × £24 = £168,000

(W11)   The value of the by-product to be credited to the process account is that which equals the saleable value of the by-product less any further costs to be incurred in selling the by-product.

Thus the value to be used is:

| | |
|---|---:|
| selling price | £9 |
| less:  further processing | (2) |
| selling/distribution | (1) |
| | £6 |

(b)

**Process BP**

| | £ | | £ |
|---|---:|---|---:|
| Process III | 2,520 | Bank (sale proceeds) | 3,780 |
| Further processing costs | 840 | | |
| Selling/Distribution | 420 | | |
| | 3,780 | | 3,780 |

Note these values are obtained by multiplying the value in (W11) (above) by 420 units of BP.

(c)     (i)

**Abnormal loss**

| | £ | | £ |
|---|---:|---|---:|
| Process I (W12) | 1,200 | Normal loss process I | 200 |
| Process III (W12) | 3,360 | Normal loss process III | 700 |
| | | P&L a/c (W19) | 3,660 |
| | 4,560 | | 4,560 |

(ii)

### Abnormal gain

|  | £ |  | £ |
|---|---|---|---|
| Normal loss process II | 120 | Process II (W12) | 480 |
| P&L a/c (W19) | 360 |  |  |
|  | —— |  | —— |
|  | 480 |  | 480 |
|  | —— |  | —— |

(W12)    The first step is to complete the double entry to the respective entries in the process accounts.

(W13)    The normal loss accounts relating to each process are as follows:

### Normal loss - Process I

|  | £ |  | £ |
|---|---|---|---|
| Process I (W14) | 1,000 | Bank (W15) | 1,200 |
| Abnormal loss (W18) | 200 |  |  |
|  | —— |  | —— |
|  | 1,200 |  | 1,200 |
|  | —— |  | —— |

### Normal loss - Process II

|  | £ |  | £ |
|---|---|---|---|
| Process II (W14) | 1,320 | Bank (W16) | 1,200 |
|  |  | Abnormal gain (W18) | 120 |
|  | —— |  | —— |
|  | 1,320 |  | 1,320 |
|  | —— |  | —— |

### Normal loss - Process III

|  | £ |  | £ |
|---|---|---|---|
| Process III (W14) | 4,200 | Bank (W17) | 4,900 |
| Abnormal loss (W18) | 700 |  |  |
|  | —— |  | —— |
|  | 4,900 |  | 4,900 |
|  | —— |  | —— |

(W14)    These entries complete the double entry to the respective process accounts.

(W15)    This is the total sales value of the actual loss which arose:

        It is calculated by:        Normal loss        1,000 units

                                    Abnormal loss       200 units

                                                          ——

                                        1,200 units × £1

(W16)    This is the total sales value of the actual loss which arose:

        It is calculated by:        Normal loss        440 units

                                      Abnormal gain     (40) units

                                                            ——

                                        400 units × £3

(W17)    This is the total sales value of the actual loss which arose:

        It is calculated by:        Normal loss        840 units

                                      Abnormal loss       140 units

                                                          ——

                                        980 units × £5

(W18)   These are balancing entries which are transferred to the corresponding abnormal loss/gain accounts. The easiest way to remember this is that there is NEVER a transfer from a NORMAL loss account to the profit and loss account.

(W19)   These are balancing entries to transfer the net cost (abnormal losses) or net benefit (abnormal gain) to the profit and loss account.

## 21    QR LTD

(a)    Net sales value = Final sales value – further processing costs

| Product | Net sales value £'000 | | | Share of joint costs | £'000 |
|---|---|---|---|---|---|
| Q | 768 – 160 | = | 608 | 608/976 × 732,000 = | 456 |
| R | 232 – 128 | = | 104 | 104/976 × 732,000 = | 78 |
| S | 32 – 0 | = | 32 | 32/976 × 732,000 = | 24 |
| T | 240 – 8 | = | 232 | 232/976 × 732,000 = | 174 |
| | | | 976 | | 732 |

### Budgeted profit statement

| | Product Q £'000 | Product R £'000 | Product S £'000 | Product T £'000 | Total £'000 |
|---|---|---|---|---|---|
| Sales | 768 | 232 | 32 | 240 | 1,272 |
| Pre-separation point costs | (456) | (78) | (24) | (174) | (732) |
| Further processing costs | (160) | (128) | - | (8) | (296) |
| Profit | 152 | 26 | 8 | 58 | 244 |

(b)

| | Product Q £'000 | Product R £'000 | Product S £'000 | Product T £'000 | Total £'000 |
|---|---|---|---|---|---|
| Sales | 512 | 144 | 32 | 180 | 868 |
| Pre-separation point costs | (456) | (78) | (24) | (174) | (732) |
| | 56 | 66 | 8 | 6 | 136 |

(c)    Further processing product Q increases profit by £96,000 (152,000 – 56,000).

Further processing product R actually reduces profit by £40,000 (26,000 – 66,000)

Further processing product T increases profit by £52,000 (58,000 – 6,000).

Product R should therefore not be further processed. This will result in the profit shown in part (a) + £40,000 = £244,000 + 40,000 = £284,000.

---

## 22　　BK CHEMICALS

(a)　(i)

|  |  | B £ | K £ | Product C £ | Total £ |
|---|---|---|---|---|---|
| Sales |  | 35,000 | 50,000 | 60,000 | 145,000 |
| Costs |  |  |  |  |  |
|  | Pre separation (W1) | 17,500 | 12,500 | 10,000 | 40,000 |
|  | Post separation | 20,000 | 10,000 | 22,500 | 52,500 |
| Profit/(loss) |  | (2,500) | 27,500 | 27,500 | 52,500 |

(ii)　The incremental revenues arising from further processing should be compared with the incremental costs of the further processing, ie, the post separation costs.

|  | Product B £ | Product K £ | Product C £ |
|---|---|---|---|
| Selling price after further processing (per litre) | 10 | 20 | 30 |
| Selling price at split-off point (per litre) | 6 | 8 | 9 |
| Incremental revenue (per litre) | 4 | 12 | 21 |
| × number of litres | × 3,500 | × 2,500 | × 2,000 |
| Incremental revenue (in total) | 14,000 | 30,000 | 42,000 |
| Incremental cost | 20,000 | 10,000 | 22,500 |
| Incremental profit | (6,000) | 20,000 | 19,500 |

Products K and C should be further processed. Product B should not. Further processing product B costs £6,000.

|  |  | B £ | K £ | Product C £ | Total £ |
|---|---|---|---|---|---|
| Sales |  | 21,000 | 50,000 | 60,000 | 131,000 |
| Costs |  |  |  |  |  |
|  | Pre separation (W1) | 17,500 | 12,500 | 10,000 | 40,000 |
|  | Post separation |  | 10,000 | 22,500 | 32,500 |
| Profit/(loss) |  | 3,500 | 27,500 | 27,500 | 58,500 |

(b)　(i)　The account of the common process would be debited with the costs incurred and credited with the sales value at split off of the output achieved. This transfer price would then be debited to the subsequent process / finished goods as appropriate and the profit arising in the process account would be transferred directly to the profit and loss account.

(ii)　Resulting profit

= (3,500 × £6) + (2,500 × £8) + (2,000 × £9) – £40,000
= £19,000

(iii)　The profit centre accounts can be used to appraise management performance more fairly because the transfer value is independent of another process's costs efficiency or inefficiency.

The processes can be evaluated to see if they are worthwhile because the profit or loss will be consistent with the incremental cost and revenue basis of decision making.

(c) (i) Any apportionment of joint costs is arbitrary and consequently any information provided which incorporates such apportionments is of doubtful value. Planning implies long term decision making or strategy, where this is based on unreliable information it may prove to be incorrect.

(ii) Control of costs is commonly thought of as being the comparison of actual and target costs. Where some of the costs are arbitrarily apportioned (as actual costs or within the target), it is because they cannot be directly attributed to the activity concerned. Thus the costs cannot be changed directly by the manager of the activity and cannot be controlled in this way.

(iii) Decisions can never be reliably made on the basis of apportioned costs because they do not relate to activities or the use of resources.

WORKING

(W1) $\dfrac{£40,000}{\text{Total output}} = \dfrac{£40,000}{(3,500+2,500+2,000)} = £5/\text{litre}$

# 23    CHEMICAL COMPOUND

(i)    **Process A**

$$\text{Cost/kg} = \frac{\text{Total costs - scrap value of normal loss}}{\text{Expected output}}$$

Total costs

| | £ |
|---|---|
| Direct material (2,000kg @ £5/kg) | 10,000 |
| Direct labour | 7,200 |
| Process plant time (140hrs @ £60/hr) | 8,400 |
| Departmental overhead (60% × £7,200) (W1) | 4,320 |
| | 29,920 |
| Scrap value of normal loss (20% × 2,000kg × £0.50/kg) | 200 |
| | 29,720 |

$$\text{Cost/kg} = \frac{£29,720}{2,000\text{kg} \times 80\%} = £18.575/\text{kg}$$

**Process A**

| | Kg | £ | | Kg | £ |
|---|---|---|---|---|---|
| Direct material | 2,000 | 10,000 | Normal loss | 400 | 200 |
| Direct labour | | 7,200 | Process B | 1,400 | 26,005 |
| Process plant hire | | 8,400 | Abnormal loss | 200 | 3,715 |
| Departmental overhead | | 4,320 | | | |
| | 2,000 | 29,920 | | 2,000 | 29,920 |

(ii)    **Process B**

Total costs

| | £ |
|---|---|
| Transfer from process A | 26,005 |
| Direct material (1,400kg @ £12/kg) | 16,800 |
| Direct labour | 4,200 |
| Process plant time (80hrs @ £72.50/hr) | 5,800 |

|  | Departmental overhead (60% × £4,200) | 2,520 |
|---|---|---|
|  |  | 55,325 |
|  | Scrap value of normal loss (2,800kg × 10% × £1.825) | (511) |
|  |  | 54,814 |

$$\text{Cost/kg} = \frac{54,814}{2,800\text{kg} \times 90\%} = £21.751587$$

### Process B

|  | Kg | £ |  | Kg | £ |
|---|---|---|---|---|---|
| Process A | 1,400 | 26,005 | Normal loss | 280 | 511 |
| Direct material | 1,400 | 16,800 | Finished goods | 2,620 | 56,989 |
| Direct labour |  | 4,200 |  |  |  |
| Process plant time |  | 5,800 |  |  |  |
| Departmental overhead |  | 2,520 |  |  |  |
| Abnormal gain | 100 | 2,175 |  |  |  |
|  | 2,900 | 57,500 |  | 2,900 | 57,500 |

(iii)
### Normal loss/gain

|  | Kg | £ |  | Kg | £ |
|---|---|---|---|---|---|
| Process A | 400 | 200 | Abnormal gain - B | 100 | 182.5 |
| Abnormal loss - A | 200 | 100 | Bank (Bal) | 780 | 628.5 |
| Process B | 280 | 511 |  |  |  |
|  | 880 | 811 |  | 880 | 811 |

(iv)
### Abnormal loss/gain

|  | Kg | £ |  | Kg | £ |
|---|---|---|---|---|---|
| Process A | 200 | 3,715 | Normal loss/gain | 200 | 100 |
| Normal loss/gain | 100 | 182.5 | Process B | 100 | 2,175 |
|  |  |  | P&L a/c (Bal fig) |  | 1,622.5 |
|  | 300 | 3,897.5 |  | 300 | 3,897.5 |

(v)
### Finished goods

|  | £ |  | £ |
|---|---|---|---|
| Process B | 56,989 |  |  |

(vi)
### Profit and Loss account (Extract)

|  | £ |  | £ |
|---|---|---|---|
| Abnormal loss/gain | 1,622.5 |  |  |

WORKINGS

(W1)  Departmental overhead absorption rate

$$= \frac{£6,840}{£7,200 + £4,200} = 60\% \text{ of direct labour cost}$$

## 24    PRODUCT COSTS

(a)    The statement identifies the fundamental problem of cost attribution in joint product processing. Beyond the separation point one should ignore any pre-separation costs. The decision concerning any processing prior to this separation should consider the value of output at the separation point and the costs of processing to that point. Due regard must then be given to the benefits arising from the most profitable further processing option on an opportunity cost basis for subsidising the pre-separation decision.

Two methods are based on:

(i)     Weight of output
(ii)    Sales value at separation point.

(b)

### Process 1

|  | Units | £ |  | | Units | £ |
|---|---|---|---|---|---|---|
| Raw material | 3,000 | 15,000 | Normal loss (W1) | | 300 | 600 |
| Additional components | | 1,000 | Output        (W2) | | 2,800 | 33,600 |
| Direct wages | | 4,000 | | | | |
| Direct expenses | | 10,000 | | | | |
| Production overhead | | 3,000 | | | | |
| Abnormal gain (W2) | 100 | 1,200 | | | | |
| | 3,100 | 34,200 | | | 3,100 | 34,200 |

### Process 2

|  | Units | £ |  | | Units | £ |
|---|---|---|---|---|---|---|
| Process 1 | 2,800 | 33,600 | Normal loss (W3) | | 140 | 700 |
| Additional components | | 780 | Output        (W4) | | 2,600 | 59,800 |
| Direct wages | | 6,000 | Abnormal loss (W4) | | 60 | 1,380 |
| Direct expenses | | 14,000 | | | | |
| Production overhead | | 7,500 | | | | |
| | 2,800 | 61,880 | | | 2,800 | 61,880 |

### Finished goods

|  | £ |  | £ |
|---|---|---|---|
| Balance b/d | 20,000 | Cost of sales (W5) | 56,800 |
| Process 2 | 59,800 | Balance c/d | 23,000 |
| | 79,800 | | 79,800 |

### Normal loss

|  | £ |  | £ |
|---|---|---|---|
| Process 1 | 600 | Cash (W6) | 400 |
| | | Abnormal gain (W7) | 200 |
| | 600 | | 600 |
| Process 2 | 700 | Cash (W8) | 1,000 |
| Abnormal loss (W9) | 300 | | |
| | | | 1,000 |
| | 1,000 | | |

**Abnormal loss**

|  | £ |  | £ |
|---|---|---|---|
| Process 2 | 1,380 | Normal loss | 300 |
|  |  | P&L a/c (W10) | 1,080 |
|  | 1,380 |  | 1,380 |

**Abnormal gain**

|  | £ |  | £ |
|---|---|---|---|
| Normal loss | 200 | Process 1 | 1,200 |
| P&L a/c (W10) | 1,000 |  |  |
|  | 1,200 |  | 1,200 |

**Profit and loss extracts**

|  | £ |  | £ |
|---|---|---|---|
| Abnormal loss | 1,080 | Abnormal gain | 1,000 |

WORKINGS

(W1)   $300 \times £2 = £600$

(W2)   $\dfrac{\text{(Total cost - scrap value of normal loss)}}{\text{Expected output}}$

$= \dfrac{3,000 \times 5 + 1,000 + 4,000 + 10,000 + 3,000 - (300 \times 2)}{3,000 - 300}$

$= \dfrac{£32,400}{2,700} = £12$

| Output | $2,800 \times £12$ | = | £33,600 |
|---|---|---|---|
| Abnormal gain | $100 \times £12$ | = | £1,200 |

(W3)   $140 \times £5 = £700$

(W4)   $\dfrac{\text{(Total cost - scrap value of normal loss)}}{\text{Expected output}}$

$= \dfrac{33,600 + 780 + 6,000 + 14,000 + 7,500 - (140 \times 5)}{2,800 - 140}$

$= £23$

| Output | $2,600 \times £23$ | = | £59,800 |
|---|---|---|---|
| Abnormal loss | $60 \times £23$ | = | £1,380 |

(W5)   Balancing figure

(W6)   Actual loss of      $200 \times £2$      =      £400

(W7)   Balancing figure

(W8)   Actual loss of      $200 \times £5$      =      £1,000

(W9)   Balancing figure

(W10)  Balancing figures

## 25     PQR LTD

*(Tutorial note:*

Process costing questions follow a common requirement to which the following series of steps should be used:

**Step 1**   Draw up the process account and enter the input quantities.

**Step 2**   Calculate the normal loss/waste quantity and enter this and the other output quantities.

**Step 3**   Balance off the quantity columns of the process account to determine the quantity of any abnormal gain or loss.

**Step 4**   Enter the input values and calculate the cost per unit (using an equivalent units table if necessary).

**Step 5**   Value the good units of output and any abnormal losses/gains.*)*

Using this series of steps the main process account is:

(a)

**Main process**

|  | kg | £ |  | kg | £ |
|---|---|---|---|---|---|
| Material input | 10,000 | 15,000 | Normal toxic waste (W1) | 500 | - |
| Direct labour |  | 10,000 | Product P (W5) | 4,800 | 16,390 |
| Variable overhead |  | 4,000 | Product Q (W5) | 3,600 | 17,210 |
| Fixed overhead |  | 6,000 | Product R (W3) | 1,000 | 1,750 |
| Normal disposal cost (W2) |  | 750 | Abnormal toxic waste | 100 | 400 |
|  | 10,000 | 35,750 |  | 10,000 | 35,750 |

(b)

**Normal toxic waste**

|  | £ |  | £ |
|---|---|---|---|
| Disposal cost (600 kg × £1.50) | 900 | Main process | 750 |
|  |  | Abnormal toxic waste | 150 |
|  | 900 |  | 900 |

**Abnormal toxic waste**

|  | £ |  | £ |
|---|---|---|---|
| Normal toxic waste | 150 | Profit and loss | 550 |
| Main process | 400 |  |  |
|  | 550 |  | 550 |

**Process 2**

|  | kg | £ |  | kg | £ |
|---|---|---|---|---|---|
| Main process | 3,600 | 17,210 | Output - Q2 (W6) | 3,300 | 26,465 |
| Fixed costs |  | 6,000 | Closing WIP (W6) | 300 | 1,920 |
| Variable costs |  | 5,175 |  |  |  |
|  | 3,600 | 28,385 |  | 3,600 | 28,385 |

(c)    The apportionment of common costs between joint products is necessary for financial accounting stock valuation, but is arbitrary and therefore is of very limited use in management accounting.

PQR Ltd uses final sales value as the basis of apportionment. This does not consider the fact that product P is sold at the point of separation and that product Q is further processed before being sold. It would seem therefore that a more equitable basis of apportionment would be to use the products' relative sales values at the point of separation. For product Q this can be calculated by deducting the further processing costs per unit of Q from its final selling price and multiplying this net value/unit by the output quantity of the main process.

(d)    Incremental revenue = £7.00/kg – £4.30/kg                    = £2.70/kg

Incremental variable cost                                         = £1.50/kg

Incremental contribution                                          = £1.20/kg

Incremental fixed costs = £6,000 × 60%                            = £3,600

Further processing breakeven volume

$$= \frac{£3,600}{£1.20} = 3,000 \text{ kg}$$

Provided the average monthly volume of Q to be processed into Q2 is at least 3,000 kg then further processing is worthwhile.

*Note:* The common costs of the main process and the unavoidable fixed further processing costs are sunk costs and therefore irrelevant to the further processing decision.

WORKINGS

(W1)    50/1,000 × 10,000 = 500 kg

(W2)    Normal waste of 500 kg @ £1.50/kg = £750

(W3)    By-product R has a value of £1.75/kg = 1,000 kg × £1.75 = £1,750

(W4)    Cost per unit

*Note:* There is no opening or closing work in process and the waste is deemed 100% complete so an equivalent units table is **NOT** required:

$$\text{Cost per unit} = \frac{\text{Input costs} + \text{Disposal cost of normal toxic waste} - \text{Sale proceeds of By-product R}}{\text{Expected output of joint products P and Q}}$$

$$= \frac{(£35,000 + £750 - £1,750)}{(850/1,000 \times 10,000)}$$

$$= £4/\text{kg}$$

The £4/kg is used to value the abnormal toxic waste and to calculate the total joint cost attributable to the joint products P and Q.

(W5)    The joint cost is (4,800 kg + 3,600 kg) × £4/kg

= 8,400 kg × £4/kg

= £33,600

This apportioned between P and Q on the basis of their **final** sales values:

| Final Sales | | Value £ | Cost £ |
|---|---|---|---|
| P | 4,800 kg × £5/kg = | 24,000 | 16,390 |
| Q | 3,600 kg × £7/kg = | 25,200 | 17,210 |
| | | 49,200 | 33,600 |

(W6)    Since there is closing WIP an equivalent units table is required:

| | Total | Main Process % | eu | Conversion % | eu |
|---|---|---|---|---|---|
| Output - Q2 | 3,300 | 100 | 3,300 | 100 | 3,300 |
| Closing WIP | 300 | 100 | 300 | 50 | 150 |
| | | | 3,600 | | 3,450 |
| Costs | | | £17,210 | | £11,175 |
| £/eu | | | £4.78 | | £3.24 |

Output    =    3,300 kg × (£4.78 + £3.24)
           =    £26,465

Closing WIP    =    (300 kg × £4.78) + (150 kg × £3.24)
                =    £1,920

# 26    ABC LTD

(a)

### Process 1

| | Kg | £ | | Kg | £ |
|---|---|---|---|---|---|
| Material W | 10,500 | 4,960 | Process 2 (W1) | 13,100 | 55,960 |
| Material X | 7,200 | 14,700 | Closing WIP (W1) | 2,000 | 5,553 |
| Direct wages | | 17,160 | Normal loss (W3) | 2,355 | - |
| Prod'n overhead | | 25,740 | Abnormal loss (W1) | 245 | 1,047 |
| | 17,700 | 62,560 | | 17,700 | 62,560 |

### Process 2

| | Kg | £ | | Kg | £ |
|---|---|---|---|---|---|
| Process 1 13,100 | 55,960 | | Finished Goods (W2) | 20,545 | 106,614 |
| Material Y | 4,050 | 15,600 | Closing WIP (W2) | 1,500 | 6,558 |
| Opening WIP | 8,400 | 21,520 | Normal loss (W3) | 2,405 | - |
| Direct labour | | 8,600 | Abnormal loss (W2) | 1,100 | 5,708 |
| Prod'n overhead | | 17,200 | | | |
| | 25,550 | 118,880 | | 25,550 | 118,880 |

(b)

### Raw material control

| | £ | | £ |
|---|---|---|---|
| Balance b/f | 15,400 | Work in progress | 35,260 |
| Purchases | 46,260 | Production overhead | 1,450 |
| | | Balance c/f | 24,950 |
| | 61,660 | | 61,660 |

### Work-in-progress control

| | £ | | £ |
|---|---|---|---|
| Balance b/f | 21,520 | Finished goods | 106,614 |
| Raw materials | 35,260 | Abnormal loss | 6,755 |
| Direct wages | 25,760 | Closing WIP | 12,111 |
| Production overhead | 42,940 | | |
| | 125,480 | | 125,480 |

### Production overhead control

| | £ | | £ |
|---|---|---|---|
| Raw materials | 1,450 | Balance b/f | 2,360 |
| Indirect wages | 2,980 | Work in progress | 42,940 |
| Creditors | 31,765 | | |
| Profit and loss | 9,105 | | |
| | 45,300 | | 45,300 |

### Abnormal loss

| | £ | | £ |
|---|---|---|---|
| Balance b/f | 1,685 | Profit and loss | 8,440 |
| Work in progress | 6,755 | | |
| | 8,440 | | 8,440 |

### Abnormal gain

| | £ | | £ |
|---|---|---|---|
| Profit and loss | 930 | Balance b/f | 930 |

### Finished goods

| | £ | | £ |
|---|---|---|---|
| Balance b/f | 27,130 | Cost of sales | 125,740 |
| Work in progress | 106,614 | Balance c/f | 8,004 |
| | 133,744 | | 133,744 |

(c) An integrated system uses one set of ledgers to record all transactions and produce reports for both financial accounting and cost accounting purposes. In contrast, an interlocking system maintains separate ledgers for each of these purposes.

As a consequence when using an interlocking system many transactions are posted more than once, resulting in increased accounting costs; a reconciliation of profits is also required. The use of two ledgers provides flexibility which results in improved management information for an administrative cost.

The use of an integrated system is less costly, but results in management information being produced as a consequence of financial accounting records and regulations.

WORKINGS

(1)    **Process 1 - Equivalent units table**

|  | | Materials | | | Conversion | |
|---|---|---|---|---|---|---|
|  | % | eu | | % | eu | |
| Output | 100 | 13,100 | | 100 | 13,100 | |
| Abnormal loss | 100 | 245 | | 100 | 245 | |
| Closing WIP | 100 | 2,000 | | 50 | 1,000 | |
|  | | 15,345 | | | 14,345 | |

| Costs | (4,960 + 14,700) £19,660 | (17,160 + 25,740) £42,900 |
|---|---|---|
| £/eu | £1.2812 | £2.9906 |

| Output | = | 13,100 × (£1.2812 + £2.9906) | = | £55,960 (rounded) |
|---|---|---|---|---|
| Abnormal loss | = | 245 × (£1.2812 + £2.9906) | = | £1,047 |
| Closing WIP | = | (2,000 × £1.2812) + (1,000 × £2.9906) | = | £5,553 |

(2)    **Process 2 - Equivalent units table**

|  | Process 1 | | Materials | | Conversion | |
|---|---|---|---|---|---|---|
|  | % | eu | % | eu | % | eu |
| Output | 100 | 20,545 | 100 | 20,545 | 100 | 20,545 |
| Abnormal loss | 100 | 1,100 | 100 | 1,100 | 100 | 1,100 |
| Closing WIP | 100 | 1,500 | 100 | 1,500 | 50 | 750 |
|  | | 23,145 | | 23,145 | | 22,395 |

| Costs | £64,680 | £17,600 | £36,600 |
|---|---|---|---|
| £/eu | £2.7946 | £0.7604 | £1.6343 |

Output = 20,545 × (£2.7946 + £0.7604 + £1.6343) = £106,614
Abnormal loss = 1,100 × (£2.7946 + £0.7604 + £1.6343) = £5,708
Closing WIP = (1,500 × (£2.7946 + £0.7604)) + (750 × £1.6343) = £6,558

(3)    Normal losses:

| Process 1: 15% of (10,500 + 7,200 − 2,000) | = | 2,355 |
|---|---|---|
| Process 2: 10% of (13,100 + 4,050 + 8,400 − 1,500) | = | 2,405 |

## 27    PAINT MANUFACTURER

(a)

**Process 2 account**

| | litres | £ | | | litres | | £ |
|---|---|---|---|---|---|---|---|
| Opening work in process | 5,000 | 60,000 | Normal loss | (W1) | 3,250 | | 6,500 |
| Process 1 | 65,000 | 578,500 | Product X | | 30,000 | (W7) | 402,180 |
| Direct labour | | 101,400 | Product Y | | 25,000 | (W7) | 369,820 |
| Variable overhead | | 80,000 | By-product Z | | 7,000 | (W4) | 24,500 |
| Fixed overhead | | 40,000 | Closing work in progress | | 6,000 | (W6) | 74,400 |
| Abnormal gain | (W2) 1,250 | (W5) 17,500 | | | | | |
| | 71,250 | 877,400 | | | 71,250 | | 877,400 |

Any question with opening/closing work in progress can **only** be solved by using an equivalent units table:

**Equivalent units table**

| Output (W3) | Process 1 | | Conversion | |
|---|---|---|---|---|
| | *%* | *eu* | *%* | *eu* |
| Started and finished | 100 | 50,000 | 100 | 50,000 |
| Opening work in progress | 0 | 0 | 60 | 3,000 |
| Closing work in progress | 100 | 6,000 | 60 | 3,600 |
| Abnormal gain | 100 | (1,250) | 100 | (1,250) |
| | | 54,750 | | 55,350 |
| Period costs incurred | | £578,500 | | £221,400 |
| Less: Normal loss value | | (6,500) | | |
| By product value (W4) | | (24,500) | | |
| | | £547,500 | | £221,400 |
| Cost per equivalent unit | | £10.00 | | £4.00 |

WORKINGS

1    Normal loss = 5% of 65,000 litres = 3,250 litres valued @ £2/litre = £6,500.

2    Abnormal gain volume is a balancing figure.

3    Output (Product X and Product Y combined) must be analysed into that which was opening work in progress and that started and finished during the period.

| | | | *Litres* | *Litres* |
|---|---|---|---|---|
| Opening work in progress | = | | | 5,000 |
| Total Output: | Product X | = | 30,000 | |
| | Product Y | = | 25,000 | |
| | | | | 55,000 |
| So started and finished | = | | | 50,000 |

4    7,000 litres @ (£4.00 − £0.50) = £24,500

5    Abnormal gain value    =    1,250 litres @ (£10.00 + £4.00)
          =    £17,500

6    Closing work in progress:                                              £

| | | | |
|---|---|---|---|
| Process 1: | 6,000 litres @ £10.00 = | 60,000 |
| Conversion: | 3,600 litres @ £4.00 = | 14,400 |
| | 74,400 | |

7    Output:                                                                    £
     Opening work in progress:
       Conversion: 3,000 litres @ £4.00 =                        12,000

     Started and finished:
       Process 1:    50,000 litres @ £10.00                    500,000
       Conversion:   50,000 litres @ £4.00                     200,000
       Opening work in progress value b/f                       60,000
                                                                              772,000

Values of joint products at point of separation:

Product X:  30,000 litres @ (£15.00 – £0.50)          435,000
Product Y:  25,000 litres @ (£18.00 – £1.50 – £0.50)   400,000

                                                       835,000

Output costs are apportioned:

|  | Value £ |  | Cost £ |
|---|---|---|---|
| Product X | 435,000 |  | 402,180 |
| Product Y | 400,000 |  | 369,820 |
|  | 835,000 |  | 772,000 |

(b)

### Abnormal gain account

| | £ | | £ |
|---|---|---|---|
| Normal loss (W8) | 2,500 | Process 2 | 17,500 |
| Profit and loss | 15,000 | | |
| | 17,500 | | 17,500 |

WORKING

8    The process account anticipates a recovery of cost from the sale of the normal loss units.  When there is an abnormal gain ie, less loss than anticipated, then there is a loss of cost recovery equal to the abnormal gain quantity valued at the normal loss scrap value:

1,250 litres @ £2.00/litre = £2,500

(c)    There are two alternative methods of apportioning common costs between joint products other than that used in part (a) above.  These are the volume and final sales value methods.

The volume method apportions the cost to each product irrespective of their relative unit values.  The cost is shared at the same rate per unit for both products.

|  | Volume | Cost £ |
|---|---|---|
| Product X | 30,000 | 455,455 |
| Product Y | 25,000 | 379,545 |
|  | 55,000 | £835,000 |

The final sales value method ignores any further processing or packaging costs incurred after the point of separation.  It can be argued that this is inequitable:

|  | Value £ | Cost £ |
|---|---|---|
| Product X:  30,000 × £15 | 450,000 | 417,500 |
| Product Y:  25,000 × £18 | 450,000 | 417,500 |
|  | £900,000 | £835,000 |

Apportionment of costs to joint products is necessary because of the need to be able to value stocks at cost (in accordance with SSAP 9).  However, all of the methods are arbitrary, and as the costs are not specific to the product, they cannot be avoided by the discontinuance of the product. As a consequence the apportionment of costs to joint products can be misleading, and if relied upon for decision making can cause incorrect decisions to be made.

(*Note:* the question only required an explanation of one alternative method of cost apportionment.)

## 28   ABC PLC

(a)

### Process 1

| | Kg | £ | | Kg | £/Kg | £ |
|---|---|---|---|---|---|---|
| Opening WIP | 3,000 | 8,144 | Normal loss | 400 | NIL | NIL |
| Material input | 4,000 | 22,000 | Output | 2,400 | 11.40 | 27,360 |
| Labour | | 12,000 | Closing WIP | 3,400 | 6.96 | 23,664 |
| Overhead absorbed (W1) | | 18,000 | Abnormal loss | 800 | 11.40 | 9,120 |
| | 7,000 | 60,144 | | 7,000 | | 60,144 |

### Process 2

| | Kg | £ | | Kg | £/Kg | £ |
|---|---|---|---|---|---|---|
| Opening WIP | 2,250 | 9,681 | Normal loss | 240 | 2.00 | 480 |
| Process 1 | 2,400 | 27,360 | Output | 2,500 | 22.10 | 55,250 |
| Labour | | 15,000 | Closing WIP | 2,600 | 13.10 | 34,060 |
| Overhead absorbed (W4) | | 22,500 | | | | |
| Abnormal gain | 690 | 15,249 | | | | |
| | 5,340 | 89,790 | | 5,340 | | 89,790 |

### Abnormal loss

| | £ | | £ |
|---|---|---|---|
| Balance b/fwd | 1,400 | Profit and loss | 10,520 |
| Process 1 | 9,120 | | |
| | 10,520 | | 10,520 |

### Abnormal gain

| | £ | | £ |
|---|---|---|---|
| Process 2 Normal loss | 1,380 | Balance b/fwd | 300 |
| Profit & Loss | 14,169 | Process 2 | 15,249 |
| | 15,549 | | 15,549 |

### Overhead control

| | £ | | £ |
|---|---|---|---|
| Costs incurred | 54,000 | Balance b/fwd | 250 |
| | | Process 1 | 18,000 |
| | | Process 2 | 22,500 |
| | | Profit & Loss | 13,250 |
| | 54,000 | | 54,000 |

### Finished goods stock

|  | £ |  | £ |
|---|---|---|---|
| Balance b/fwd | 65,000 | Cost of sales | 60,250 |
| Process 2 | 55,250 | Balance c/fwd | 60,000 |
|  | 120,250 |  | 120,250 |

### Cost of sales

|  | £ |  | £ |
|---|---|---|---|
| Balance b/fwd | 442,500 | Profit & Loss | 502,750 |
| Finished goods stock | 60,250 |  |  |
|  | 502,750 |  | 502,750 |

### Sales

|  | £ |  | £ |
|---|---|---|---|
| Profit & Loss | 637,000 | Balance b/fwd | 585,000 |
|  |  | Debtors | 52,000 |
|  | 637,000 |  | 637,000 |

### Profit and loss
### For the year

|  | £ | £ |
|---|---|---|
| Sales |  | 637,000 |
| Cost of sales |  | 502,750 |
| Gross profit |  | 134,250 |
| Abnormal gain |  | 14,169 |
|  |  | 148,419 |
| Abnormal loss | 10,520 |  |
| Overhead under absorbed | 13,250 |  |
|  |  | (23,770) |
| Net profit |  | 124,649 |

WORKINGS

(W1)

150% of labour cost, so £12,000 × 150% = £18,000.

(W2)

### Process 1 Equivalent units table

|  | Total | Materials | | Conversion | |
|---|---|---|---|---|---|
|  | Total | % | eu | % | eu |
| Output | 2,400 | 100 | 2,400 | 100 | 2,400 |
| Abnormal loss | 800 | 100 | 800 | 100 | 800 |
| Closing WIP | 3,400 | 100 | 3,400 | 40 | 1,360 |
|  |  |  | 6,600 |  | 4,560 |

|  | £ | £ |
|---|---|---|
| Costs: b/f | 4,400 | 3,744 |
| Period | 22,000 | 30,000 (W3) |
|  | 26,400 | 33,744 |
| Cost per equivalent unit | £4.00 | £7.40 |

| Valuations: | Total £ | Material £ | Conversion £ |
|---|---|---|---|
| Output | 27,360 | 9,600 | 17,760 |
| Abnormal loss | 9,120 | 3,200 | 5,920 |
| Closing WIP | 23,664 | 13,600 | 10,064 |

(W3)

Labour and overhead costs.

(W4)

150% of labour cost so, £15,000 × 150% = £22,500

(W5)

### Process 2 Equivalent units table

|  | Total | Process 1 % | eu | Conversion % | eu |
|---|---|---|---|---|---|
| Output | 2,500 | 100 | 2,500 | 100 | 2,500 |
| Abnormal loss | (690) | 100 | (690) | 100 | (690) |
| Closing WIP | 2,600 | 100 | 2,600 | 40 | 1,040 |
|  |  |  | 4,410 |  | 2,850 |

|  | £ | £ |
|---|---|---|
| Costs: b/f | 4,431 | 5,250 |
| Period | 27,360 | 37,500 |
| Normal loss scrap | (480) |  |
|  | 31,311 | 42,750 |
| Cost per equivalent unit | £7.10 | £15.00 |

| Valuations: | Total £ | Process 1 £ | Conversion £ |
|---|---|---|---|
| Output | 55,250 | 17,750 | 37,500 |
| Abnormal gain | (15,249) | (4,899) | (10,350) |
| Closing WIP | 34,060 | 18,460 | 15,600 |

(b)

| Field name | Type | Length |
|---|---|---|
| Date | Alpha/Numeric | 6 |
| Account name | Alpha | 15 |
| Account code | Numeric | 8 |
| Value | Numeric | 12 |
| Description | Alpha | 30 |

## 29    XY LTD

(*Tutorial notes:*

(1)    Firstly draw lines to open up the T accounts.  Use abbreviations for the heading and narratives for the transactions **but** make sure the examiner will be able to understand them.  The main priority is to record the transactions; if you do not know where one goes leave it out (come back to it **if** you have time at the end).

(2)    The transactions are numbered in the solution to assist understanding.

(3)    A quick glance at the figures in the question indicates that it will be quicker to show figures in £'000.

(4)    Balance sheet format - use formats learnt in Financial Accounting but don't be too fussy!)

(a) & (b)

### Share capital

| | | £'000 | | | £'000 |
|---|---|---|---|---|---|
| | Balance c/d | 500 | | Balance b/d | 500 |

### Fixed assets

| | | £'000 | | | | £'000 |
|---|---|---|---|---|---|---|
| | Balance b/d | 275 | 10 | Production overhead | | 15 |
| | | | | Balance c/d | | 260 |
| | | 275 | | | | 275 |

### Bank

| | | | £'000 | | | £'000 |
|---|---|---|---|---|---|---|
| | | Balance b/d | 225 | 2 | Wages | 500 |
| 11 | | Trade debtors | 520 | 3 | Production overhead | 20 |
| | | | | 3 | Selling overhead | 40 |
| | | | | 3 | Administration overhead | 25 |
| | | | | 12 | Trade creditors | 150 |
| | | | | | Balance c/d | 10 |
| | | | 745 | | | 745 |

### Production overhead

| | | £'000 | | | £'000 |
|---|---|---|---|---|---|
| 1 | Trade creditors | 47.5 | 6 | Work in progress: | |
| 3 | Bank | 20 | | Dept A | 110 |
| 4 | Raw material | 65 | | Dept B | 120 |
| 5 | Wages | 42.5 | | | |
| 7 | Accrual c/d | 26 | | | |
| 10 | Fixed assets (Dep'n) | 15 | | | |
| | P&L a/c - over recovery | 14 | | | |
| | | 230 | | | 230 |

### Raw material stock

| | | £'000 | | | | £'000 |
|---|---|---|---|---|---|---|
| 1 | Trade creditors | 525 | 4 | Work in progress | | |
| | | | | - Dept A | 180 | |
| | | | | - Dept B | 192.5 | |
| | | | 9 | Production overhead | 65 | |
| | | | | Balance c/d | 87.5 | |
| | | 525 | | | | 525 |

### Work in progress Dept A

| | | £'000 | | | £'000 |
|---|---|---|---|---|---|
| 4 | Raw material | 180 | 8 | Finished goods | 570 |
| 5 | Wages | 300 | | | |
| 6 | Production overhead | 110 | | Balance c/d | 20 |
| | | 590 | | | 590 |

### Work in progress Dept B

| | | £'000 | | | £'000 |
|---|---|---|---|---|---|
| 4 | Raw material | 192.5 | 8 | Finished goods | 555 |
| 5 | Wages | 260 | | | |
| 6 | Production overhead | 120 | | Balance c/d | 17.5 |
| | | 572.5 | | | 572.5 |

### Trade creditors

| | | £'000 | | | £'000 |
|---|---|---|---|---|---|
| 12 | Bank | 150 | 1 | Raw materials | 525 |
| | | | | Production overhead | 47.5 |
| | Balance c/d | 422.5 | | | |
| | | 572.5 | | | 572.5 |

### Wages

| | | £'000 | | | £'000 |
|---|---|---|---|---|---|
| 2 | Bank | 500 | 5 | Work-in-progress: | |
| 2 | PAYE etc. | 175 | | - Dept A | 300 |
| | | | | - Dept B | 260 |
| | | | | Production overhead | 42.5 |
| | | | | Selling overhead | 47.5 |
| | | | | Administration overhead | 25 |
| | | 675 | | | 675 |

### PAYE etc

| | £'000 | | | £'000 |
|---|---|---|---|---|
| Balance c/d | 175 | 2 | Wages | 175 |

## Trade debtors

|   |       | £'000 |            |            | £'000 |
|---|-------|-------|------------|------------|-------|
| 9 | Sales | 870   |            | Bank       | 520   |
|   |       |       |            | Balance c/d| 350   |
|   |       | 870   |            |            | 870   |

## Selling overhead

|   |       | £'000 |             | £'000 |
|---|-------|-------|-------------|-------|
| 3 | Bank  | 40    | P&L account | 87.5  |
| 5 | Wages | 47.5  |             |       |
|   |       | 87.5  |             | 87.5  |

## Administration overhead

|   |          | £'000 |             | £'000 |
|---|----------|-------|-------------|-------|
| 3 | Bank     | 25    | P&L account | 89    |
| 5 | Wages    | 25    |             |       |
| 7 | Accruals | 39    |             |       |
|   |          | 89    |             | 89    |

## Finished goods stock

|   |                   | £'000 |   |               | £'000 |
|---|-------------------|-------|---|---------------|-------|
| 8 | Work-in-progress: |       | 9 | Cost of sales | 700   |
|   | Dept A            | 570   |   | Balance c/d   | 425   |
|   | Dept B            | 555   |   |               |       |
|   |                   | 1,125 |   |               | 1,125 |

## Profit and loss account

|             | £'000 |             | £'000 |
|-------------|-------|-------------|-------|
| Balance c/d | 7.5   | P&L account | 7.5   |

## Sales account

|             | £'000 |   |               | £'000 |
|-------------|-------|---|---------------|-------|
| P&L account | 870   | 9 | Trade debtors | 870   |

## Cost of sales

|   |               | £'000 |             | £'000 |
|---|---------------|-------|-------------|-------|
| 9 | Finished goods| 700   | P&L account | 700   |

(c)     (i)     **Profit statement for the 3 months ended 30 April**

|               | £'000 |
|---------------|-------|
|               |       |
| Sales         | 870   |
| Cost of sales | (700) |
|               |       |
| Gross profit  | 170   |

|  |  |  |
|---|---|---|
| Selling overhead | (87.5) | |
| Administration overhead | (89) | |
| (Under)/over recovery of production overhead | 14 | |
| | — | |
| Net profit | 7.5 | |
| | — | |

(ii)    **Balance sheet as at 30 April**

| | £'000 | £'000 |
|---|---|---|
| **Fixed assets** | | |
| Cost | | 275 |
| Depreciation | | (15) |
| | | — |
| | | 260 |
| **Current assets** | | |
| Stock    -    Raw materials | 87.5 | |
|       -    Work-in-progress (20 + 17.5) | 37.5 | |
|       -    Finished goods | 425 | |
| Trade debtors | 350 | |
| Cash at bank | 10 | |
| | — | |
| | 910 | |
| **Creditors: amounts falling due within 1 year** | | |
| Trade creditors | 422.5 | |
| PAYE etc | 175 | |
| Accruals £(39 + 26) | 65 | |
| | — | |
| | 662.5 | 247.5 |
| | — | — |
| | | 507.5 |
| | | — |
| **Capital and reserves** | | |
| Share capital | | 500 |
| Profit and loss account | | 7.5 |
| | | — |
| | | 507.5 |
| | | — |

(*Tutorial note:* the £39,000 management consultant's fee could alternatively have been charged to production overhead.)

# 30    VARIOUS POINTS

(a)    A notional cost is one that does not involve a real cashflow but which improves the information provided to management by its inclusion in management reports.

It is difficult to incorporate notional costs into an integrated accounting system because the system is used to produce financial accounting as well as cost accounting statements. In the case of interlocking systems the inclusion of notional costs in the cost accounts was merely an item to be entered on the reconciliation statement, but with integrated systems it requires the use of careful coding systems to obtain these benefits. Examples of notional costs include:

(i)    A charge of interest for the use of internal funds, whilst there is no charge being paid to an outside lender the use of funds may appear to be free, but in reality the cost is the opportunity cost of the funds which at the very least is the deposit rate which could be earned by investing them in a bank deposit account.

(ii)    If a factory is owned then notional rent may be charged to make its production costs comparable with those of a similar rented factory, it is also a measure of the opportunity cost of investing in land and buildings.

(b)    Banks, like many other organisations provide a wide range of services to their customers, some of these are provided at branch level whilst others require the support of the branch network and head office.

The costs of banks are largely fixed since they comprise the land and building related costs and their staff costs, these will not easily be identifiable with a particular product or service. Nevertheless the bank will incur these costs as a result of its existing to provide facilities to its customers.

The only means available is to attempt to measure the services provided, apart from specialist services which are clearly time related. The most common methods in use are the number of transactions processed or the value of lodgements. Most banks use one of these methods as a means of charging their business customers.

The difficulties of such techniques are that they are arbitrary, the bank must therefore give careful consideration to the potential reaction of its customers to the charges it seeks to impose.

(c)    Spreadsheets may be used to produce numerical reports and then by changing some of the basic assumptions the effect on the final result will be calculated automatically. This is especially useful for planning.

The use of electronic mail can greatly enhance world-wide communications far more cheaply than the use of facsimile machines.

Integrated packages allow the combination of information from a database, spreadsheet and text presentations which improve the quality of a management report.

The cost of portable or laptop computers is such that they may be used in environments not traditionally compatible with the use of computers. This has extended the working day and led to more efficient and up-to-date responses to current data.

## 31    NB LTD

(a)    **Process 1**

$$OAR = \frac{\text{Budgeted overheads}}{\text{Budgeted level of activity}} = \frac{£125,000}{£50,000} = 250\% \text{ of direct labour cost}$$

(from work in process figures)

**Process 2**

$$OAR = \frac{£105,000}{£70,000} = 150\% \text{ of direct labour cost}$$

(b)

**Freehold buildings at cost**

|  | £'000 |  | £'000 |
|---|---|---|---|
| Bal b/f | 800 | | |

**Plant and equipment**

|  | £'000 |  | £'000 |
|---|---|---|---|
| Bal b/f | 480 | | |

### Provision for depreciation on plant and equipment

| | £'000 | | £'000 |
|---|---|---|---|
| Bal c/f | 108 | Bal b/f | 100 |
| | | Production overhead control | 8 (W1) |
| | ___ | | ___ |
| | 108 | | 108 |
| | ___ | | ___ |
| | | Bal b/f | 108 |

### Raw materials

| | £'000 | | £'000 |
|---|---|---|---|
| Bal b/f | 400 | Creditors | 10 |
| Creditors | 210 | Work in Process 1 | 136 |
| | | Work in Process 2 | 44 |
| | | Bal c/f | 420 |
| | ___ | | ___ |
| | 610 | | 610 |
| | ___ | | ___ |
| Bal b/f | 420 | | |

### Work in Process 1

| | £'000 | | £'000 |
|---|---|---|---|
| Bal b/f | 246 | Abnormal loss | 20 (W3) |
| Raw materials | 136 | Work in Process 2 | 483 (W2) |
| Wages | 84 | Bal c/f | 173 |
| Production overhead control | 210 (W4) | | |
| | ___ | | ___ |
| | 676 | | 676 |
| | ___ | | ___ |
| Bal b/f | 173 | | |

### Work in Process 2

| | £'000 | | £'000 |
|---|---|---|---|
| Bal b/f | 302 | Abnormal loss | 33 (W6) |
| Raw materials | 44 | Finished goods | 908 (W7) |
| Wages | 130 | Bal c/f | 213 |
| Work in Process 1 | 483 (W2) | | |
| Production overhead control | 195 (W5) | | |
| | ___ | | ___ |
| | 1,154 | | 1,154 |
| | ___ | | ___ |
| Bal b/f | 213 | | |

### Finished goods

| | £'000 | | £'000 |
|---|---|---|---|
| Bal b/f | 60 | Cost of sales | 844 |
| Work in Process 2 | 908 (W7) | Bal c/f | 124 |
| | ___ | | ___ |
| | 968 | | 968 |
| | ___ | | ___ |
| Bal b/f | 124 | | |

### Debtors

|          | £'000 |          | £'000 |
|----------|------:|----------|------:|
| Bal b/f  | 1,120 | Bank     | 1,140 |
| Sales    | 1,100 | Bal c/f  | 1,080 |
|          | 2,220 |          | 2,220 |
| Bal b/f  | 1,080 |          |       |

### Capital

|  | £'000 |          | £'000 |
|--|------:|----------|------:|
|  |       | Bal b/f  | 2,200 |

### Profit retained

|  | £'000 |          | £'000 |
|--|------:|----------|------:|
|  |       | Bal b/f  | 220   |

### Creditors

|               | £'000 |               | £'000 |
|---------------|------:|---------------|------:|
| Raw materials | 10    | Bal b/f       | 300   |
| Bank          | 330   | Raw materials | 210   |
| Bal c/f       | 170   |               |       |
|               | 510   |               | 510   |
|               |       | Bal b/f       | 170   |

### Bank

|          | £'000 |                                   | £'000 |
|----------|------:|-----------------------------------|------:|
| Debtors  | 1,140 | Bal b/f                           | 464   |
| Bal c/f  | 466   | Wages                             | 200   |
|          |       | Production overhead control       | 170   |
|          |       | Production overhead control       | 250   |
|          |       | Creditors                         | 330   |
|          |       | Administration overhead           | 108   |
|          |       | Selling and distribution overhead | 84    |
|          | 1,606 |                                   | 1,606 |
|          |       | Bal b/f                           | 466   |

### Sales

|          | £'000 |          | £'000 |
|----------|------:|----------|------:|
| Bal c/f  | 2,300 | Bal b/f  | 1,200 |
|          |       | Debtors  | 1,100 |
|          | 2,300 |          | 2,300 |
|          |       | Bal b/f  | 2,300 |

## Cost of sales

|              | £'000 |          | £'000 |
|--------------|------:|----------|------:|
| Bal b/f      | 888   | Bal c/f  | 1,732 |
| Finished goods | 844 |          |       |
|              | 1,732 |          | 1,732 |
| Bal b/f      | 1,732 |          |       |

## Abnormal loss

|                  | £'000    |          | £'000 |
|------------------|---------:|----------|------:|
| Bal b/f          | 9        | Bal c/f  | 62    |
| Work in Process 1 | 20 (W3) |          |       |
| Work in Process 2 | 33 (W6) |          |       |
|                  | 62       |          | 62    |
| Bal b/f          | 62       |          |       |

## Production overhead under/over absorbed

|                           | £'000 |          | £'000 |
|---------------------------|------:|----------|------:|
| Production overhead control | 23  | Bal b/f  | 21    |
|                           |       | Bal c/f  | 2     |
|                           | 23    |          | 23    |
| Bal b/f                   | 2     |          |       |

## Administration overhead

|          | £'000 |          | £'000 |
|----------|------:|----------|------:|
| Bal b/f  | 120   | Bal c/f  | 228   |
| Bank     | 108   |          |       |
|          | 228   |          | 228   |
| Bal b/f  | 228   |          |       |

## Selling and distribution overhead

|          | £'000 |          | £'000 |
|----------|------:|----------|------:|
| Bal b/f  | 80    | Bal c/f  | 164   |
| Bank     | 84    |          |       |
|          | 164   |          | 164   |
| Bal b/f  | 164   |          |       |

## Wages

|          | £'000 |                   | £'000 |
|----------|------:|-------------------|------:|
| Bank     | 200   | Work in Process 1 | 84    |
| Bal c/f  | 14    | Work in Process 2 | 130   |
|          | 214   |                   | 214   |
|          |       | Bal b/f           | 14    |

### Production overhead control

|  | £'000 |  |  | £'000 |
|---|---|---|---|---|
| Bank | 170 | Work in Process 1 | | 210 (W4) |
| Bank | 250 | Work in Process 2 | | 195 (W5) |
| Depreciation | 8 (W1) | Underabsorption | | 23 |
|  | 428 |  |  | 428 |

(c)    An abnormal loss is a loss greater than that expected under efficient working conditions.  It indicates inefficiency.  Possible reasons:

1        The materials were processed at too high or low a pressure or temperature.

2        A machine breakdown caused an unusual amount of defective output.

WORKINGS

(1)      Depreciation is 20% straight-line. $\therefore$ Charge for month $= 20\% \times 480,000 \times \frac{1}{12} = £8,000$

(2)      *(Tutorial note:*  A nasty trick here, the examiner does not mention overheads but they must be included.)

Transfer from process 1 to process 2 =

| | |
|---|---|
| 154,000 | Materials |
| + 94,000 | Wages |
| + 250% × 9,400 | Overheads |
| £483,000 | |

(3)      *(Tutorial note:*  Same trick again.)

Abnormal loss    $= 6,000 + 4,000 + (250\% \times 4,000)$
$= £20,000.$

(4)      Overheads absorbed    =    £84,000 × 250% = £210,000

(5)      Overheads absorbed    =    £130,000 × 150% = £195,000

(6)      Abnormal loss    =    18,000 + 6,000 + (150% × 6,000)
=    £33,000

(7)      Transfer to finished goods    =    558,000 + 140,000 + (140,000 × 150%)
=    £908,000

## 32    RETAIL DEPARTMENT STORE

*(Tutorial notes:*

**Overall**

The mark allocations on this question are disproportionate to the time required.  Part (a) is tight on time, (b) is realistic, (c) the time is generous therefore savings would have been possible.  (d) one could easily spend 1 hour answering this so one must be strict.  It is important to make an attempt to (d) since few students like stating their views so it is relatively easy to impress the examiner!

On reading the requirements at the start, (c) refers to gross profit, therefore, this should be included in answer (a) to save time and (d) asks for alternative action which should be borne in mind as you work through the question.

**Part (a)**

The key here is to focus on the requirements which ask for two things ie:

(i)     Presentation of the information in a more meaningful way to aid decision making, and

(ii)    Include statistics or indicators of performance which are considered useful.

The answer should therefore be geared to providing information which is as specific as possible to the individual departments so as to identify where profits are being earned/losses incurred. The answer should consider the rate at which profit is being earned and should focus on the principal budget factor which is floor area.

Initial points on first read of question:

(i)     The store is currently making a loss!

(ii)    No figures given showing the amount of profit/loss of each department.

(iii)   Two proposals put forward as possible ways to improve the situation.*)*

(a)    **Results for year ended 31 January 19X0**

| | Ladies wear | | Mens' wear | | General | | Toys | | Restaurant | | Total | |
|---|---|---|---|---|---|---|---|---|---|---|---|---|
| | £'000 | £'000 | £'000 | £'000 | £'000 | £'000 | £'000 | £'000 | £'000 | £'000 | £'000 | £'000 |
| Sales | | 800 | | 400 | | 2,200 | | 1,400 | | 200 | | 5,000 |
| Cost of sales: | | | | | | | | | | | | |
| Purchases | 506 | | 220 | | 1,290 | | 1,276 | | 167 | | | |
| Stock (Increase)/decrease | (10) | | 20 | | 30 | | (100) | | (1) | | | |
| | | (496) | | (240) | | (1,320) | | (1,176) | | (166) | | (3,398) |
| Gross profit | | 304 | | 160 | | 880 | | 224 | | 34 | | 1,602 |
| Allocable direct fixed costs: | | | | | | | | | | | | |
| Wages | 96 | | 47 | | 155 | | 59 | | 26 | | 383 | |
| Expenses | 38 | | 13 | | 35 | | 20 | | 10 | | 116 | |
| Sales and promotion | 10 | | 5 | | 30 | | 75 | | - | | 120 | |
| | | (144) | | (65) | | (220) | | (154) | | (36) | | (619) |
| Profit/(loss) | | 160 | | 95 | | 660 | | 70 | | (2) | | 983 |
| Other costs: | | | | | | | | | | | | |
| Office wages | | | | | | | | | | | 70 | |
| Delivery | | | | | | | | | | | 200 | |
| Directors' salaries and fees | | | | | | | | | | | 120 | |
| Store capacity costs | | | | | | | | | | | 488 | |
| Interest | | | | | | | | | | | 20 | |
| Discounts allowed | | | | | | | | | | | 25 | |
| Bad debts | | | | | | | | | | | 15 | |
| Miscellaneous expenses | | | | | | | | | | | 75 | |
| | | | | | | | | | | | | (1,013) |
| Loss | | | | | | | | | | | | (30) |

## Performance Indicators

|  | Ladies | Mens | General | Toys | Restaurant |
|---|---|---|---|---|---|
| **Gross profit %** |  |  |  |  |  |
| $\dfrac{\text{Gross profit}}{\text{Sales}} \times 100$ | $\dfrac{304}{800} \times 100$ | $\dfrac{160}{400} \times 100$ | $\dfrac{880}{2{,}200} \times 100$ | $\dfrac{224}{1{,}400} \times 100$ | $\dfrac{34}{200} \times 100$ |
|  | = 38% | = 40% | = 40% | = 16% | = 17% |

Gross profit per 1% of floor space

|  | Ladies | Mens | General | Toys | Restaurant |
|---|---|---|---|---|---|
|  | $\dfrac{304}{20}$ | $\dfrac{160}{15}$ | $\dfrac{880}{20}$ | $\dfrac{224}{35}$ | $\dfrac{34}{10}$ |
| £'000 | = 15.2 | = 10.67 | = 44 | = 6.4 | = 3.4 |

(Gross profit – direct fixed costs) per 1% of floor space

|  | Ladies | Mens | General | Toys | Restaurant |
|---|---|---|---|---|---|
|  | $\dfrac{160}{20}$ | $\dfrac{95}{15}$ | $\dfrac{660}{20}$ | $\dfrac{70}{35}$ | $\dfrac{(2)}{10}$ |
| £'000 | = 8 | = 6.33 | = 33 | = 2 | = (0.2) |

Sales per 1% of floor space

|  | Ladies | Mens | General | Toys | Restaurant |
|---|---|---|---|---|---|
| £'000 | 40 | 26.67 | 110 | 40 | 20 |

(b)    *(Tutorial note: care should be taken to show and explain the effect.)*

**Effect on profit for a full year of closing Toys Department**

|  | – £'000 | + £'000 |
|---|---|---|
| Lost sales | 1,400 |  |
| Saving in cost of sales |  | 1,176 |
| Saving in    –    Wages |  | 59 |
| –    Expenses |  | 20 |
| –    Sales and promotions |  | 75 |
|  | 1,400 | 1,330 |
|  | 1,330 |  |
| Net reduction in profit | 70 |  |

The department store would show a loss of £100,000 if the toys department is closed as it is making a £70,000 contribution to overheads.

**Assumptions**

The whole of the department expenses and sales and promotion costs can be avoided by closing the department.

The aim here is to show the incremental effect of closing the department. Hence store capacity costs are omitted as it is assumed they will be unaffected by the closure.

(c)    **Calculation of increase in sales needed to maintain gross profits**

|                          | *Ladies Wear* | | *Mens' Wear* | |
| ------------------------ | --- | --- | --- | --- |
| Effect on gross profit % | % | | % | |
| Selling price            | $100 - 5 =$ | 95 | $100 - 5 =$ | 95 |
| Cost of sales            | 62 | 62 | 60 | 60 |
| Gross profit             | 38 | 33 | 40 | 35 |

$$\text{Revised gross profit \%} = \frac{33}{95} \times 100 \qquad\qquad \frac{35}{95} \times 100$$

$$= 34.7\% \qquad\qquad\qquad = 36.8\%$$

Hence sales value needed to maintain gross profit

$$= \text{Gross profit} \times \frac{100}{\text{gross profit \%}} \qquad = 304 \times \frac{100}{34.7} = 876 \qquad 160 \times \frac{100}{36.8} = 435$$

|                          | | |
| ------------------------ | --- | --- |
| Original sales           | 800 | 400 |

(i)    Increase in sales value £'000            76            35

(ii)   Increase in sales as % of 19X0 sales.

$$\frac{76}{800} \times 100 \qquad\qquad \frac{35}{400} \times 100$$

$$= 9\tfrac{1}{2}\% \qquad\qquad = 8\tfrac{3}{4}\%$$

(d)    *(Tutorial note*

This part of the question requires discipline.

The answer should cover the proposals and any other points which may have occurred to you as you worked through the question. Reference where appropriate should be made to the figures prepared in (a) ie, use your answer.*)*

(i)    **Closure of toy department**

The working in (b) indicates that profits would be reduced by this closure. The calculations are slightly unrealistic in that alternative uses for the space presently occupied by the department have been ignored.

(ii)   **Reduce selling prices in Ladies Wear and Mens' Wear**

This proposal is dependent on being able to assess the effect of the reduction in selling prices on demand; if the effect is greater than $9\tfrac{1}{2}\%$ and $8\tfrac{3}{4}\%$ then this proposal will result in an improvement in profits.

(iii)  **Alternative action**

The following should be evaluated:

(1)    The most profitable department is the General department. Can this be expanded?

(2)    The restaurant is not promoted at present. Advertising may boost turnover and consequently increase the number of people entering the store. The fact that the restaurant is likely to attract people into the store is a strong argument for keeping it open at existing sales volumes even though there is at present a loss incurred on its operation.

# 33   GLASS BOTTLES

(a)  (i)   **Absorption costing**

|  | September | | October | |
|---|---|---|---|---|
|  | £'000 | £'000 | £'000 | £'000 |
| Sales |  | 2,784 |  | 3,232 |
| Opening stock | Nil |  | 730.24 |  |
| Direct materials | 920 |  | 624 |  |
| Direct labour | 828 |  | 561.60 |  |
| Variable production overhead | 386.40 |  | 262.08 |  |
| Fixed production overhead | 864.80 |  | 586.56 |  |
|  | 2,999.20 |  | 2,764.48 |  |
| Closing stock | (730.24) | (2,268.96) | (130.4) | (2,634.08) |
| Gross profit |  | 515.04 |  | 597.92 |
| Over/(under) absorption |  | 208.80 |  | (45.44) |
|  |  | 723.84 |  | 552.48 |
| Fixed selling costs | 120 |  | 120 |  |
| Fixed admin costs | 80 | (200) | 80 | (200) |
| Net profit |  | 523.84 |  | 352.48 |

(ii)   **Marginal costing**

|  | September | | October | |
|---|---|---|---|---|
|  | £'000 | £'000 | £'000 | £'000 |
| Sales |  | 2,784 |  | 3,232 |
| Opening stock | Nil |  | 519.68 |  |
| Direct materials | 920 |  | 624 |  |
| Direct labour | 828 |  | 561.60 |  |
| Variable production overhead | 386.40 |  | 262.08 |  |
|  | 2,134.40 |  | 1,967.36 |  |
| Closing stock | (519.68) | (1,614.72) | (92.80) | (1,874.56) |
| Contribution |  | 1,169.28 |  | 1,357.44 |
| Fixed costs |  |  |  |  |
| Production | 656 |  | 632 |  |
| Selling | 120 |  | 120 |  |
| Administration | 80 | (856) | 80 | (832) |
| Net profit |  | 313.28 |  | 525.44 |

(b)   Marginal costing separates fixed costs and reports them as a cost of the period in which they are incurred. This causes an immediate effect on the profit of the period and therefore highlights the effect of variable costs on contribution and of the fixed costs on the final profit. This should assist in the control of costs.

Marginal costing will not smooth out the fluctuations in profit which occur when sales fluctuate. If production is constant changes in the level of sales will cause a change in stock levels, so the valuation of stock at variable cost only under a marginal costing system will cause greater fluctuations in profit than absorption costing.

Profits are maximised by the maximisation of contribution in periods of constant fixed costs. The use of marginal costing highlights contribution and management may use this to identify profitable operating levels and thereby improve profitability.

## 34    THREE PRODUCTS

(a)

| Unit costs | Product X £ | Product Y £ | Product Z £ | Total £ |
|---|---|---|---|---|
| Direct materials | 50 | 120 | 90 | |
| Direct labour:     A | 70 | 40 | 75 | |
| B | 24 | 18 | 30 | |
| C | 32 | 16 | 60 | |
| Variable overhead | 12 | 7 | 16 | |
| | 188 | 201 | 271 | |
| Selling price | 210 | 220 | 300 | |
| Contribution per unit | 22 | 19 | 29 | |
| | | | | |
| Sales volume (units) | 7,500 | 6,000 | 6,000 | |
| Total contribution (£) | 165,000 | 114,000 | 174,000 | 453,000 |
| Less fixed costs | | | | 300,000 |
| Profit | | | | 153,000 |

(b)

| | X | Y | Z |
|---|---|---|---|
| Contribution/unit | £22 | £19 | £29 |
| Department B hours/unit | 4 | 3 | 5 |
| Contribution/hr | £5.50 | £6.33 | £5.80 |
| Ranking | (3) | (1) | (2) |

Maximum Dept B hours

$$= (7,500 \times 4) + (6,000 \times 3) + (6,000 \times 5)$$
$$= 78,000 \text{ hours}$$

∴ Manufacture:

| | |
|---|---|
| 7,500 units of Y uses | 22,500 hours |
| 8,000 units of Z uses | 40,000 hours |
| 3,875 units of X uses | 15,500 hours (W1) |
| | 78,000 |

This yields a contribution of:

| | £ |
|---|---|
| X: 3,875 × £22 = | 85,250 |
| Y: 7,500 × £19 = | 142,500 |
| Z: 8,000 × £29 = | 232,000 |
| | 459,750 |
| Less fixed costs | 300,000 |
| Profit | 159,750 |

(c)     (1)     It has been assumed that the fixed costs are not affected by the increased volume of products Y and Z and reduction in volume of product X.

        (2)     It relies on the sales director's demand estimates.

        (3)     It ignores the effects of reducing the production of X such as the effect on customers' goodwill, and the position of the company in the market for X.

WORKINGS

(W1)     This is the balancing number of department B hours available.

---

## 35    CD LTD

(a)     (i)

**Step 1**     Identify whether the limiting factor is department 1 hours; or department 2 hours.

Dept 1 - maximum production:

     Robroy   100,000/5         = 20,000
     Trigger   100,000/7.5     = 13,333.

Dept 2 - maximum production:

     Robroy   160,000/7.5     = 21,333
     Trigger   160,000/10      = 16,000.

Therefore, without the use of sub-contractors department 1 hours are the limiting factor.

**Step 2**     Rank the contribution per dept 1 hour for each product:

|  | *Robroy* | | *Trigger* | |
|---|---|---|---|---|
|  | £ | £ | £ | £ |
| Selling price |  | 300 |  | 430 |
| Direct costs: |  |  |  |  |
|    Dept 1 | 85 |  | 135 |  |
|    Dept 2 | 90 |  | 120 |  |
| Variable overhead: |  |  |  |  |
|    Dept 1 | 10 |  | 15 |  |
|    Dept 2 | 18 |  | 24 |  |
|  |  | (203) |  | (294) |
| Contribution/unit |  | 97 |  | 136 |
|  |  |  |  |  |
| Dept 1 hours/unit |  | 5 |  | 7.5 |
| Contribution/dept 1 hour |  | £19.40 |  | £18.13 |
| Ranking |  | 1 |  | 2 |

Since Robroy has the highest contribution per dept 1 hour this product should be preferred.

Production is limited to 20,000 units which will yield profits of:

|  | £'000 |
|---|---|
| Contribution (20,000 × £97) | 1,940 |
| Fixed costs (800,000 + 400,000) | (1,200) |
| Profit | 740 |

(ii)

**Step 1**    consider the hours

(1)    there are insufficient hours in both departments to make these quantities without using sub-contractors, therefore both Jason and Nadira must be used to achieve either of these volumes.

(2)    the balance of the required production can be achieved without difficulty:

**Dept 1**

12,000 Robroy - 5 hours each       = 60,000 hours

**or**

10,000 Trigger - 7.5 hours each      = 75,000 hours

**Dept 2**

15,600 Robroy - 7.5 hours each      = 117,000 hours

**or**

14,000 Trigger - 10 hours each      = 140,000 hours.

Thus there is no longer an hours constraint.

**Step 2**    consider the contributions:

(1)    using the existing values for contribution per unit:

22,000 Robroy @ £97/unit= £2,134,000

**or**

18,000 Trigger @ £136/unit      = £2,448,000.

Thus Trigger provides the greater total contribution, subject to sub-contractor prices exceeding the internal variable cost.

(2)

|        | *Robroy* | | *Trigger* | |
|        | *Internal* | *Sub-con* | *Internal* | *Sub-con* |
|        | £ | £ | £ | £ |
|--------|------|------|------|------|
| Dept 1 | 95 | 110 | 150 | 170 |
| Dept 2 | 108 | 120 | 144 | 154 |
| Total  | 203 | 230 | 294 | 324 |

This table shows the differences in cost between using the sub-contractors rather than manufacturing internally on a cost/unit basis.

(3)    Revised contributions would be:

|  | £'000 | £'000 |
|---|---|---|
| **Robroy** | | |
| As per (1) above | | 2,134 |
| Adjustments: | | |
| Jason:  10,000 × (£110 – £95) | 150 | |
| Nadira:  6,400 × (£120 – £108) | 76.8 | |
| | | 226.8 |
| Revised contribution | | 1,907.2 |

**Trigger**

|  |  |
|---|---|
| As per (1) above | 2,448 |
| Adjustments: |  |

| | | |
|---|---|---|
| Jason: 8,000 × (£170 – £150) | 160 | |
| Nadira: 4,000 × (£154 – £144) | 40 | |
| | | (200) |
| Revised contribution | | 2,248 |

On the basis of the above, if using sub-contractors CD Ltd should concentrate on product Trigger.

However, these values assume that the sub-contractors are used for their respective maximum capacities. This is not necessary and because the internal cost is less than the buying price then the contractors would be used as follows:

Jason: 2,000 Robroy **or** 4,666.66 Trigger

Nadira: 666.66 Robroy **or** 2,000 Trigger.

The additional costs would therefore be either:

| | | | £ | £ |
|---|---|---|---|---|
| Robroy: | 2,000 × (£110 – £95) | = | 30,000 | |
| | 666.66 × (£120 – £108) | = | 8,000 | |
| | | | | 38,000 |

**or**

| | | | £ | £ |
|---|---|---|---|---|
| Trigger: | 4,666.66 × (£170 – £150) | = | 93,333 | |
| | 2,000 × (£154 – £144) | = | 20,000 | |
| | | | | 113,333 |

Each of these need to be deducted from their corresponding contributions in (1) above:

| | Robroy £'000 | Trigger £'000 |
|---|---|---|
| Original contributions | 2,134 | 2,448 |
| Adjustment | (38) | (113.333) |
| Revised contribution | 2,096 | 2,334.667 |

On the basis of the above Trigger should be the product sold, resulting in a profit of:

| | £ |
|---|---|
| Contribution | 2,334,667 |
| Less: Fixed costs | (1,200,000) |
| Profit | 1,134,667 |

(b)     (i)     The conclusion is based on budgeted estimates of hours available. If these are found to be overstated (by as little as 6.25% in dept 2) then the production of 20,000 Robroy cannot be achieved.

(ii)     Care must be taken to ensure that the quality of the work undertaken by the sub-contractors is acceptable.

(c)     Marginal costing is a system of cost accounting which distinguishes between fixed and variable costs.

In decision making relevant costs are those which are both future and differential. Such costs are most likely to be classified as variable costs because it is these costs which are related to the level of activity.

Thus a system of marginal costing is likely to provide costs which are useful for decision making purposes.

## 36     PQ LTD

*Note:* the following profit statements are prepared assuming that cost structure and revenue per unit during the first quarter of the year were as budgeted.

(a)     (i)     **Marginal costing**

|  | £ | £ |
|---|---|---|
| Sales [40,000 × £40 (W1)] |  | 1,600,000 |
| Variable production costs [55,000 × £16 (W2)] | 880,000 |  |
| Closing stock (15,000 × £16) | 240,000 |  |
| Production variable cost of sales |  | (640,000) |
|  |  | 960,000 |
| Variable selling, distribution, admin [40,000 × £8 (W3)] |  | (320,000) |
| Contribution |  | 640,000 |
| Less:   Fixed costs |  |  |
| Production | 200,000 |  |
| Selling, distribution, admin | 300,000 |  |
|  |  | (500,000) |
| Net profit |  | 140,000 |

(ii)     **Absorption costing**

|  | £ | £ |
|---|---|---|
| Sales [as (i)] |  | 1,600,000 |
| Variable production costs [as (i)] | 880,000 |  |
| Fixed production costs (W4) | 275,000 |  |
|  | 1,155,000 |  |
| Closing stock [15,000 × (£16 + £5)] | (315,000) |  |
| Cost of sales |  | (840,000) |
| Gross profit |  | 760,000 |
| Over absorption of fixed production costs |  | 75,000 |
|  |  | 835,000 |
| Less:   Selling, distribution, admin |  |  |
| Variable [as (i)] | 320,000 |  |
| Fixed [as (i)] | 300,000 |  |
|  |  | (620,000) |
| Net profit |  | 215,000 |

(b)      The difference in the reported profit depending upon whether marginal or absorption costing is used arises out of the stock valuation.

As can be seen from (a) above, under marginal costing stock is valued at its variable production cost, whereas the absorption costing method is based on total production cost.

The absorption costing method is based on the requirements of SSAP 9. SSAP 9 states that stock should be valued at cost (or net realisable value if lower) and that the cost should be the total cost incurred in bringing the product to its present location and condition. SSAP 9 further explains that this total cost should include an appropriate proportion of fixed production costs, and that the appropriate proportion should be based on normal levels of activity.

For these purposes the budgeted production level is usually considered to equal the normal level of activity, so the absorption rate per unit is calculated using the budgeted production level.

Thus in summary the difference between marginal and absorption costing lies in the amount of cost which is included in the valuation of the asset of stock (in the balance sheet) and the amount treated as a cost (in the periodic profit and loss account).

Under the three scenarios:

(i)      If sales and production volumes are equal, then the opening and closing stocks will be equal, so both systems will report the same profit.

(ii)      If sales exceed production, this means that stocks will decrease and so some previous period(s) costs, which had been deferred by including them in the stock valuation, will be brought into the period's profit and loss account.

Since absorption costing defers a larger cost per unit than marginal costing, the release of this larger deferred cost will result in lower profits being reported under absorption costing than under marginal costing.

(iii)      This is the opposite of (ii) and is illustrated by part (a) of this question. Absorption costing defers a greater cost per unit and thus will have higher reported profits than marginal costing.

(c)

| | £ |
|---|---|
| Budgeted profit | 400,000 |
| Budgeted fixed costs | 800,000 |
| Budgeted contribution | 1,200,000 |

Contribution per unit = (£80 – £20 - £10) = £50

Budgeted volume (£1,200,000/£50) = 24,000

The three strategies are:

| | Volume | Selling price | Contribution per unit | Total |
|---|---|---|---|---|
| 1 | 26,400 | £76 | £46 | £1,214,400 |
| 2 | 28,800 | £74 | £44 | £1,267,200 |
| 3 | 30,000 | £72 | £42 | £1,260,000 |
| Now | 24,000 | £80 | £50 | £1,200,000 |

Since the fixed costs are unaffected by the decision, any change in contribution will equal the change in profit.

Therefore, provided cost structures remain unchanged, strategy 2 is recommended because it will increase profits by £67,200.

## WORKINGS

(W1)   $\dfrac{£6,400,000}{160,000} = £40/unit$

(W2)   $\dfrac{£2,560,000}{160,000} = £16/unit$

(W3)   $\dfrac{£1,280,000}{160,000} = £8/unit$

(W4)   Absorption rate $= \dfrac{£800,000}{160,000} = £5/unit$

Amount absorbed in the first quarter is:

| | £ |
|---|---:|
| 55,000 units × £5 per unit | 275,000 |
| Amount incurred | (200,000) |
| Over absorption | 75,000 |

---

## 37   AZ TRANSPORT GROUP PLC

(a)

| | W | X | Y | Z | Total |
|---|---:|---:|---:|---:|---:|
| Fares charged (W1) | 187,200 | 262,080 | 386,100 | 171,600 | 1,006,980 |
| Fuel & repairs (W2) | 24,570 | 21,060 | 25,740 | 22,230 | 93,600 |
| Gross contribution | 162,630 | 241,020 | 360,360 | 149,370 | 913,380 |
| Drivers wages (W3) | 74,880 | 74,880 | 74,880 | 74,880 | 299,520 |
| Vehicle fixed cost | 4,000 | 4,000 | 4,000 | 4,000 | 16,000 |
| | 78,880 | 78,880 | 78,880 | 78,880 | 315,520 |
| Net contribution | 83,750 | 162,640 | 281,480 | 70,490 | 597,860 |
| General fixed costs | | | | | 300,000 |
| Profit | | | | | 297,860 |

(b)   (i)   proposed fare change would alter the income per return journey to:

$$((15 - 20\%) \times £3.75) + ((10 - 20\%) \times £1.50) = £57$$

This is less than the present journey income of £60.

Contribution would reduce by £3 per journey, a total of (£3 × 3,120 journeys) **£9,360**

(ii)   The fare should **not** be changed.

WORKINGS

(W1)   Each route comprises: 2 buses × 5 return journeys × 6 days × 52 weeks = 3,120 return journeys.

Income per return journey is:

| | | |
|---|---|---|
| Route W : | (15 × £3.00) + (10 × £1.50) | = £60.00 |
| Route X : | (10 × £6.00) + ( 8 × £3.00) | = £84.00 |
| Route Y : | (25 × £4.50) + ( 5 × £2.25) | = £123.75 |
| Route Z : | (20 × £2.20) + (10 × £1.10) | = £55.00 |

Total income for each route = 3,120 return journeys × income per return journey
ie, Route W – 3,120 × £60.

(W2)    Fuel and repair cost = 3,120 return journeys × return travel distance × £0.1875
ie,  Route W = 3,120 × 42 × £0.1875

(W3)    Each route has 2 vehicles ie, 2 drivers × 6 days × 52 weeks × £120.

(c)    (i)

|  |  | £ |
|---|---|---|
| Labour costs: |  |  |
| 2 fitters @ £15,808 |  | 31,616 |
| Supervisor |  | 24,000 |
|  |  |  |
| Material costs: |  |  |
| Safety checks: |  |  |
| 6 per annum per vehicle × £75 |  | 6,300 |
| Servicing: |  |  |
| Buses (W4)  499,200/4,000 × £100 |  | 12,480 |
| Taxis  128,000/4,000 × £100 × 6 taxis |  | 19,200 |
|  |  | 93,596 |

(ii)    If the garage is awarded the contract, the cost will be:

| *Year 1* | £ | *Subsequent years* | £ |
|---|---|---|---|
| Garage | 90,000 | Garage | 90,000 |
| Fitters - redundancy | 15,808 |  | Nil |
|  | 105,808 |  | 90,000 |

| *Summary* |  | £ |
|---|---|---|
| In house: | Present costs | 93,596 |
|  | New employee | 20,000 |
|  |  | 113,596 |
|  |  |  |
| Garage: | As above year 1 | 105,808 |
|  | Supervisor retained | 24,000 |
|  |  | 129,808 |

in subsequent years the cost is reduced to

| | £ |
|---|---|
| Garage cost | 90,000 |
| Supervisor retained | 24,000 |
|  | 114,000 |

On financial grounds there is little difference in subsequent years between retaining the work in-house or contracting it to the garage.  In the first year it is cheaper to retain the work because of the redundancy payments.

The work should be retained.

(iii)    There are a number of factors to consider, including:

- if work is sub-contracted the control of the work scheduling is lost.

- if the work is sub-contracted employee skills will be lost and AZ will have a weaker negotiating position with any external supplier

-     if the work is retained in-house, more planned maintenance may be introduced to reduce the amount of breakdowns.

-     if the work is retained, the maintenance division may tender for outside work to utilise any spare capacity.

-     cost increases, in-house and externally must also be considered.

(W4)     Route W :   3,120 journeys × 42 km   = 131,040 km
       Route X :   3,120 journeys × 36 km   = 112,320 km
       Route Y :   3,120 journeys × 44 km   = 137,280 km
       Route Z :   3,120 journeys × 38 km   = 118,560 km

                                        499,200 km

---

## 38     JK LTD

(a)

|  | Product | | | | |
|---|---|---|---|---|---|
|  | J | K | L | M | Total |
|  | £'000 | £'000 | £'000 | £'000 | £'000 |
| Sales | 200 | 400 | 200 | 200 | 1,000 |
| Variable costs | 140 | 80 | 210 | 140 | 570 |
| Contribution | 60 | 320 | (10) | 60 | 430 |

(b)     Calculate the contribution/sales ratios and plot each product starting with the product having the greatest C/S ratio.

|  | J | K | L | M |
|---|---|---|---|---|
|  | 30% | 80% | (5%) | 30% |

**Contribution - Sales graph**

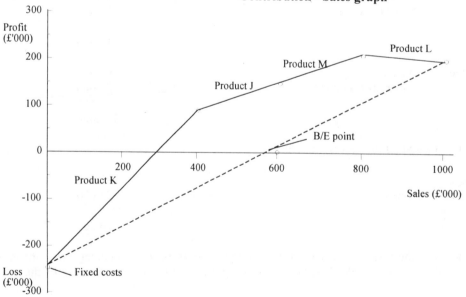

(c)     The products are plotted in the order of their c/s ratios. The steeper the line for an individual product the greater the c/s ratio for that product. Thus it can be seen that product K provides the greatest contribution with respect to sales value.

It can be seen from the graph that product L should be dropped as it provides negative contribution.

The breakeven point can be calculated using the c/s ratio of the mix. This can also be approximately seen from the graph.

$$\text{B/E} = \frac{\text{Fixed costs}}{\text{c/s ratio of the mix}}$$

$$= \frac{240,000}{430/1,000}$$

$$= £558,140$$

(d)     The overall ratio could be improved by:

   (i)     increasing the selling prices

   (ii)    decreasing the sales of products J, L or M

   (iii)   automating the process. This would increase fixed costs but would reduce variable costs thus increasing contribution.

---

## 39      PE LTD

(a)     (i)     Each unit of P yields a contribution of £5
                Each unit of E yields a contribution of £2

                Therefore one sales batch of 4P and 3E yields contribution of:

                (4 × £5) + (3 × £2)                      = £26
                Fixed cost                              = £561,600

                Therefore breakeven $= \dfrac{£561,600}{£26} = 21,600$ sales batches

                This is

                        21,600 × 4 = 86,400 of P @ £10 =        £864,000
                and
                        21,600 × 3 = 64,800 of E @ £12 =        £777,600

                        Breakeven sales revenue                 £1,641,600

   (ii)    Using the same principles each sales batch yields:

                (4 × £5) + (4 × £2) = £28

                Therefore breakeven $= \dfrac{£561,600}{£28} = 20,057.14$ batches

                = 80,228.571 or 80,229 of each product

                The sales revenue is; 80,229 × £22 = £1,765,038

   (iii)   The product mix of 4P to 3E has a lower total sales value requirement to breakeven, but requires more sales of P and less of E to breakeven than the mix of 4P to 4E. The solution depends on the market demand for each product. Whilst product P is more profitable per unit than product E if the market for P cannot support a demand of 86,400 units the second mix is preferable, if this demand for product P does exist then mix (i) is preferable because it is more profitable.

(iv)

|  | Product | |
|---|---|---|
|  | P | E |
| Contribution/unit | £5 | £2 |
| Hours/unit | 0.4 | 0.1 |
| Contribution/hour | £12.50 | £20 |

When there is a shortage of machine hours product E yields the better return per hour than product P. Thus production should concentrate on product E. If all time is spent on product E then (32,000/0.1) 320,000 units can be made which yields a contribution of £640,000 and a net profit of £78,400.

(b)    A conventional breakeven chart shows costs, revenues and profit/loss but does not show how increases in activity earn contribution which is used firstly to cover fixed costs and then to earn profits.

**Conventional breakeven chart**

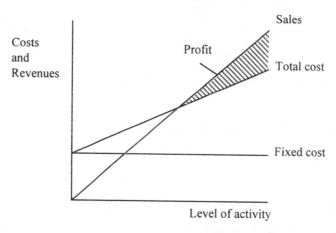

**Contribution breakeven chart**

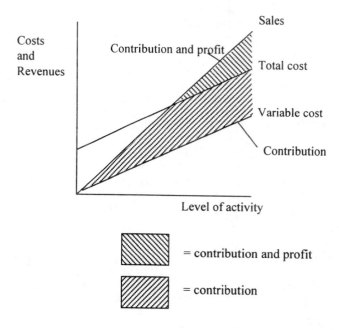

## 40     PREMIER HOTEL

(a)     **Accountants' conventional breakeven chart**

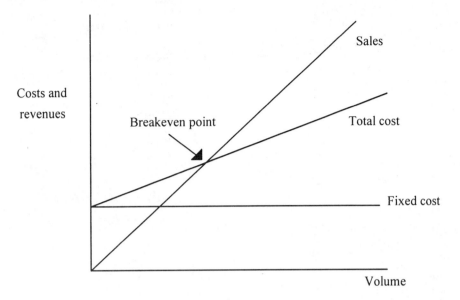

The accountants' breakeven chart shown above makes the following assumptions:

(i)     Selling prices are constant per unit;
(ii)    variable costs vary proportionately with the level of activity;
(iii)   fixed costs do not change over the different level of activity.

With the accountants' breakeven chart, we have assumed that the sales, variable costs, fixed costs and thus total cost have a linear relationship with volume.

With the economists' breakeven chart, we do not make these assumptions and thus the total cost line and sales line are curvi-linear.

**Economists' breakeven chart**

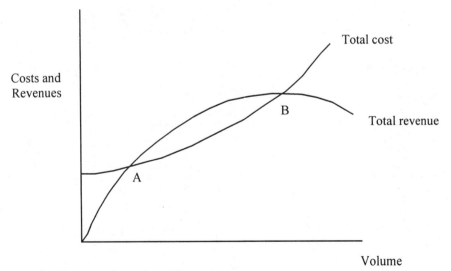

There are two breakeven points - A and B.

The total revenue line is curvi-linear.  The selling price per unit is not constant.  In order to sell more units it would be necessary to decrease the selling price per unit.

The total cost line is curvi-linear.  At first there are economies of scale and then later on, diseconomies of scale.

The economists' model is correct in that it does not make the limiting assumptions that the accountants' model does and thus it would seem that the accountants' model is wrong. The accountants' model, however, is very similar to the economists' model over the **relevant range**. (Individual companies do not operate over the entire possible range of activities, but only within a small portion, known as the relevant range - within the relevant range linearity assumptions work very well.)

If we compare the above two models on one diagram we can see the similarities.

**Economists' and accountants' models compared**

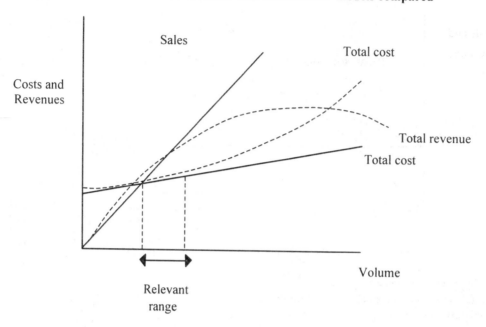

The relevant range in breakeven analysis is often taken to be between the breakeven point and the budgeted level of activity.

The diagram above shows the similarities between the two models over the relevant range, but one further difference not yet mentioned is that the economists' model includes an allowance for a normal level of profit as part of the total cost. This would not be included in the accountants' model.

(b)   (i)   Budgeted room occupancy ratio   $= \dfrac{\text{Budgeted room lettings}}{\text{Potential room lettings}} \times 100\%.$

For April to September   $= \dfrac{218,400}{256,200} \times 100\% \qquad = \qquad 85\%$

For October to March   $= \dfrac{165,200}{254,800} \times 100\% \qquad = \qquad 65\%$

(ii)   Budgeted no of rooms rented   $= \dfrac{\text{Budgeted income}}{\text{rental per room}}$

For April to September   $= \dfrac{218,400}{35} \qquad = \qquad 6,240 \text{ rooms}$

For October to March   $= \dfrac{165,200}{35} \qquad = \qquad 4,720 \text{ rooms}$

Fixed costs = 9,000 + 5,500 + 4,800 + 2,700 + 3,000 = 25,000 per month
= £150,000 for a six-month period.

|  | | April to September | | October to March | |
|---|---|---|---|---|---|
|  |  | £ | £ | £ | £ |
| Sales |  |  | 218,400 |  | 165,200 |
| Variable costs |  |  |  |  |  |
| 6 × 6,240 |  | 37,440 |  |  |  |
| 6 × 4,720 |  |  |  | 28,320 |  |
| Fixed costs |  | 150,000 |  | 150,000 |  |
|  |  |  | 187,440 |  | 178,320 |
| Profit/(loss) |  |  | 30,960 |  | (13,120) |

(iii)   Contribution per room   =   rent – variable costs

=   35 – 6

=   £29

Breakeven point   =   $\dfrac{\text{Fixed costs}}{\text{Contribution / month}}$

=   $\dfrac{25,000}{29}$

=   862 rooms

(iv)   The fixed costs are irrelevant as to whether or not the hotel should be shut down for January and February as they will be incurred anyway. The focus should be on contribution. As the hotel provides contribution it should be kept open. If some of the fixed costs were avoidable, they would have to be compared with the contribution. Provided contribution exceeds the avoidable fixed costs, the hotel should be kept open.

(v)   The question does not make it clear whether PM Ltd owns other hotels. If it does there may be a company-wide arrangement for maintenance and insurance, but if individual hotels choose their own maintenance and insurance contracts, the manager of the Premier can compare his costs with those of the other hotels.

The manager could also contact a number of insurance and maintenance companies and see whether he could get a similar or better service for a cheaper price.

# 41   BUDGET PROFIT STATEMENT

(a)   (i)   Breakeven point in sales value

=   $\dfrac{\text{Fixed cost}}{(\text{Sales} - \text{Variable costs})} \times \text{Sales}$

=   $\dfrac{78}{(288 - 171)} \times £288,000$

=   0.667 × £288,000

=   £192,000

Breakeven point in units

=   $\dfrac{\text{B / E point in sales value}}{\text{Selling price per unit}}$

$$= \frac{192,000}{32}$$

$$= \quad 6,000 \text{ units}$$

(ii)     **Contribution/volume or profit volume graph**

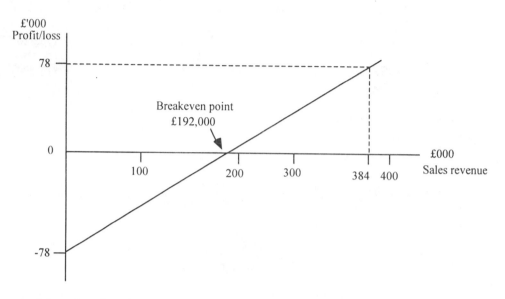

(iii)    Anticipated profit at full capacity (ie, sales of 12,000 × £32 = £384,000) from the graph is £78,000

(b)

|  |  | | (i) £ | | (ii) £ |
|---|---|---|---|---|---|
| Sales |  | 10,800 × £28 | 302,400 | 12,000 × £27.20 | 326,400 |
|  |  | £ | | £ | |
| Less: | Direct materials (W1) | 64,800 | | 72,000 | |
|  | Direct wages (W2) | 86,400 | | 96,000 | |
|  | Production overhead variable (W3) | 21,600 | | 24,000 | |
|  | Selling overhead variable (W4) | 32,400 | | 36,000 | |
|  |  |  | 205,200 | | 228,000 |
| Contribution |  |  | 97,200 | | 98,400 |
| Fixed overhead (42,000 + 36,000) |  |  | 78,000 | (42,000 + 36,000 83,000 +5,000) | |
| Profit |  |  | 19,200 | | 15,400 |

The respective profits are:       Original plan        £39,000
                                  Alternative (i)      £19,200
                                  Alternative (ii)     £15,400

Management should continue with its original budget, operating at 75% of capacity, as this produces the greatest profit.

(c)    (i)                                   £

|                                          | £       |
|------------------------------------------|---------|
| Sales 12,000 at £32                      | 384,000 |
| Less: Marginal cost (from (b)(ii)        | 228,000 |
| Contribution                             | 156,000 |
| Fixed overhead                           | 93,000  |
| Profit                                   | 63,000  |

This proposal would generate a greater profit than any of the others and should be implemented.

(ii)     A major reservation is in the reliability of the forecast. This would depend on the track record of the company carrying out the market research study. More useful information may be given if the probability of the success of this campaign could be forecast.

WORKINGS

| | | | | | | | | |
|---|---|---|---|---|---|---|---|---|
| (W1) | Cost/unit | = | £54,000/9,000 | = | £6 | £6 × 10,800 | = | £64,800 |
|      |           |   |               |   |    | £6 × 12,000 | = | £72,000 |
| (W2) | Cost/unit | = | £72,000/9,000 | = | £8 | £8 × 10,800 | = | £86,400 |
|      |           |   |               |   |    | £8 × 12,000 | = | £96,000 |
| (W3) | Cost/unit | = | £18,000/9,000 | = | £2 | £2 × 10,800 | = | £21,600 |
|      |           |   |               |   |    | £2 × 12,000 | = | £24,000 |
| (W4) | Cost/unit | = | £27,000/9,000 | = | £3 | £3 × 10,800 | = | £32,400 |
|      |           |   |               |   |    | £3 × 12,000 | = | £36,000 |

## 42    BUDGETED PROFIT STATEMENT

(a)    Before starting the answer, the production overhead costs must be analysed into their fixed and variable components, and the stock valuations adjusted (W1).

|                                        | January to June 1997 | | July to December 1997 | |
|----------------------------------------|-------:|-------:|-------:|-------:|
|                                        | £'000  | £'000  | £'000  | £'000  |
| Sales                                  |        | 540    |        | 360    |
| Opening stock (W1)                     | 90     |        | 144    |        |
| Direct materials                       | 108    |        | 36     |        |
| Direct labour                          | 162    |        | 54     |        |
| Variable production overhead (W1)      | 54     |        | 18     |        |
|                                        | 414    |        | 252    |        |
| Closing stock (W1)                     | (144)  |        | (72)   |        |
|                                        | 270    |        | 180    |        |
| Variable distribution overhead (W2)    | 15     |        | 10     |        |
|                                        |        | 285    |        | 190    |
| Contribution                           |        | 255    |        | 170    |

Fixed costs
    Selling (W3)            50               50
    Administration (W3)      80               80
    Production (W1)       24               24
    Distribution (W2)      30               30

                                 (184)            (184)

    Profit/(Loss)                     71             (14)

(b)

|  | Jan - June 1997 | July - Dec 1997 |
|---|---|---|
| Increase/(Decrease) in stock units | 3,000 | (4,000) |
| Fixed production overhead/unit (FOAR) | £2.00 | £2.00 |
| Stock movement × FOAR | £6,000 | (£8,000) |
| Marginal costing profit | £71,000 | (£14,000) |
| Absorption costing profit | £77,000 | (£22,000) |

(c)

|  | £ |
|---|---|
| Absorption profit Jan - June 1997 | 77,000 |
| Reduced contribution due to volume reduction [5,000 units × £17 (W4)] | (85,000) |
|  | (8,000) |
| Fixed cost deferred in Jan - June due to stock increase (£160,000 – £100,000) × 10% (W1) | (6,000) |
| Fixed cost brought back in July - Dec due to stock decrease (£160,000 – £80,000) × 10% (W1) | (8,000) |
| Absorption profit July - Dec 1997 | (£22,000) |

(d)    Breakeven point $= \dfrac{\text{Fixed costs}}{\text{Contribution / unit}}$

$$= \frac{£184,000 \text{ (per 6 months)}}{£17}$$

$$= \frac{£368,000}{£17} \text{ (per annum)}$$

$$= 21,647 \text{ units per annum}$$

(e)    Marginal costing emphasises the variability of costs relative to levels of activity. Since most decisions involve changes to activity levels this emphasis (together with the avoidance of arbitrary attribution of fixed costs to cost units) means that the relevant costs of the decision will more closely follow marginal rather than absorption costing values.

**WORKINGS**

(W1)   *Production units*                                  *18,000*       *6,000*

| | £ | £ |
|---|---|---|
| Overhead absorbed | 90,000 | 30,000 |
| (Over)/Under absorption | (12,000) | 12,000 |
| Overhead cost | £78,000 | £42,000 |

Using high and low points:

| | Units | £ |
|---|---|---|
| High | 18,000 | 78,000 |
| Low | 6,000 | 42,000 |
| | 12,000 | £36,000 |

$$\text{Variable cost} = \frac{£36,000}{12,000} = £3 \text{ per unit produced}$$

By substituting fixed cost = £78,000 − (18,000 × £3) = £24,000

Under marginal costing stock is valued at variable cost only:

| | | £/unit |
|---|---|---|
| D - Materials | (£108,000/18,000) | 6 |
| D - Labour | (£162,000/18,000) | 9 |
| V - Overhead | (as above) | 3 |
| | | 18 |

The fixed overhead included in the absorption costing stock valuation can be found by calculating the overhead absorption rate and analysing it into its fixed and variable components:

$$\frac{\text{Overhead absorbed}}{\text{Production units}} = \frac{£90,000}{18,000} = \qquad £5 \text{ per unit}$$

Since the variable part (see below) =           £3 per unit

Fixed production overhead                 £2 per unit

Added to the variable cost of £18 per unit gives an absorption stock valuation of £20 per unit.

In other words, the marginal costing stock values are 90% (£18/£20) of the absorption stock values.

(W2)   

| Sales units | 15,000 | 10,000 |
|---|---|---|
| Distribution costs | £45,000 | £40,000 |

Using the high/low points method:

$$\text{Variable cost} = \frac{£5,000}{5,000} = £1 \text{ per unit sold}$$

and by substitution the fixed costs =

£45,000 − (15,000 × £1) = £30,000

(W3)   Selling and administration costs are constant and therefore are both fixed costs.

(W4)

| | £ | £ |
|---|---|---|
| Selling price = £540,000/15,000 | | 36 |
| Variable production cost | 18 | |
| Variable distribution cost | 1 | |
| | | 19 |
| Contribution/unit | | 17 |

## 43    Z PLC

(a)    (i)

| | Sales £ | Cost of sales £ |
|---|---|---|
| Highest | 90,000 | 55,000 |
| Lowest | 80,000 | 50,000 |
| | 10,000 | 5,000 |

$$\text{Variable cost} = \frac{£5,000}{£10,000} = 50\% \text{ of sales}$$

By substitution:

| | | | |
|---|---|---|---|
| Lowest: | Variable cost = 50% × £80,000 | = | £40,000 |
| | Fixed cost (balance) | = | £10,000 |
| | Total cost | = | £50,000 |

(ii)

| | Sales £ | Sell/Dist £ |
|---|---|---|
| Highest | 90,000 | 9,000 |
| Lowest | 80,000 | 8,000 |
| | 10,000 | 1,000 |

$$\text{Variable cost} = \frac{£1,000}{£10,000} = 10\% \text{ of sales}$$

By substitution:

| | | | |
|---|---|---|---|
| Lowest: | Variable cost = 10% × £80,000 | = | £8,000 |
| | Fixed cost (balance) | = | £Nil |
| | Total cost | = | £8,000 |

(iii)

| | Sales £ | Admin £ |
|---|---|---|
| Highest | 90,000 | 15,000 |
| Lowest | 80,000 | 15,000 |
| | 10,000 | Nil |

$$\text{Variable cost} = \frac{\text{£NIL}}{\text{£10,000}} = \text{NIL}$$

By substitution:

| Lowest: | Variable cost | = | £Nil |
|---|---|---|---|
| | Fixed cost (balance) | = | £15,000 |
| | Total cost | = | £15,000 |

(b)

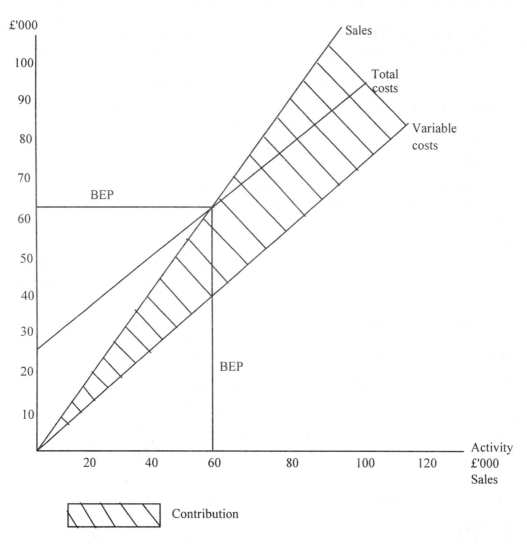

Z plc
Contribution breakeven chart

Break-even point = £62,500 of sales

(c)    Breakeven value = £62,500/month
Margin of safety = 30%
Average monthly sales = £62,500 × 1.3 = £81,250

If sales = £81,250:

| Variable costs = 60% of sales | = | £48,750 |
|---|---|---|
| Fixed costs | = | £25,000 |
| Total costs | = | £73,750 |

Monthly profit averages £81,250 – £73,750 = £7,500

Annual profit = £7,500 × 12 = £90,000

(d)    Contribution from existing outlet per month
       = 40% of sales
       = 40% of £81,250
       = £32,500

This is an annual contribution of £32,500 × 12 = £390,000.

By opening the second outlet 10% of this is transferred ie, £39,000.

Therefore to make the same overall profit the contribution from the second outlet must equal:

| | |
|---|---:|
| Contribution transferred | £39,000 |
| Fixed costs of new outlet | £100,000 |
| | £139,000 |

Since contribution = 40% of sales, the sales required are:

$$\frac{£139,000}{40\%} = £347,500$$

(e)    A retail organisation needs to identify the costs and revenues associated with each of its products (or at least product ranges) in order to determine their profitability. This is measured relative to their consumption of resources (eg, space occupied).

For multi-site retail organisations costs and revenues should be separately recorded for each site. Managers will then have responsibility for the costs and revenues which they can control at their respective sites. In this regard it is important to clearly identify controllable and non-controllable items in any performance reports, which will probably be linked to budgets.

## 44    EXE PLC

(a)    (*Note*: A marginal costing format should be used to assist management decision making).

| | W £ | X £ | Y £ | Z £ | Total £ |
|---|---:|---:|---:|---:|---:|
| Sales | 30,000 | 20,000 | 35,000 | 15,000 | 100,000 |
| Variable cost of sales | (4,800) | (1,600) | (13,200) | (5,000) | (24,600) |
| Variable selling overhead (W1) | (3,000) | (2,000) | (3,500) | (1,500) | (10,000) |
| Gross contribution | 22,200 | 16,400 | 18,300 | 8,500 | 65,400 |
| Specific fixed cost (W2) | (5,200) | (2,400) | (1,800) | (2,000) | (11,400) |
| Net contribution | 17,000 | 14,000 | 16,500 | 6,500 | 54,000 |

| | | | | |
|---|---|---|---|---|
| Non-specific fixed costs | : Production | | | (20,000) |
| | : Selling | | | (20,000) |
| | : Administration | | | (8,000) |
| Net Profit | | | | 6,000 |

(b)    (i)

| | W | X | Y | Total |
|---|---|---|---|---|
| Net Contribution | 17,000 | 14,000 | 23,280 (W3) | 54,280 |
| Non specific fixed costs (as before) | | | | 48,000 |
| Net profit | | | | 6,280 |

(ii)    Increase in net contribution from Y

| | |
|---|---|
| (23,280 – 16,500) | 6,780 |
| Lost contribution from Z | 6,500 |
| Increase in total net contribution and profit | 280 |

(c)    There are a number of factors which should be considered:-

(i)    There may be a need to retrain staff to enable them to produce product Y rather than product Z. Some staff may need to be made redundant, thus lowering the morale of the workforce.

(ii)    The loss of product Z will erode the skills of employees gradually until the knowledge of this product is eliminated.

(iii)    Product Z may be a complimentary product to W, X or Y and thus its removal may cause the sale of these other products to reduce.

(iv)    Customers who previously bought product Z and one or more of the other products may take all of their business to a competitor.

(v)    The deletion of product Z may provide an opportunity for a competitor to enter the market.

(d)

**Contribution / Breakeven Chart Product Y**

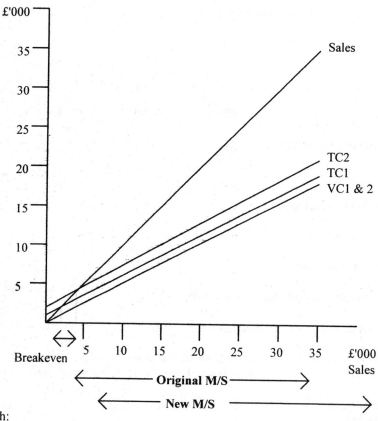

From the graph:

the breakeven point increases from £3,500 to £4,500 sales value, an increase of £1,000

the margin of safety increases from £31,500 (£35,000 – £3,500) to £44,500 (£49,000 – £4,500), an increase of £13,000.

**W1**

|                          | W       | X       | Y       | Z       |
|--------------------------|---------|---------|---------|---------|
| Per question             | 8,000   | 7,000   | 8,500   | 6,500   |
| Non-specific fixed cost  | (5,000) | (5,000) | (5,000) | (5,000) |
|                          | 3,000   | 2,000   | 3,500   | 1,500   |

**W2**

|                          | W       | X       | Y       | Z       | *Total*  |
|--------------------------|---------|---------|---------|---------|----------|
| Per question             | 11,200  | 6,400   | 8,800   | 5,000   | 31,400   |
| Non-specific (20% of sales) | (6,000) | (4,000) | (7,000) | (3,000) | (20,000) |
| Specific                 | 5,200   | 2,400   | 1,800   | 2,000   | 11,400   |

W3

|  |  | Y |
|---|---|---|
| Previous gross contribution |  | 18,300 |
| 40% increase |  | 7,320 |
|  |  | 25,620 |
| Previous specific fixed cost | 1,800 |  |
| 30% increase | 540 | (2,340) |
| Revised net contribution |  | 23,280 |

## 45　X LTD

(a) Generally the classification of costs as fixed or variable identifies those costs which change in total when activity changes (variable costs) and those whose total remains constant (fixed costs).

Relevant costs are those which are affected by a decision, and since most decisions affect activity levels, variable costs (which change when activity changes) can be seen to be relevant costs.

However, it does not automatically follow that fixed costs are not relevant. Some fixed costs may be specific to a product or department and therefore may be avoidable. For example, a decision to discontinue a product will cause the product specific fixed cost to be saved, but a reduction in volume (but not to nil) will have no effect on the fixed cost.

Thus each decision must be considered individually. Whilst variable costs will be relevant, fixed costs will generally not be relevant but there will be circumstances when they must be considered relevant, due to their avoidability.

(b)　(i)

|  | | *Product* | | | |
|---|---|---|---|---|---|
|  | A | B | C | D | Total |
| Contribution/unit | £46.00 | £55.00 | £61.00 | £54.00 |  |
| Hours/unit $\left(\dfrac{\text{Direct labour cost}}{\text{£6/hour}}\right)$ | 3.00 | 2.50 | 4.00 | 4.50 |  |
| Contribution/hour | £15.33 | £22.00 | £15.25 | £12.00 |  |
| Ranking | 2nd | 1st | 3rd | 4th |  |
| We *must* produce 20 litres of each which uses (hours) | 60 | 50 | 80 | 90 | 280 |

The balance of hours are allocated according to rankings, subject to maximum demand levels

| Product B first |  |  |  |  |
|---|---|---|---|---|
| (150 – 20) = 130 litres |  | 325 hours |  | 325 |
|  |  |  |  | 605 |
| Then Product A |  |  |  |  |
| (200 – 20) = 180 litres | 540 hours |  |  | 540 |
|  |  |  |  | 1,145 |
| Then Product C |  |  |  |  |
| (100 – 20) = 80 litres, but we only have time for 200/4 = 50 litres |  |  | 200 hours | 200 |
|  |  |  |  | 1,345 |

The production plan is thus:

|   |           |
|---|-----------|
| A | 200 litres |
| B | 150 litres |
| C | 70 litres |
| D | 20 litres |

The contribution is:

|   |                    |         |
|---|--------------------|---------|
|   |                    | £       |
| A | 200 litres × £46   | 9,200   |
| B | 150 litres × £55   | 8,250   |
| C | 70 litres × £61    | 4,270   |
| D | 20 litres × £54    | 1,080   |
|   |                    | 22,800  |
| Less: | Fixed overhead (1,600 hours × £8) | 12,800 |
| Profit |               | 10,000  |

*Note:* the hourly rate for fixed overhead is calculated from product costs (eg, for A: $\dfrac{£24}{3 \text{ hours}}$ = £8 per hour)

(ii)    The buying price of product C is greater than its variable manufacturing cost, so it should continue to be produced so far as resources allow. However, the buying price is less than X Ltd's selling price, so whilst production is limited, X Ltd should buy the units needed to satisfy the maximum demand.

The extra fixed cost will be specific to product D. Product D has the lowest contribution per labour hour and, at the minimum production level, the extra fixed cost exceeds the contribution earned (£6,000 ÷ 4 = £1,500 per quarter).

If production of product D were to cease, the extra fixed cost could be avoided and the labour resources released used to increase production of product C.

Since product D can be bought in for £100 per litre, a profit can be made by re-selling it for £120 per litre so the maximum demand of 120 litres should be met by this approach.

The labour hours released are 90 hours [see (b)(i)] which can be used to make a further 22.5 litres of product C.

Thus the revised contribution is:

|   |                                               |           |
|---|-----------------------------------------------|-----------|
|   |                                               | £         |
| A | 200 litres × £46                              | 9,200.00  |
| B | 150 litres × £55                              | 8,250.00  |
| C | 92.5 litres × £61 (manufactured)              | 5,642.50  |
| C | 7.5 litres × £15 (£120 – £105) (bought)       | 112.50    |
| D | 120 litres × £20 (£120 – £100) (bought)       | 2,400.00  |
|   |                                               | 25,605.00 |

An increase of £2,805 (£25,605 – £22,800).

| 46 | **BVX LTD** |
|----|-------------|

(a)

|                                                  | Chair  | Bench  | Table  | Total    |
|--------------------------------------------------|--------|--------|--------|----------|
| Contribution/unit (W1)                           | £8.00  | £17.50 | £16.00 |          |
| Timber/unit (m²) (W2)                            | 2.5    | 7.5    | 5      |          |
| Contribution/m²                                  | £3.20  | £2.33  | £3.20  |          |
| Ranking                                          | 1st    | 3rd    | 1st    |          |
| Minimum units to avoid penalty                   | 500    | 100    | 150    |          |
| Timber required for minimum units (m²)           | 1,250  | 750    | 750    | 2,750    |
| Number of units to maximum demand/ production resources (W3) | 3,500  | 233    | 1,350  |          |
| Timber used for production above minimum units   | 8,750  | 1,747.5| 6,750  | 17,247.5 |
| Timber used                                      |        |        |        | 19,997.5 |
| Timber available                                 |        |        |        | 20,000   |
| Total number of units to be produced             | 4,000  | 333    | 1,500  |          |

|                  |                    |            | £         |
|------------------|--------------------|------------|-----------|
| Contribution from: |                  |            |           |
| Chairs           | 4,000 × £8.00      |            | 32,000.00 |
| Benches          | 333 × £17.50       |            | 5,827.50  |
| Tables           | 1,500 × £16.00     |            | 24,000.00 |
|                  |                    |            | 61,827.50 |
| Fixed costs (W4) |                    |            | 54,000.00 |
| Profit           |                    |            | 7,827.50  |

Since the optimum plan includes production of sufficient quantities of each item to meet the order comprising the minimum demand, and production of the most profitable items already meets the maximum demand there is no need to consider the financial penalty.

(b)     The maximum price which should be paid for the timber, a scarce resource, is also known as its shadow price.

The shadow price is the price at which the purchaser makes a nil contribution from its use, therefore to answer the question it is necessary to consider the use of any additional timber acquired.

The present situation is that demand for chairs and tables are fully satisfied from the existing resources, but there is some unsatisfied demand for benches. Thus any additional timber would be used to manufacture more benches.

Based on the current input cost of £2.00 per m² each m² of timber earns a contribution of £2.33. Thus the maximum price to be paid is the sum of these values ie, £4.33 per m².

However, there is no benefit in obtaining more timber than can be used to satisfy the total demand for benches, so this shadow price of £4.33 (m² only applies for up to 12,500 m² of timber (W5) thereafter there is no use for the timber so its shadow price is nil.

(c)        Briefing paper for management meeting

All of the terms listed are terms used in the context of decision making, though some of them apply to other areas of management accounting too.

| | |
|---|---|
| Variable costs | are costs which change in total when the level of activity changes. Many direct costs eg, materials are variable costs because the greater the level of activity the greater are the raw materials required. |
| Relevant costs | are costs which are affected by the decision being taken. Examples include the purchase of specialist materials for a particular job. This is a cost which is only incurred if the work is undertaken and so the cost is relevant to the decision. |
| Avoidable costs | are those costs which are saved or avoided as a result of a particular decision. For example a reduction in the heating/lighting cost of a hotel if it closes during the winter. |
| Incremental costs | are extra costs incurred because of a decision. For example a decision to increase production may make it necessary to lease additional machines. |
| Opportunity costs | are benefits foregone by choosing a particular course of action. For example when dealing with scarce resource problems the opportunity cost, is the contribution which could be earned from the next best use of the resource. |

Thus it can be seen that variable costs will be relevant costs in all decisions because most decisions involve changes to the level or mix of activity. But this does not mean that all relevant costs are variable, fixed costs are relevant if they change due to the decision. When fixed costs reduce they are described as avoidable, if they increase they are said to be incremental. Lastly when decisions involve choosing between alternative uses of limited resources, the opportunity cost of the limited resource is relevant to the decision.

(W1)

|  | Chair £ | Bench £ | Table £ |
|---|---|---|---|
| Selling price | 20.000 | 50.000 | 40.000 |
| Timber cost | 5.00 | 15.000 | 10.000 |
| Direct labour cost | 4.00 | 10.00 | 8.00 |
| Var, overhead, cost | 3.00 | 7.50 | 6.00 |
|  | 12.00 | 32.50 | 24.00 |
| Contribution/unit | 8.00 | 17.50 | 16.00 |

(W2)    Timber cost/£2 per square metre

(W3)    After identifying the timber required to meet the minimum order there remains a balance of timber available. This is allocated to the products according to their rank order, highest first.

There is sufficient timber to produce sufficient chairs and tables to meet the maximum demand after which 1,750 m$^2$ of timber remain. This is used to make 233 further benches, leaving a balance of 2.5m$^2$ of timber which is insufficient to make another unit.

(W4)    $(4,000 \times £4.50) + (2,000 \times £11.25) + (1,500 \times £9.00)$

(W5)

| | | | |
|---|---|---|---|
| Maximum demand for benches | = | 2,000 | benches |
| Existing production | = | 333 | benches |
| Maximum extra production | | 1,667 | benches |
| Timber required for extra production: | | | |
| 1,667 benches × 7.5 m$^2$/bench | = | 12,502.5m$^2$ | |
| Unused stock of timber | | | |
| (20,000 m$^2$ – 19,997.5m$^2$) | = | 2.5m$^2$ | |
| Maximum additional timber | = | 12,500m$^2$ | |

## 47    PRINCIPAL BUDGET FACTORS

(a)    Machine time required for annual demand:

|  |  |
|---|---|
| Product A  24,000 units × 2 hours | 48,000 |
| Product B  24,000 units × 4 hours | 96,000 |
|  | 144,000 |

Capacity:

| | | |
|---|---|---|
| July: | 2,000 of A @ 2 hours | 4,000 |
| August: | 1,000 of A @ 2 hours | 2,000 |
| Sept - | | |
| June: | 4,000 of A × 10 months @ 2 hours | 80,000 |
| | | 86,000 |

| | |
|---|---|
| Machine hours are the limiting factor by | 58,000 hours |

(b)

### Sales/production budget in units

| | Hours Capacity | Product A Units | Hours | Product B Units | Hours |
|---|---|---|---|---|---|
| July | 4,000 | 2,000 (W1) | 4,000 | Nil | Nil |
| August | 2,000 | 1,000 (W1) | 2,000 | Nil | Nil |
| September | 8,000 | 2,400 (W2) | 4,800 | 800 | 3,200 (W4) |
| October | 8,000 | 1,000 (W3) | 2,000 | 1,500 | 6,000 (W4) |
| November | 8,000 | 1,000 (W3) | 2,000 | 1,500 | 6,000 (W4) |
| December | 8,000 | 1,000 (W3) | 2,000 | 1,500 | 6,000 (W4) |
| | | 8,400 | | 5,300 | |

WORKINGS

1    These are limited by the machine hours available.

2    Limited to maximum sales (7,200/3 = 2,400/month).

3    Limited to maximum sales (3,000/3 = 1,000/month).

4    Balance of hours available divided by 4 hours per unit to determine the number of units.

(c)    If equal quantities of A and B are to be sold this will equal the lower of the monthly sales demand for A or B subject to the production capacity/stocks available.

The first priority for production will be to meet sales demand for the period, thereafter items will be made for stock.

| | Hours capacity | Production of A & B (units of each) | Sales of A & B (units of each) |
|---|---|---|---|
| July | 4,000 | 667 (W1) | 667 (W2) |
| August | 2,000 | 333 (W1) | 333 (W2) |
| September | 8,000 | 1,333 (W1) | 1,333 (W2) |
| October | 8,000 | 1,333 (W1) | 1,000 (W3) |
| November | 8,000 | 1,333 (W1) | 1,000 (W3) |

| December | 8,000 | 1,333 (W1) | 1,000 (W3) |
|---|---|---|---|
| | | | 5,333 |

As sales of A and B are to be in equal quantities, then production would be equal, one unit of each of A and B requires 6 machine hours.

WORKINGS

1        Restricted by machine capacity.
2        Restricted by production.
3        Restricted by demand for product A.

(d)

| | Product A £ | Product B £ |
|---|---|---|
| Selling price | 10.00 | 8.00 |
| Variable costs/unit | 5.50 | 7.60 |
| Contribution/unit | 4.50 | 0.40 |
| Units sold (b) | 8,400 | 5,300 |
| Units sold (c) | 5,333 | 5,333 |
| Difference in units sold | 3,067 | (33) |
| Effect on contribution | £13,801.50 reduction | £13.20 increase |

Overall effect on contribution and profit (assuming that fixed costs are not affected by the change) is £13,801.50 − £13.20 = £13,788.30 reduction.

# 48    PDR PLC

(a)

| Product | A | B | C | D |
|---|---|---|---|---|
| Contribution/unit | £16 | £17 | £23 | £22 |
| Machine hrs/unit | 4 | 3 | 4 | 5 |
| Contribution per machine hour | £4.00 | £5.67 | £5.75 | £4.40 |
| Rank | 4th | 2nd | 1st | 3rd |
| Plan: Units | Nil | 180 | 250 | 92 |
| Hours | Nil | 540 | 1,000 | 460 |

**Profit statement**

| | £ | £ |
|---|---|---|
| Contribution from product: | | |
| B | 3,060 | |
| C | 5,750 | |
| D | 2,024 | |
| | | 10,834 |
| Less: fixed costs: | | |
| 1,000 hours × £8/hour | | (8,000) |
| Profit | | 2,834 |

(b)

# REPORT

| | |
|---|---|
| **To:** | Marketing Director |
| **From**: | Management Accountant |
| **Subject:** | Production strategies |
| **Date:** | 26 May 1999 |

### Introduction

Further to your request I have considered the proposed strategies to overcome our production constraints and set out my findings below.

### Findings

(i)      The overtime option increases the variable costs and thus reduces unit contribution.

        The reductions are:

| | |
|---|---|
| Product A | £3.50/unit |
| Product D | £7.00/unit |

        Each product still has a positive unit contribution of:

| | |
|---|---|
| Product A | £12.50/unit |
| Product D | £15.00/unit |

        Overtime of 216 hours/week would enable the company to meet the full demand. This is equivalent to around 8 hours/week per employee so it is a feasible alternative.

(ii)      If product B were to be bought-in this would release 540 machine hours. These could be used to make:

         8 units of product D
       125 units of product A

        which yields contribution of:

| | |
|---|---|
| Product A: 125 × £16 | £2,000 |
| Product D:   8 × £22 | £176 |
| | £2,176 |

        **But** the buying price of product B is £7/unit more than its variable production cost:

        180 units × £7           (£,1,260)

        This option does **not** meet all of the demand.

### Conclusion

Only option (i) meets our demand requirements, but working overtime is not a long-term solution and there may be wear and tear costs in using the machinery for longer hours.

Option (ii) allows us to meet much of the demand but other factors such as

-      supplier reliability
-      supplier quality
-      loss of production control/expertise

must be considered.

## 49     CHOICE OF CONTRACTS

(a)

| Note | | North East | | South Coast | |
|---|---|---|---|---|---|
| | | £ | £ | £ | £ |
| | Contract price | | 288,000 | | 352,000 |
| (1) | Material X: stock | 19,440 | | | |
| (2) | Material X: firm orders | 27,360 | | | |
| (3) | Material X: not yet ordered | 60,000 | | | |
| (4) | Material Y | | | 49,600 | |
| (5) | Material Z | | | 71,200 | |
| (6) | Labour | 86,000 | | 110,000 | |
| (8) | Staff accommodation and travel | 6,800 | | 5,600 | |
| (9) | Penalty clause | | | 28,000 | |
| (10) | Loss of plant hire income | | | 6,000 | |
| | | | 199,600 | | 270,400 |
| | Profit | | 88,400 | | 81,600 |

The company should undertake the North-east contract. It is better than the South coast contract by £6,800 (£88,400 - £81,600).

(b)

Note 1     Material X can be used in place of another material which the company uses. The value of material X for this purpose is 90% × £21,600 = £19,440. If the company undertakes the North-east contract it will not be able to obtain this saving. This is an opportunity cost.

Note 2     Although the material has not been received yet the company is committed to the purchase. Its treatment is the same therefore as if it was already in stock. The value is 90% × £30,400 = £27,360.

Note 3     The future cost of material X not yet ordered is relevant.

Note 4     The original cost of material Y is a sunk cost and is therefore not relevant. If the material was to be sold now its value would be 24,800 × 2 × 85% = £42,160, ie, twice the purchase price less 15%, however, if the material is kept it can be used on other contracts, thus saving the company from future purchases. The second option is the better. The relevant cost of material Y is 2 × 24,800 = £49,600. If the company uses material Y on the South coast contract, it will eventually have to buy an extra £49,600 of Y for use on other contracts.

Note 5     The future cost of material Z is an incremental cost and is relevant.

Note 6     As the labour is to be sub-contracted it is a variable cost and is relevant.

Note 7     Site management is a fixed cost and will be incurred whichever contract is undertaken (and indeed if neither is undertaken), and is therefore not relevant.

Note 8     It is assumed that the staff accommodation and travel is specific to the contracts and will only be incurred if the contracts are undertaken.

Note 9     If the South-coast contract is undertaken the company has to pay a £28,000 penalty for withdrawing from the North-east contract. This is a relevant cost with regard to the South-coast contract.

Note 10     The depreciation on plant is not a cash flow. It is therefore not relevant. The opportunity cost of lost plant hire is relevant, however.

Note 11    It is assumed that the notional interest has no cash flow implications.

Note 12    It is assumed that the HQ costs are not specific to particular contracts.

---

## 50    JASON

*(Tutorial note: part (a) involves description of opportunity cost and out of pocket cost, the latter term widely used by people in general. The question asks students to provide a numerical example using their own figures. The golden rule here is keep it simple.*

*Part (b) involves application of the terms in part (a).*

*Part (c) involves understanding of cost behaviour. The sales volume has changed (not sales price), therefore it can be assumed that the variable costs will retain the same relationship with sales revenue for all volumes. The fixed cost figures are calculated as a percentage of the original sales figure, since they are unaffected by volume. Also, 'marginal costing' format means show contribution.)*

(a)    An opportunity cost is 'the value of the benefit sacrificed when one course of action is chosen, in preference to an alternative' (*CIMA Terminology*). It is an imputed cost which does not involve an actual cash flow but rather a cash flow that would have been achieved if the alternative course of action had been pursued. For example, a contract needs 100 hours of skilled labour which is normally incurred at the basic rate of £4. This type of labour is in short supply and if it is used on the contract production and sale of product X will be reduced. Details of product X:

|  | £ | £ |
|---|---|---|
| Selling price |  | 30 |
| Direct material | 5 |  |
| Direct labour (skilled): |  |  |
| 2 hours @ £4 | 8 |  |
| Variable overhead | 2 | 15 |
| Contribution |  | 15 |

$$\text{Contribution per labour hour} = \frac{15}{2} = £7.50$$

Opportunity cost of labour for contract

$$= \quad £7.50 \times 100 \text{ hours}$$
$$= \quad £750$$

An 'out of pocket cost' is 'a current or near-future outlay made to meet costs incurred because of a specific decision' (*Horngren*), ie it is a cost which involves an actual cash outlay/payment and is a conventional concept of cost with which people are familiar. An example would be the cost of raw material that has to be purchased in order to undertake the above contract. If the contract needs 400 kilos of material A, none of which is in stock, and the current purchase price is £2, then the 'out of pocket cost' of material A for the contract would be 400 × £2 = £800.

(b)    Evaluation of Debbie's offer to Jason (per quarter)

*(Tutorial note: for information the costs/benefits are marked as opportunity costs (OC) or out of pocket costs (OOP).)*

|  | Costs £ | Benefits £ |
|---|---|---|
| Contribution to car expenses (OOP) |  | 120 |
| Season ticket avoided (OC) |  | 188 |
|  |  | 308 |
| Petrol and oil (OOP) | 128 |  |
| Tyres and miscellaneous (OOP) | 52 | 180 |
| Net benefit |  | 128 |

Therefore the offer should be accepted.

The above conclusion assumes that the extra mileage on the car does not cause the car to decline in value more than it would if just used for college and weekends, ie depreciation is unaffected by the decision.

(c)    **Statement of amended sales and cost structure**

|  | % | £'000 | £'000 |
|---|---|---|---|
| Sales | 100 |  | 2,560 |
| Direct material | 32 | 819.2 |  |
| Direct wages | 18 | 460.8 |  |
| Variable production overhead | 6 | 153.6 |  |
| Variable administration and selling costs | 3 | 76.8 | 1,510.4 |
| Contribution | 41 |  | 1,049.6 |
| Fixed costs: |  |  |  |
| Production $(2{,}560 \times \dfrac{100}{80} \times 24\%)$ | 30 | 768 |  |
| Administration and selling $(2{,}560 \times \dfrac{100}{80} \times 7\%)$ | 8.75 | 224 | 992 |
| Profit | 2.25 |  | 57.6 |

# 51    PUBLISHING COMPANY

(a)

| | *Reasons* | £ |
|---|---|---|
| Paper | Book value is irrelevant because it is a sunk cost, as there is no other use replacement would not occur so the opportunity cost or scrap sale proceeds is the relevant value. | 2,500 |
| Ink | Since this involves a future cost if the work is undertaken the purchase price should be used. Since the remaining stock has no foreseeable use it has no value so the entire purchase cost is used. | 3,000 |
| Skilled labour | Since the weekend working is caused if the work is undertaken the full cost is relevant: | |

|  |  |
|---|---|
| 125 hours @ £4/hr = | £500 |
| 125 hours @ £5/hr = | £625 |

|  |  | 1,125 |
|---|---|---|
| Unskilled labour | The weekend work results in 50 hours time off in lieu, this with the 75 other hours worked totals 125 hours which is less than the 200 hours of idle time which are already being paid for, thus there is no incremental cost. | Nil |
| Variable overhead | This is a future cost which will be incurred if the work is undertaken | 1,400 |

| Printing press | - | The depreciation is a past cost and should be ignored, however, the use of the press has an opportunity cost. If this work is undertaken then the press is not available for hire. The opportunity cost is the contribution which would be earned from hiring: | |
|---|---|---|---|
| | | 200 hours @ (£6 – £3) | 600 |
| Production fixed costs | - | As these costs are unaffected by the decision they should be ignored | Nil |
| Estimating costs | - | These costs are past or sunk costs and should be ignored. | Nil |
| MINIMUM PRICE | | | £8,625 |

(b)   Contribution is the difference between sales and variable costs, both of which are dependent on activity. Fixed costs, which tend to be independent of activity, are ignored.

Since most decisions involve changes in the level of activity the relevant costs and revenues are those affected by changes in the level of activity. Thus the net effect of these relevant costs and revenues is contribution.

(c)   An opportunity cost is the value which represents the cost of the next best alternative or the benefit forgone by accepting one course of action in preference to others when allocating scarce resources.

If there is only one scarce resource, decisions can be made by ranking alternatives according to their contributions per unit of the scarce resource. However, in reality there will be many scarce resources, and different alternatives will use alternative combinations of those scarce resources. In these situations opportunity costs are used to identify the optimum use of those resources.

## 52   EXE PLC

| | | | £ | REASONING |
|---|---|---|---|---|
| (a) | Direct materials | : steel | 55.00 | This is in regular use, so use replacement value. |
| | | : brass | 20.00 | Future transaction value. |
| | Direct labour | : skilled (W1) | 300.00 | The overtime is the cheaper alternative. |
| | | : semi-skilled | Nil | The idle time is already being paid, so there is no further cost. |
| | Variable overhead | | 7.50 | The only cost which is specific to this job is the power cost. |
| | Fixed overhead | | Nil | These are not affected by the work. |
| | Estimation costs | | Nil | These are a sunk cost. |
| | Administration costs | | Nil | These are not affected by the work. |
| | Profit | | Nil | This is not needed to breakeven. |
| | Relevant cost | | 382.50 | |

WORKING

1      Overtime cost: 25 hours × £8 × 1.5 = £300
       Lost contribution: 25 hours × £13 = £325

(b)   If the order is to form part of normal production then the pricing of such an order would be on a different basis to that used in the above estimate. The problem therefore is the difficulties that would arise from an attempt to change the price in future.

With this in mind, there would need to be a thorough review of the resources estimate, and they would need to be valued on a long-term basis. This is in comparison to the short-term relevant cost basis which is appropriate when there is a need to utilise idle capacity.

Before entering into any longer term agreements it is also important to consider the likelihood of alternative, more profitable work from the same resources. The pricing of future work must recognise the real value of such alternatives.

(c)    Example

| Product | X | Y |
|---|---|---|
| Contribution/unit | £10 | £8 |
| Labour hours/unit | 4 | 2 |
| Contribution/hour | £2.50 | £4 |

Thus product Y is the more profitable use of the labour and would be ranked 1st.

If an opportunity cost approach is used then:

(i)    if one unit of X is made we lose the contribution from 2 units of Y.

(ii)    if one unit of Y is made, we lose the average contribution from 0.5 units of X.

|  | X £ | Y £ |
|---|---|---|
| Contribution/unit | 10 | 8 |
| Opportunity contribution lost: |  |  |
| 2 Y | 16 |  |
| 0.5 X |  | 5 |
|  | (£6) | £3 |

It can be seen that by introducing an opportunity cost product X has a negative contribution per unit whereas product Y's contribution per unit is still positive, showing that it is worthwhile despite the alternative.

# 53    CASH BUDGET

(a)

|  | January £'000 | February £'000 | March £'000 |
|---|---|---|---|
| Receipts (W1) | 1,195 | 1,190 | 1,090 |
| **Payments** |  |  |  |
| Wages and salaries | 60 | 60 | 60 |
| Materials creditors | 240 | 210 | 240 |
| Variable overhead (W2) | 224 | 196 | 175 |
| Fixed overhead (W2) | 200 | 161 | 200 |
| Selling and admin overhead | 110 | 115 | 115 |
| Corporation tax | 750 | - | - |
| Dividend | - | - | 500 |
| VAT (W3) | 13 | 84 | 58 |
| Capital expenditure | 1,000 | - | 700 |
|  | 2,597 | 826 | 2,048 |
| Net cash flow for month | (1,402) | 364 | (958) |
| Opening cash balance | 1,450 | 48 | 412 |
| Closing cash balance | 48 | 412 | (546) |

WORKINGS

(W1)

| | November £'000 | December £'000 | January £'000 | February £'000 | March £'000 |
|---|---|---|---|---|---|
| Sales | 1,100 | 1,000 | 1,400 | 1,200 | 1,100 |
| 60% current month | | | 840 | 720 | 660 |
| 30% +1 month | | | 300 | 420 | 360 |
| 5% +2 months | | | 55 | 50 | 70 |
| Receipts | | | 1,195 | 1,190 | 1,090 |

(W2)

| | | December £'000 | January £'000 | February £'000 | March £'000 |
|---|---|---|---|---|---|
| Total overheads | | 640 | 560 | 500 | 560 |
| Variable part (× 35%) | | 224 | 196 | 175 | 196 |
| Fixed overheads | | 416 | 364 | 325 | 364 |
| Depreciation | | 164 | 164 | 164 | 164 |
| Fixed overheads (cash items) | | 252 | 200 | 161 | 200 |

Note that depreciation is not a cash flow and should not appear in a cash budget.
The fixed overhead is paid in the month incurred and the variable in the following month.

(W3)

| | December £'000 | January £'000 | February £'000 | March £'000 |
|---|---|---|---|---|
| Sales | 1,000 | 1,400 | 1,200 | |
| Output tax ($7/47$ ths - 1 month delay) | - | 149 | 209 | 179 |
| Input tax | | 136 | 125 | 121 |
| Payment | | 13 | 84 | 58 |

(b)  (i)   More careful control of debtors might result in less bad debts and the earlier settlement of bills.  Bad debts for January - March will eventually amount to £185,000 (5% × (1.4m + 1.2m + 1.1m)).  Any reduction in the level of bad debts would be useful.

One of the main purposes of a cash budget is to identify any cash surpluses.  It is important that any surpluses are invested to best advantage.

(ii)   The most obvious change that could be made is the delayed purchase of the capital equipment or at least a delay in payment for it.

It might be possible to renegotiate the credit terms available for the purchase of raw materials and/or for the overheads.  Extending the credit period would be a temporary cash flow improvement.

## 54   D LTD

(a)  (i)

**Sales budget**
**Year ended 31 December 1994**

| Quarter | Units | £'000 |
|---|---|---|
| 1 | 40,000 | 6,000 |
| 2 | 50,000 | 7,500 |
| 3 | 30,000 | 4,800 |
| 4 | 45,000 | 7,200 |
| | 165,000 | 25,500 |

(ii)

**Production budget**
**Year ended 31 December 1994**

| | | Quarters (units) | | | |
|---|---|---|---|---|---|
| | *1* | *2* | *3* | *4* | *Total* |
| Required by sales | 40,000 | 50,000 | 30,000 | 45,000 | 165,000 |
| Closing stock | 5,000 | 3,000 | 4,500 | 4,000 | 4,000 |
| | 45,000 | 53,000 | 34,500 | 49,000 | 169,000 |
| Opening stock | (9,000) | (5,000) | (3,000) | (4,500) | (9,000) |
| Production | 36,000 | 48,000 | 31,500 | 44,500 | 160,000 |

(iii)

**Material usage budget**
**Year ended 31 December 1994**

| | | Quarters (units) | | | |
|---|---|---|---|---|---|
| | *1* | *2* | *3* | *4* | *Total* |
| Component R | 144,000 | 192,000 | 126,000 | 178,000 | 640,000 |
| Component T | 108,000 | 144,000 | 94,500 | 133,500 | 480,000 |
| Shell S | 36,000 | 48,000 | 31,500 | 44,500 | 160,000 |

(iv)

**Production cost budget**
**Year ended 31 December 1994**

| | | | Quarters | | | |
|---|---|---|---|---|---|---|
| | | *1* | *2* | *3* | *4* | *Total* |
| | | £'000 | £'000 | £'000 | £'000 | £'000 |
| Direct material: | R | 1,152 | 1,689.6 | 1,108.8 | 1,566.4 | 5,516.8 |
| | T | 540 | 792 | 519.75 | 734.25 | 2,586 |
| | S | 1,080 | 1,440 | 945 | 1,335 | 4,800 |
| Direct labour | | 1,080 | 1,440 | 945 | 1,388.4 | 4,853.4 |
| Variable overhead | | 360 | 480 | 315 | 445 | 1,600 |
| Fixed overhead | | 54 | 72 | 47.25 | 66.75 | 240 |
| | | 4,266 | 5,913.6 | 3,880.80 | 5,535.8 | 19,596.2 |

(b)   The principal budget factor is the factor which limits the organisation within the budgeting period. This may be one or more production resources which limit production or it may be demand for its products, ie, sales.

When this factor has been identified this budget must be prepared first and the other budgets derived from it.

Assuming sales to be the limiting factor a forecast of likely sales demand must be made for the budget period. Such forecasts may use both external and internal data.

External data would include

- feedback from existing customers; and
- the results of market research.

These could be entered onto a database or statistics package on a computer and analysed by consumer group, age and various other classifications.

Internal data will be based on past records of sales volumes and prices. These may be analysed using time series techniques to identify seasonal and underlying trends. Such trends may be compared with other internal and external data to establish any correlation which may exist.

Again this analysis can be improved by using statistical and modelling (ie, spreadsheet) packages on a microcomputer. This analysis can be used to predict future sales based on trends.

## 55   SUPERMARKET

### *Answer plan*

(a) Sales by till
Sales by section
Exceptional figures/
variances

Comparison of Sales v
prev weeks

Discrepancies
Customer complaints
Stock outs

Cash statement

(b) Sales by section

Exceptional figures/ variances

Comparison v prev week

Stock report
Absenteeism report
Details of price rises expected
Competitor prices

Report on any promotions

(c) Sales by section

Exceptional figures/
variances

Comparison v prev mths
Comparison v budget
Comparison v last year
Year to date figures

Profit statement

### REPORT

**To:**       Manager

**From:**     Management Accountant

**Date:**     23 November 19X3

**Subject:**  **Information needs for efficient running of business**

---

I have listed below, various reports which I think should prove useful in the running of the supermarket. I have broken the report into three categories - daily reports, weekly reports and monthly reports.

(a)   **Daily reports**

(i)     Sales per till.

(ii)    Sales per section (frozen foods, bakery, greengrocery, etc).

(iii)   Any exceptional figures or variances for individual products or groups of products (the figures will have to be very unusual to be highlighted, as on a daily basis, there can be big fluctuations, and we don't want to highlight too many products).

(iv)    Comparison of sales figures with the same day's sales figures in previous weeks.

(v)     Discrepancies on tills.

(vi)    Customer complaints broken down by product or by service problems.

(vii)   Stock out report.

(viii)  Cash statement.

(b)   **Weekly reports**

(i)     Sales per section.

(ii)    Any exceptional figures or variances for individual products or groups of products. (This will be a more detailed report than the corresponding daily report as over a week there should be less fluctuations and we will therefore set higher limits upon our expectations.)

(iii)      Comparison of sales figures with previous weeks' sales.

(iv)      Stock report, including out-of-date product details.

(v)      Customer complaint summary.

(vi)      Labour report, especially detailing absenteeism numbers.

(vii)      Details of expected or actual supplier price increases.

(viii)      Information on competitors' prices.

(ix)      Details on success or otherwise of any special promotions.

(c)     **Monthly reports**

(i)      Sales per section.
(ii)      Sales per product.
(iii)      Comparison with previous year.
(iv)      Comparison with previous months.
(v)      Comparison with budgets.
(vi)      Year to date figures.
(vii)      Exceptional figures/variances.
(viii)      Profit statement.

With the vast number of different products that we have, it is important that you do not become bogged down with too much detail and that management-by-exception principles are followed. The above suggestions will of course be augmented by any necessary ad-hoc reports.

MANAGEMENT ACCOUNTANT

## 58    TJ LTD

(a)     It is firstly necessary to identify the behavioural aspects of each item of cost - this is done using the high and low points technique:

(i)

|  | £ | Activity % |
|---|---|---|
| Direct materials | 1,153,800 | 75 |
|  | 846,200 | 55 |
|  | 307,600 | 20 |

Variable cost = $\dfrac{£307,600}{20}$ = £15,380 per 1%

By substitution, the total variable cost at 55% =

|  | £ |
|---|---|
| £15,380 × 55 | 845,900 |
| Therefore fixed cost | 300 |
| Total as above | 846,200 |

(ii)

|  | £ | Activity % |
|---|---|---|
| Direct wages | 2,019,150 | 75 |
|  | 1,480,850 | 55 |
|  | 538,300 | 20 |

$$\text{Variable cost} = \frac{£538{,}300}{20} = £26{,}915 \text{ per } 1\%$$

By substitution, the total variable cost at 55% =

|  | £ |
|---|---|
| £26,915 × 55 | 1,480,325 |
| Therefore fixed cost | 525 |
| Total as above | 1,480,850 |

(iii)

|  | £ | Activity % |
|---|---|---|
| Production overhead | 703,830 | 75 |
|  | 596,170 | 55 |
|  | 107,660 | 20 |

$$\text{Variable cost} = \frac{£107{,}660}{20} = £5{,}383 \text{ per } 1\%$$
By substitution, the total variable cost at 55% =

|  | £ |
|---|---|
| £5,383 × 55 | 296,065 |
| Therefore fixed cost | 300,105 |
| Total as above | 596,170 |

(iv)

|  | £ | Activity % |
|---|---|---|
| Selling and distribution overhead | 207,690 | 75 |
|  | 192,310 | 55 |
|  | 15,380 | 20 |

$$\text{Variable cost} = \frac{£15{,}380}{20} = £769 \text{ per } 1\%$$
By substitution, the total variable cost at 55% =

|  | £ |
|---|---|
| £769 × 55 | 42,295 |
| Therefore fixed cost | 150,015 |
| Total as above | 192,310 |

(v)    Administration overhead

This cost is constant at all activity levels so it is a fixed cost.

**Flexible budget**

| | Activity level 85% £ | £ |
|---|---|---|
| Sales (W10) | | 5,911,092 |
| Variable costs | | |
|     Direct materials (W1) | 1,385,738 | |
|     Direct wages (W2) | 2,356,408 | |
|     Production overhead (W3) | 489,584 | |
|     Selling and distribution overhead (W4) | 69,940 | |
| | | 4,301,670 |
| Contribution | | 1,609,422 |

Fixed costs
    Direct materials (W5)                     318
    Direct wages (W6)                        541
    Production overhead (W7)           330,115
    Selling and distribution overhead (W8)  161,266
    Administration overhead (W9)      132,000

                                          624,240

Profit                                985,182

(b)      The change in activity level may give rise to the following problems:

     (i)    **Market based problem**

The industry sector is recovering from the recent recession and it is possible that market demand will not increase in line with expectations unless the selling price is reduced. This may make such an increase in volume unprofitable.

     (ii)   **Production resource problem**

The direct workers are currently employed on production for an average of 40 hours per week. The proposed increase to 85% (approximately one-third increase above existing levels) will require the recruitment of additional workers and/or additional machinery. In the latter case, such investment may lead to increased fixed costs.

     (iii)  **Financing problem**

The increase will result in higher working capital (stocks and debtors). These will need to be funded.

(c)      The committee will comprise:

     (i)    Accountant
     (ii)   Production manager
     (iii)  Marketing manager
     (iv)  Personnel manager

The role of the committee is to co-ordinate the preparation of the budget, to ensure that it is completed in accord with the budget timetable, and to allocate responsibilities for the preparation of functional budgets.

## WORKINGS

(W1)   ($£15,380 \times 85) \times 1.06$    =   £1,385,738

(W2)   ($£26,915 \times 85) \times 1.03$    =   £2,356,408

(W3)   ($£5,383 \times 85) \times 1.07$     =   £489,584

(W4)   ($£769 \times 85) \times 1.07$      =   £69,940

(W5)   $£300 \times 1.06$             =   £318

(W6)   $£525 \times 1.03$             =   £541

(W7)   $£300,105 \times 1.10$       =   £330,115

(W8)   $£150,015 \times 1.075$     =   £161,266

(W9)   $£120,000 \times 1.10$       =   £132,000

(W10)   Total cost $\times \dfrac{100\%}{(100\% - 16\frac{2}{3}\%)}$

$= £4,925,910 \times \dfrac{100\%}{83\frac{1}{3}\%}$      $=$      £5,911,092

## 57   XYZ LTD

(a)

| | Sept<br>£ | Oct<br>£ | Nov<br>£ | Dec<br>£ | Jan<br>£ | Feb<br>£ |
|---|---|---|---|---|---|---|
| **RECEIPTS** | | | | | | |
| Cash sales (W1) | 18,240 | 15,200 | 17,100 | 16,720 | 15,960 | 19,000 |
| Credit sales (W2) | 30,000 | 28,800 | 24,000 | 27,000 | 26,400 | 25,200 |
| Capital | | 8,000 | | | | |
| | 48,240 | 52,000 | 41,100 | 43,720 | 42,360 | 44,200 |
| **PAYMENTS** | | | | | | |
| Purchases (W3) | 18,800 | 19,600 | 17,600 | 17,000 | 19,800 | 17,200 |
| Wages (W4) | 6,800 | 6,000 | 6,500 | 6,400 | 6,200 | 7,000 |
| Fixed costs (W5) | 6,000 | 6,000 | 6,000 | 6,000 | 6,000 | 6,000 |
| Capital | 15,000 | | 10,000 | | | 4,000 |
| Corporation tax | | | 44,000 | | | |
| | 46,600 | 31,600 | 84,100 | 29,400 | 32,000 | 34,200 |
| Surplus/(Deficit) | 1,640 | 20,400 | (43,000) | 14,320 | 10,360 | 10,000 |
| Balance b/f | 5,000 | 6,640 | 27,040 | (15,960) | (1,640) | 8,720 |
| Balance c/f | 6,640 | 27,040 | (15,960) | (1,640) | 8,720 | 18,720 |

(b)      A spreadsheet is a computer modelling package which comprises rows and columns which intersect to form cells in a matrix. It can be seen that this is the layout used in (a) above.

Each cell may be used to store either a label (description); a value; or a formula. The formula may be referenced to the contents of other cells which can automate the calculation of many values in applications such as the cash budget in (a) above.

The spreadsheet may be used simply as an efficient and powerful calculator; however, it is also a powerful presentations device with graphic representations of the data being available. In this regard the user must segregate the output presentation and data entry areas of the spreadsheet.

Using part (a) as an example, the row and column headings would be as shown above. The sales values for each month would then be inserted into an input area together with the percentages for cash/credit sales etc. The equivalent of working 3 would also be included in this area.

Formulae would then be entered in the input area to calculate intermediate values (eg, stock used in W3) and in the output area to link with the input area. Some values (eg, the capital receipt and payments) would be keyed directly into the output area since no further calculations are required. Where the same formula is used for a number of time periods, then it would be entered once and copied to the columns of the other periods.

Any of the input variables may then be changed and the effect on the final output will be automatically calculated, this is known as What-If analysis.

(c)      Feed forward is the comparison of expected output based on budgets and forecasts with organisational objectives or constraints. For example it may be that in part (a) the overdraft facility is only £10,000. This initial cash budget identifies an expected overdraft of £15,960 at the end of November. The plan would need to be reconsidered **before** it is implemented. This is feedforward control.

Feedback is the comparison of actual and target performance **after** the budget has been implemented. For example in October the actual and budget sales receipts for September could be compared and the reasons for any differences investigated.

WORKINGS

(W1)    Since 60% of sales are credit sales, 40% are cash sales, eg,

|  | £ |
|---|---|
| September cash sales = £48,000 × 40% = | 19,200 |
| 5% discount on £19,200 | 960 |
|  | 18,240 |

(W2)    August credit sales are paid in September, and so on.

Credit sales = 60% so the September receipt = 60% × £50,000 = £30,000

| (W3) | July | Aug | Sept | Oct | Nov | Dec |
|---|---|---|---|---|---|---|
| Sales: | | | | | | |
| Stock used | | | | | | |
| (40% of sales) | 17,600 | 20,000 | 19,200 | 16,000 | 18,000 | 17,600 |
| Opening stock | | | | | | |
| (50% of 40% of sales) | (8,800) | (10,000) | (9,600) | (8,000) | (9,000) | (8,800) |
| Closing stock | | | | | | |
| (50% of 40% of | | | | | | |
| next months sales) | 10,000 | 9,600 | 8,000 | 9,000 | 8,800 | 8,400 |
| Extra stock | | | | | 2,000 | |
| PURCHASES | 18,800 | 19,600 | 17,600 | 17,000 | 19,800 | 17,200 |
| Paid in | Sept | Oct | Nov | Dec | Jan | Feb |

(W4)    10% of sales + £2,000

eg, September:
        (10% × £48,000) + £2,000 = £6,800

(W5)    £7,500 – £1,500 Depreciation : £6,000

# 58      BUDGETED SALES VALUES

|  | May £ | June £ | July £ |
|---|---|---|---|
| Receipts | 401,700 | 450,280 | 425,880 |
| Payments | | | |
| Materials (W3) | 161,640 | 172,440 | 166,320 |
| Labour (W2) | 86,040 | 86,400 | 79,920 |
| Variable overhead (W4) | 26,592 | 28,728 | 27,936 |
| Fixed overhead | 75,000 | 75,000 | 75,000 |
| Capital expenditure | – | 190,000 | – |
|  | 349,272 | 552,568 | 349,176 |
| Surplus/(deficit) | 52,428 | (102,228) | 76,704 |
| Balance b/f | 40,000 | 92,428 | (9,860) |
| Balance c/f | 92,428 | (9,860) | 66,844 |

## WORKINGS

(W1)   Production

| | April £'000 | May £'000 | June £'000 | July £'000 | August £'000 |
|---|---|---|---|---|---|
| Sales | 400 | 450 | 520 | 420 | 480 |
| Variable cost of sales (60%) | 240 | 270 | 312 | 252 | 288 |
| Current production (60%) | 144 | 162.0 | 187.2 | 151.2 | 172.8 |
| Previous month production (40%) | 108 | 124.8 | 100.8 | 115.2 | N/A |
| Total production | 252 | 286.8 | 288.0 | 266.4 | N/A |

(W2)   Labour

| | | | | | |
|---|---|---|---|---|---|
| Labour costs (30%) | 75.6 | 86.04 | 86.4 | 79.92 | |

(W3)   Materials

| | | | | | |
|---|---|---|---|---|---|
| Materials used (60%) | 151.2 | 172.08 | 172.8 | 159.84 | |
| Current purchases (50%) | 75.6 | 86.04 | 86.40 | 79.92 | |
| Previous month purchases (50%) | 86.04 | 86.04 | 79.92 | N/A | |
| Total purchases | 161.64 | 172.44 | 166.32 | N/A | |

(W4)   Variable overhead

| | | | | | |
|---|---|---|---|---|---|
| Incurred (10%) | 25.2 | 28.68 | 28.8 | 26.64 | |
| Current paid | 10.08 | 11.472 | 11.520 | 10.656 | |
| Following paid | N/A | 15.120 | 17.208 | 17.280 | |
| | | 26.592 | 28.728 | 27.936 | |

(W5)   Fixed overhead

$$\frac{(£1,200,000 - £300,000)}{12} = £75,000 \text{ per month}$$

## 59    FLEXIBLE

## Answer Plan

(a)    Definitions, differences between types of budget.

A fixed budget is a budget showing the costs and/or revenues at a single level of activity.

A flexible budget is a budget showing the costs and/or revenues at more than one level of activity.

As can be seen from the above definitions a flexible budget provides more information than a fixed budget by recognising the behavioural characteristics of different items of cost/revenue.

# *Answer Plan*

(b)     Types of cost, purposes of budgetary control, advantages/disadvantages.

## REPORT

To:         Board of Directors
From:       Management Accountant
Re:         Budgets and budgetary control              Date: X-X-19XX

Costs may be analysed and classified in a number of different ways. It is usual for them to be classified by function eg, Production, Selling, Administration, Research, and then for them to be further analysed into fixed costs and variable costs.

Production costs are likely to include significant values of both fixed and variable costs, whereas in other areas of the business the value of variable costs is often much less if they exist at all.

Budgetary control is the process of comparing actual and budgeted costs and revenues, however there are often distinct purposes of budgetary control which are not the same for all costs.

Where costs are associated with producing goods or services for resale the objective is often to ensure that resources are used efficiently rather than to limit expenditure. For example if there is demand for more units from customers, production is encouraged to expand to meet that demand provided it can be done both efficiently and profitably.

However, with other items such as research and advertising expenditure the purpose of budgetary control is often to limit expenditure.

The two purposes are well served by the use of both fixed and flexible budgets. Flexible budgets are designed to provide cost allowances for different levels of activity having regard to the behavioural characteristics of the costs. This type of budget is thus ideally suited to controlling the efficiency of costs and resources.

Fixed budgets provide pre-set expenditure limits and are thus suitable for controlling discretionary costs such as research and advertising expenditure.

The other main advantage of a fixed budget is that it provides a target in terms of activity levels, costs and revenues. Whilst this target may change in order to effect appropriate control over production related items, without an initial target the activities of the organisation could not be co-ordinated.

# *Answer Plan*

(c)     Spreadsheet, sales budget, input areas, formulae, output area.

A spreadsheet is a matrix comprising rows and columns which intersect to form cells. Each cell may be used to store a description, a value, or a formula.

A sales budget shows the quantity of each product to be sold, the selling price per unit, and the consequent sales value. These values may be analysed in many ways, for example by sales person, geographical region, etc.

When using a spreadsheet for complex budgets of large organisations it is important to create a formalised structure comprising an input area, a working area, and an output area.

As its name suggests an input area is the area of the spreadsheet which is used to receive the data upon which the sales budget is to be based. The basic data for a sales budget are the volume of sales and the selling price. However the volume may be analysed between different sales persons, in different geographical areas, for each product, for each accounting period. Selling prices will probably be different for each product and may be different in different geographical areas and at different times of the year.

The working area will be used to store the results of intermediate calculations based upon the data entered. These calculations will be the subject of formulae which act on the data values.

The output area will be that part of the spreadsheet which provides the final sales budget report, this can be in the form of a table of values and/or a graphical output.

Spreadsheets are used for these tasks because they can calculate and re-calculate values very quickly and any change made in the input area of the spreadsheet will automatically update the values in the output area.

Furthermore actual values may be exported from the general ledger accounting system into the spreadsheet. Here they may be linked to the budget data and a variance report prepared.

## 60    Q PLC

(a)

| | Jan £ | Feb £ | Mar £ |
|---|---|---|---|
| **Receipts** | | | |
| Sales | 69,600 | 56,944 | 56,470 |
| Interest (W2) | | | 37 |
| | 69,600 | 56,944 | 56,507 |
| **Payments** | | | |
| Capital | | | 30,000 |
| Admin and selling | 15,000 | | |
| Labour (W1) | 15,000 | 16,500 | 9,750 |
| Overhead (W1) | 15,000 | 12,600 | 10,800 |
| Materials (W1) | 21,000 | 17,500 | 16,500 |
| Interest (W2) | | 64 | |
| | 66,000 | 46,664 | 67,050 |
| Surplus / (Deficit) | 3,600 | 10,280 | (10,543) |
| Balance B/fwd | (5,000) | (1,400) | 8,880 |
| Balance C/fwd | (1,400) | 8,880 | (1,663) |

(b)    Feedforward is the comparison of a budget with an objective to see if the proposed course of action achieves the objective set. If it does not then consideration can be given to changing the proposed course of action.

Feedback control is the comparison of a budget with the actual results to see if the target has been achieved.

Thus a cash budget can be used initially as part of a feedforward control system, and then once it has been agreed and thus become the target to be achieved, it is used as part of a feedback control system when it is compared with actual results.

**W1** Production Cost

|  | January £ | February £ | March £ | April £ |
|---|---|---|---|---|
| Total | 50,000 | 55,000 | 32,500 | 50,000 |
| Materials 40% of total | 20,000 | 22,000 | 13,000 | 20,000 |

50% 50% 50% 50% 50% 50% 50% 50%

| Paid Dec | Paid Jan | Paid Feb | Paid March | Paid April |
|---|---|---|---|---|

|  |  |  |  |  |
|---|---|---|---|---|
| 10,000 | 10,000 | 11,000 | 6,500 | |
| | 11,000 | 6,500 | 10,000 | |
| | 21,000 | 17,500 | 16,500 | |

| Labour 30% of total | 15,000 | 16,500 | 9,750 |
|---|---|---|---|
| | Paid Jan | Paid Feb | Paid March |

| Production overhead (remainder = 30%) | 15,000 | 16,500 | (9,750) |
|---|---|---|---|
| Fixed | (5,000) | (5,000) | (5,000) |
| Variable | 10,000 | 11,500 | 4,750 |
| Creditor | | | |

40% 60% 40% 60% 40%

| | Paid Jan | Paid Feb | Paid March |
|---|---|---|---|
| B/FWD (per question) (11,000 - 2000 fixed) | 4,000 | 6,000 | 6,900 |
| | 9,000 | 4,600 | 1,900 |
| | 2,000 | 2,000 | 2,000 |
| Fixed Payable (5,000 - 3,000 depreciation) | 15,000 | 12,600 | 10,800 |

**W2** Interest:

February: $\left(\dfrac{(5,000) + (1,400)}{2}\right) \times 2\% = 64$ payable in February

March: $\left(\dfrac{(1,400) + 8,880}{2}\right) \times 1\% = 37$ receivable in March

---

# 61 X PLC

(a) (i) **Sales budget**

| Volume | 1,300 units |
|---|---|
| Selling price | £250 |
| Sales value | £325,000 |

(ii)     **Production budget**

|  |  |
|---|---:|
| Required by sales | 1,300 |
| Add: Closing stock (W1) | 225 |
|  | 1,525 |
| Less: Opening stock (W2) | (200) |
| Good units required | 1,325 |
| Wastage $\frac{10}{90} \times 1,325$ | 147 |
| Target production | 1,472 |

(iii)    **Raw material usage budget**

Material A : 1,472 × 3 kgs = 4,416 kgs
Material B : 1,472 × 2 kgs = 2,944 kgs
Material C : 1,472 × 4 kgs = 5,888 kgs

(iv)    **Raw material purchases budget**

|  | A<br>£ | B<br>£ | C<br>£ |
|---|---:|---:|---:|
| Required by production | 4,416 | 2,944 | 5,888 |
| Add closing stock (W3) | 1,200 | 480 | 720 |
|  | 5,616 | 3,424 | 6,608 |
| Less: Opening stock | (1,000) | (400) | (600) |
| Purchase quantity | 4,616 | 3,024 | 6,008 |
| Material cost/kg | £3.50 | £5.00 | £4.50 |
| Purchase value | £16,156 | £15,120 | £27,036 |
| (Total £58,312) | | | |

(v)     **Labour requirements budget**

|  |  |
|---|---:|
| Hours required by production:<br>1,472 units × 8 hours | 11,776 |
| Supporting activity hours:<br>$\frac{20}{80} \times 11,776$ | 2,944 |
| Attendance hours | 14,720 |
| Hourly rate | £8.00 |
| Labour cost | £117,760 |

WORKINGS

(W1)    50% of October sales = 225 units
(W2)    50% of July sales = 200 units
(W3)    Opening stock + 20%

(b)     The principal budget factor (or limiting factor) is the factor which limits the activity level of the organisation during the budget period. It may be the level of sales demand at the intended selling price or the availability of resources such as materials or labour/machine hours.

Its identification is an important part of the budget preparation process because all of the budgets are based upon its value. If this were not so, the budgets prepared would be unachievable and thus of little or no use for control purposes.

(c)     The spreadsheet would comprise two areas, an input area and an output area, these are illustrated below:

Input area

| | Z | AA |
|---|---|---|
| 1 | 8.00 | hours per unit |
| 2 | 0.20 | % of attendance time support in decimal |
| 3 | 8.00 | labour rate per hour |
| 4 | 1,472 | target production |

*Note:* Z4 value could be copied from the production budget spreadsheet, other values are input data.

Output area

| | | |
|---|---|---|
| 1 | Production hours | = Z1 * Z4 |
| 2 | Support hours | = (Z2/1 – Z2) * B1 |
| 3 | Total hours | = B1 + B2 |
| 4 | Hourly rate | = Z3 |
| 5 | Labour cost | = B3 * B4 |

## 62  MAZ HOTEL

(a)     A spreadsheet is a computer program which comprises row, columns and pages to provide cells into which data or formulae may be entered.

A database is a computer program based around files, records and fields. Each field contains data relating to a particular record. Similar records are kept in the same file.

Spreadsheets are better for planning because plans are summaries of expected future transactions. For these a 2-3 dimensional storage medium is sufficient. The planning process involves a series of iterations and changes before the final plan is agreed. Spreadsheets are ideal for re-calculating values after changing different input variables.

Databases are more suited to the storage of volumes of data. Actual accounting data will consist of many similar transactions having similar attributes. Databases can be used to store the data, then sort it according to user defined parameters. Selected data can then be summarised and output reports produced.

(b)

**MAZ Hotel – Week 38**

| Cost item | Flexible budget £ | Actual cost £ | Variance £ |
|---|---|---|---|
| Food costs | 2,400 | 2,490 | 90 A |
| Heating, lighting, power | 750 | 710 | 40 F |
| Cleaning | 1,300 | 1,440 | 140 A |
| Administration | 3,000 | 2,850 | 150 F |
| | 7,450 | 7,490 | 40 A |

## 63  BUDGETS AND STANDARDS

### Answer plan

Definitions, standards feed into budget, budgets change, standards don't so much, relate to future, must be quantified, control, planning, motivation and evaluation aspects, expected or motivational, standards most often for materials and labour, relate to single units or segments of the business.

A budget is a quantitative or financial plan relating to the future. A standard is a predetermined measurable quantity set in defined conditions.

**Similarities**

1  Both budgets and standards relate to the future.

2  Both budgets and standards must be quantified.

3  Both are used in planning.

4  Both are used in controlling the activities of the business. Actual results are compared against the budget or standard and if a significant difference occurs, the reasons behind the difference are investigated and if possible and desirable, corrective action taken.

5  Both may be used as a basis for evaluating performance. Managers and workers may be judged on their performance vs the expected result.

6  Neither budgets nor standards should be prepared as just 'cold' mathematical exercises, the computational/numerate aspects should be considered in conjunction with motivational effects of budgets and standards used as targets.

7  Both budgets and standards can be designed to show purely the expected results for a forthcoming period or may be designed to provide a more difficult target in order to motivate managers/workers.

**Differences**

1  The biggest difference between budgets and standards, is that standards tend to be expressed per unit, whereas budgets are for much bigger entities such as departments, functions or resources.

2  Standards are most often set for materials and labour (but can be set for variable overheads and fixed overheads). Budgets cover a much greater variety of costs and entities, such as cash, fixed assets, research and development etc.

3  Standards usually relate to two variables - quantity and price. Although both variables may be difficult to predict, usually they will not be capable of varying too much. Budgets tend to depend upon many factors and the cumulative effect of possible differences can have a profound effect.

4  Once standards are set, they do not require much effort to update from year to year. With budgets, the setting of a new budget involves much more work.

5  Standards are often set up in order to prepare the budget.

## 64  RS LTD

(a)

**Standard product cost**

|  |  | £ |
|---|---|---|
| Material R | 10 kgs @ £30 | 300 |
| Material S | 6 kgs @ £45 | 270 |
| Direct labour | 30 hrs @ £5.50 | 165 |

|  |  |  |
|---|---|---|
| Production overhead (W1) | | 210 |
| | | 945 |
| Standard gross profit (W3) | | 255 |
| Standard selling price (W2) | | 1,200 |

(b)     **Material R**

**Price variance**

| | | |
|---|---|---|
| Standard price | = | £30.00 |
| Actual price (£35,000/1,100) | = | £31.82 (rounded) |
| | | 1.82 (A) |

Price variance = $(300 + 1,100 - 375) \times £1.82$   =   £1,866 (A)

**Usage variance**

| | | |
|---|---|---|
| Standard usage = 100 units × 10 kgs | = | 1,000 kg |
| Actual usage | = | 1,025 kg |
| | | 25 kg (A) |

Usage variance = 25 kg × £30   =   £750 (A)

**Material S**

**Price variance**

| | | |
|---|---|---|
| Standard price | = | £45.00 |
| Actual price (£15,180 / 345) | = | £44.00 |
| | | 1.00 (F) |

Price variance = $(460 + 345 - 225) \times £1$   =   £580 (F)

**Usage variance**

| | | |
|---|---|---|
| Standard usage = 100 units × 6 kgs | = | 600 kg |
| Actual usage | = | 580 kg |
| | | 20 kg (F) |

Usage variance = 20 kg × £45   =   £900 (F)

**Direct labour**

**Rate variance**

| | | |
|---|---|---|
| Standard rate | = | £5.50 |
| Actual rate (£17,325/3,300) | = | £5.25 |
| | | 0.25 (F) |

Rate variance = 3,300 hrs × £0.25   =   £825 (F)

**Efficiency variance**

| | | | |
|---|---|---|---|
| Standard hours = 100 units × 30 hrs | | = | 3,000 |
| Actual hours | | = | 3,300 |
| | | | 300 (A) |

| | | | |
|---|---|---|---|
| Efficiency variance = 300 hrs × £5.50 | | = | £1,650 (A) |

**Fixed production overhead**

**Expenditure variance**

| | | | |
|---|---|---|---|
| Budget cost (£252,000/12) | | = | £21,000 |
| Actual cost | | = | £22,000 |
| Expenditure variance | | | £1,000 (A) |

(c)

| | | £ A | £ F | £ |
|---|---|---|---|---|
| Budgeted gross profit (W4) | | | | 25,500 |
| Cost variances | | | | |
| Material R | Price | 1,866 | | |
| | Usage | 750 | | |
| Material S | Price | | 580 | |
| | Usage | | 900 | |
| Direct labour | Rate | | 825 | |
| | Efficiency | 1,650 | | |
| Production overhead | Expenditure | 1,000 | | |
| | | 5,266 | 2,305 | 2,961 A |
| Actual gross profit | | | | 22,539 |

(d)     Direct labour rate variance £825 (F)

This variance is controllable by the personnel manager who appears to have settled a wage rate of 25 pence per hour less than that which was anticipated.

The manager may have employed staff of a lower grade than expected.

Direct labour efficiency variance £1,650 (A)

The variance is controllable by the production manager, it means that a total of 300 more hours were used than should have been for the output achieved.

Insufficient training may have been given to the workers.

WORKINGS

(W1)   £252,000/1,200 = £210

(W2)   £120,000/$\dfrac{1,200}{12}$ = £1,200

(W3)   Balancing figure

(W4)   Budget gross profit = 100 units × £255 = £25,500

## 65    USES AND LIMITATIONS

(a)    Standard costs are the estimated future costs of producing a single cost unit. They may be prepared using the principles of marginal or absorption costing.

Standard costs are normally incorporated into the organisation's accounting system, which reconciles to the actual costs by the inclusion of variances. This enables certain aspects of accounting to be simplified, for example, the recording of stock movements and their valuation.

Standard costs may also be used as part of the planning process, both in predicting costs and controlling actual results against the standards. These standards may also be used to motivate employees as part of the performance appraisal process.

The limitations of standard costs are largely related to the reliability of the standard set; both from the difficulty of establishing the standard and subsequently maintaining its accuracy.

In addition, if standards are to be used for performance appraisal of employees and to plan for the future of the organisation there may be a conflict between the target and a realistic expectation of future performance.

(b)                                          **MEMORANDUM**

**To:**          Production manager

**From:**       Assistant accountant

**Date:**       X-X-19XX

**Subject:**    Standard costing under inflationary conditions

---

I have been requested by the managing director to respond to your comment on standard costing in times of inflation.

Standard costs are made up of two elements, a quantity of a resource required per unit of the finished product, and an estimated price per unit of the resource. When setting a value for the price element two possibilities exist:

(i)       to use the price prevailing at the start of the year; or
(ii)      to estimate an average price to be paid during the year ahead.

Both methods cause difficulties. Method (i) will inevitably cause adverse (often uncontrollable) price variances as inflation causes prices to rise. Method (ii) would (in theory) cause favourable variances in the early periods of a year and adverse variances in the later periods of a year which will (if the estimated average price is accurate) total to a nil variance for the year. Either of these techniques will allow an analysis of the trends of costs to be recognised.

A further alternative is to revise the price element of the standard cost each accounting period, but this makes trend analysis very difficult.

Thus the price element of standard costing and the resulting price related variances may be of limited use under inflationary conditions. Instead emphasis should be placed on the usage or resource quantity aspects of the technique, which, if measured in physical rather than monetary units, are not affected by inflation.

(c)

|  | Actual £ | Standard £ |  | Variance £ (F) | £ (A) |
|---|---|---|---|---|---|
| Sales | 259,000 | 245,000 Price (W3) | 14,000 |  |  |
| Production costs |  |  |  |  |  |
| Direct materials | 65,570 | 64,000 Price (W4) | 830 ✓ |  |  |
|  |  | Usage (W5) |  |  | 2,400 ✓ |
| Direct labour | 107,100 | 96,000 Rate (W6) |  |  | 5,100 ✗ |
|  |  | Eff (W7) |  |  | 6,000 ✓ |
| Variable overheads | 18,800 | 19,200 Expend (W8) | 1,600 ✗ |  |  |
|  |  | Eff (W9) |  |  | 1,200 ✓ |

| | | | | |
|---|---|---|---|---|
| Fixed overheads | 39,000 | 32,000 Expend (W10) | 1,000 | |
| | | (Volume (W11) | | 8,000 |
| Royalties | 8,000 | 6,400 Expend (W12) | | 1,600 |
| Production cost | 238,470 | 217,600 | | |
| Closing stock (W2) | 27,200 | 27,200 | | |
| Operating profit | 47,730 | 54,600 | | |
| Selling and dist | 12,000 | 14,000 Expend (W13) | 2,000 | |
| | 35,730 | 40,600 | 19,430 | 24,300 |
| Total (W14) | | | | 4,870(A) |

WORKINGS

(W1)   Sales = 7,000 kgs @ £35 = £245,000
       Costs = 8,000 kgs produced × respective cost / kg given in the question

(W2)   £238,470 × 1,000 / 8,000

(W3)   Standard price                              =        £35
       Actual price                                =        £37
                                                             2 (F)

       7,000 kg @ £2 per kg                         =    £14,000 (F)

(W4)   Standard price                              =       £8.00
       Actual price                                =       £7.90
                                                            0.10 (F)

       8,300 kgs @ £0.10 per kg                     =      £830 (F)

(W5)   Standard usage 8,000 × 1                     =    8,000 kg
       Actual usage                                 =    8,300 kg
                                                          300 kg (A)

       300 kg @ £8.00                               =    £2,400 (A)

(W6)   Standard rate                                =     £6.00 /hr
       Actual rate:  £107,100/17,000                =     £6.30 /hr
                                                          0.30 /hr (A)

       £17,000 hrs @ £0.30                          =    £5,100 (A)

(W7)   Standard hours:  8,000 kgs × 2 hrs           =   16,000 hrs
       Actual hrs                                   =   17,000 hrs
                                                        1,000 hrs (A)

       1,000 hrs @ £6.00 / hr                       =    £6,000 (A)

(W8)

|  | £ |
|---|---|
| Standard cost of actual hours 17,000 × 1.20 | 20,400 |
| Actual cost | 18,800 |
|  | 1,600 F |

(W9)

|  | Hr |
|---|---|
| Standard hours of actual output 8,000 × 2 | 16,000 |
| Actual hours | 17,000 |
|  | 1,000 A |
| × standard VOAR | × £1.20 |
|  | £1,200 A |

(W10)

|  | £ |
|---|---|
| Budgeted overheads 10,000 × 4 | 40,000 |
| Actual overheads | 39,000 |
|  | 1,000 F |

(W11)   Fixed overhead absorption rate per kg = £4

Difference between budget and actual output:

| 10,000 – 8,000 | = | 2,000 kg |
|---|---|---|
| 2,000 kg @ £4/kg | = | £8,000 (A) |

(W12)   £6,400 – £8,000        =   £1,600 (A)

(W13)   £14,000 – £12,000      =   £2,000 (F)

(W14)   £24,300 – £19,430      =   £4,870 (A)

## 66   JB PLC

(a)   (i)

|  | (W1) Original budget I £ | (W2) Flexed budget II £ | Actual costs III £ | Total variance IV £ |  |
|---|---|---|---|---|---|
| Direct material | 480,000 | 444,000 | 442,650 | 1,350 | Fav |
| Direct labour | 140,000 | 129,500 | 129,940 | 440 | Adv |
| Variable production overhead | 60,000 | 55,500 | 58,800 | 3,300 | Adv |
| Fixed production overhead | 100,000 | 100,000 | 104,000 | 4,000 | Adv |
|  | 780,000 | 729,000 | 735,390 | 6,390 | Adv |

(ii)   **Material price variance**

|  | £ |
|---|---|
| Standard cost of actual quantity of material 113,500 kg × £4 kg | 454,000 |
| Actual cost | 442,650 |
|  | 11,350   Fav |

**Material usage variance**

| | kg | |
|---|---|---|
| Standard usage of actual output | | |
| 18,500 units × 6 kg/unit | 111,000 | |
| Actual usage | 113,500 | |
| | 2,500 | Adv |
| × Standard price    × 4 | | |
| | £10,000 | Adv |

**Labour rate variance**

| | £ | |
|---|---|---|
| Standard cost of actual hours | | |
| 17,800 hours × £7/hr | 124,600 | |
| Actual cost | 129,940 | |
| | 5,340 | Adv |

**Labour efficiency variance**

| | hrs | |
|---|---|---|
| Standard hours of actual output | | |
| 18,500 × 1hr/unit | 18,500 | |
| Actual hours | 17,800 | |
| | 700 | Fav |
| × Standard rate | × 7 | |
| | £4,900 | Fav |

(b)    A rolling forecast is a continuously updated forecast whereby each time actual results are reported, a further forecast period is added and intermediate period forecasts are updated.

*(Tutorial note:* the above exact CIMA definition does not have to be given.*)*

Its main uses are in volatile environments where forecasts need constant updating or in businesses where it is always useful to have at least 9 or 10 months worth of forecast.

WORKINGS

(W1)    £24/unit, £7/unit and £3/unit × budgeted 20,000 units.
(W2)    £24/unit, £7/unit and £3/unit × actual 18,500 units.

---

## 67    SK LTD

(a)    **Standard cost of 18,000 units of Jay**

| | £ |
|---|---|
| Direct material (£48 × 18,000) | 864,000 |
| Direct labour (£35 × 18,000) | 630,000 |
| Variable production overhead (£10 × 18,000) | 180,000 |
| Fixed production overhead (£50 × 18,000) | 900,000 |
| | 2,574,000 |

(b)

| Cost item | Standard cost £ | Variances Adverse £ | Favourable £ | Actual cost £ |
|---|---|---|---|---|
| Direct materials | 864,000 | | | 836,000 |
|    Price variance (W1) | | | 76,000 | |
|    Usage variance (W2) | | 48,000 | | |
| Direct labour | 630,000 | | | 604,800 |
|    Rate variance (W3) | | 16,800 | | |
|    Efficiency variance (W4) | | | 42,000 | |
| Variable production overhead | 180,000 | | | 172,000 |
|    Expenditure variance (W5) | | 4,000 | | |
|    Efficiency variance (W6) | | | 12,000 | |
| Fixed production overhead | 900,000 | | | 1,030,000 |
|    Expenditure variance (W7) | | 30,000 | | |
|    Volume variance (W8) | | 100,000 | | |
| | 2,574,000 | 198,800 | 130,000 | 2,642,800 |

(c)    Such a report identifies the extent of the difference between standard and actual costs, and how it may be attributed to the effects of price and resource utilisation.

The report provides the starting point for managers to investigate why the variance occurred and improve future performance. However, it does not identify managerial responsibilities or controllability. Changing the report to identify these aspects would allow the report to be directed to the appropriate manager.

## WORKINGS

(W1)

| | £ |
|---|---|
| 76,000 kgs should cost £12/kg | 912,000 |
| Actual cost | 836,000 |
| | 76,000 F |

(W2)

| | kgs |
|---|---|
| 18,000 units should use 4 kgs each | 72,000 |
| Actual usage | 76,000 |
| | 4,000 A |
| 4,000 kgs × £12/kg | £48,000 A |

(W3)

| | £ |
|---|---|
| 84,000 hours should cost £7/hour | 588,000 |
| Actual cost | 604,800 |
| | 16,800 A |

(W4)

| | Hours |
|---|---|
| 18,000 units should use 5 hours each | 90,000 |
| Actual time taken | 84,000 |
| | 6,000 F |
| 6,000 hours × £7/hour | £42,000 F |

| (W5) | | £ |
|---|---|---:|
| 84,000 hours should cost £2/hour | | 168,000 |
| Actual cost | | 172,000 |
| | | 4,000 A |

| (W6) | | Hours |
|---|---|---:|
| 18,000 units should use 5 hours each | | 90,000 |
| Actual time taken | | 84,000 |
| | | 6,000 F |
| 6,000 hours × £2/hour | | £12,000 F |

| (W7) | | £ |
|---|---|---:|
| Budget cost = 20,000 × £50/unit | | 1,000,000 |
| Actual cost | | 1,030,000 |
| | | 30,000 A |

| (W8) | | Units |
|---|---|---:|
| Budget volume | | 20,000 |
| Actual volume | | 18,000 |
| | | 2,000 A |
| 2,000 units × £50/unit | | £100,000 A |

## 68    DL HOSPITAL TRUST

(a)    **Cost reconciliation statement**

| | | | £ |
|---|---|---|---:|
| Budget cost (20 × £2,000 × 250%) | | | 100,000 |
| Activity adjustment (100,000 × 2/20) | | | 10,000 |
| | | | 110,000 |

| Cost variances: | Adv. | Fav. | |
|---|---:|---:|---|
| Surgical team fees: | | | |
| Rate variance (W1) | | 2,600 | |
| Efficiency variance (W1) | 3,000 | | |
| Variable overhead: | | | |
| Expenditure variance (W2) | | 725 | |
| Efficiency variance (W2) | 1,875 | | |
| Fixed overhead: | | | |
| Expenditure variance (W3) | 1,950 | | |
| Volume variance (W3) | | 3,500 | |
| | 6,825 | 6,825 | |

| | | | |
|---|---|---|---:|
| | | | Nil |
| Actual cost | | | 110,000 |

(b)   Budgetary control is based on controlling total costs whereas standard costing is based on controlling unit costs.

In service organisations it is common for its activities to be varied and consequently it may be difficult to find a standard measure of activity. It may also be difficult to identify costs with particular activities.

The disadvantage of using only budgetary control is that whilst it limits expenditure it does not provide a basis for monitoring the efficiency of expenditure.

In contrast standard costing provides a basis for monitoring such efficiency without limiting expenditure.

If possible therefore both budgetary control and standard costing should be used, though the latter may not be appropriate for some of the organisation's activities.

(c)                                             **REPORT**

**To:**          Managing Director

**From:**        Management Accountant

**Date:**        X XXX 19XX

**Subject:**     Overhead absorption

---

Surgical team fees are representative of the direct labour cost of the DL Hospital Trust. This basis of absorption implies that all of the overhead costs arise due to the surgical team fees cost. Clearly this is likely to be an unjustifiable assumption. However, it does provide an administratively convenient method of attributing overhead costs to surgical operations.

However, management may review the causes of the overhead costs and improve their information provision by attributing costs according to various cost drivers. This would be via an Activity Based Costing system.

WORKINGS

(1)   Surgical team fees:

Rate variance          $= £44,400 - (£2,000/10 \times 235)$
                       $= £2,600 \text{ (F)}$

Efficiency variance    $= (235 - (22 \times 10)) \times £2,000/10$
                       $= £3,000 \text{ (A)}$

(2)   Variable overhead:

Expenditure variance   $= £28,650 - (235 \times (2,000/10 \times 62.5\%))$
                       $= £725 \text{ (F)}$

Efficiency variance    $= (235 - (22 \times 10)) \times £2,000/10 \times 62.5\%$
                       $= £1,875 \text{ (A)}$

(3)   Fixed overhead:

Expenditure variance   $= £36,950 - (£2,000 \times 20 \times 87.5\%)$
                       $= £1,950 \text{ (A)}$

Volume variance        $= (22 - 20) \times (£2,000 \times 87.5\%)$
                       $= £3,500 \text{ (F)}$

## 69     ABC LTD

(a)     (i)     Budgeted volume $= \dfrac{\text{Budgeted profit}}{\text{budgeted profit / unit}}$

$= \dfrac{£30,000}{£3} = 10,000$ units

Difference between actual and budget volume equals

$\dfrac{\text{Fixed overhead volume variance}}{\text{Standard fixed overhead / unit}}$

$= \dfrac{£24,500}{£14} = 1,750$ units, and since the variance is adverse actual volume is less than budgeted:

$10,000 - 1,750 = \underline{8,250}$ units

(ii)     Actual production should take:

| | |
|---|---:|
| 8,250 units × 4 hours/unit = | 33,000 hours |

Difference between actual and standard hours

$= \dfrac{\text{labour efficiency variance}}{\text{standard labour rate}}$

| | |
|---|---:|
| $= \dfrac{£4,000}{£4} =$ | 1,000 hours |
| Actual hours | 34,000 |

(iii)     Actual production should use

| | | |
|---|---|---:|
| 8,250 units × 5 litres | = | 41,250 litres |

Difference between actual and standard usage

$= \dfrac{\text{material usage variance}}{\text{standard material price}}$

| | | |
|---|---|---:|
| $= \dfrac{£400}{£0.20}$ | = | 2,000 litres |
| Actual usage | | 39,250 litres |
| Less: | | |
| Decrease in stock | = | 800 litres |
| ACTUAL PURCHASES | | 38,450 litres |

(iv)     Standard cost of variable overhead

| | £ |
|---|---:|
| = 8,250 units × £6/unit | 49,500 |
| Total variance (£1,000 F + £1,500 A) | 500 A |
| Actual cost | 50,000 |

(v)    Budgeted fixed overhead cost                                    £
       = budgeted units × £14/unit
       = 10,000 units × £14/unit                              =   140,000

       Expenditure variance                                   =       500 F

       Actual fixed overhead cost                                     139,500

(b)    Standard costs are targets per unit, whereas budgets are total costs set for a single or a range of activity levels.

This distinction means that if using standard costs those costs not clearly related to cost units are unitised using some form of absorption technique; this is not necessary when using budgets. However, both are used as targets against which actual values may be compared.

In manufacturing organisations it is likely that the output units will be homogeneous and easily measured whereas in non-manufacturing (service) organisations there are likely to be various forms of output which may not be easy to measure. Also non-manufacturing organisations are likely to have a greater proportion of indirect costs than manufacturing organisations. These two distinctions and difficulties make the use of standard costing in non-manufacturing organisations less appropriate than in manufacturing organisations because of the imposed attribution of standard costs to cost units.

However, a significant distinction between budgets and standard costs is that budgets set a limit on total expenditure which cannot be exceeded without authorisation whereas standard costs measure the efficiency of unit costs without limiting total expenditure.

In conclusion then standard costs are appropriate to control variable costs in all types of organisation but budgets are a more appropriate means of controlling fixed or discretionary costs which are not related to activity. It is for these reasons that some organisations use both standard costs and budgetary control systems.

## 70    TUR PLC

(a)    (i)     Material price

                                                                      £
       Standard cost 4,800 kgs × £3.50                        16,800
       Actual cost                                            18,240

                                                              1,440 (A)

       (ii)    Material usage

                                                                      kgs
       Standard: 965 units × 5 kgs                            4,825
       Actual                                                 4,840

                                                              15 kgs

       15 kgs × £3.50                                         £52.50 (A)

       (iii)   Labour rate

                                                                      £
       Standard cost 4,000 × £4.50                            18,000
       Actual cost 4,000 × £4.60                              18,400

                                                              400 (A)

(iv)  Labour efficiency

|  |  | Hours |
|---|---|---|
| Standard: 965 units × 4 hours | | 3,860 |
| Actual | | 4,000 |
| | | 140 hours |

140 hours × £4.50                                          £630 (A)

(v)  Variable overhead expenditure

|  |  | £ |
|---|---|---|
| Standard cost 4,000 hrs × £1.50 | | 6,000 |
| Actual cost | | 5,950 |
| | | 50 (F) |

(vi)  Variable overhead efficiency

|  |  | Hours |
|---|---|---|
| Standard: 965 × 4 hours | | 3,860 |
| Actual | | 4,000 |
| | | 140 hours |

140 hours × £1.50 per hour                             £210 (A)

(vii)  Fixed overhead expenditure

|  |  | £ |
|---|---|---|
| Budgeted: 1,000 units × £10 | | 10,000 |
| Actual | | 9,900 |
| | | 100 (F) |

(viii)  Fixed overhead volume

|  |  | Units |
|---|---|---|
| Volume difference: | Budget | 1,000 |
| | Actual | 965 |
| | | 35 units |

35 units × £10                                             £350 (A)

(b)  (i)

**Raw material stock**

| | £ | | £ |
|---|---|---|---|
| Balance b/d | 8,750 | Work in progress | 16,940 |
| | | Price variance | 1,440 |
| Purchases | 18,240 | Balance c/d | 8,610 |
| | 26,990 | | 26,990 |

(ii)

**Work in progress**

|  | £ |  | £ |
|---|---|---|---|
| Materials | 16,940 | Material usage* | 52.5 |
| Labour | 18,400 | Labour rate* | 400.0 |
| Variable overhead | 5,950 | Labour efficiency* | 630.0 |
| Fixed overheads | 9,900 | Variable overhead efficiency* | 210.0 |
| Variable overhead expenditure* | 50 | Fixed overhead volume* | 350.0 |
| Fixed overhead expenditure* | 100 | Finished goods | 49,697.5 |
|  | 51,340 |  | 51,340.0 |

* Variances from part (a)

*Note:* The transfer to finished goods is 965 units × £51.50 = £49,697.50

## 71    Q PLC

(a)    **Price variance**

|  | £ |
|---|---|
| 4,000 kgs should cost £3/kg | 12,000 |
| Actual cost | 12,800 |
|  | £800 A |

**Usage variance**

700 units of finished product should use 5 kgs of material R/unit

|  | kgs |
|---|---|
| 700 × 5 | 3,500 kgs |
| Actual usage (4,000 – 320) | 3,680 |
| An extra | 180 kgs |

180 kgs @ £3 (standard price) = £540 A

(b)

|  | Dr | Cr |
|---|---|---|
| Raw material control | 12,800 |  |
| Creditor |  | 12,800 |

Being purchase of raw materials

|  | Dr | Cr |
|---|---|---|
| Material price variance | 800 |  |
| Raw material control |  | 800 |

Being extraction of variance

|  | Dr | Cr |
|---|---|---|
| Work in progress | 11,040 |  |
| Raw material control |  | 11,040 |

Being actual usage of material at standard price (3,680 kgs @ £3)

|  | Dr | Cr |
|---|---|---|
| Material usage variance | 540 |  |
| Work in progress |  | 540 |

Being recognition of usage variance

(c)  **Advantages**

    (i)     Since stocks will be valued at standard prices the need to keep detailed stock valuation records is avoided.

    (ii)    As the variance is extracted on purchase it is more easily recognised by the buyer because it occurs at the point of activity.

    **Disadvantages**

    (i)     The valuation of stocks at standard prices is not acceptable for published accounts if the material price variance is significant. Under such circumstances, a separate stock valuation using actual stock costs would be required.

    (ii)    If materials are bought in bulk, rather than on a regular basis, the recognition of any price variance at the time of purchase may distort the results of that accounting period.

(d)  The standard usage needs to be adjusted for the normal wastage of 5%:

    5 kg × 100/95 = 5.263 kg

    700 units of product should use:

|  | kgs |
|---|---|
| 700 × 5.263 kg | 3,684 |
| Actual usage | 3,680 |
| Saving | 4 kgs |

    4 kgs @ £3 (standard price) = £12 F

    This shows that when the adjusted standard is used then the usage variance is negligible. If the ideal (ie, zero wastage) standard is used for performance measurement, management may waste time and costs investigating a variance which does not arise from operational performance.

(e)  An ideal standard is one which makes no allowance for normal wastage, normal inefficiency, etc and is therefore impossible to achieve other than in very short periods. The initial material usage standard was an example of such a standard.

    An attainable standard is one which takes account of normal wastage and inefficiency. An example is the revised material usage standard. As is illustrated by the answer to earlier parts of the question, this standard is more appropriate as a basis of performance appraisal and thus any variances which arise are more meaningful and more useful to management.

## 72   SALES/OVERHEAD VARIANCES

(a)    (i)     Under marginal costing the difference between the budgeted and actual number of units sold is valued using the standard contribution per unit to determine the sales volume variance, so:

| | |
|---|---|
| Budgeted sales (units) | 10,000 |
| Actual sales (units) | 9,500 |
| Difference | 500 |

$$\frac{\text{Sales volume variance (marginal)}}{\text{Difference}} = \text{Standard contribution / unit}$$

$$= \frac{£7,500}{500} = £15$$

(ii)    Under absorption costing the sales volume variance is the difference between the actual and budgeted units sold valued at the standard profit per unit, so

$$\frac{\text{Sales volume variance (absorption)}}{\text{Difference}} = \text{standard profit/unit}$$

$$= \frac{£4,500}{500} = £9$$

(iii)   The fixed overhead absorption rate (based on budgets) is the difference between the standard contribution per unit and the standard profit per unit:

£15 – £9 = £6

The absorption rate is £6 per unit
Budgeted production = 10,000 units

| | | |
|---|---|---|
| So budgeted cost | = | 10,000 units × £6/unit |
| | = | £60,000 |
| Expenditure variance | = | 2,500 F   (deduct because it is favourable) |
| Actual cost | = | £57,500 |

## Answer Plan

(b)    Plan: purpose of variance calculations, absorption v marginal costing, the implications for variances.

Variances are calculated in order to reconcile the budgeted profit with the actual profit. This reconciliation is achieved by comparing the actual and budgeted levels of activity, and the actual costs incurred and resources used with the costs and resources expected for the level of activity achieved.

Absorption and marginal costing take differing views on the treatment of fixed production overhead costs. Under absorption costing such costs are considered to be necessarily incurred by production, and consequently they are attributed to individual cost units using an absorption rate based on budgeted expenditure and activity levels. The effect of this treatment is that under absorption costing stocks are valued at their total production cost (including a share of fixed production overhead costs).

Under marginal costing the fixed production overhead costs are not recognised as being necessarily incurred by production because the cost is fixed, and therefore its total value is not affected by the level of production activity. Consequently the fixed production overhead cost is not attributed to individual cost units. Instead it is treated as an expense of the period in which it is incurred, and wholly written off in the period's profit and loss account. The effect of this treatment is that stocks are valued at variable production cost only.

The effect of these different stock valuations is that in periods when the level of stock increases or decreases (as occurs in this question) the profit reported by the two systems will be different. Since the purpose of variances is to reconcile profits then if the profits reported are different then at least some of the variances are different.

In fact most of the variances calculated in respect of these two systems are the same. All of the variable cost variances are the same, and as is shown by the data in the question the selling price variance and fixed production overhead expenditure variance are the same. But under marginal costing there is no fixed production overhead volume variance. It is not applicable to marginal costing because it arises due to the attribution of such costs to cost units, and as stated above marginal costing does not do this. Instead marginal costing emphasises contribution and thus the sales volume variance is valued differently.

Using the data from the question it can be seen that during September 1996 production exceeded sales by 200 units. The effect of this is that absorption costing would report higher profits than marginal costing due to its having a higher stock valuation per unit. The difference in the profits would be

|  |  |  |  |
|---|---|---|---|
| 200 units × £6/unit (absorption rate) (see (a) (iii)) | = | £1,200 | |

The difference between the sales volume variances under the two systems is (£4,500A – £7,500A) = £3,000 (more adverse under marginal costing)

The fixed overhead volume variance does not exist under marginal costing = £(1,800) (less adverse under marginal costing)

Difference in profits as above                         £1,200

---

## Answer Plan

(c)        How the fixed overhead volume variance arises, the meaning of the fixed overhead volume variance.

The fixed overhead volume variance under absorption costing arises due to the use of an absorption rate based on budgeted costs and activity levels. This is used to attribute fixed production overhead costs to cost units as they are produced.

The rate is designed so that if the actual costs and activity levels are exactly as predicted then there will be no variances. In practice of course this is rarely the case, and it is a difference between the actual and budgeted production volume which gives rise to the fixed overhead volume variance.

The variance is calculated by multiplying the difference in units by the absorption rate per unit, hence in the question:

(10,000 units – 9,700 units) × £6/unit = £1,800

The variance in the question is adverse because the actual units produced were less than budgeted. The important thing is to establish why there is this difference in volume. Only then will the full consequences of the variance be understood and the usefulness to management be derived.

For example was the lower level of activity deliberate? The level of actual sales was lower than budgeted and lower than the actual production achieved, was a decision made to lower production in order to avoid increasing stock levels, or was there a machine breakdown which prevented production from taking place.

In the question the variance was adverse, this is usually thought of as being inefficient because profits will be lower than expected with the opposite view being taken of favourable variances. However, a favourable fixed overhead volume variance means that more units have been produced than expected - is this a benefit if they cannot be sold?

In conclusion it is not the variance itself which is useful to management but the reason why the production volume achieved differs from that budgeted and the consequential effects of that volume difference.

---

## Answer Plan

(d)        Activity Based Costing, cost pools, cost driver rates, cost control, benefits to management.

Activity Based Costing (ABC) is a system of full costing which recognises that the more traditional method of absorption costing using cost centre absorption rates may not provide accurate product costs.

ABC identifies the activities of a production process and the extent to which individual products make use of those activities. Costs are then estimated for each of these activities which are referred to as cost pools. The number of times which the activity is expected to be carried out is also estimated and a cost driver rate calculated:

$$\frac{\text{Estimated cost of cost pool}}{\text{Estimated number of times activity is to be performed}}$$

An individual product will probably make use of a number of different activities, and a proportion of the cost of each activity will be attributed to the product using these pre-determined cost driver rates.

The actual costs of each cost pool together with the number of times the activity is performed will be collected and a comparison made with the corresponding estimated values. This is similar to the comparison of actual and budgeted costs and volumes using the traditional absorption costing approach except that there are likely to be a greater number of cost driver rates using ABC than the one per cost centre absorption rate found in traditional absorption costing.

## 73     PDC LTD

(a)

Plan:     Flexible budgets, Controllability, Trend, Significance, Causes of variances

### REPORT

To:          Management Team
From:        Management Accountant
Date:        21 May 1997
Subject:     Monthly Variance Reports

Further to our recent meeting I have been asked to comment on the content and format of the monthly variance reports currently in use.

The present report compares the actual results with the budget approved by the board of directors. However this budget was based on a different level of activity from that actually achieved. Whilst it is important to identify the difference in activity, care must be taken to ensure that an appropriate comparison of costs is made, otherwise the resulting variances will be meaningless.

The budget which has been approved is based on a single level of activity and is therefore a fixed budget. This is acceptable as a basis of controlling costs which are not affected by the level of activity, but where costs vary with activity levels a meaningful comparison can only be made by comparing the actual costs with the expected cost of actual activity using a flexible budget.

The report should also identify those items of cost and revenue which are controllable by the recipient of the report. Further analysis of the causes of this can be identified. However it is unfair to make managers responsible for something which they cannot control, and if they are not responsible it can be misleading to imply from the report that this is the case.

The report only shows the results with a single period, whilst it is important to report monthly it is also important to identify the overall situation and how the current period fits into the trend. For example the loss of sales in March may be due to the advancement of a delivery to a customer of goods originally intended to be sold in the first week of March but despatched on the last day of February. If a cumulative year to date report is prepared in addition to the month's report it will help to eliminate periodic fluctuations not worthy of investigation and will identify overall trends.

The inclusion of % values as well as £s is useful because it identifies the significance of the variances. Random fluctuations are to be expected in any system due to either the method of setting standard costs (which usually use an annual average) or errors in recording actual data. Thus variances which are small in percentage terms are not worthy of further investigation unless they are part of a consistent trend over time.

Finally an analysis of cost variance by its cause (ie, price and quantity aspects) is recommended as this will assist in identifying the manager responsible for it. However, caution must be exercised to see if there is any interdependence of variances before identifying responsibilities.

The layout of a revised report is in Appendix A below.

**APPENDIX A**

### MONTHLY VARIANCE REPORT

| | Original Budget | Activity Adjustment | Flexed Budget | Actual Results | Total Variance £ | % | Quantity Variance £ | % | Price Variance £ | % |
|---|---|---|---|---|---|---|---|---|---|---|
| **Volumes** | | | | | | | | | | |
| Sales | | | | | | | | | | |
| Production | | | | | | | | | | |
| | | | | | | | | | | |
| **Costs/Revenues** | | | | | | | | | | |
| Sales | | | | | | | | | | |
| Direct materials | | | | | | | | | | |
| Direct labour | | | | | | | | | | |
| Stock adjustment | | | | | | | | | | |
| Contribution | | | | | | | | | | |

Separate reports are prepared for the month and year to date.

(b)    The main difference between budgeting control and standard costing is that the former uses budgets as the basis of comparison whereas the latter uses standard costs. Budgets provide a total cost/revenue target for a stated level of activity whereas standard costs are costs estimated for a single unit.

A less important difference is that standard costing is a system which is integrated with the actual accounting system whereas budgetary control operates as a reporting system external to the accounting system.

The significance of the total versus unit principles of budgetary control and standard costs lies in the controlling of costs. Budgetary control acts to limit total expenditure to the level approved in the budget. Standard costing controls the efficiency of resource procurement and utilisation by controlling the cost per unit without limiting the total sum.

It can be seen that budgetary control and standard costing provide different controls. For this reason an organisation can usefully use both techniques. In particular budgetary control is appropriate for discretionary costs such as research, advertising and for non-activity related costs such as administration. Standard costing is more appropriate for activity related costs such as those illustrated in part (a).

(c)    In order to produce a report such as that illustrated in part (a) it is necessary to collect data on the levels of activity (production and sales) and the monetary values of the transactions which have occurred.

For many organisations the above data will be provided from many different sources, and will need to be collected and combined to produce the report.

If a database system were used then the information would be held in different parts of the system, but could be retrieved and formatted into the report without the risk of transcription errors or errors of omission. Much of the data required is related to a monetary transaction (ie, sales quantity, kgs of materials, labour hours) so this could be collected at the same time as the monetary value by use of a sub-coding system and separate quantity fields on the appropriate accounting records.

## 74    SEW

(a)    (i)    Budgeted profit    =    £20,000 – £4,500 – £4,500 – £2,250 – £4,500 = £4,250

Budgeted units    =    1,500

Budget profit/unit    =    $\dfrac{£4,250}{1,500}$ = £2.8333

Actual sales volume    =    $\dfrac{\text{Std profit on actual sales}}{\text{Budgeted profit / unit}} = \dfrac{£3,400}{£2.8333}$ = 1,200 units

(ii)    Standard usage $= \dfrac{750\text{kgs}}{1,500} = 0.5\text{kgs/unit}$

Actual production should use:

| | |
|---|---|
| 1,550 units × 0.5kgs/unit | 775 kgs |

Usage variance = £150 (A)

| | |
|---|---|
| $£150 \div \left(\dfrac{£4,500}{750\text{kgs}}\right)$ | 25 kgs |

| | |
|---|---|
| Actual usage | 800 kgs |

(iii)   1,000 kgs should cost £6/kg (£4,500/750 kgs)

| | |
|---|---|
| 1,000 kgs × £6/kg | £6,000 |
| Price variance | £1,000 (F) |
| Actual cost | £5,000 |

(iv)    Standard time/unit $= \dfrac{1,125 \text{ hours}}{1,500 \text{ units}}$    0.75 hrs

| | |
|---|---|
| 1,550 units should take 1,550 × 0.75 hrs | 1162.5 hrs |

Efficiency variance = £150 (A)

| | |
|---|---|
| $£150 \div \left(\dfrac{£4,500}{1,125\text{ hrs}}\right)$ | 37.5 hrs |

| | |
|---|---|
| Actual hours | 1,200 hrs |

(v)     1,200 hours should cost £4/hr (£4,500/1,125 hrs)

| | |
|---|---|
| 1,200 hours × £4/hr | = £4,800 |
| Rate variance | = £200 (A) |
| Actual cost | £5,000 |

(vi)    Standard variable overhead cost/unit = £2,250/1,500 units = £1.50/unit

| | |
|---|---|
| 1,500 units should cost £1.50/unit | £2,325 |
| Total variance = £6,000 (A) + £75 (A) | £675 (A) |
| Actual cost | £3,000 |

(vii)

| | |
|---|---|
| Budgeted cost | £4,500 |
| Expenditure variance | 2,500 (F) |
| Actual cost | = £2,000 |

(b)     The direct material usage variance, being adverse, means that the actual quantity of materials used was higher than expected. This may be caused by using a lower quality material resulting in a higher level of wastage.

The direct labour rate variance, being adverse, means that the actual rate paid per hour was higher than expected. This might be because of a pay increase which was not included in the standard cost.

The sales volume variance, being adverse, means that the actual number of units sold was less than budgeted. This may be caused by a general reduction in the demand for the product or the effect of a competitor reducing their prices.

# 75   OVERHEAD VARIANCES

(a)   Machine related variable overhead:

|  | £ |
|---|---|
| Expenditure variance: | |
| 22,000 machine hours should cost £8.00/hr | 176,000 |
| Actual cost | 176,000 |
| | £Nil |

| Efficiency variance: | |
|---|---|
| 5,450 units should use 4 hours each | 21,800 hours |
| Actual | 22,000 hours |
| An extra | 200 hours |
| 200 hours @ £8.00/hour | £1,600 (A) |

Labour related variable overhead:

|  | £ |
|---|---|
| Expenditure variance: | |
| 10,800 labour hours should cost £4.00/hour | 43,200 |
| Actual cost | 42,000 |
| | £1,200 (F) |

| Efficiency variance: | |
|---|---|
| 5,450 units should use 2 hours each | 10,900 hours |
| Actual | 10,800 hours |
| A saving of | 100 hours |
| 100 hours @ £4.00/hour | £400 (F) |

Fixed overhead:

|  | £ |
|---|---|
| Expenditure variance: | |
| Budget cost = 5,500 units × £20.00/unit | 110,000 |
| Actual cost | 109,000 |
| | £1,000 (F) |

| Volume variance: | |
|---|---|
| Budget units | 5,500 |
| Actual units | 5,450 |
| Shortfall | 50 units |
| 50 units × £20.00 = | £1,000 (A) |

(b)    Machine related efficiency variance:  the machines were operated at a lower speed than expected.

Labour related expenditure variance:  the cost of the related employment costs were lower than expected per hour.

Labour related efficiency variance:  a higher grade of labour was used which took less time to complete the tasks.

(c)    Such an approach is beneficial because it identifies overhead costs with their cause, rather than assuming that they are all driven by a single cause.

This should enable management to control such costs more easily, the variances reported will be more meaningful and this will help management to control costs.

## 76    T PLC

(a)    **Profit Calculations**

Budgeted Profit:-

|  |  | £/Unit |
|---|---|---|
| Selling price |  | 10.00 |
| Direct materials $\dfrac{10,000\text{kgs}}{5,000\text{units}} \times £0.50$ |  | 1.00 |
| Direct labour 0.5 hours × £4.00 |  | 2.00 |
| Production overhead : $\dfrac{£10,000}{5,000 \text{ units}}$ |  | 2.00 |
|  |  | 5.00 |
| Profit per unit |  | £5.00 |

| | |
|---|---|
| Total Profit 5,000 units × £5 = | £25,000 |
| Less Administration | 3,000 |
| Budgeted profit | £22,000 |

Actual Profit:-

|  | £ | £ |
|---|---|---|
| Sales 4,900 × £11.00 |  | 53,900 |
| D Material 10,600 kgs × £0.60 | 6,360 |  |
| D Labour 5,400 × 0.55 hrs × £3.80 | 11,286 |  |
| Fixed Overhead | 10,300 |  |
|  | 27,946 |  |
| Closing stock 500 units × £5.00 | (2,500) | (25,446) |
| Gross Profit |  | (28,454) |
| Administration |  | (3,100) |
| Net Profit |  | 25,354 |

**Note:** In a standard costing system stocks are valued at standard (ie. budgeted) cost.

**Variance calculations**

Selling price:

| | |
|---|---:|
| 4,900 units should sell for £10 each | £49,000 |
| Actual sales | £53,900 |
| | £4,900 F |

Sales volume:

| | |
|---|---:|
| Budgeted sales | 5,000 units |
| Actual sales | 4,900 units |
| Shortfall | 100 units |
| 100 units × standard profit of £5 / unit = | £500 A |

Material price:

| | |
|---|---:|
| 10,600 kgs should cost £0.50/kg | £5,300 |
| but cost £0.60/kg | £6,360 |
| | £1,060 A |

Material usage:

| | |
|---|---:|
| 5,400 units should use $\dfrac{10,000\text{kgs}}{5,000\text{ units}}$ each | 10,800 kgs |
| Actual usage | 10,600 kgs |
| Saving | 200 kgs |
| 200 kgs × standard price of £0.50/kg | £100 F |

Labour rate

Actual hours     = 5400 units × 0.55 hours / unit
                  = 2970 hours

| | |
|---|---:|
| 2970 hours should cost £4.00 / hour | £11,880 |
| but cost £3.80 / hour | £11,286 |
| | 594 F |

Labour efficiency

| | |
|---|---:|
| 5400 units should use 0.50 hours each | 2700 hours |
| Actual hours | 2970 hours |
| An extra | 270 hours |
| 270 hours × standard rate of £4.00 / hour | £1080 A |

Production overhead expenditure

| | |
|---|---:|
| Budgeted cost | £10,000 |
| Actual cost | £10,300 |
| | £300 A |

Production overhead volume

| | |
|---|---:|
| Budgeted production units | 5,000 |
| Actual production units | 5,400 |
| | |
| An extra | 400 units |
| | |
| 400 units × Absorption rate of £2 / unit | £800 F |

Administration overhead cost

| | |
|---|---:|
| Budgeted cost | £3,000 |
| Actual cost | £3,100 |
| | |
| | £100 A |

## Reconciliation Statement

| | £ |
|---|---:|
| Budgeted profit | 22,000 |
| Sales volume profit variance | 500 A |
| | |
| Standard profit on actual sales | 21,500 |
| Selling price variance | 4,900 F |
| | |
| | 26,400 |

Cost Variances:

| | A £ | F £ | |
|---|---:|---:|---:|
| Material price | 1060 | | |
| Material usage | | 100 | |
| Labour rate | | 594 | |
| Labour efficiency | 1080 | | |
| Production overhead:- | | | |
|   Expenditure | 300 | | |
|   Volume | | 800 | |
| | | | |
| Administration overhead | 100 | | |
| | 2,540 | 1,494 | 1,046 A |
| | | | |
| Actual Profit | | | 25,354 |

(b)   (i)     The material usage variance, being favourable, indicates that the amount of material used was less than expected for the actual output achieved. This could be caused by the purchase of higher quality materials, which resulted in less wastage than normal.

       (ii)    The labour rate variance, being favourable, indicates that the hourly wage rate paid was lower than expected. This could be due to employing a lower grade of employee than was anticipated in the budget.

      (iii)    The sales volume profit variance, being adverse, indicates that the number of units sold was less than budgeted. This may have been caused by the increased sales price of £11 (compared to a budgeted price of £10) which has reduced customer demand; or the actions of competitors.

(c)     Interdependence of variances is the term used to describe the situation when there is a single cause of a number of variances.

For example, the use of a higher grade of labour than was anticipated is likely to cause an adverse labour rate variance, a favourable labour efficiency variance, and possibly a favourable material usage variance (due to more experience of working with materials).

It is important that when variances are reported, the possibility that some of them may have a common cause should be acknowledged, and managers encouraged to work together for the benefit of the organisation.

## 77   RESTAURANT

(a)

| | |
|---|---:|
| Budget selling price | £7.50 |
| Budgeted costs | £3.00 |
| Profit per set menu | £4.50 |
| Budget volume | 750 |
| Budget profit (750 × £4.50) | £3,375 |

(b)

| | |
|---|---:|
| Sales 860 × £7 | £6,020 |
| Costs per question | £2,548 |
| Profit | £3,472 |

(c)      *Variance calculations*

Sales price:

| | |
|---|---:|
| 860 meals should sell for £7.50 = | £6,450 |
| Actual ((b) above) = | £6,020 |
| | £430 A |

Sales volume:

| | |
|---|---:|
| Budgeted volume = | 750 |
| Actual volume = | 860 |
| | 110 |
| 110 × £4.50 = | £495 F |

Mushroom price:

| | |
|---|---:|
| 90 kgs should cost £3/ kg = | £270 |
| Actual = | £300 |
| | £30 A |

Mushroom usage:

| | |
|---|---:|
| 860 menus should use 100g = | 86 kg |
| Actual = | 90 kg |
| | 4 kg |
| 4 kg × £3/kg = | £12 A |

Cream – total

| | |
|---|---:|
| 860 menus should cost £0.20 = | £172 |
| Actual = | £160 |
| | 12 F |

Beef price:

| | |
|---|---:|
| 70 kg should cost £15/kg = | £1,050 |
| Actual = | £1,148 |
| | £98 A |

Beef usage:
   860 menus should use 0.1 kg =                                    86 kg
   Actual =                                                         70 kg
                                                                           _____
                                                                           16 kg
                                                                           _____

16 kg @ £15.00/kg =                                                        £240 F
                                                                           _____

Potatoes price:
   180 kg should cost £0.25/kg =                                    £45
   Actual =                                                         £40
                                                                           _____
                                                                           £5 F
                                                                           _____

Potatoes usage:
   860 menus should use 0.2 kg =                                    172 kg
   Actual =                                                         180 kg
                                                                           _____
                                                                           8 kg
                                                                           _____

8 kg @ £0.25/kg -                                                          £2 A
                                                                           _____

Vegetables price:
   270 kgs should cost £0.90/kg =                                   £243
   Actual =                                                         £250
                                                                           _____
                                                                           £7 A
                                                                           _____

Vegetable usage:
   860 menus should use 0.3 kgs =                                   258 kgs
   Actual =                                                         270 kgs
                                                                           _____
                                                                           12 kgs
                                                                           _____

12 kgs @ £0.90/kg =                                                        £10.80 A
                                                                           _____

Other – total
   860 menus should cost £0.23 =                                    £197.80
   Actual =                                                         £200.00
                                                                           _____
                                                                           £2.20 A
                                                                           _____

Fresh fruit price
   140 kgs should cost £3/kg =                                      £420
   Actual =                                                         £450
                                                                           _____
                                                                           £30 A
                                                                           _____

Fresh fruit usage:
   860 menus should use 0.15 kgs =                                  129 kgs
   Actual =                                                         140 kgs
                                                                           _____
                                                                           11 kgs
                                                                           _____

11 kgs @ £3/kg =                                                           £33 A
                                                                           _____

**Reconciliation statement**

|  | £ |
|---|---|
| Budgeted profit | 3,375 |
| Sales volume variance | 495 F |
|  | 3,870 |
| Selling price variance | 430 A |
|  | 3,440 |

| Cost variances: |  | A | F |  |
|---|---|---|---|---|
| Mushroom | : price | 30 |  |  |
|  | : usage | 12 |  |  |
| Cream | : total |  | 12 |  |
| Beef | : price | 98 |  |  |
|  | : usage |  | 240 |  |
| Potatoes | : price |  | 5 |  |
|  | : usage | 2 |  |  |
| Vegetables | : price | 7 |  |  |
|  | : usage | 10.80 |  |  |
| Other | : total | 2.20 |  |  |
| Fresh fruit | : price | 30 |  |  |
|  | : usage | 33 |  |  |
|  |  | 225 | 257 | 32 F |
| Actual profit |  |  |  | 3,472 |

(d)

**Report**

To:      Restaurant Manager                          From:  Management Accountant

Subject: Set Menu Profitability

Date:     25 November 1998

**Introduction**

Further to our meeting, I have considered the monthly variance report concerning our set menus.

**Findings**

1.       By measuring each variance as a percentage of its target value, the most significant variances are those relating to the price and usage of beef.

2.       I have discussed this with the chef who advises me that the price increase was, in his opinion, due to the anticipated European demand following the lifting of the UK beef export ban.

3.       In order to maintain the profitability of the set menu, the chef thus reduced the portion size to compensate for this extra price.

**Conclusion**

It seems that our chef should be thanked for his attention to detail and his prompt action to maintain profitability.

## 78    RBF TRANSPORT LTD

(a)    (i)    Budgeted fixed overhead cost/mile

$$= \frac{(£15,600 + £400)}{200,000} \quad = \quad £0.08/\text{mile}$$

| | | |
|---|---|---|
| Volume variance | = | £1,760 (A) |
| Volume difference | = | 22,000 miles (A) |
| Actual miles | = | 200,000 − 22,000 |
| | = | 178,000 |

(ii)    Standard rate/hr   =   $\dfrac{£0.08}{0.02}$

                            =   £4/hour

        Rate variance      =   £1,086 F

                            =   $\dfrac{£1,086}{3,620} = £0.30/\text{hr (F)}$

        Actual rate        =   £4.00 − £0.03 = £3.70/hr

(iii)    Standard price/litre   =   $\dfrac{£0.04}{0.1}$

                            =   £0.40/litre

| | | |
|---|---|---|
| Actual price/litre | = | £0.42/litre |
| Price variance/litre | = | £0.02 (A) |
| Total price variance | = | £420 (A) |

        Actual number of litres =   $\dfrac{£420}{£0.02} = 21,000$

(iv)    178,000 miles should cost £0.06/mile = £10,680

        Total variable overhead variance    =   £100 F

        Actual cost                     = £10,580

(b)    **To:**        Transport Operations Manager

        **From**:    Management Accountant

        **Date:**

        **Subject:**   Standard costs

**Introduction**

This report explains the type of standard cost which may be set and importance of keeping standards meaningful and relevant.

**Types of standard**

A standard cost is a prediction of the cost per unit expected in a future period. It is dependant on estimates of resource requirements per output unit and the price to be paid per resource unit.

There are three types of standard which may be set – these are often referred to as:

- current standard;
- attainable standard; and
- idea standard

The current standard uses existing efficiency and achievement levels as the standard for the future period. This does not encourage improvement and may also allow existing inefficiencies to continue unnoticed.

The attainable standard sets a target which requires improvements in performance if it is to be achieved, but these are small and are considered to be achievable (or attainable). This form of standard is believed to be the best motivator to a manager.

The ideal standard assumes a perfect working environment (which never exists for a prolonged period). This is impossible to achieve.

**Keeping standards useful**

Standards are useful as a basis for performance evaluation. If such comparisons are to be valid the standard must reflect the current method of working **AND** resource prices which are unrealistic. If standards are not kept up to date they are no longer meaningful and thus their usefulness is reduced.

**Conclusion**

I recommend that attainable standards should be used, and that they should be reviewed regularly. Please contact me if you wish to discuss this further.

---

## 79   ANSWERS TO MULTIPLE CHOICE QUESTIONS

1    Scarce resource – 7,000 labour hours

|  | A | B | C |
|---|---|---|---|
| Labour hours per unit | 2.5 | 6 | 7.5 |
| Contribution per unit | £6.50 | £6.80 | £15 |
| Contribution per labour hour | £2.60 | £1.13 | £2 |
| Ranking | 1 | 3 | 2 |

Production plan

|  |  |  | Hours |
|---|---|---|---|
| Maximum demand for |  |  |  |
| A | 1,000 units × 2.5 |  | 2,500 |
| C | 200 units × 7.5 hours |  | 1,500 |
| B | 500 units × 6 hours |  | 3,000 (balance) |

Therefore C.

2    $0.10 \times \dfrac{120{,}000}{6{,}000 \times (0.05 + 0.10)} + 0.25 \times \dfrac{72{,}000}{6{,}000 \times (0.20 + 0.25)} = £20$

Therefore D.

3    $1{,}500 \times 60\% + (18{,}000 - 1{,}500) + 3{,}000 \times 80\% = 19{,}800$

Therefore C.

4     Equivalent units = $100 \times 70\% + (1,900 - 100) + 200 \times 40\% = 1,950$
Cost per unit = $1,930,500 \div 1,950 = £990$
Cost of completed production = $38,600 + (70 + 1,800) \times 990 = £1,889,900$
Cost per unit of completed production = $1,889,900 \div 1,900 = £995$

Therefore B.

5     Cost in period and b/f = £100,000
Equivalent units in period = $800 + 6,500 + 1,500 = 8,800$
Cost per unit = $100,000 \div 8,800 = £11.36$
Value of closing WIP = $1,500 \times 11.36 = £17,000$

Therefore A.

6     $2,000 + 42,300 - (1,500 + 40,100 + 400) = 2,300$

Therefore D.

7

|  | Sales revenue £ | Joint costs £ |
|---|---|---|
| UB-1 | 62,400 | 35,862 |
| UB-2 | 76,800 | 44,138 |
|  | £139,200 | £80,000 |

Closing stock valuation = $35,862 \times \dfrac{8}{208} + (44,138 + 38,400) \times \dfrac{12}{192} = £6,500$

Therefore C.

8     Opening work in progress   + Started   = Finished   + Closing work in progress
=            20,000        + 110,000   = 90,000     +            40,000

Cost per car = $\dfrac{132,000}{90,000 + 0.5 \times 40,000} = £1.20$

Therefore B.

9     B/E point = $\dfrac{1,000 \times (4.60 + 5.80)}{24.90 - (5.60 + 3.40)} = 654$

Therefore C.

10     $(300,000 - 3,000 \times 0.5) \times \dfrac{2}{10} = £59,700$

Therefore C.

11     $\dfrac{3,300}{400 \times 0.7 + 1,800 + 200 \times 0.6} = £1.50$

Therefore B.

12

|  | Kilts | Skirts | Dresses |  |
|---|---|---|---|---|
| Contribution per hour | 4 | 5.50 | 7 | = 1,000 dresses |

Therefore C.

13      $26,000 \div [(6 + 5 + 2) \div 6] \times \frac{1}{2} = 6,000$

Therefore A.

14      400 units started and finished + 600 units 75% complete = 850 units

Therefore C.

15      Budgeted contribution = $18,000 \times 40 = £720,000$
Budgeted fixed costs = $580,000 + 20,000 = £600,000$
Budgeted profit = $720,000 - 600,000 = £120,000$

Therefore A.

16      If EUs down, CPU up and cost of finished goods up.

Therefore D.

17      $(500 \times 3 - \text{Quantity used}) \times 2 = + £200$
Quantity used = 1,400 kg
Quantity purchased = $1,400 + 300 - 100 = 1,600$ kg

Therefore C.

18      $50,000 \times 20\% + 40,000 \times 60\% + 60,000 \times 10\% = £40,000$

Therefore C.

19      $25,000 \times 20\% + 20,000 \times 65\% + 30,000 \times 10\% = £21,000$

Therefore C.

20      (a)     Iron        $= 2 \times (800 \times 5 - 3,900) =$        200 F
                Copper      $= 3 \times (800 \times 3 - 2,600) =$        600 A

                Net                                                   £400 A

        Therefore B.

        (b)     Labour rate = $3,400 \times 7 - (2,000 \times 7 + 1,400 \times 7.20) = £280$ A

        Therefore A.

        (c)     Variable overhead rate = $3,400 \times 3 - 10,000 = £200$ F

        Therefore A.

        (d)     Fixed overhead expenditure = $(2 \times 4,000) - 8,800 = £800$ A

        Therefore C.

        (e)     Fixed overhead volume = $8 \times (800 - [4,000 \div 4]) = £1,600$ A

        Therefore D.

21      Variable cpu = $(6,000 - 5,000) \div (4m - 2m) = £500$ million
Fixed cost per quarter = $5,000 - 2 \times 500 = £4,000$
$\therefore$ Cost of 5m units = $4,000 + 5 \times 500 = £6,500$

Therefore B.

22    Break-even number of units = $\dfrac{\text{Fixed costs}}{\text{Contribution per unit}}$

If selling price per unit and variable cost per unit rise by 10%, then contribution per unit rises by 10%.

∴ Break-even number of units will decrease
    (assuming a positive contribution in the first place!)

Therefore C.

23

|  | £ |
|---|---|
| Selling price | 40 |
| VC | 32 |
| Contribution | 8 |

Increase in fixed cost = £8,000
∴ Increase in B/E point = £8,000 ÷ 8 = 1,000 units

Therefore C.

24

| | Dept A £ | Dept B £ | Total £ |
|---|---|---|---|
| Direct materials | 20,000 | 16,000 | 36,000 |
| Direct labour | 24,000 | 20,000 | 44,000 |
| Production overhead | 20,000 | 25,000 | 45,000 |
| Full production cost | | | 125,000 |
| Other overheads 20% | | | 25,000 |
| Cost of job | | | 150,000 |
| Profit (20% of sales = 25% of cost) | | | 37,500 |
| Sales price | | | £187,500 |

Therefore D.

25    Statement A is correct.  Job costs are identified with a particular job, whereas process costs (of units produced and work in process) are averages, based on equivalent units of production.

Statement B is also correct.  The direct cost of a job to date, excluding any direct expenses, can be ascertained from materials requisition notes and job tickets or time sheets.

Statement C is correct, because without data about units completed and units still in process, losses and equivalent units of production cannot be calculated.

Statement D is incorrect, because the cost of normal loss will usually be incorporated into job costs as well as into process costs.  In process costing this is commonly done by giving normal loss no cost, leaving costs to be shared between output, closing stocks and abnormal loss/gain.  In job costing it can be done by adjusting direct materials costs to allow for normal wastage, and direct labour costs for normal reworking of items or normal spoilage.

Therefore D.

26    Statement (c) would be correct *except* that the profit in each year depends partly on opening and closing stock values of finished goods and WIP.  Opening stock + Costs of production − Closing stock = Cost of sales. Since unit overhead costs will differ if 'actual' overhead costs are used, rather than pre-determined overhead absorption rates, opening and closing stock values will differ.

Statement (d) is correct because 'actual' overhead costs, based on actual overhead expenditure and actual activity for the period, cannot be determined until after the end of the period (the month, or the year).

Therefore C.

27     Contribution margin $= \dfrac{SP - VC}{SP} = \dfrac{SP - 60}{SP} = 0.52$

$\Rightarrow SP = £125$

Profit this year $= (125 - 60) \times 1,000 - 25 \times 1,000 = £40,000$

| Increases | Selling price | $= 125 \times 1.08$ | $=$ | £135 |
|---|---|---|---|---|
| | Variable costs | $= 60 \times 1.05$ | $=$ | £63 |
| | Fixed costs | $= 25 \times 1,000 \times 1.05$ | $=$ | £26,250 |

Break-even point in units $= \dfrac{26,250 + 40,000}{(135 - 63)} = 921$

Therefore D.

28     The correct answer is D.

29

|  | £ |
|---|---|
| Overhead absorbed $= 72,600 \times 6.40$ | 464,640 |
| Overhead incurred | 472,560 |
| Overhead under-absorbed | £7,920 |

Overhead was under-absorbed because absorbed overhead is less than actual costs incurred.

Therefore B.

30     (a)     The coding system is

| Digits 1 and 2 | Location code |
|---|---|
| Digits 3 and 4 | Function code |
| Digits 5, 6 and 7 | Type of expense |

Thus for (1) Birmingham (2) production and (3) factory depreciation we have 3112450.

Therefore D.

(b)     The accountant is an expense of the Manchester office, and hotel costs will be classified as subsistence costs (rather than travel or entertainment).

Thus for (1) Cardiff (2) finance and (3) subsistence we have 3217920.

Therefore C.

31     Item B describes *costs* of an activity or cost centre. Item A describes *cost units*. Item D describes *budget centres*. A cost centre is defined in the CIMA *Official Terminology* as 'a production or service location, function, activity or item of equipment for which costs are accumulated'.

Therefore C.

32     Continuous stocktaking is defined in the question. Perpetual inventory is a stock recording system whereby each movement in or out of stock is recorded as it occurs, and so stock records for *every* item are always up-to-date. ABC inventory analysis is a stock control system which categorises stock items into three categories, according to the proportion and value of total stock usage of the item. The stock items in category A which represent the largest proportion of stock usage by value (but the smallest number of items) merit the greatest

amount of stock control effort. Low-value or small usage items in category C merit the least amount of stock control.

Therefore A.

33    62,965 + 13,600 = £76,565. The only direct costs are the wages paid to direct workers for ordinary time, plus the basic pay for overtime. Overtime premium and shift allowances are usually treated as overheads. However, if and when overtime and shiftwork are incurred specifically for a particular cost unit, they are classified as direct costs of that cost unit. Sick pay is treated as an overhead and is therefore classified as an indirect cost.

Therefore B.

34    With LIFO, if newer stocks cost more to buy from suppliers than older stocks, the costs of materials issued and used will be higher. It follows that the cost of sales will be higher and the profit lower.

Closing stocks with LIFO will be priced at the purchase price of earlier items that were received into stock. In a period of rising prices, this means that closing stocks will be valued at old, out-of-date and low prices.

Therefore A.

35    Use of the last in, first out stock valuation method results in closing stocks being valued at the oldest prices. Since prices are rising, the oldest prices will be the lowest prices. Next in, first out uses the next price to be paid for materials, which in this case is likely to be the highest price of all, for both materials issued and for closing stock valuations.

Therefore B.

36

|  | £ |
|---|---|
| Sales 625 × 4 | 2,500 |
| Gross profit | 1,250 |
| Material cost of sales | £1,250 |

| Cost of units sold | |
|---|---|
| First 200 units (× 1.80) | 360 |
| Next 300 units (× 2.10) | 630 |
|  | 990 |
| Total cost of 625 units sold | 1,250 |
| Balance cost of last 125 units sold | £260 |

Cost per unit 260 ÷ 125 = £2.08

Therefore D.

37    The unit price of parts received was

| 3 April | £6.00 |
|---|---|
| 7 April | £6.60 |
| 11 April | £8.00 |
| 24 April | £7.00 |

(a)     Value of parts issued, using FIFO

|  |  | £ | £ |
|---|---|---|---|
| 16 Aug | 1,000 @ 5.60 each (opening stock) | 5,600 | |
|  | 2,000 @ 6 each | 12,000 | |
|  | 1,000 @ 6.60 each | 6,600 | |

|  |  |  |  | 24,200 |
|---|---|---|---|---|
| 30 Aug | 2,000 @ 6.60 each | | 13,200 | |
| | 2,000 @ 8 each | | 16,000 | |
| | 1,000 @ 7 each | | 7,000 | |
| | | | | 36,200 |
| Total value of parts issued | | | | £60,400 |

Therefore A.

(b) Value of parts issued, using LIFO

|  |  | £ | £ |
|---|---|---|---|
| 16 Aug | 2,000 @ 8 each | 16,000 | |
| | 2,000 @ 6.60 each | 13,200 | |
| | | | 29,200 |
| 30 Aug | 3,000 @ 7 each | 21,000 | |
| | 1,000 @ 6.60 each | 6,600 | |
| | 1,000 @ 6 each | 6,000 | |
| | | | 33,600 |
| Total value of parts issued | | | £62,800 |

Therefore C.

38    The high-low method identifies the expected variable and fixed elements.

Therefore A.

39    Revenue is most likely to be based on the quantity delivered and the distance travelled. Cost per tonne miles gives a measure of both quantity and distance.

Therefore C.

40    Such a cost is not real, it is imputed so that a reliable comparison can be made. Only C relates to such a cost, the distractors refer to alternative classifications of real costs.

The correct answer is **C.**

41    Distractor A is incorrect because it is the cost of modification not the opportunity value of V.

Distractor B is the scrap value of V and could be the relevant cost. However, it does not represent the next best alternative and thus is not correct.

Distractor D is the cost of the alternative material and would be relevant if an equal quantity of V could be used without further processing costs being incurred.

Distractor E is incorrect because it is a past historic cost.

The answer is C because

| | |
|---|---|
| Replacement material cost saved (2 kg @ £4.50) | £9.00 |
| Less further processing cost (£1 × 3 kg) | £3.00 |
| | £6.00 |

£6.00/3 kg = £2.00 per kg.

The correct answer is **C.**

42      Absorption rate $= \dfrac{£100,000}{20,000} = £5/\text{unit}$

Difference in volume    =    20,000 – 19,500
                        =    500 units

Volume variance         =    500 units × £5/unit
                        =    £2,500 (A)

It is adverse because actual volume is less than that budgeted.

The correct answer is **B**.

43      Standard contribution/unit = £10.00 – £5.60 = £4.40
        Volume difference = 5,000 – 4,500 = 500 units.

Variance = 500 × £4.40 = £2,200 Adverse.

The correct answer is **B**.

44      The difference between the stock valuations of these systems is the treatment of the fixed overhead costs. It is this which causes the profit difference. The question cannot be answered without an analysis of the fixed and variable costs.

The correct answer is **E**.

45      Contribution per unit = £20 × 40% = £8.

Breakeven point $= \dfrac{£60,000}{£8} = 7,500$ units.

The correct answer is **E**.

46      Common cost attributed to P is:

| | £ |
|---|---|
| $\dfrac{£117,000}{\text{Total output}} \times 4,500 = \dfrac{£117,000}{9,750} \times 4,500 =$ | 54,000 |
| Further processing cost 4,500 × £9 = | 40,500 |
| | 94,500 |
| Sales revenue (4,500 – 10%) × £25 | 101,250 |
| Profit | 6,750 |

The correct answer is **A**.

47

| | £ |
|---|---|
| Value certified | 1,300,000 |
| Cost of work certified | 1,000,000 |
| | 300,000 |

$$£300,000 \times \frac{\text{Cash received}}{\text{Value certified}}$$

$$= £300,000 \times \frac{£1,200,000}{£1,300,000}$$

$$= \underline{£276,923}$$

The correct answer is **B**.

48    Distractors A, B, and C are incorrect because the price variance is adverse and therefore should be debited to the variance account.

Distractor E is incorrect because in such a system price variances are recorded in the raw material control account so that stock is valued at standard prices.

The correct answer is **D**.

49    Job costing involves carrying out work to a customer's specification where the time taken on an individual job is relatively short.

Thus (ii) and (iii) only are correct.

The correct answer is **C**.

50    Weighted average c/s ratio equals

$$\frac{(1 \times 40\%) + (3 \times 50\%)}{4} = 47.5\%$$

$$\text{Breakeven point} = \frac{\text{Fixed costs}}{\text{c / s ratio}} = \frac{£120,000}{0.475} = 252,632$$

The correct answer is **C**.

51

| Product | X | Y | Z |
|---|---|---|---|
| Contribution/unit | £41 | £54 | £50 |
| Materials (kg/unit) | 2 | 1 | 3 |
| Contribution/kg | £20.50 | £54 | £16.66 |
| Ranking | 2 | 1 | 3 |

The correct answer is **B**.

52    Contract costing is used when the work is customer specific and takes a long time to complete (usually more than one year).

Thus only (ii) is correct.

The correct answer is **E**.

53   Price variance:                                                                          £

        8,200 kg should cost £0.80/kg           =                    6,560
        Actual cost                             =                    6,888
                                                                     ─────
                                                                     328  (A)
                                                                     ─────

     Usage variance:

        870 units should use 8 kg each          =                    6,960 kg
        Actual usage                            =                    7,150 kg
                                                                     ─────────
                                                                     190 kg
                                                                     ─────────

        190 kg @ £0.80/kg                        =                    £152  (A)
                                                                     ─────────

     The correct answer is **D**.

54   60% of August sales less 2% discount:
        £60,000 × 60% × 98%  =                                       35,280
     25% of July sales:
        £40,000 × 25%                                                10,000
     12% of June sales:
        £35,000 × 12%                                                4,200
                                                                     ──────
                                                                     49,480
                                                                     ──────

     The correct answer is **D**.

55   Service industries use composite cost units eg, passenger miles because it is difficult to measure their output activity using a single measure. It is difficult to identify costs with cost units for the same reason. Equivalent units are used in connection with work in progress stocks which does not apply in service costing so B is correct.

     The correct answer is **B**.

56   Increase in cost = £1,800

     Increase in production = 1,000 units

     Variable cost = $\dfrac{£1,800}{1,000}$ = £1.80/unit

     Variable cost of 2,000 units = 2,000 × £1.80 =          £3,600
     Total cost of 2,000 units =                             £11,100
                                                             ───────
     Fixed cost                                              7,500
                                                             ───────

     Variable cost of 4,000 units = 4,000 × £1.80 =          £7,200
     Fixed cost                                              £7,500
                                                             ───────
                                                             £14,700
                                                             ───────

     The correct answer is **B**.

57   Fixed cost per unit = $\dfrac{£60,000}{30,000}$ =                                  £2.00/unit

Variable cost/unit =                                                                   £9.50/unit
                                                                                       ————
                                                                                       £11.50/unit
                                                                                       ————

Profit/unit = £15.00 − £11.50 = £3.50/unit
Sales units = 2,400 − 180 = 2,220 units
Profit = 2,220 × £3.50 =                                                               £7,770
Less under absorption:

$\left(\dfrac{30,000}{12} - 2,400\right) \times £2 =$                                 £200
                                                                                       ————
                                                                                       £7,570
                                                                                       ————

The correct answer is **B**.

58   Budget cost = $\dfrac{£120,000}{12}$ =                                             £10,000
     Actual cost =                                                                     £9,800
                                                                                       ————
                                                                                       £200      (F)
                                                                                       ————

The correct answer is **B**.

59   A non-integrated system is one in which the only asset/liability accounts are those representing stocks. Thus at the beginning of a year the stock and work-in-progress accounts will contain debit balances and a credit balance will be found in the cost ledger control account.

The correct answer is **E**.

60

**Process account (units only)**

|  | £ |  | £ |
|---|---|---|---|
| Opening WIP | 600 | Normal loss | 500 |
| Input (balancing figure) | 15,200 | Output | 14,500 |
|  |  | Closing WIP | 800 |
|  | ——— |  | ——— |
|  | 15,800 |  | 15,800 |
|  | ——— |  | ——— |

**Equivalents units table**

|  |  | Total | Materials | | Conversion | |
|---|---|---|---|---|---|---|
|  |  |  | % | eu | % | eu |
| Output | - O/WIP | 600 | 20 | 120 | 40 | 240 |
|  | - S&F | 13,900 | 100 | 13,900 | 100 | 13,900 |
| Closing WIP |  | 800 | 70 | 560 | 40 | 320 |
|  |  |  |  | ——— |  | ——— |
|  |  |  |  | 14,580 |  | 14,460 |
|  |  |  |  | ——— |  | ——— |

The correct answer is **A**.

61   Since the process account is debited with the production value, the abnormal gain account is credited with this value to complete the double entry. The scrap proceeds lost are then debited to the abnormal gain account so that the resulting balance represents the net gain of the lesser loss.

The correct answer is **C**.

62   Only the incremental costs and revenues are relevant which are (iii), (iv) and (v), so the answer is B

63    Breakeven point = Fixed costs $\times \dfrac{1}{c/s \text{ ratio}} = £48,000 \times \dfrac{1}{40\%} = £120,000$

If actual sales = £140,000, then the margin of safety is £20,000 (£140,000 − £120,000)

Since the selling price is £10 per unit this is equivalent to 2,000 units and so the answer is **A**

64    Direct materials and direct labour costs are both wholly variable because their cost per unit is constant.

**Production overhead - Department 1**

| Volume | Cost total |
|--------|-----------|
| 1,000  | £6,000    |
| 2,000  | £8,400    |

Since the cost per unit *and* the total cost are different, this must be a semi-variable cost. Using the high/low points technique:

$$\frac{\text{Difference in total cost}}{\text{Difference in volume}} = \frac{£2,400}{1,000} = £2.40 \text{ per unit}$$

By substitution:

|                                  | £     |
|----------------------------------|-------|
|                                  | £     |
| Variable cost of 1,000 units     | 2,400 |
| Total cost of 1,000 units        | 6,000 |
|                                  | ----- |
| Fixed cost element               | 3,600 |

**Production overhead - Department 2**

| Volume | Cost total |
|--------|-----------|
| 1,000  | £4,000    |
| 2,000  | £4,000    |

Since the cost total is the same, this is a wholly fixed cost. So to summarise:

|                          | Fixed<br>£ | Variable<br>£ |
|--------------------------|-----------|---------------|
| Direct materials         |           | 4.00          |
| Direct labour            |           | 3.50          |
| Production overhead - 1  | 3,600     | 2.40          |
| Production overhead - 2  | 4,000     |               |
|                          | -----     | -----         |
|                          | 7,600     | 9.90          |

The correct answer is **E**

65    Maximum stock level = Reorder level + Reorder quantity − Minimum usage in the lead time

Reorder level = Maximum usage × Maximum lead time = 10 × 5 = 50 units

Reorder quantity = EOQ = $\sqrt{\dfrac{2\text{CoD}}{\text{Ch}}}$

where    Co    =    cost of an order
         D     =    annual demand
         Ch    =    cost of holding one item for one year

So EOQ = $\sqrt{\dfrac{2 \times 50 \times 1,750}{2}} = \sqrt{87,500} \cong 296$

Maximum stock level = $50 + 296 - (4 \times 3) = 334$

So:

| | | |
|---|---|---|
| | Closing stock | 334 |
| | Usage | 140 |
| | | 474 |
| | Less: Opening stock | 170 |
| | Purchases | 304 |

The correct answer is **B**

66    Rate variance:

| | £ |
|---|---|
| Standard cost of actual hours (13,450 × £6) | 80,700 |
| Actual cost | 79,893 |
| | 807 (F) |

Efficiency variance:

| | |
|---|---|
| Standard hours produced (3,350 × 4) | 13,400 |
| Actual hours | 13,450 |
| Extra hours | 50 (A) |

Variance    $= 50 \times £6 = £300$ (A)

The correct answer is **D**

67    

| | |
|---|---|
| 850 units should sell at £9 each | £7,650 |
| Actual sales value | £7,480 |
| Selling price variance | £170 A |

Volume difference is 50 units, under marginal costing these are valued using the standard contribution per unit of £5 (£9 − £4).

So the volume variance is $50 \times £5 = £250$ (F).

It is favourable because actual sales volume exceeds budget volume.

The correct answer is **E**

68    Material price variance:

Calculated based on purchases because an integrated standard costing system is in use:

Cost saving per unit = £0.20 (£4.50 − £4.70)

Total saving = $5,000 \times £0.20 = £1,000$

This is a favourable variance and will be credited to the variance account.

2,400 units of the finished product should use 4,800 units of material (2,400 × 2).

Actual usage was 50 units more (4,850 – 4,800), so the usage variance is:

50 × £4.70 (standard price) = £235 (A)

This will be debited to the variance account so the answer is **D**.

69      Stocks are valued at standard prices, so the material price variance must be calculated by reference to the quantity purchased.

**Price variance**

|  | kgs |
|---|---|
| Actual quantity used | 4,100 |
| Reduction in stock | 300 |
| Quantity purchased | 3,800 kgs |

|  | £ |
|---|---|
| 3,800 kgs should cost £4.50/kg | 17,100 |
| Actual cost | 14,400 |
| Price variance | £2,700 F |

**Usage variance**

1,040 finished units should use:

|  | kgs |
|---|---|
| 4 kgs each | 4,160 |
| Actual usage | 4,100 |
| Saving | 60 kgs |

60 kgs @ £4.50/kg (standard price) = £270 F

Therefore the answer is B.

70

|  | H £ | J £ | K £ |
|---|---|---|---|
| Contribution/unit | 30 | 42 | 38 |
| Labour cost/unit | 10 | 15 | 10 |
| Contribution/labour cost | 3.0 | 2.8 | 3.8 |
| Ranking | 2 | 3 | 1 |

K is the most profitable and J the least profitable - the answer is B.

71      Absorption costing values stocks inclusive of a proportion of fixed production overhead costs, so stock values will be higher than those of marginal costing.

When stocks increase part of the fixed production overhead cost is carried in the balance sheet stock valuation if absorption costing is used, so absorption costing profits will be higher than those of marginal costing.

The answer is B.

72   Although the breakeven sales value can be calculated from the data provided it is not possible to calculate the number of units required to breakeven, so the answer is E.

73   Since material R is in regular use and is readily available in the market, its relevant cost is the replacement price of £6/kg.

So 1,000 kgs × £6/kg = £6,000 = D.

74   The value of the abnormal gain is not used to reduce the cost of the process. The answer is A.

75   **Rate variance**

| | £ |
|---|---|
| 11,700 hours should cost £6.40/hour | 74,880 |
| Actual cost | 64,150 |
| Price variance | £10,730 F |

**Efficiency variance**

| | Hours |
|---|---|
| 2,300 units should use 4.5 hours each | 10,350 |
| Actual hours | 11,700 |
| An extra | 1,350 hours |

1,350 hours @ £6.40/hour (standard rate) = £8,640 A

The answer is D.

76   **Expenditure variance**

| | |
|---|---|
| Monthly budgeted production (10,800/12) | 900 units |
| | £ |
| Monthly budgeted expenditure | |
| 900 × £4 | 3,600 Fixed |
| 800 × £6 | 4,800 Variable |
| | £8,400 |
| Actual expenditure | £8,500 |
| Expenditure variance | £100 A |

**Volume variance**

This only applies to fixed overhead costs:

Difference in volume = 100 units
100 units × £4 per unit = £400 A

The answer is E.

77 The effect of the changes in stock levels on profits are:

£

Financial accounts
£5,000 – £4,000 + £9,800 – £7,900     2,900 Dr   Profit & loss
Cost accounts
£6,400 – £5,200 + £9,600 – £7,600     3,200 Dr   Profit & loss

Additional Dr in cost accounts     £300    in Profit & loss

So the answer is A.

78

### Process account (units only)

| | Units | | Units |
|---|---|---|---|
| Opening WIP | 2,000 | Normal loss | 2,400 |
| Input | 24,000 | Output | 19,500 |
| | | Closing WIP | 3,000 |
| | | Abnormal loss (balance) | 1,100 |
| | 26,000 | | 26,000 |

### Equivalents units table

| | Materials % | eu | Conversion % | eu |
|---|---|---|---|---|
| Output | 100 | 19,500 | 100 | 19,500 |
| Abnormal loss | 100 | 1,100 | 100 | 1,100 |
| Closing WIP | 100 | 3,000 | 45 | 1,350 |
| | | 23,600 | | 21,950 |

The answer is E.

79 The abnormal loss is a form of output, and the only form of output valued at its scrap value is the normal loss.

Therefore the answer is D.

80 If a sales value of £100 per unit is assumed then the original and revised situations will be:

| | Original £ | Revised £ |
|---|---|---|
| Selling price | 100 | 110 |
| Variable cost/unit | 60 | 60 |
| Contribution/unit | 40 | 50 |

Fixed costs do not affect contribution and if sales volume is unchanged then the overall change in contribution can be measured using the contribution per unit:

$$\frac{(50-40)}{40} = 25\%$$

Therefore the answer is D.

81    A flexible budget is a budget which recognises which costs remain constant and which change when the level
      of activity changes.  From this analysis a budget is prepared which shows the total costs expected at different
      levels of activity.

      Therefore the answer is C.

82    The fixed overhead variances are:

      Expenditure:        Budget cost
                            2,400 standard hours × £5            =         £12,000
                          Actual cost                            =         £13,100
                                                                           ————
                          Adverse variance of                              £1,100
                                                                           ————

      Volume:             Budget standard hours                           2,400
                          Actual standard hours                           2,350
                                                                          ————
                          Shortfall                                          50
                                                                          ————

      50 standard hours × £5 = £250 adverse

      Fixed overhead variances are entered in the fixed overhead control account and the respective variance
      accounts.  Adverse variances are debits to the variance account with the corresponding credit being made in
      the fixed overhead control account.

      Therefore the answer is E.

83    The distinction between direct and indirect costs is that the former can be economically identified with a unit
      of the item being costed (the cost unit), whereas indirect costs cannot be so identified and are treated as
      overhead costs.

      Therefore the answer is B.

84    To determine the most and least profitable use of the material each product must be ranked on its contribution
      per £1 of material used:

|                                      | L       | M       | N       |                   |
|--------------------------------------|---------|---------|---------|-------------------|
|                                      | £       | £       | £       |                   |
| Selling price                        | 60      | 85      | 88      | *Sum of direct    |
| Variable cost per unit*              | (30)    | (43)    | (50)    | material,         |
|                                      | ——      | ——      | ——      | direct labour,    |
| Contribution/unit                    | 30      | 42      | 38      | variable          |
|                                      | ——      | ——      | ——      | overhead          |
| D Material/unit                      | 15      | 20      | 30      |                   |
| Contribution per £1 of direct material | 2.00  | 2.10    | 1.27    |                   |
| Ranking                              | 2nd     | 1st     | 3rd     |                   |

      Therefore the answer is E.

85    The term 'master budget' is used to describe the set of summary budgets.

      Therefore the answer is B.

86    To answer this question requires the preparation of an equivalent units table:

|  | Materials | | Conversion | |
|---|---|---|---|---|
|  | % | eu | % | eu |
| Output: |  |  |  |  |
| Opening WIP | 0 | 0 | 60 | 1,200 |
| Started & finished | 100 | 17,500 | 100 | 17,500 |
| Closing WIP | 100 | 3,000 | 45 | 1,350 |
| Abnormal loss (see below) | 100 | 1,100 | 100 | 1,100 |
|  |  | 21,600 |  | 21,150 |

**Process account**
**(litres only)**

| Opening WIP | 2,000 | Normal loss | 2,400 |
|---|---|---|---|
| Input | 24,000 | Output | 19,500 |
|  |  | Closing WIP | 3,000 |
|  |  | Abnormal loss (bal) | 1,100 |
|  | 26,000 |  | 26,000 |

Therefore the answer is C.

87    The first step is to rank the products based upon their respective contributions per kg of material to establish the production priority:

$$\text{Quone } £8.00 / \left(\frac{£6.00}{£2.00}\right) = £2.66/kg = 2\text{nd}$$

$$\text{Qutwo } £8.50 / \left(\frac{£5.00}{£2.00}\right) = £3.40/kg = 1\text{st}$$

Since Qutwo is ranked 1st any materials will be used on this product which has unlimited demand.

The opportunity cost equals the benefit of the extra material ie, the contribution which would be earned if it were to be available.

Therefore the answer is D.

88    The relevant internal manufacturing cost in this make versus buy decision comprises three elements:

| (i) | the variable manufacturing cost | £8.00 |
|---|---|---|
| (ii) | the unitised specific fixed cost (W1) | £2.50 |
| (iii) | the opportunity cost of the labour (W2) | £5.00 |
|  |  | £15.50 |

Therefore the answer is E.

**WORKINGS**

(W1)    The unitised specific fixed cost is included because it is specific to the component.

(W2)    The opportunity cost is the alternative contribution from the same amount of labour.

$£10/£8 = £1.25$ per £1 of labour cost.

The component has a labour cost of £4.00 so the alternative contribution is:
$£1.25 \times 4 = £5.00$

89    The quantity of goods available for sale comprises the sales quantity plus the required closing stock. Some of these are provided from the opening stock.

      The correct answer is B.

90    A standard marginal costing system does not use absorption rates so statement (i) is incorrect. Only statements (ii) and (iii) are true.

      The correct answer is C.

91    Sales variances are **never** recorded in ledger accounts.

      The correct answer is E.

92    Absorption rate/unit            $=$       $\dfrac{£48,000}{4,800}$       $=$       £10/unit

      Under absorption             $=$       £8,000
      Expenditure variance         $=$       £2,000                    Adverse

      Volume variance              $=$       £6,000                    Adverse

      Volume difference in units   $=$       $\dfrac{£6,000(A)}{£10/\text{unit}}$   $=$   600 units less than budget

      Budgeted units               $=$       4,800
      Volume difference            $=$        600

      Actual units                 $=$       4,200

      The correct answer is C.

93    The material is in regular use so its resale value is irrelevant. Past values are always irrelevant. If the material is used it must be replaced, but the excess of 400 kgs due to the purchase of 1,000 kgs is not relevant because the material is in regular use.

      Thus the relevant cost is: 600 kgs $\times$ £3.25 = £1,950

      The correct answer is D.

94    An abnormal gain means that the actual loss in process was less than expected so the resulting benefit will be credited to the profit and loss account.

      Abnormal gains and losses are valued at the same rate as good units:

                                                                              £
              Materials                                                     9.40
              Conversion £11.20 $\times$ 75%                                 8.40

                                                                          17.80

      But being an abnormal gain there is also the lost opportunity of selling units as scrap at £2.00/litre.

      Thus the benefit per litre   $=$       £17.80 – £2.00 = £15.80
                                              160 litres $\times$ £15.80 = £2,528

      The correct answer is C.

95    The direct costs are wholly variable because their cost/unit is the same at both activity levels (£7.00/unit)

The overhead costs are either wholly fixed or semi-variable because their cost/unit changes. The total overhead costs are:

| | | | |
|---|---|---|---|
| 1,000 units | × | £4.50 = | £4,500 |
| 2,000 units | × | £3.00 = | £6,000 |

Since the total cost also differs it is semi-variable. The high and low points method is used:

| | Units | £ |
|---|---|---|
| | 2,000 | 6,000 |
| | 1,000 | 4,500 |
| Difference | 1,000 | 1,500 |

The variable cost $= \dfrac{£1,500}{1,000} = £1.50/\text{unit}$

By substitution:

| | £ |
|---|---|
| Variable cost of 2,000 units | |
| (2,000 × £1.50) | 3,000 |
| Fixed cost (to balance) | 3,000 |
| Total cost | 6,000 |

| | | | |
|---|---|---|---|
| Thus variable cost/unit = £7.00 + £1.50 | = | £8.50 | |
| Fixed cost | = | £3,000 | |

The correct answer is E.

96    First calculate the contribution to sales ratio for Cee:

| | | | | | |
|---|---|---|---|---|---|
| Aye | 40% | × | ⅓rd | = | 13.33% |
| Bee | 50% | × | ⅓rd | = | 16.67% |
| Cee | 54% | × | ⅓rd | | |
| (balancing figure) | | | | = | 18.00% |
| Total | | | | = | 48.00% |

By changing the mix the overall ratio becomes:

| | | | | | |
|---|---|---|---|---|---|
| Aye | 40% | × | 40% | = | 16.00% |
| Bee | 50% | × | 25% | = | 12.50% |
| Cee | 54% | × | 35% | = | 18.90% |
| Total | | | | = | 47.40% |

The correct answer is C.

*Note*: Fixed costs are irrelevant.

97    A fixed budget provides details of costs, revenues and resource requirements for a single level of activity.

The correct answer is A.

98      Sales receipts comprise cash and credit sale receipts.                                    £

        In May 1997 cash sales are £55,000 × 40% =                                              22,000

        In May credit sale receipts comprise:

        April sales       £70,000 × 60% × 70% × 98%      =        28,812
        March sales       £60,000 × 60% × 27%            =         9,720
                                                                  _____
                                                                            38,532
                                                                            _____
        Total receipts                                                      60,532
                                                                            _____

        The correct answer is C.

99      A direct cost is a cost which can be economically identified with the cost unit. A cost unit is the item being
        costed so the answer is B.

100     Absorption rate    $= \dfrac{\text{Budgeted cost}}{\text{Budgeted output}} = \dfrac{£100,000}{10,000} = £10$ per standard hour

        Actual output is 1,000 standard hours less than budget so this produces an under absorption due to volume of:

        1,000 standard hours × £10 = £10,000 under.

        The actual expenditure, compared to budget because it is a fixed cost, was £1,400 more than budget, this is the
        under absorption caused by expenditure.

        Therefore the answer is C.

101     Relevant production costs are those which are variable or, if fixed, are product specific.

        The relevant costs are thus:

        |                                  | M1 £/unit | M2 £/unit |
        |----------------------------------|-----------|-----------|
        | Variable costs                   | 4.60      | 4.40      |
        | Fixed cost:  £2,500/12,500 units |           | 0.20      |
        |                                  | _____     | _____     |
        |                                  | 4.60      | 4.60      |
        |                                  | _____     | _____     |

        Answer B.

102     Present fixed cost comprises general fixed cost and specific fixed costs of M2. The specific fixed cost of M2
        would not be incurred if only M1 were purchased.

        General fixed costs is:

                                                                              £

                £1.20 × 10,000 units of M1                                 12,000
                £0.80* × 12,500 units of M2                                10,000
                                                                          _____
                                                                           22,000
                                                                          _____

        *  (£1.00 – £0.20 specific to M2).

        The contribution required to achieve a profit of £50,000 = £50,000 + £22,000 = £72,000.

Contribution/unit = £10.00 − £4.60 = £5.40.

So the units required = £72,000/£5.40 = 13,333 units.

Answer = C.

103    The relevant cost is the lower of the relevant costs of each option.

|  |  | £ |
|---|---|---:|
| Recruitment: | 4 employees @ £40,000 = | 160,000 |
|  | Manager (no change) | Nil |
|  |  | £160,000 |
| Retrain and replace: | Training | 15,000 |
|  | Replacement | 100,000 |
|  |  | £115,000 |

The answer is B.

104    Relevant costs are future and differential. A common cost is one which is shared by cost centres, activities, or cost units; since it is non-specific it is unlikely to be affected by a decision. An unavoidable cost is a cost which is incurred irrespective of the decision.

The answer is D.

105    Since material stocks are valued using standard purchase price, the price variance would be calculated using the quantity purchased. Therefore:

|  | £ |
|---|---:|
| Actual cost of 7,800 kg | 16,380 |
| Price variance | 1,170 (A) |
| Standard cost of 7,800 kg | £15,210 |

$$\text{Standard price per kg} = \frac{£15,210}{7,800 \text{ kg}} = £1.95/\text{kg}$$

Answer is A.

106

|  | £ |
|---|---:|
| Actual sales revenue | 99,000 |
| Expected revenue from sales: |  |
| 11,000 units × £8.00 | 88,000 |
| Selling price variance | 11,000 (F) |

Since an absorption costing system is used any sales volume difference will be valued using budgeted (ie, standard) profit per unit.

|  | Units |
|---|---:|
| Budgeted sales £100,000/£8.00 = | 12,500 |
| Actual sales | 11,000 |
| Shortfall | 1,500 |

1,500 units shortfall × £2.50/unit = £3,750 (A)

Answer is A.

107     The rank order is found by determining the contribution per unit of the scarce resource ie, labour:

| | Z1 | Z2 | Z3 |
|---|---|---|---|
| Selling price/unit | 15.00 | 18.00 | 17.00 |
| Variable costs/unit | 7.00 | 11.00 | 12.70 |
| Contribution/unit | 8.00 | 7.00 | 4.30 |
| Labour cost/unit | 2.00 | 4.00 | 1.80 |
| Contribution per £1 of labour cost | £8.00/£2.00 = £4.00 | £7.00/£4.00 = £1.75 | £4.30/£1.80 = £2.39 |
| Ranking | 1st | 3rd | 2nd |

Answer is D.

108

| | £ |
|---|---|
| Actual cost was | 98,350 |
| 19,100 hours should cost: | |
| 19,100 × £5.40 | 103,140 |
| Rate variance | 4,790 (F) |

| | Hours |
|---|---|
| Actual hours | 19,100 |
| 4,650 units should require: | |
| 4,650 × 4 hours | 18,600 |
| An extra | 500 |
| 500 hours × £5.40 (standard rate) | £2,700 (A) |

Answer is E.

109     Since a fixed cost remains constant in total the level of activity multiplied by the cost per unit is always the same. This means that the area under the cost curve is always the same so the answer is D.

110     A joint product is one which arises at the same time as other products of similar value so the answer is C.

111     Contract costing is a form of specific order costing, differentiated from job costing by the time taken to complete the work. Statements two and three are correct so the answer is B.

112     The difference between the profit reported under marginal and absorption costing always equals the change in the stock level multiplied by the fixed overhead absorption rate per unit.

When stock levels increase, absorption costing reports a higher profit. The profit reported is lower when stock levels decrease.

In the period production exceeded sales by 2,500 units; therefore stock levels increased.

The difference in profit equals 2,500 units x £8 / unit = £20,000.

Since stock levels increased, absorption costing will report higher profits, so the marginal costing profit is:-
£42,000 - £20,000 = £22,000

The answer is B

113    Over-absorption measures the combined effect of differences in expenditure and volume in the process of absorbing costs.

An adverse expenditure variance means that the actual cost exceeded the expected cost and thus this would lead to an under-absorption. Since the overall total was an over absorption of £12,000; the volume effect must equal an over-absorption of £15,000.

Absorption rates are always based on budgets:-

$$\frac{\text{Fixed production overhead cost}}{\text{Production units}} = \frac{£72,000}{7,200}$$

$$= £10 / \text{unit}$$

The difference in units is therefore

$$\frac{£15,000}{£10/\text{unit}} = 1,500 \text{ units}$$

As the volume effect creates an over-absorption, this means that the actual volume was greater than the budgeted volume, so the actual volume was 7,200 units + 1,500 units = 8,700 units.

The answer is E.

114    This question requires the use of the high and low points technique:-

| No of units | £ / unit | Total cost |
|---|---|---|
| 800 | 5.875 | 4700 |
| 500 | 7.000 | 3500 |
| Difference   300 | | 1200 |

$$\text{Variable cost / unit} = \frac{£1,200}{300} = £4 / \text{unit}$$

By substitution:-

| | £ |
|---|---|
| Variable cost of 500 units = | 2,000 |
| Fixed cost (balance) | 1,500 |
| Total cost of 500 units = | 3,500 |

The answer is E

115    Direct costs are those attributable to a cost unit, which can be economically identified with the unit. The answer is B.

116    A by-product is usually treated in the same way as a normal loss with its resale value being the equivalent of the scrap value of a normal loss.

The answer is C.

117/
118    The solution of these questions requires an equivalent units table:-

|  | Litres |  | Material |  | Conversion |  |
|---|---|---|---|---|---|---|
| Output:- |  |  |  |  |  |  |
| Opening WIP | 1,000 |  | NIL | 30% | 300 |  |
| Started & finished | 23,000 | 100% | 23,000 | 100% | 23,000 |  |
| Closing WIP | 3,500 | 100% | 3,500 | 80% | 2,800 |  |
| Abnormal loss | 500(W1) | 100% | 500 | 60% | 300 |  |
| Equivalent units |  |  | 27,000 |  | 26,400 |  |

**WI**

**Process account (litres)**

|  | £ |  | £ |
|---|---|---|---|
| Opening WIP | 1,000 | Normal loss (10%) | 3,000 |
| Input | 30,000 | Ouput | 24,000 |
|  |  | Closing WIP | 3,500 |
|  |  | Abnormal loss (bal.) | 500 |
|  | 31,000 |  | 31,000 |

Thus the answers are:-

117    C
118    A

119    Contract costing is used for work specific to customer requirements which takes a long time to complete, often straddling a financial year-end.

The answer is E.

120    September credit sale receipts are:

|  |  | £ |
|---|---|---|
| August sales × 70% × 97% | = | 61,110 |
| July sales × 20% | = | 12,000 |
| June sales × 8% | = | 4,200 |
|  |  | 77,310 |

The answer is C.

121    Use the high/low points method to identify the extent of the fixed and variable costs:

|  | Activity | £ |
|---|---|---|
| High | 3,000 | 20,640 |
| Low | 2,000 | 17,760 |
| Differences | 1,000 units | 2,880 |

Variable cost/unit = $\dfrac{£2,880}{1,000}$ = £2.88/unit

By substitution:

|  | £ |
|---|---|
| Variable cost of 2,000 units @ £2.88 = | 5,760 |

|  |  |  |
|---|---|---|
| Fixed cost (balancing figure) | = | 12,000 |
|  |  | 17,760 |

Allowance for 4,000 units is:
|  |  |
|---|---|
| Variable cost 4,000 × £2.88 = | 11,520 |
| Fixed cost | 12,000 |
|  | 23,520 |

The answer is B.

**122**   

| Product | L £ | M £ | N £ |
|---|---|---|---|
| Selling price | 97.50 | 123.50 | 123.50 |
| Variable costs | (44.20) | (53.30) | (58.50) |
| Contribution | 53.30 | 70.20 | 65.00 |
| Material/unit | 13.00 | 6.50 | 19.50 |
| Contribution per £ of material | 4.10 | 10.80 | 3.33 |
| Ranking | 2nd | 1st | 3rd |

The answer is B

**123**   Breakeven sales value is

$$\frac{\text{Fixed costs}}{{}^{c}/_{s}\text{ ratio}} = \frac{£76,800}{40\%} = £192,000$$

| Sales were | £224,000 |
|---|---|
| Margin of safety | = £32,000 |

$$\text{Number of units} = \frac{£32,000}{£16} = £2,000 \text{ units}$$

The answer is A.

**124**   This decision requires a comparison of incremental costs and revenues.
The answer is B.

**125**   
$$\text{Budgeted cost } \frac{£240,000}{12 \text{ months}} = £20,000$$

| Actual cost | = | £19,600 |
|---|---|---|
|  |  | £400 F |

The answer is B.

**126**   Budgeted volume/period is

$$\frac{\text{Budgeted cost/period}}{\text{Absorption rate/unit}} = \frac{£20,000}{£40} = 500$$

| Actual units | = | 450 |
|---|---|---|
| Shortfall |  | 50 units |

50 units × £40/unit = £2,000 A

The answer is D.

127     13,450 hours should cost $\dfrac{£117,600}{(4 \text{ hrs} \times 3,500 \text{ units})}$ per hour

                                               =      £112,980

Actual cost                              =      £111,850

                                                     £1,130 F

The answer is B.

128     3,350 units should take 4 hours each  =        13,400 hrs
       Actual                               =         13,450 hrs

                                                        50 hrs

50 hours × $\dfrac{£117,600}{(4 \times 3,500)}$          =         £420 A

The answer is A.

129     Direct costs are those which can be traced to a single cost unit.

The answer is B.

130     A flexible budget is a budget which shows costs/revenues at more than one activity level.

The answer is C.

131     The term master budget is used to describe the summary budgets.

The answer is B.

132     Weighted average $\dfrac{C}{S}$ ratio is:

$$\dfrac{[(2 \times 40\%) + (6 \times 50\%)]}{8}$$

$$= \dfrac{380\%}{8} = 47.5\%$$

Breakeven $= \dfrac{£60,000}{47.5\%} = £126,316$

Answer is C.

133     Product

| | P | Q | R |
|---|---|---|---|
| | £ | £ | £ |
| Contribution/unit | 82 | 108 | 100 |
| Materials/unit | 4 kg | 2 kg | 6 kg |
| Contribution/kg | £20.50 | £54 | £16.66 |

The answer is B.

134       Since stock is valued at standard cost, the price variance is extracted at the time of purchase.

Price variance:

| | |
|---|---:|
| 8,200 kg should cost £0.80/kg = | £6,560 |
| Actual cost | £6,888 |
| | £328 A |

Usage variance:

| | |
|---|---:|
| 870 units should use 8 kg/unit = | 6,960 kg |
| Actual usage | 7,150 kg |
| | 190 kg |

190 kg @ £0.80/kg - £152 A

Answer is D.

135       Equivalent units table

| | *Materials* | | *Conversion* | |
|---|---|---|---|---|
| | % | eu | % | eu |
| Output: | | | | |
| O/WIP | 20 | 60 | 40 | 120 |
| Started in period | 100 | 6,950 | 100 | 6,950 |
| Closing WIP | 70 | 280 | 40 | 160 |
| | | 7,290 | | 7,230 |

Answer is A.

136       Variable cost per unit equals:

$$\frac{\text{Difference in costs}}{\text{Difference in units}} = \frac{£1,800}{2,000}$$
$$= £0.90/\text{unit}$$

Budget cost allowance
$$= £12,900 + [(8,000 - 6,000) \times £0.90]$$
$$= £14,700$$

Answer is B.

137       Contribution/unit = £5.50

Marginal costing profit
$$= (2,220 \times £5.50) - (£60,000/12)$$
$$= £12,210 - £5,000$$
$$= £7,210$$

Stock levels increased by 180 units so absorption profit will be higher than marginal profit by

180 units × (£60,000/30,000 units) = £360.

Absorption profit = £7,210 + £360
                      = £7,570

Answer is B.

138       Since stock is maintained at standard cost, the price variance is extracted on purchase.

Price variance:
   5,000 units × (£4.50 − £4.70)    =    £1,000 F

Usage variance:

| | | |
|---|---|---|
| 2,400 units should use 2 units | = | 4,800 units |
| Actual usage | = | 4,850 units |
| | | 50 units |

50 units @ £4.70 = £235 A

Favourable variances are credit to variance accounts, adverse variances are debited to variance accounts.

The answer is D.

# 6

*Stage 2*

*Operational Cost Accounting*

*OCA*

24 November 1999
morning

INSTRUCTIONS TO CANDIDATES

Read this page before you look at the questions.

---

*You are allowed three hours to answer this question paper.*

*Answer the ONE question in section A (consisting of ten sub-questions).*

*Answer the TWO questions in section B.*

*Answer ONE question ONLY from section C.*

**NOVEMBER 1999 EXAMINATION**

*OPERATIONAL COST ACCOUNTING*

SPECIAL ANSWER SHEET FOR SECTION A

| | | | | | |
|---|---|---|---|---|---|
| 1.1 | A | B | C | D | E |
| 1.2 | A | B | C | D | E |
| 1.3 | A | B | C | D | E |
| 1.4 | A | B | C | D | E |
| 1.5 | A | B | C | D | E |
| 1.6 | A | B | C | D | E |
| 1.7 | A | B | C | D | E |
| 1.8 | A | B | C | D | E |
| 1.9 | A | B | C | D | E |
| 1.10 | A | B | C | D | E |

SECTION A — 20 MARKS
ANSWER *ALL* TEN SUB-QUESTIONS

*Each of the sub-questions numbered from 1.1 to 1.10 inclusive, given below, has only ONE right answer.*

**Requirement:**

*On the SPECIAL ANSWER SHEET provided, place a circle "O" around the letter (either A, B, C, D or E) that gives the right answer to each sub-question.*

*If you wish to change your mind about an answer, block out your first attempt and then encircle another letter. If you do not indicate clearly your final choice, or if you encircle more than one letter, no marks will be awarded for the sub-question concerned.*

## 80    MULTIPLE CHOICE QUESTIONS

1.1    When comparing the profits reported under marginal and absorption costing during a period in which the level of stocks increased,

   A    absorption costing profits will be higher and closing stock valuations lower than those under marginal costing.

   **B**    absorption costing profits will be higher and closing stock valuations higher than those under marginal costing.

   C    marginal costing profits will be higher and closing stock valuations lower than those under absorption costing.

   D    there is no difference in the stock valuations, but the profit reported will be different.

   E    there is no difference in the profit reported, but the valuation of closing stock will be different.

1.2    In order to utilise some spare capacity, Z Limited is preparing a quotation for a special order which requires 1,000 kgs of material R.

   Z Limited has 600 kgs of material R in stock (original cost £5.00 per kg).

   Material R is used in the company's main product Q.
   Each unit of Q uses 3 kgs of material R, and based on an input value of £5.00 per kg of R, each unit of Q yields a contribution of £9.00.

   The resale value of material R is £4.00 per kg. The present replacement price of material R is £6.00 per kg. Material R is readily available in the market.

   The relevant cost of the 1,000 kgs of material R to be included in the quotation is

   A    £4,000.    B    £5,000.    C    £5,400.    **D**    £6,000.    E    £8,000.

**1.3**    In process costing, the cost attributed to any abnormal gain units is

   A    debited to the process account and credited to the abnormal gain account.
   B    debited to the abnormal gain account and credited to the normal loss account.
   C    debited to the normal loss account and credited to the abnormal gain account.
   D    debited to the abnormal gain account and credited to the process account.
   E    debited to the scrap sales account and credited to the abnormal gain account.

**1.4**    The following data have been taken from the books of CB plc, which uses a non-integrated accounting system:

|  | Financial accounts £ | Cost accounts £ | |
|---|---|---|---|
| Opening stock of materials | 5,000 | 6,400 | 1400 |
| Closing stock of materials | 4,000 | 5,200 | 1200 |
| Opening stock of finished goods | 9,800 | 9,600 | (200) |
| Closing stock of finished goods | 7,900 | 7,600 | (300) |
|  | 3300 | 3200 | |

The effect of these stock valuation differences on the profit reported by the financial and cost accounting ledgers is

   A    the financial accounting profit is £300 greater than the cost accounting profit.
   B    the financial accounting profit is £2,100 greater than the cost accounting profit.
   C    the cost accounting profit is £300 greater than the financial accounting profit.
   D    the cost accounting profit is £900 greater than the financial accounting profit.
   E    the cost accounting profit is £2,100 greater than the financial accounting profit.

**1.5**    The following details relate to the main process of X Limited, a chemical manufacturer:

| | |
|---|---|
| Opening work-in-progress | 2,000 litres, fully complete as to materials and 40% complete as to conversion. |
| Material input | 24,000 litres |
| Normal loss is 10% of input. | |
| Losses arise at the end of processing. | |
| Output to process 2 | 19,500 litres |
| Closing work-in-progress | 3,000 litres, fully complete as to materials and 45% complete as to conversion. |

The number of equivalent units to be included in X Limited's calculation of the cost per equivalent unit, using a **weighted average basis** of valuation, are

| | *Materials* | *Conversion* |
|---|---|---|
| A | 21,400 | 19,750 |
| B | 21,400 | 20,850 |
| C | 22,500 | 21,950 |
| D | 22,500 | 20,850 |
| E | 23,600 | 21,950 |

**1.6**    When deciding, purely on financial grounds, whether or not to process further a joint product, the information required is:

    (i)    the value of the common process costs;
    (ii)   the method of apportioning the common costs between the joint products;
    (iii)  the sales value of the joint product at the separation point;
    (iv)  the final sales value of the joint product;
    (v)   the further processing cost of the joint product.

Which of the above statements are correct?

    A    (i), (ii) and (iii) only.
    B    (iii), (iv) and (v) only.
    C    (iv) and (v) only.
    D    (i), (ii), (iv) and (v) only.
    E    All of them.

**1.7**    The following data have been extracted from the budget working papers of BL Limited:

| Production volume | 1,000 units<br>£ per unit | 2,000 units<br>£ per unit |
|---|---|---|
| Direct materials | 4.00 | 4.00 |
| Direct labour | 3.50 | 3.50 |
| Production overhead – department 1 | 6.00 | 4.20 |
| Production overhead – department 2 | 4.00 | 2.00 |

The total fixed cost and the variable cost per unit are as follows:

| | Total fixed cost<br>£ | Variable cost per unit<br>£ |
|---|---|---|
| A | 3,600 | 7.50 |
| B | 3,600 | 9.90 |
| C | 4,000 | 11.70 |
| D | 7,600 | 7.50 |
| E | 7,600 | 9.90 |

**1.8**    State which of the following are characteristics of contract costing:

    (i)    identical products,
    (ii)   customer-driven production,
    (iii)  short timescale from commencement to completion of the cost unit.

    A    None of them
    B    (i) and (ii) only.
    C    (ii) and (iii) only.
    D    (i) and (iii) only.
    E    (ii) only.

**1.9**     The following details have been extracted from the debtor collection records of C Limited:

|                                              |      |
|----------------------------------------------|------|
| Invoices paid in the month after sale        | 60%  |
| Invoices paid in the second month after sale | 25%  |
| Invoices paid in the third month after sale  | 12%  |
| Bad debts                                    | 3%   |

Invoices are issued on the last day of each month.

Customers paying in the month after sale are entitled to deduct a 2% settlement discount.

Credit sales values for December 1999 to March 2000 are budgeted as follows:

| *December* | *January* | *February* | *March* |
|------------|-----------|------------|---------|
| £35,000    | £40,000   | £60,000    | £45,000 |

The amount budgeted to be received from credit sales in March 2000 is

**A**   £47,280.    **B**   £47,680.    **C**   £48,850.    **D**   £49,480.    **(E)**   £50,200.

**1.10**    The following extract is taken from the production cost budget of S Limited:

| *Production*     | *2,000 units* | *3,000 units* |
|------------------|---------------|---------------|
| Production cost  | £11,100       | £12,900       |

The budget cost allowance for an activity level of 4,000 units is

**A**     £7,200.
**B**     £14,700.
**C**     £17,200.
**(D)**   £22,200.
**E**     none of these values.                                                  **(20 marks)**

Rec      JAN   Feb   MAR
21000   8750  4200
24000  10000
36000
─────
5020

1400

24000

## SECTION B — 55 MARKS

## ANSWER *BOTH* QUESTIONS

---

| **81     XYZ PLC (Q2 of examination)** |
|---|

XYZ plc provides engineering services to a number of small businesses in Wyetown.

Its services comprise milling, turning and grinding, each of which is a separate cost centre within XYZ plc. The company prepares its accounts annually to 31 October, and extracted the following balances from its trial balance on 30 September 1999:

|  | Dr £'000 | Cr £'000 |
|---|---|---|
| Sales |  | 1,650 |
| Cost of sales | 1,095 |  |
| Work-in-progress | 22 |  |
| Production overhead |  | 12 |
| Finished goods | 3 |  |
| Selling and administration costs | 48 |  |

XYZ plc operates an absorption costing system using the following machine hour absorption rates:

| Milling | £7.50 |
|---|---|
| Turning | £8.00 |
| Grinding | £9.00 |

During October 1999 XYZ plc had the following transactions:

| *Incurred costs*: | £'000 |
|---|---|
| Direct materials | 40 |
| Indirect materials | 8 |
| Direct labour | 60 |
| Indirect labour | 12 |
| Indirect production expenses | 24 |
| Selling and administration costs | 5 |

The valuation of work-in-progress and finished goods stock on 31 October 1999 was:

|  | £'000 |
|---|---|
| Work-in-progress | 20 |
| Finished goods | 4 |

During October 1999 the sales made to customers achieved gross profit of 25% of sales value.

The number of machine hours during October 1999 were:

| Milling | 2,400 hours |
|---|---|
| Turning | 1,800 hours |
| Grinding | 1,600 hours |

**Requirements:**

(a)    Explain briefly the main reasons why organisations such as XYZ plc use absorption costing rather than marginal costing.    **(4 marks)**

(b)    Write up the following ledger accounts commencing with the balances on 30 September 1999:

> Work-in-progress;
> Finished goods;
> Production overhead.    **(12 marks)**

(c)    Prepare XYZ plc's profit and loss account for the year ended 31 October 1999.    **(5 marks)**

(d)    XYZ plc is now considering its production overhead budgets for the year 2000. The company has estimated the following production overhead costs and machine hours:

|  | £'000 | Hours |
|---|---|---|
| Milling | 200 | 25,000 |
| Turning | 190 | 22,000 |
| Grinding | 220 | 18,000 |
| Maintenance | 44 | |
| Stores | 54 | |

The Maintenance and Stores departments are regarded as production service departments. It is expected that during 2000 the proportion of work performed for each department will be as follows:

|  | *Maintenance* | *Stores* |
|---|---|---|
| Milling | 40% | 30% |
| Turning | 20% | 20% |
| Grinding | 25% | 40% |
| Maintenance | n/a | 10% |
| Stores | 15% | n/a |

**Requirement:**

Calculate appropriate machine hour overhead absorption rates for the year 2000.    **(9 marks)**
    **(Total: 30 marks)**

---

## 82    DH (Q3 of examination)

---

DH is considering the purchase of a bar/restaurant which is available for £130,000. He has estimated that the weekly fixed costs will be as follows:

|  | £ |
|---|---|
| Business rates | 125 |
| Electricity | 75 |
| Insurances | 60 |
| Gas | 45 |
| Depreciation | 125 |
| Telephone | 50 |
| Advertising | 40 |
| Postage and stationery | 20 |
| Motor expenses | 20 |
| Cleaning | 10 |

He has estimated that his average weekly sales of drinks will amount to £1,500 and that these will have a contribution to sales ratio of 60%.

He expects to serve 40 customers per week in the restaurant, with each customer spending an average of £20. This excludes the value of any drinks which are included in the weekly estimate of drinks sales above. It is expected that the contribution to sales ratio in the restaurant will be 60%.

There are no specific fixed costs attributable to the sale of drinks or customer sales.

**Requirements:**

**(a)**     Calculate the weekly breakeven sales value of the business.                          **(3 marks)**

**(b)**     Prepare a statement showing the annual profit based on the above cost and revenue estimates. Use a marginal costing format and assume that the business operates for 50 weeks per year.     **(10 marks)**

**(c)**     Calculate the weekly sales value required to achieve a profit of £500 per week.     **(3 marks)**

**(d)**     Assume that DH purchases the bar/restaurant in December 1999, and expects to open for business on 1 January 2000. DH is now finalising his budgets for 2000. He is particularly concerned about his bar purchases. Based upon the estimated sales above, he believes that of the total weekly drinks sales:

>        60% will be beer sales;
>        25% will be soft drink sales; and
>        15% will be wine/spirits sales.

Purchase prices are expected to be equal to 30% of sales value. Initially, stocks are required to be as follows, and these will be purchased in December 1999:

>        Beer            0.5 week's sales
>        Soft drinks     2.0 weeks' sales
>        Wine/spirits    1.0 week's sales

but these are to be reduced by 10% at the end of week 2.

A loss of 5% of purchases due to wastage and spillage is expected.

**Requirement:**

Prepare the bar purchase budget for week 2, showing clearly the purchase values of each type of item sold.
**(9 marks)**
**(Total:  25 marks)**

## SECTION C — 25 MARKS

## ANSWER **ONE** QUESTION ONLY

---

| 83 | PQR PLC (Q4 of examination) |
|---|---|

PQR plc is preparing its budgets for next year. It has already prepared forecasts of demand levels for its product range. These are as follows:

|  | Forecast 1 | | Forecast 2 | |
|---|---|---|---|---|
|  | *Price*<br>£ | *Quantity* | *Price*<br>£ | *Quantity* |
| Product A | 10.00 | 500 | 15.00 | 350 |
| Product B | 20.00 | 800 | 25.00 | 700 |
| Product C | 30.00 | 2,200 | 40.00 | 1,000 |

You are to assume that *only one of either* forecast 1 *or* forecast 2 can be accepted.

The expected variable unit costs of each product are as follows:

|  | *Product A*<br>£ | *Product B*<br>£ | *Product C*<br>£ |
|---|---|---|---|
| Direct materials (50p per kg) | 2.00 | 3.50 | 7.00 |
| Direct labour | 3.00 | 5.00 | 7.40 |
| Variable overhead | 1.50 | 2.50 | 3.70 |
|  | 6.50 | 11.00 | 18.10 |

No specific fixed costs are expected for any product.

General fixed costs are budgeted as £20,000 for the year.

All three products use the same direct material which is expected to be limited in supply to a maximum of 22,020 kgs in the budget year.

**Requirements:**

(a) Recommend, with supporting calculations, whether forecast 1 or forecast 2 should be adopted for the budget period. **(15 marks)**

(b) Prepare a report, addressed to the Managing Director, to explain the budget preparation process, with particular reference to:

  (i)   the principal budget factor;
  (ii)  the budget manual; and
  (iii) the role of the budget committee. **(10 marks)**

**(Total: 25 marks)**

## 84    WYE (Q5 of examination)

Data from the October 1999 standard cost card of product Wye, the only product of Exe plc, is as follows:

|  |  |  | £ |
|---|---|---|---|
| Direct materials | 4 kg | @ £2.50 per kg | 10.00 |
| Direct labour | 3 hours | @ £6.00 per hour | 18.00 |
| Variable overhead | 3 hours | @ £4.00 per hour | 12.00 |
| Fixed overhead |  |  | 20.00 |
|  |  |  | 60.00 |
| Standard profit |  |  | 15.00 |
| Standard selling price |  |  | 75.00 |

Budgeted fixed overhead cost for October 1999 was £25,000.

The operating statement for October 1999, when raw material stock levels remained unchanged, was as follows:

|  | £ Adverse | £ Favourable | £ |
|---|---|---|---|
| Budgeted profit |  |  | 17,250 |
| Sales volume profit variance |  |  | 750 (Adverse) |
|  |  |  | 16,500 |
| Selling price variance |  |  | 5,500 (Favourable) |
|  |  |  | 22,000 |
| Cost variances: |  |  |  |
| Direct materials  - price | 535 |  |  |
|                  - usage | 375 |  |  |
| Direct labour  - rate | 410 |  |  |
|                - efficiency | 1,200 |  |  |
| Variable overhead  - expenditure |  | 820 |  |
|                - efficiency | 800 |  |  |
| Fixed overhead  - expenditure |  | 1,000 |  |
|                - volume |  | 1,000 |  |
|  | 3,320 | 2,820 | 500 (Adverse) |
| Actual profit |  |  | 21,500 |

**Requirements:**

**(a)**    Calculate:

| | | |
|---|---|---|
| (i) | actual sales units; | **(3 marks)** |
| (ii) | actual production units; | **(3 marks)** |
| (iii) | actual selling price per unit; | **(2 marks)** |
| (iv) | actual material price per kg; | **(2 marks)** |
| (v) | actual labour hours; | **(2 marks)** |
| (vi) | actual variable overhead cost; | **(3 marks)** |
| (vii) | actual fixed overhead cost. | **(3 marks)** |

**(b)**      Prepare a report addressed to the Operations Manager which explains the meaning and possible causes of the two most significant variances which occurred in October 1999.      **(7 marks)**

**(Total: 25 marks)**

# NOVEMBER 1999 EXAMINATION ANSWERS

| 80 | MULTIPLE CHOICE ANSWERS |
|---|---|

1.1　Absorption costing includes a proportion of fixed production overhead costs in stock valuations whereas marginal costing does not. Thus absorption costing results in a higher stock valuation than marginal costing.

The answer is B.

1.2　Material R is readily available in the market so there is no opportunity loss in relation to product Q. The relevant cost is the replacement price of R.

The answer is D.

1.3　Abnormal gains arise when the actual loss is less than expected, thus they are, in effect, a negative cost.

The answer is A.

1.4　The effect on costs in the profit and loss account is:

|  | Financial accounts £ | Cost accounts £ |
|---|---|---|
| Materials stock |  |  |
| Opening | 5,000 | 6,400 |
| Closing | (4,000) | (5,200) |
| Finished stock |  |  |
| Opening | 9,800 | 9,600 |
| Closing | (7,900) | (7,600) |
|  | 2,900 | 3,200 |

The cost accounts have a greater cost value so the financial accounts will show a higher profit.

The answer is A.

1.5　Equivalent units table:

|  | Materials % | Materials eu | Conversion % | Conversion eu |
|---|---|---|---|---|
| Output | 100 | 19,500 | 100 | 19,500 |
| Closing WIP | 100 | 3,000 | 45 | 1,350 |
| Abnormal loss (W1) | 100 | 1,100 | 100 | 1,100 |
|  |  | 23,600 |  | 21,950 |

W1　Normal loss = $24,000 \times 10\% = 2,400$ litres

Abnormal loss = $2,000 + 24,000 - 2,400 - 19,500 - 3,000 = 1,100$

The answer is E.

1.6　Relevant data comprises costs/revenues which are product specific (ie post separation). Items (iii); (iv); and (v) are relevant.

The answer is B.

1    The high/low points method is used:

|  | 1,000 units £ | 2,000 units £ |
|---|---|---|
| Total cost/unit | 17.50 | 13.70 |
| Total cost | 17,500 | 27,400 |

Difference in total cost

$$\text{Difference in units} = \frac{£9,900}{1,000} = £9.90 \text{ variable cost per unit}$$

By substitution:

|  | £ |
|---|---|
| Variable cost of 1,000 units | 9,900 |
| Fixed costs (balance) | 7,600 |
| Total cost of 1,000 units | 17,500 |

The answer is E.

1.8    Contract costing is used for customer specific projects of duration which often span more than one financial year.

The answer is E.

1.9    The amount to be received is:

|  | £ |
|---|---|
| 60% of February sales | 36,000 |
| 25% of January sales | 10,000 |
| 12% of December sales | 4,200 |
|  | 50,200 |
| Less: 2% discount on February collections | (720) |
|  | 49,480 |

The answer is D

1.10    $\dfrac{\text{Difference in cost}}{\text{Difference in units}} = \dfrac{£1,800}{1,000} - £1.80/\text{unit}$

4,000 units  $= £12,900 + (1,000 \times £1.80)$
           $= £14,700$

The answer is B.

---

## 81    XYZ PLC

(a)    There are two main reasons why organisations such as XYZ plc use absorption costing.

(1)    Companies are regulated to produce financial accounts which comply with SSAP 9. As absorption costing complies with SSAP 9 and marginal costing does not, the use of absorption costing avoids the need to produce duplicate accounts – one set for external reporting and another for internal reporting.

(2)    Absorption costing is a form of total costing so by using this method managers are aware of the total cost of the product/service when making decisions.

(b)

### Work in progress

| | £'000 | | £'000 | |
|---|---|---|---|---|
| Balance b/fwd | 22 | Finished goods | 148.8 | (balance) |
| Direct materials | 40 | Balance c/fwd | 20 | |
| Direct labour | 60 | | | |
| Overhead absorbed: | | | | |
| Milling | 18 | | | (2,400 × 7.50) |
| Turning | 14.4 | | | (1,800 × 8.00) |
| Grinding | 14.4 | | | (1,600 × 9.00) |
| | 168.8 | | 168.8 | |

### Finished goods

| | £'000 | | £'000 | |
|---|---|---|---|---|
| Balance b/fwd | 3 | Cost of sales | 147.8 | (balance) |
| Work in progress | 148.8 | Balance c/fwd | 4 | |
| | 151.8 | | 151.8 | |

### Production overhead

| | £'000 | | £'000 | |
|---|---|---|---|---|
| Indirect materials | 8 | Balance b/fwd | 12 | |
| Indirect labour | 12 | Work in progress: | | |
| Indirect expenses | 24 | Milling | 18 | |
| Profit & Loss (balance) | 14.8 | Turning | 14.4 | (see above) |
| | | Grinding | 14.4 | |
| | 58.8 | | 58.8 | |

(c)

### Profit and Loss

| | £ | |
|---|---|---|
| Sales | 1,847,066 | (1,650,000 + 197,066) |
| Cost of sales | 1,242,800 | (1,095,000 + 147,800) |
| Gross profit | 604,266 | |
| Production overhead over absorbed | 14,800 | |
| | 619,066 | |
| Selling & Administration | 53,000 | (48,000 + 5,000) |
| Net profit | 566,066 | |

Sales of period are: £147,800 × $\frac{100}{75}$ = 197,066

(d)     All figures in £'000

$M = 44 + 0.1S$
$S = 54 + 0.15M$

$M = 44 + 0.1 (54 + 0.15M)$
$M = 44 + 5.4 + 0.015M$
$0.985 M = 49.4$

$M = 50.152$

$S = 54 + (0.15 \times 50.152)$
$S = 61.523$

|         | Milling | Turning | Grinding | Maint.    | Stores    |
|---------|---------|---------|----------|-----------|-----------|
| Costs   | 200     | 190     | 220      | 44        | 54        |
| M       | 20.061  | 10.030  | 12.538   | (50.152)  | 7.523     |
| S       | 18.457  | 12.305  | 24.609   | 6.152     | (61.523)  |
|         | 238.518 | 212.335 | 257.147  | nil       | nil       |

|         | Milling | Turning | Grinding |
|---------|---------|---------|----------|
| Hours   | 25,000  | 22,000  | 18,000   |
| £/hour  | 9.54    | 9.65    | 14.29    |

---

## 82   DH

(a)   Weekly fixed costs    = £570

Breakeven sales value    = £570/0.6
= £950

(b)   Sales:

|                                    | £       | £        |
|------------------------------------|---------|----------|
| Drinks (£1,500 × 50)               | 75,000  |          |
| Food (40 × £20 × 50)               | 40,000  |          |
|                                    |         | 115,000  |
| Variable costs (40% of sales)      |         | (46,000) |
| Contribution (60% of sales)        |         | 69,000   |
| Fixed costs (£570 × 50)            |         | (28,500) |
| Profit                             |         | 40,500   |

(c)   Weekly sales value $= \dfrac{\text{Fixed cost} + \text{profit}}{^{C}\!/_{S}\ \text{ratio}}$

$= \dfrac{£570 + £500}{0.6} = £1,783.33$

(d)   Bar purchase budget for week 2

|                                    | Beer £ | Soft Drinks £ | Wines/ Spirits £ |
|------------------------------------|--------|---------------|------------------|
| Sales                              | 900    | 375           | 225              |
| Stocks @ selling price             |        |               |                  |
|   Opening                | (450)  | (750)         | (225)            |
|   Closing                | 405    | 675           | 202.5            |
| Gross purchases @ selling price    | 855    | 300           | 202.5            |
| Gross purchases @ cost (30% of above) | 256.5 | 90          | 60.75            |
| Waste                              | 13.5   | 4.74          | 3.20             |
| Purchases value                    | 270.0  | 94.74         | 63.95            |

## 83    PQR PLC

(a)    **Forecast 1**

| | | | | |
|---|---|---|---|---|
| 500 A | × | 4 kg | = | 2,000 kg |
| 800 B | × | 7 kg | = | 5,600 kg |
| 2,200 C | × | 14 kg | = | 30,800 kg |
| | | | | 38,400 kg |

Material is the limiting factor

**Forecast 2**

| | | | | |
|---|---|---|---|---|
| 350 A | × | 4 kg | = | 1,400 kg |
| 700 B | × | 7 kg | = | 4,900 kg |
| 1,000 C | × | 14 kg | = | 14,000 kg |
| | | | | 20,300 kg |

Demand is the limiting factor

For forecast 1 product ranking is required:

| | A | B | C |
|---|---|---|---|
| Price | 10.00 | 20.00 | 30.00 |
| Variable cost | 6.50 | 11.00 | 18.10 |
| Contribution | 3.50 | 9.00 | 11.90 |
| Materials | 4 kg | 7 kg | 14 kg |
| Net contribution Per kg of material | £0.875 | £1.28 | £0.85 |
| RANKING | 2nd | 1st | 3rd |
| Make | 500 | 800 | 1,030 |
| Uses | 2,000 kg | 5,600 kg | 14,420 kg |
| Yields: | | | |
| CONTRIBUTION | £1,750 | £7,200 | £12,257 |

TOTAL CONTRIBUTION                    £21,207

The contribution from forecast 2 is:

| | | | £ |
|---|---|---|---|
| A | 350 × | (£15.00 – £6.50) | 2,975 |
| B | 700 × | (£25.00 – £11.00) | 9,800 |
| C | 1,000 × | (£40.00 – £18.10) | 21,900 |
| | | | 34,675 |

Forecast 2 pricing is recommended because it yields a higher contribution.

b)

| | | |
|---|---|---|
| **To**: | Managing Director |
| **From**: | Management Accountant |
| **Subject**: | Budget Preparation |
| **Date**: | 24$^{th}$ November 1999 |

**Introduction**

Further to our brief discussions I explain below the budget preparation process with particular reference to the areas you highlighted.

**Details**

The budget preparation process starts when the organisational objectives are set by the Board of Directors. These objectives are communicated to a budget committee which comprises a representative of each functional area of the business, plus an accountant who usually acts as Budget Officer. The Budget Officer co-ordinates the work of the committee.

The committee does not produce the budgets, but controls and co-ordinates the budget preparation process. The committee issues guidelines in the form of a budget manual. This manual is provided to all managers who have budgeting responsibilities.

Typically the manual comprises:

(i)         an organisation chart, showing the budget responsibilities of each manager;
(ii)        prices, wage rates, and inflation estimates to be used in the budgets;
(iii)       a timetable for the preparation of the budgets.

The first step in the detailed aspects of budget preparation is the identification of the principal budget factor. This is also known as the limiting factor because it is the factor which limits the activities of the organisation during the budget period.

Typically this limiting factor is either:

(i)         sales demand at a particular price; or
(ii)        a production resource.

When this has been identified the first budget to be produced is that relating to the limiting factor. When this is done, the other budgets can then be produced.

When the budgets have been produced they are sent to the Board of Directors for approval.

**Conclusion**

There are many other factors which we can discuss, if you wish please contact me.

---

## 84    WYE

(a)   (i)

| Budgeted sales | $=\dfrac{\text{Budgeted profit}}{\text{Standard profit}}$ | |
|---|---|---|
| | $=\dfrac{£17,250}{£15}$ | =   1,150 units |
| Sales volume variance | $=\dfrac{£750\,(A)}{£15}$ | =    50 units (A) |
| ACTUAL SALES | | 1,100 units |

(ii)    Budgeted production    $= \dfrac{\text{Budgeted fixed cost}}{\text{Absorption rate}}$

$= \dfrac{£25,000}{£20}$    $=$    1,250 units

Fixed overhead volume variance    $= \dfrac{£1,000\,(F)}{£20}$    $=$    50 units (F)
_____

ACTUAL PRODUCTION                    1,300 units
_____

(iii)   Sales price variance    $=$    £5,500 (F)
        Actual sales    $=$    1,100 units

Variance    $=$    £5/unit (F)

Standard price    $=$    £75/unit

Actual price    $=$    £80/unit

(iv)    1,300 units should use 4 kg each    $=$    5,200 kg
        Usage variance    $=$    £375 (A)
        valued at standard price of £2.50/kg    $=$    150 kg
_____

Actual usage    $=$    5,350 kg
_____

Price variance    $=$    £535 (A)

Variance    $=$    £0.10/kg (A)

Standard price    $=$    £2.50/kg

ACTUAL PRICE    $=$    £2.60/kg

(v)     1,300 units should use 3 hours each    $=$    3,900 hours

Efficiency variance    $=$    £1,200 (A)
valued at standard rate of £6/hour    $=$    200 hours
_____

ACTUAL HOURS    4,100 hours
_____

(vi)    Standard variable overhead cost of 1,300 units:

1,300 units × £12/unit    $=$    £15,600
Total variance    $=$    £20 (F)
_____

ACTUAL COST    £15,580
_____

(vii)   Budgeted cost    $=$    £25,000
        Expenditure variance    $=$    £1,000 (F)

ACTUAL COST    £24,000
_____

b)       **To**:            Operations Manager
         **From**:        Management Accountant
         **Subject**:     Variance Report – October 1999
         **Date**:        24th November 1999

**Introduction**

Further to our discussions I have considered the performance during October 1999 and set out my findings below.

**Findings**

The two most significant variances were the selling price variance and direct labour efficiency variance.

The selling price was higher than budgeted. This may be a deliberate policy to counteract the effects of inflation and cost increases.

The labour efficiency variance may be caused by problems of working with poorer quality materials.

**Conclusion**

I would be pleased to discuss this with you further. Please contact me if you wish to do this.

# CIMA

**AT FOULKS LYNCH**

## HOTLINES

Telephone: 00 44 (0) 20 8844 0667
Enquiries: 00 44 (0) 20 8831 9990
Fax: 00 44 (0) 20 8831 9991

## AT FOULKS LYNCH LTD

Number 4, The Griffin Centre
Staines Road, Feltham
Middlesex TW14 0HS

| Intended Examination Date: May 2000 ☐  November 2000 ☐ | Textbooks (Pub'd July 99) | Exam Kits (Pub'd Jan 2000) | Lynchpins (Pub'd Jan 2000) | Tracks (Audio Tapes) | Distance Learning Excludes Tracks |
|---|---|---|---|---|---|
| **Stage One** | | | | | |
| 1 Financial Accounting Fundamentals | £17.95 ☐ | £9.95 ☐ | £5.95 ☐ | £10.95 ☐ | £85.00 ☐ |
| 2 Cost Accounting & Quantitative Methods | £17.95 ☐ | £9.95 ☐ | £5.95 ☐ | £10.95 ☐ | £85.00 ☐ |
| 3 Economic Environment | £17.95 ☐ | £9.95 ☐ | £5.95 ☐ | £10.95 ☐ | £85.00 ☐ |
| 4 Business Environment & Info Technology | £17.95 ☐ | £9.95 ☐ | £5.95 ☐ | £10.95 ☐ | £85.00 ☐ |
| **Stage Two** | | | | | |
| 5 Financial Accounting | £17.95 ☐ | £9.95 ☐ | £5.95 ☐ | £10.95 ☐ | £85.00 ☐ |
| 6 Operational Cost Accounting | £17.95 ☐ | £9.95 ☐ | £5.95 ☐ | £10.95 ☐ | £85.00 ☐ |
| 7 Management Science Applications | £17.95 ☐ | £9.95 ☐ | £5.95 ☐ | £10.95 ☐ | £85.00 ☐ |
| 8 Business & Company Law | £17.95 ☐ | £9.95 ☐ | £5.95 ☐ | £10.95 ☐ | £85.00 ☐ |
| **Stage Three** | | | | | |
| 9 Financial Reporting | £18.95 ☐ | £10.95 ☐ | £5.95 ☐ | £10.95 ☐ | £85.00 ☐ |
| 10 Management Accounting Applications | £18.95 ☐ | £10.95 ☐ | £5.95 ☐ | £10.95 ☐ | £85.00 ☐ |
| 11 Organisational Mgt & Development | £18.95 ☐ | £10.95 ☐ | £5.95 ☐ | £10.95 ☐ | £85.00 ☐ |
| 12 Business Taxation* FA99 May/Nov 2000 | £18.95 ☐ | £9.95 ☐ | £5.95 ☐ | £10.95 ☐ | £85.00 ☐ |
| **Stage Four** | | | | | |
| 13 Strategic Financial Management | £18.95 ☐ | £10.95 ☐ | £5.95 ☐ | £10.95 ☐ | £85.00 ☐ |
| 14 Strategic Mgt Accountancy & Marketing | £18.95 ☐ | £10.95 ☐ | £5.95 ☐ | £10.95 ☐ | £85.00 ☐ |
| 15 Information Management | £18.95 ☐ | £10.95 ☐ | £5.95 ☐ | £10.95 ☐ | £85.00 ☐ |
| 16 Management Accounting Control Systems | £18.95 ☐ | £10.95 ☐ | £5.95 ☐ | £10.95 ☐ | £85.00 ☐ |

*Paper 12 Kit and Lynchpin published Aug 99

| P & P + Delivery | Textbooks | Exam Kits | Lynchpins | Tracks | Distance Learning |
|---|---|---|---|---|---|
| UK Mainland | £2.00/book | £1.00/book | £1.00/book | £1.00/tape | £5.00/pack |
| NI, ROI & EU Countries | £5.00/book | £3.00/book | £3.00/book | £1.00/tape | £15.00/pack |
| Rest of world standard air service | £10.00/book | £8.00/book | £8.00/book | £2.00/tape | £25.00/pack |
| Rest of world courier service† | £22.00/book | £20.00/book | Not applicable | Not applicable | £47.00/pack |

**SINGLE ITEM SUPPLEMENT FOR TEXTBOOKS AND EXAM KITS:**

If you only order 1 item, INCREASE postage costs by £2.50 for UK, NI & EU Countries or by £15.00 for Rest of World Services

| TOTAL | | | | | |
|---|---|---|---|---|---|
| Sub Total £ | | | | | |
| Post & Packing £ | | | | | |
| Total £ | | | | | |

†*Telephone number essential for this service*     ***Payments in Sterling in London***     Order Total £

## DELIVERY DETAILS

☐ Mr  ☐ Miss  ☐ Mrs  ☐ Ms   Other

Initials                Surname

Address

Postcode

Telephone                Deliver to home ☐

Company name

Address

Postcode

Telephone                Fax

Monthly report to go to employer ☐    Deliver to work ☐

## PAYMENT

1  I enclose Cheque/PO/Bankers Draft for £_____
   Please make cheques payable to AT Foulks Lynch Ltd.

2  Charge Mastercard/Visa/Switch A/C No:

Valid from: ☐☐☐☐     Expiry Date: ☐☐☐☐

Issue No: (Switch only) ☐☐

Signature                Date

## DECLARATION

I agree to pay as indicated on this form and understand that AT Foulks Lynch Terms and Conditions apply (available on request). I understand that AT Foulks Lynch Ltd are not liable for non-delivery if the rest of world standard air service is used.

Signature                Date

| **Please Allow:** | UK mainland | - 5-10 w/days |
|---|---|---|
| | NI, ROI & EU Countries | - 1-3 weeks |
| | Rest of world standard air service | - 6 weeks |
| | Rest of world courier service | - 10 w/days |

**Notes:** All delivery times subject to stock availability. Signature required on receipt (except rest of world standard air service). Please give both addresses for Distance Learning students where possible.

*Form effective at December 99*     *All details correct at time of printing*     ***Source: CIMAKTJ0***